INSIGHT GUIDE

BOSTON

Discovery CHANNEL

APA PUBLICATIONS L
Part of the Langenscheidt Publishing Group

ABOUT THIS BOOK

Editorial

Project Editor
Brian Bell
Update Editor
Alan Andres

Distribution

UK & Ireland
GeoCenter International Ltd
The Viables Centre , Harrow Way
Basingstoke, Hants RG22 4BJ
Fax: (44) 1256-817988

United States
Langenscheidt Publishers, Inc.
46–35 54th Road, Maspeth, NY 11378
Fax: (718) 784-0640

Canada
Prologue Inc.
1650 Lionel Bertrand Blvd., Boisbriand
Québec, Canada J7H 1N7
Tel: (450) 434-0306. Fax: (450) 434-2627

Australia & New Zealand
Hema Maps Pty. Ltd.
24 Allgas Street, Slacks Creek 4127
Brisbane, Australia
Tel: (61) 7 3290 0322. Fax: (61) 7 3290 0478

Worldwide
Apa Publications GmbH & Co.
Verlag KG (Singapore branch)
38 Joo Koon Road, Singapore 628990
Tel: (65) 865-1600. Fax: (65) 861-6438

Printing

Insight Print Services (Pte) Ltd
38 Joo Koon Road, Singapore 628990
Tel: (65) 865-1600. Fax: (65) 861-6438

©2000 Apa Publications GmbH & Co.
Verlag KG (Singapore branch)
All Rights Reserved
First Edition 1991
Second Edition 2000

CONTACTING THE EDITORS
Although every effort is made to
provide accurate information, we
live in a fast-changing world and
would appreciate it if readers
would call our attention to any
errors or outdated information
that may occur by writing to:
Insight Guides, P.O. Box 7910,
London SE1 1WE, England.
Fax: (44 20) 7403-0290.
e-mail:
insight@apaguide.demon.co.uk

This guidebook combines the
interests and enthusiasms of
two of the world's best known information providers: Insight Guides,
whose titles have set the standard
for visual travel guides since 1970,
and Discovery Channel, the world's
premier source of nonfiction television programming.

The editors of Insight Guides provide both practical advice and
general understanding about a destination's history, culture and
people. Discovery Chan-
nel and its Web site,
www.discovery.com,
help millions of viewers
explore their world from
the comfort of their
home and also encourage them to
explore it first hand.

How to use this book

This fully updated edition of *Insight
Guide: Boston* is structured to convey
an understanding of the city and its
culture as well as to guide readers
through its sights and activities:

◆ The **Features** section, indicated
by a yellow bar at the top of each
page, covers the city's history, culture and people in a series of
informative essays.

◆ The main **Places** section, indicated by a blue
bar, is a full guide to all
the sights and areas
worth visiting. Places of

special interest are coordinated by number with the maps.

◆ The **Travel Tips** listings section, with an orange bar, provides information on travel, hotels, shops, restaurants and more. An index to the section is on the back flap.

The contributors

This major revision of *Insight Guide: Boston* combined the talents of Boston-based editor **Alan Andres** and Insight's editorial director **Brian Bell**. Andres, who has been an antiquarian bookseller, magazine editor and a marketing and editorial acquisitions executive for a leading Boston book publisher, supervised the commissioning of new text and

the thorough updating of the remaining material. Bell directed the book's new, improved design and the selection of many new photographs reflecting Boston's ever changing urban landscape.

Updaters include **Glenn Stout**, who revised the section on Boston's sporting legacy and has written books on baseball legends Ted Williams and Jackie Robinson; **Ken Mallory**, who contributed to the chapter on the harbor islands and oversees publications for the New England Aquarium; Cambridge-based urban planning writer **Peter Strupp**, who wrote on architecture; and **Jon Marcus**, a senior editor at *Boston Magazine* who was responsible for the chapter on education.

This edition builds on the success of the first edition, edited by **Marcus Brooke**, a Scot who was on the faculties of Harvard University and the Massachusetts Institute of Technology before becoming a roving writer and photographer.

The text of several other writers has been updated for this edition. **John Gattuso**, who wrote some of the History and Places chapters, is now series editor for the Discovery Adventure books jointly produced by Insight Guides and Discovery Channel. **Michael Wentworth**, curator of painting and sculpture at the Boston Athenaeum, wrote the original chapter on the visual arts. **William Schofield**, the writer and reporter who invented the concept of the Freedom Trail, and **Dana Berg**, an artist and art historian, each wrote Places chapters.

Given such a wealth of local expertise, Insight Guides can only commend their work and echo the words of Rudyard Kipling: "I have learned never to argue with a Bostonian."

EXPLORE YOUR WORLD
Discovery
CHANNEL

Map Legend

– – – –	State/Neighborhood Boundary
–•– •–	National Park/Reserve
– – – –	Ferry Route
●	Subway
✈ ✈	Airport: International/ Regional
🚌	Bus Station
■	Parking
●	Tourist Information
✉	Post Office
✝ † ⴕ	Church/Ruins
†	Monastery
☾	Mosque
✡	Synagogue
🏰 ⌂	Castle/Ruins
∴	Archeological Site
∩	Cave
1	Statue/Monument
★	Place of Interest

The main places of interest in the Places section are coordinated by number with a full-colour map (e.g. ❶), and a symbol at the top of every right-hand page tells you where to find the map.

INSIGHT GUIDE
BOSTON

CONTENTS

Frog Pond,
Boston Common

Insight on ...

Information panels

Places

Travel Tips

THE HUB OF THE UNIVERSE

Life, liberty and the pursuit of happiness are all very well,
but what really counts in Boston is self-esteem

Consider the sentiments of a Proper Bostonian, so called because she lives in downtown "Boston Proper," the old "walking city" of the 17th century. "Like it? Why, I never thought of it that way. Liking Boston is like saluting the flag."

Justifiable pride? Insufferable arrogance? Perhaps visitors' reactions to Boston and Bostonians reveal more about themselves than about the city and its inhabitants, but it is certain that no other American city has provoked so many polarized opinions. Writers in particular have always flocked to Boston, drawn by its strong literary tradition, so the quality of both praise and invective is of an uncommonly high standard.

Boston is "a state of mind," said Mark Twain (or perhaps Ralph Waldo Emerson, or possibly Thomas Appleton, for Bostonians can always find something to disagree about). It's "a moral and intellectual nursery," said (again, arguably) the Spanish philosopher George Santayana. "A museum piece," thought Frank Lloyd Wright. "A hole," wrote Robert Browning.

A hard sell

Maybe Boston simply oversold itself. Even today, when city halls all over America house marketing teams intent on promoting their "product" with the publicity tools once dedicated to breakfast cereals and sun-tan oils, no copywriter would dare claim for the city the status that Oliver Wendell Holmes, author, philosopher and professor of anatomy at Harvard, gave it in 1860: that "it is the thinking center of the continent, and therefore of the planet." To the scholars at Harvard, this seemed scandalously faint praise and in no time at all this small northeastern corner of the new republic had extended its sphere of influence to become nothing less than the Hub of the Universe.

The Hub hit harder times in the 20th century and, between 1950 and 1970, its population slumped from more than 800,000 to 563,000 as more people abandoned the decaying inner city for better housing in the suburbs. Successive mayors and city planners campaigned to reverse the decline, and soaring modern architecture and a revived waterfront began to signal a new confidence. With the help of the research laboratories and high-tech industries of Cambridge, and the renewed vitality of the arts, Boston avoided relegation to the status of an outdoor museum of history and once again began to play a leading role in the nation's affairs. Self-esteem had been restored. ❏

PRECEDING PAGES: British ships on the warpath in 1776; Boston is a thriving seaport by 1855; Boston Harbor in the late 19th century; the harbor today.
LEFT: the Prudential Center in Back Bay.

Decisive Dates

1625 William Blackstone, 29, an Anglican clergyman and Boston's first European settler, builds a log cabin on what is now Boston Common.
1630 John Winthrop, recently elected governor of the Massachusetts Bay Company, leads the *Arbella* and 10 other Puritan ships into Boston Harbor after a three-month trip from England.
1631 Boston court officials create America's first police force by putting watchmen on duty from sunset to sunrise.

1635 Boston Latin School, the nation's first public school, is founded.
1636 The Puritans show their commitment to education by founding a college at New Towne, later Cambridge. It was subsequently to be named after its benefactor, John Harvard.
1640 Stephen Day, a locksmith and ironworker turns printer, publishes the first book produced in the colonies, *Bay Psalm Book.*
1660 A Quaker, Mary Dyer, is hanged on the Boston Common. The Quakers were denounced by the Puritans as a "cursed sect."
1684 Massachusetts Bay Colony charter is revoked, ending Puritan independence from royal control.

1690 The first American newspaper, *Publick Occurances: Both Foreign and Domestic*, is published in Boston.
1692 Salem Witch Trials begin.
1717 Boston Light, the oldest lighthouse in the nation, is erected in the harbor.
1761 Boston lawyer James Otis declares: "Taxation without representation is tyranny."
1764 The Sugar Act and the Stamp Act arouse anti-royalist sentiments.
1770 The Boston Massacre, in which British troops fire on a rock-throwing mob, killing five.
1773 Phillis Wheatley, a young slave living with a wealthy Boston family, becomes the first published African-American poet. Boston Tea Party, in which a shipment of tea is thrown into the harbor in protest against a new three-pence tax on tea.
1775 Paul Revere's ride and Battles of Lexington and Concord spark American Revolution. Battle of Bunker Hill. George Washington takes command of Continental Army at Cambridge.
1776 British troops evacuate Boston. The Declaration of Independence is read from the State House balcony.
1780 John Adams drafts the Massachusetts Constitution including a Bill of Rights; John Hancock is the first governor of the Commonwealth of Massachusetts.
1795 On Beacon Hill, Paul Revere and Samuel Adams lay the cornerstone for the new State House by Charles Bulfinch, America's first professional architect.
1812 War of 1812 against British paralyzes the city's commerce.
1814 American Industrial Revolution begins at Robert Cabot Lowell's first mill on the Charles River in Waltham.
1815 The Handel & Haydn Society, now the nations's oldest continuously performing arts organization, gives its first concert.
1822 Boston is incorporated as a city.
1831 William Lloyd Garrison begins publishing an abolitionist journal, *The Liberator*. Mount Auburn Cemetery, the nation's first garden cemetery, opens in Cambridge.
1845 Henry David Thoreau begins his three-year spell at Walden Pond.
1846 First operation under general anesthesia performed at Massachusetts General Hospital.
1852 Boston Public Library, the first free city library supported by taxes, opens.
1857 Filling of Back Bay begins, cleaning up a foul-smelling 580-acre public dump.

1861 Massachusetts Institute of Technology is granted charter.

1863 The 54th Massachusetts Voluntary Infantry, the first African-American regiment, is formed. The Oneida Club first plays American-style football on Boston Common.

1868 Louisa May Alcott of Concord publishes *Little Women.*

1872 Great Fire of Boston destroys downtown, killing 33 people and razing 776 buildings.

1876 First words are spoken over telephone by Alexander Graham Bell.

1877 Swan boats launched at Public Garden.

1879 Radcliffe College founded for women.

1881 Boston Symphony Orchestra founded. Frederick Law Olmsted, landscape architect, begins work on Emerald Necklace park system.

1886 Henry James publishes *The Bostonians.*

1892 First Church of Christ, Scientist, established in Boston by Mary Baker Eddy.

1897 First Boston Marathon. The first subway in America opens at Park Street.

1903 Boston Pilgrims defeat Pittsburgh Pirates in first baseball World Series.

1909 Filene's Automatic Bargain Basement opens in Washington Street.

1919 Strike of 1,300 Boston police. Breaking it brings to national prominence Massachusetts Governor Calvin Coolidge.

1920 Red Sox sell Babe Ruth to New York Yankees for $125,000.

1927 Italian immigrants Nicola Sacco and Bartolomeo Vanzetti are executed in a Charlestown prison for alleged killings and holdups. The case became a model for social injustice in the 1920s.

1942 Fire in a Bay Village nightclub kills 490.

1944 The computer age dawns in Cambridge laboratories as a 50-ft-long calculating machine gets its sums right.

1945 James Michael Curley, although under indictment for fraud, wins fourth term as mayor.

1946 John Fitzgerald Kennedy, 29, elected to US Congress from Charlestown and Cambridge.

1947 Polaroid founder Edwin Land demonstrates first instant camera in Cambridge.

1950 A Brinks armored car is robbed in North End. Thieves net $2.7 million. Eight men are convicted six years later.

PRECEDING PAGES: the State House and State Street, *circa* 1801. **LEFT:** the Pilgrims come ashore. **RIGHT:** detail from the Café du Barry mural by Josh Viner on Newbury Street, Back Bay.

1953 The world's first kidney transplant is performed at Brigham Hospital. The recipient lives for seven years.

1955 Martin Luther King is awarded a PhD from Boston University.

1959 The Boston Redevelopment Authority begins razing the old West End, long a center for gambling dens, burlesque halls and brothels but home to 7,000 people, and starts building Government Center and luxury apartments.

1962 The "Boston Strangler" begins a 21-month rape and murder spree, killing 13 women.

1972 After 75 years as a men-only race, the

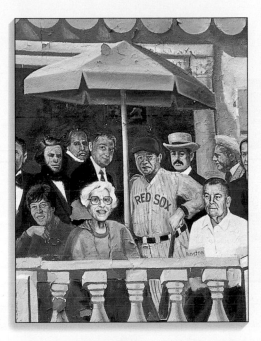

Marathon acknowledges first women's winner.

1973 Robert Parker publishes *The Godwulf Manuscript,* the first "Spenser" detective novel.

1978 A blizzard dumps 27.1 inches (69 cm) of snow on Boston and 48 inches (122 cm) in parts of the state. City drifts reach 15 ft (4.6 meters).

1990 In the largest art heist in history, thieves remove $200 million in paintings from Isabella Stewart Gardner Museum.

1992 The road-burying Big Dig (*see pages 44–45*), begins. It is due for completion in 2004.

1993 The TV series *Cheers,* set in a fictional Boston bar, ends after 275 episodes.

1996 The Harbor Islands are designated a national park area. ❑

BEGINNINGS

Boston's founders, escaping oppression in England, created their own climate of religious intolerance. But soon trade became more important than theology

American cities have a way of effacing history. The present is so jammed with information, and reminders of the past are so glibly destroyed, that people have trouble remembering what happened last year in their cities, much less a century ago. It's rare indeed to hear anyone talking about "old Los Angeles" or "old New York" – unless of course it's in the sense of the "old neighborhood," which everyone agrees "ain't what it used to be."

But Boston is different. Here's a city whose identity is still firmly rooted in the past. Every schoolboy knows that Boston is the cradle of American independence. Adams, Revere, Hancock – they are more than historical figures, they are players in a national mythology. Americans look to the patriots for a sense of who they are. And they look to Boston as the birthplace of the nation.

Native Americans

At the time of European contact, the New England coast was inhabited by several loosely affiliated Algonquin tribes, including the Massachusetts in the Boston area and the Wampanoag near Cape Cod. They led fairly settled lives, moving seasonally within tribal boundaries and making their livelihood from hunting, fishing and planting. By the time English settlers arrived, they had already suffered greatly from European diseases introduced by traders. Between 1616 and 1617 a smallpox epidemic wiped out nearly one-third of the native population and put the coastal tribes at the mercy of their inland enemies. The devastation was so complete at some Wampanoag villages that settlers found only bones scattered on the ground because there was no one left to bury the dead.

At first, the Indians and whites managed to sustain reasonably peaceful relations. With the help of Tisquantum (Squanto), who had learned English after being sold into slavery by the

Europeans, the Wampanoag sachem Massasoit negotiated an alliance with the settlers at Plimoth Plantation – the Indians supplying food and instruction, the whites supplying defense against threatening tribes to the east. But, as English settlements expanded, relations between Indians and whites grew hostile.

Finally, in 1675, Massasoit's son Pometacom (King Philip) led a raid against a small settlement on Narragansett Bay, launching a bloody three-year conflict. Although Boston was never attacked, King Philip's War devastated about 50 other towns in New England. In the end, Pometacom was captured and beheaded, and the Wampanoag were decimated.

The City upon a Hill

At the time of Pometacom's defeat, Boston was already a bustling seaport and the undeclared capital of New England. Nearly 40 years earlier, John Winthrop came to the site with a group of Puritans determined to create a new society

LEFT: reenactment of John Winthrop signing a charter giving rights to the area. **RIGHT:** Myles Standish established contact with the native indians.

– a "visible kingdom of God." While still aboard the *Arbella*, halfway between the Old World and the New, Winthrop addressed his fellow colonists, clearly laying out for them the terms of their covenant with the Almighty.

"We must be knit together, in this work, as one man," he told them. "We must entertain each other in brotherly affection. We must be willing to abridge ourselves of our superfluities, for the supply of other's necessities… We must delight in each other; make other's conditions our own; rejoice together; mourn together; labor and suffer together." And if they stood by this commitment, Winthrop said, they would be rewarded with divine benefaction and the admiration of the world. "For we must consider that we shall be as a City upon a Hill. The eyes of all people are upon us."

The great adventure

To the small group of gallant colonists gathered on deck, Winthrop's words must have resounded with a comforting sense of purpose. The motherland had long since receded beyond the horizon, and most of them would never see it again. They were alone in unfamiliar waters with nothing but wind and waves in every direction, heading towards a wilderness that

must have seemed impossibly remote.

Although many of the colonists didn't know each other before boarding the ship, they held a common body of convictions. They saw themselves as religious reformers, followers of a strict brand of Calvinism that sought to purge the Anglican Church of its "papist" trappings and to free English society from its licentious ways. They wanted to purify the English church and to develop a "holy commonwealth" where they could live and worship as God would wish. But by 1629, the Puritans were so oppressed in England that even men of considerable wealth such as John Winthrop, a Suffolk lawyer, were thinking about leaving. Together with several

EARLIER EXPLORERS

As the Puritan leadership planned their migration, they had the benefit of more than100 years of interest in the region. In 1524 Giovanni da Verrazano was the first European to explore the American coast north of the Carolinas, and he was followed in 1525 by Estevan Gomez. Oddly, the European powers didn't pay much further attention to New England until the early 1600s, when several expeditions were launched at much the same time, including the voyage of Captain John Smith in 1614. Smith made a detailed survey of the Massachusetts Bay region, and returned to England enthusiastic about the potential of colonization.

other middle-class Puritans, Winthrop purchased a charter issued by the king a year earlier. The charter entitled the group – known as the Massachusetts Bay Company – to occupy a strip of land between the Charles and Merrimack Rivers and stretching from the Atlantic to the Pacific Oceans. Much to their credit, they also arranged to "transfer the government of the plantation to those that shall inhabit there," which meant that for all practical purposes the company would be self-governing.

OPPRESSED IN ENGLAND

After King James I assumed the throne in 1603, he scorned the Puritans as non-conformists, charged them with seditious behavior, and promised "to harry them from the land."

called Naumkeag. Five years later, John Endicott arrived at Naumkeag with a second group of settlers, and the village was renamed Salem.

When Winthrop set out from England on March 29, 1630, with a fleet of 11 ships and about 750 colonists, there was some talk of joining Endicott's people at Salem. When they arrived more than two months later, however, they found the town in such a "sad and unexpected condition" that they decided to move south to Charlestown and build a settlement

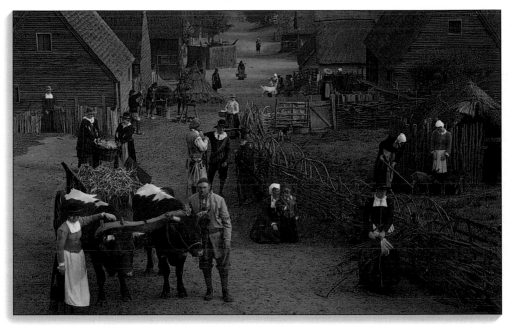

The Plimoth Plantation

After several failed attempts to establish trading posts in the region, the first permanent settlement was founded at Plimoth by the so-called "Pilgrims," a small group of religious dissenters (even more radical than the Puritans) who fled from England to Holland in 1606 and then sailed to the New World in 1620. The Pilgrims were followed in 1623 by a small party of Puritans who settled north of Massachusetts Bay at a place

FAR LEFT: 8-year-old Anne Pollard, the first white woman to set foot in Boston (1630). **LEFT:** John Winthrop, the Cambridge-educated Puritan leader. **ABOVE:** Pilgrims at Plimoth Plantation.

of their own. This first camp was overcrowded and riddled with disease, and it gradually broke up, a few small groups heading up the Charles River to the sites of Watertown and Newtown, others moving to Saugus, Medford, Dorchester and Roxbury.

For his part, Winthrop took up the invitation of an eccentric minister named William Blackstone who had been living in solitude across the Charles River on a hilly peninsula the Indians called Shawmut. Together with 150 settlers, Winthrop moved to the site which, at the first meeting of "freemen" on September 7, was officially named Boston after their home town in Lincolnshire.

An age of intolerance

The town grew remarkably fast. There were about 300 people in 1632, 600 in 1635 and 1,200 in 1640 – most living in wood houses huddled around Town Cove or in the market-place near present-day North Square. Although democratic in structure, the government was basically a theocracy. Only male church-members could vote, and the ministers were consulted on all but administrative matters. The Rev. John Cotton, minister of the First Church of Boston, was a major influence on Governor Winthrop, who considered himself a "sacred student" under Cotton's direction. In later years, ministerial power shifted to the "Mather dynasty" (Richard, Increase, Cotton and Samuel) which ruled from the pulpit of the Second Church of Boston for the better part of four generations.

Although the Puritans were themselves religious dissenters, they showed no tolerance for non-orthodox beliefs. Both Roger Williams and Anne Hutchinson tried to introduce theological innovations, and were banished from the colony. The Quakers who came to Boston were whipped or had an ear cut off, and were then kicked out. A few brave enough to return from banishment, including the heroic Mary Dyer, were hanged from the Great Elm on the Common.

WHAT THE PURITANS BELIEVED

To the Puritans, people were naturally sinful and required unrelenting discipline. Work, frugality and humility were highly valued, while "harmless" distractions such as dance, music and stylish clothes were scorned as frivolities. Education was considered essential, and within six years of their arrival the Puritans established a public school for children and a college for ministers (which later became Harvard University).

The corner-stone of Puritan theology was the Calvinist doctrine of predestination, a belief that God preordained who was saved and who was damned. The key to acceptance in Puritan society was to demonstrate through pious demeanor that you were, in fact, one of God's chosen people. Because a saint was thought to despise sin in others, much effort was put into reforming those who didn't quite measure up.

Making a public display of just how much they detested sin was also believed to be a good way of protecting the town from divine retribution, and as a result wayward members of the community were often cruelly punished for their deeds.

Even minor offenses like cursing or gossiping could be punished by whipping, branding or being placed in the stocks. Ironically, the stock-maker, who gave the General Court an inflated bill, was the first to be locked in his contraption. A sailor just returned from a long voyage was whipped for kissing his wife in public.

Despite such hardships of Puritan life, settlers continued to pour into Boston. Many, however, were more interested in the condition of their purses than the condition of their souls. In the face of so many outsiders, the churches closed themselves off, and before long a rift developed between members and non-members, saints and sinners. At its inception, Winthrop envisioned Boston as a town where citizens would be committed to a common purpose by the bonds of "brotherly affection." But by the time he died in 1649, Boston had become quite a different place, with an "aristocracy of saints" commanding most of the political power and the remainder of

Interference from England

In its first 30 years the Massachusetts Bay Colony enjoyed virtual autonomy from the mother country. With English politics being rocked by Oliver Cromwell, England was much too preoccupied with business at home to monitor its colonial backwaters.

But when Charles II assumed the throne in 1660, this age of benign neglect came suddenly to an end. Among the new monarch's first acts was to rein in the New England colonies, which were not only governing themselves like a sovereign nation, but doing business like one too. There wasn't much sense for a king to have col-

the community getting by as best it could.

Although many settlers planned to make their living as farmers, it quickly became clear that Boston's future was tied to the sea. By the late 1630s, Boston ships were carrying loads of codfish to England, Spain and Portugal and were returning with much needed manufactured goods. Merchants were also exporting to the West Indies, which, by the late 1600s, was supplying molasses to Boston rum distilleries and slaves to wealthy land-owners.

LEFT: reconstruction of an early kitchen at Plimoth Plantation. **ABOVE:** the trial of George Jacobs, accused of witchcraft in 1692.

onies if they didn't produce good revenues, so Charles set about putting them on a money-making basis. First, he used the Navigation Acts to force colonial merchants to do business exclusively with England. And then, in order to hamstring the Puritan leadership, he ordered voting rights in Massachusetts be granted to all men of "good estate" regardless of church membership.

Although the Puritans made a fuss over the change in suffrage, most merchants simply ignored the Navigation Acts and continued trading with whomever they wished. When Charles got wind of just how widespread smuggling had become, he answered the colonists' audacity by revoking the Massachusetts Bay charter in 1684 and transforming the whole of New England into a single royal colony.

Charles died before he could finish this work, but his brother, James II, picked up where he left off by appointing Sir Edmund Andros governor-general of the Dominion of New England in 1686. To Bostonians, Andros was a particularly contemptible man. In his first few weeks as governor, he not only converted the Old South Meeting House into an Anglican Church – sacrilege to the Puritan clergy – he also limited town meetings to one a year and forced all property-holders to make new payments on land titles.

COTTON MATHER

Cotton Mather (1663–1728), whose life was "a continual conversation with heaven." fought for inoculation against smallpox, a controversial treatment. When he inoculated his own son, his house was bombed.

would be allowed to elect their own representatives, but suffrage would be extended to all property-holders, irrespective of religion, and the crown would appoint the governor. It was a blow to the authority of the Puritan clergy, but it was the best deal Mather could get.

The Salem witches

When Mather returned to Boston, he found a bizarre situation brewing that was to damage the clergy's authority even further. In 1692, in the town of

The colonists were furious. When word reached them that King James had been ousted during the "Glorious Revolution," they staged an insurrection of their own. Andros was forced out of office, thrown in jail and shipped back to England.

In the meanwhile, Boston's most prominent minister, Increase Mather, was sent off to England to make the Puritans' case against Andros. When William and Mary took over the crown, he begged them to restore the original charter. The new monarchs were sympathetic, but unwilling to relinquish so much power. They offered Mather a compromise. The colonists

Salem, several young girls fell victim to a strange malady, causing them to writhe in pain and "make most piteous outcries of burnings, of being cut with knives, beat, etc. and the marks of wounds were afterwards to be seen."

The ministers attending the children declared them to be bewitched, and in the process of finding the culprits, touched off a flurry of accusations that quickly developed into full-blown hysteria. Even the brilliant Cotton Mather (Increase's son) was convinced of the sorcery, and he fanned the flames of paranoia with blistering sermons about the breakdown of Puritan law and the artful designs of Satan. Even so, he didn't believe that the hysterical testimony of young girls was sufficient evidence to condemn a person to death.

By the time a new governor arrived and put an end to witch-hunting, hundreds had been accused and 19 had been executed. The credibility of the clergy, and the church in general, suffered irreparable damage. The age of Winthrop's "city upon a hill" came to an inglorious end. Puritan ideals were still very much an integral part of everyday Boston life, but a new class of men were already rising to power.

THE "TRIANGLE TRADE"

Merchants like Thomas Hancock, Peter Faneuil and James Otis made fortunes on the "triangle trade," shipping fish and crafted goods to Europe and picking up molasses and slaves in the West Indies

jects like Faneuil Hall, which was funded by Peter Faneuil and donated to the city.

Although Boston merchants were doing well, the rest of the city was not. The economic slow-down was partly due to competition from other colonial towns, especially New York and Philadelphia, which were steadily creeping into Boston markets. Boston was also taking the brunt of England's colonial battles – the so-called French and Indian Wars which had raged intermittently since the late 1600s and

The rise of the merchant class

With suffrage now open to property-holders, a class of wealthy merchants emerged as an influential force in Boston's affairs. The town had always made its living from the sea, but by the early 1700s shipbuilding and codfishing thrived and Boston dominated coastal and international trade. Vast fortunes were being accumulated on the "triange trade" (see panel above). The merchants' newly acquired wealth was put into handsome homes like Thomas Hancock's mansion atop Beacon Hill as well as into civic pro-

---

LEFT: Cambridge colleges in 1743.
ABOVE: Long Wharf and part of Boston Harbor, 1764.

flared again in 1740 (King George's War) and 1754 (the Seven Years' War).

These wars were an enormous drain on Boston. Hundreds of men were killed, ships were destroyed, and the city was overburdened with the care of widows and orphans. Then an earthquake in 1755 toppled buildings and terrified the populace. And five years later, the town was devastated by the worst fire in colonial history, leaving at least 1,000 people homeless.

By the time the French were defeated in 1763, Boston was a shambles. Just as it began to recover, the British renewed the old tug-of-war by trying to impose further taxes. In doing so, they lit a fuse that would detonate a revolution. ❑

THE ROAD TO REVOLUTION

What's the point of having colonies, England argued, if not to collect taxes?

In that case, Bostonians argued, it was time to cease being a colony

England, having subdued the French for the time being, turned its attention again to the colonies. And, as always, its aim was to get as much money out of them as possible. In 1763, King George III launched the effort with a battery of legislation that prohibited colonial currency and cracked down on the lucrative sugar trade between Boston and the West Indies. Before New Englanders could mount an effective protest, parliament also passed the Stamp Act (1765) requiring colonists to pay taxes on legal documents.

To the fiesty Bostonians, these restrictions were worse than the old Navigation Acts and smacked of the same arbitrary use of power. The rallying cry went out, "No taxation without representation," as mobs took the protest into the streets. They looted the Lieutenant Governor's home and terrorized tax collectors. By the time the stamps arrived in Boston there wasn't an official in town brave enough to distribute them.

The unlikely conspirators

At the heart of the uproar in Boston was a loose organization of agitators known as the Sons of Liberty, which included Paul Revere, John Hancock, Dr Joseph Warren, and their leader, Samuel Adams. They were as unlikely a collection of conspirators as one could imagine. Sam Adams was a disheveled middle-aged man who, despite a genius for political organization, had managed to squander a sizable inheritance on several failed businesses and spent much of his life in what he called "honorable poverty."

His protégé, John Hancock, on the other hand, was the wealthiest man in New England. He was much younger than Adams, not a particularly deep thinker, and known for his vanity and dandified manners. As one observer described him, his "brains were shallow and pockets deep." The other two members also made an unusual

LEFT: part of Paul Revere's engraving showing British troops opening fire in King Street.
RIGHT: Samuel Adams (1722–1803), spokesman for the Patriots during the Revolution.

pair. Joseph Warren was an upper-class, Harvard-trained physician. And Paul Revere was a working-class Renaissance man – a gifted craftsmen, a courageous patriot and, with a hand in just about everything, an indefatigable public servant.

While the Sons of Liberty were raising hell in Boston, the hastily formed Stamp Act Congress

called for an American boycott against British goods. By March 1766, the boycott had caused so much damage to British commerce that King George relented and lifted the tax.

When news of the Stamp Act's demise reached the colonies, Boston was overjoyed. John Hancock even opened his magnificent Beacon Hill estate and supplied Madeira wine to the commoners who gathered in the yard. But George III didn't take defeat lightly. In 1767 his new chancellor of the exchequer, Charles Townshend, lashed out with a new tax on imported items such as paper, lead and tea. Again, the town reacted with predictable fervor. When the Massachusetts House of Representatives issued

Sam Adams' "circular letters" denouncing the Townshend Acts, the governor closed it down – and Bostonians hit the streets.

Four thousand British soldiers were sent to quell the unruly mobs, and a series of skirmishes followed between Redcoats and civilians. For more than a year, the taunting and bullying became an ugly game of brinkmanship that finally erupted into all-out violence. It happened on March 5, 1770, when a group of Redcoats fired into a threatening crowd. This "Boston Massacre" (*see page 140*) claimed the lives of five colonists and wounded several others. Ironically, the Townshend Acts were repealed in England on that very day. It wasn't a total surrender, however. As a symbol of the "supremacy of Parliament," a nominal tax on tea remained.

The Boston Tea Party

The tea tax won no friends in Boston, and when the first loads arrived in Boston Harbor, the Sons of Liberty were ready to prevent the cargo from reaching colonial teapots. On December 16, 1773, about 50 townsmen disguised as Indians boarded the cargo ships and dumped the tea into Boston Harbor while a crowd of thousands cheered from the wharves.

The Boston Tea Party was more than the

THE POWER OF THE PRESS

In 1639 a printing press was assembled in Cambridge. Its early releases included the *Bay Psalm Book*, the *New England Primer*, and the freeman's oath of loyalty to Massachusetts. In 1690, the colonies' first newspaper, *Publick Occurrences Both Foreign and Domestick*, appeared in Boston but was succeeded by the more popular *Boston News-Letter* in 1704. Other memorable tabloids, including the *Rehearsal*, the *Massachusetts Spy* and the *Independent Advertiser*, kept New England informed, if not always accurately, as the country roared to revolution. By the 1850s, the region hosted no fewer than 424 periodical publications.

British could tolerate. They unveiled the Coercive Acts, closing Boston Harbor, dissolving the government of Massachusetts, installing General Thomas Gage as military governor and providing for the use of private homes to quarter British troops. Thousands of people moved out of Boston, and the town ground to a halt.

In September 1774, the First Continental Congress met in Philadelphia and voted to form a colonial army. In and around Boston, colonials stockpiled guns and ammunition in preparation for war. When General Gage heard of a weapons cache in Concord, 20 miles (32 km) west of Boston, he sent 800 Redcoats to capture it.

While the troops prepared to move out, Paul

Revere was already paddling across the Charles River to warn the countryside of the British march. He arranged for a friend, Robert Newman, to place lanterns in the steeple of Christ Church as a signal of the soldiers' direction. When Revere reached Charlestown he borrowed a horse and rode into the countryside warning villagers that the British were coming.

At Lexington he found Sam Adams and John Hancock hiding out together, hoping to evade capture before attending the Second Continental Congress. Revere also met two other messengers, William Dawes and young Dr. Samuel Prescott, and together they rode toward Con-

The British marched on to Concord, destroyed the few weapons they found there, and tried to return the same way they came. But by then rebels were hidden along the road and peppered the Redcoats with musket fire all the way back to Charlestown. By the time the troops returned to Boston, 73 Redcoats had been killed and 200 wounded.

The Battle of Bunker Hill

As news of the confrontation at Lexington spread out from Boston, thousands of colonials poured into the area, forming an arching line of siege between Charlestown and Boston Neck. On June

cord until they ran into a British patrol. Dawes and Prescott escaped, but Revere was captured, only to be released a few hours later.

By the time the British regulars reached Lexington green en route to Concord, 70 local "minutemen" – armed civilians pledged to fight at a minute's notice – were assembled. The rebels were ordered to lay down their weapons, but refused. The British fired, the rebels scattered, and all hell broke loose. When the smoke finally cleared, eight minutemen lay dead and 10 had been wounded.

LEFT: Joseph Warren dies in the Battle of Bunker Hill.
ABOVE: General Howe's army abandons Boston.

17, 1775, more than 2,600 Redcoats tried to break the siege by storming a rebel position on Breed's Hill (adjacent to Bunker Hill). British artillery flattened Charlestown as the colonials repelled two attacks and then, running out of ammunition, retreated on the third. It was a technical victory for the British, but with more than 1,300 casualties, and an enormous boost in American spirits, it was hardly decisive.

Less than a month after the Battle of Bunker Hill, General George Washington arrived in Cambridge and took command of the colonial forces. The siege of Boston continued through the bitter winter of 1775–76, until Washington forced out the British with a clandestine placement of artillery on Dorchester Heights, over-looking the British flotilla in Boston Harbor. On March 17, 1776, nearly 9,000 Redcoats and 1,000 Tories boarded 78 vessels and sailed away while American militiamen re-occupied the town.

The Revolutionary War raged for seven more years and, although Boston was spared its hor-rors, the population was reduced from 20,000 to 6,000 residents who survived as best they could.

Bulfinch and Brahmins

In the spring of 1787, a young man of means by the name of Charles Bulfinch returned to Boston after two years abroad. The town he surveyed

was in many respects still the colonial seaport of his boyhood – a cluster of narrow streets and wooden buildings gathered haphazardly around the waterfront. Since the Revolutionary War, Boston had returned to business as usual. Wealthy merchants were still in control of local affairs, and they still earned their riches from the sea, although many were now engaging in the China trade, sailing around the tip of South America to lucrative Asian markets.

During his European travels, young Bulfinch acquired a taste for architecture, and he began offering "gratuitous advice" to friends who were building new homes in the West End. Although no one could have guessed from so humble a

beginning, it was the start of a career that would ultimately change the face of Boston.

Between 1795 and 1818, Bulfinch launched an architectural renaissance that, perhaps more than anything else, expressed the ambitions of Federalist Boston and solidified the ascendency of the ruling class. Although an early failure in the South End caused him financial troubles throughout much of his career (he even spent a month in debtor's prison), he worked with extra-ordinary energy. As well as designing churches, homes and public buildings, he rehabilitated Faneuil Hall, nearly tripling it in size, and spear-headed the development of Beacon Hill. His crowning achievement, however, was the mag-nificent domed State House, now a Boston icon.

In 1818 Bulfinch was commissioned by the federal government to design the new capitol in Washington, DC. He left Boston, not as he found it, but a transformed place, no longer an 18th-century town of wooden houses and crooked lanes, but a 19th-century city of cob-blestone and brick.

Jefferson challenges the elitists

Bulfinch's work gave Boston a new sense of gravity that was immediately appealing to upper-class families, many of whom moved out of the North End into prestigious homes on Beacon Hill. Politically, the Brahmin class was wedded to the Federalist notion of government by "the wise, the well-born, and the good," a policy near and dear to their pocketbooks as well as their conceits. Since the Revolution, Massachusetts Federalists had played a major role in crafting the new government, and they had always kept a firm grip on the reins of city politics. But when Thomas Jefferson was elected President in 1800, all that seemed to change. Jefferson was a clas-sic democrat, and his belief in the principles of equality were anathema to the Brahmins.

Worse yet was his foreign policy. In 1807, hostilities with England led to the Embargo Act, which nearly strangled the lucrative China trade. "Jimmy Madison's War" with England (the War of 1812) only made a bad situation worse, and once again, Boston ships were left to languish in the harbor while merchants scrambled for new opportunities in which to invest their capital.

Always enterprising, several high-ranking Brahmin families, including the Lowells, Apple-tons and Amorys, began diverting their money into small textile plants that had been established some years before as an entrepreneurial experiment. Their timing was impeccable. With European trade impaired by the war, Americans were clamoring for manufactured goods. Factories were built in outlying towns, and the Brahmins were soon making a killing in the textile industry.

As was customary in this closely knit society, the financial alliances that were necessary to get this enterprise off the ground were forged with wedding vows. By the 1850s, a number of new family names were added to Boston's social register,

THE BRAHMIN TRADITION

Boston's bluebloods inherited many of the old Puritan values, such as modesty and frugality – and a sense of self-importance.

min paternalism took on a more ardent quality. The wind of change began with the growing popularity of the Unitarian church. As defined by the Rev. William Ellery Channing, Unitarianism did away with the old Calvinist notions of predestination and original sin, stressing instead the benevolence of God and the potential for human perfectibility. The road to salvation, he argued, was through the exercise of conscience, rationality and tolerance.

The Unitarian spirit was driven to its loftiest heights by a school of thought known as Tran-

and a sub-class of nouveaux riches manufacturers was planted in the loam of Brahmin society.

The spirit of reform

The infusion of fresh blood into Brahmin veins produced both new capital and new ideas. From the days of the Puritans, Boston's ruling class acknowledged its obligation to improve the conditions of the less fortunate, if not by actual material assistance, then by the power of example.

But in the early years of the new century Brah-

LEFT: the first Declaration of Independence in Boston. ABOVE: this section of a painting by John White Allen Scott (1815–1907) shows Broad Street in 1853.

scendentalism, espoused in its most beautiful and stirring form by the "sage of Concord," Ralph Waldo Emerson. Emerson contended that truth wasn't to be found in the scriptures but in the workings of the natural world; salvation wasn't to be achieved by blind obedience to the social and religious hierarchy, but by actively fighting oppression and poverty. It was this vision that set the stage for the intellectual renaissance that swept through New England in the mid-1800s, nurturing the genius of writers such as Henry David Thoreau, Henry Wadsworth Longfellow and Nathaniel Hawthorne.

Within official circles, the reform movement was advanced by Mayor Josiah Quincy, who engineered a major overhaul of city services. On the fringes, however, the new activism took on a more radical edge. To the shock of Brahmin society, women began taking a leading role in temperance, health care and prison-reform movements. Early feminists like Margaret Fuller and Lydia Maria Child took up the cause of womens' rights, demanding a full stake in educational, political and economic opportunities.

The fight against slavery

The most significant new movement was William Lloyd Garrison's crusade against slavery. In 1831, Garrison began publishing an anti-

slavery newspaper, *The Liberator,* from a tiny office on Washington Street. Obscure at first, Garrison's blistering diatribes inflamed Southerners as well as Brahmins who were dependent on Southern cotton for their textile mills.

On one occasion Garrison was yanked out of a meeting by a mob, tied up, and nearly trampled. He speculated later that the assault "was planned and executed not by the rabble, or the workingmen, but by 'gentlemen of property and standing from all parts of the city'."

The abolitionists stirred even more controversy when they attacked discrimination against blacks within Boston itself. The polarizing issue was the segregation of public schools. Encour-

aged by Garrison's work, Benjamin F. Roberts sued the Boston School Board for denying his daughter admission to a white school. Although unsuccessful, the suit revitalized the drive for legislative action, and in April 1854 – after five years of intensive lobbying – a law was passed prohibiting the segregation of schools on the basis of "race, color, or religious opinions."

Meanwhile, Garrison's movement was beginning to have national repercussions. Hostility over slavery continued to mount between North and South, and even conservative Yankees joined the protest against its expansion into western territories. The underground railroad routinely smuggled slaves through "safe houses" in various parts of the city, and when a black Bostonian named Anthony Burns was captured by a slave-catcher, the whole town turned out to watch him being marched to the docks while 2,000 troops guarded against a riot.

In November, 1860, Abraham Lincoln was elected president without a single Southern electoral vote. Five months later Fort Sumter was bombarded by Confederate artillery. The Civil War was on, and New England responded dutifully to Lincoln's call for volunteers. ❑

LEFT: the abolitionists make a stand.
ABOVE: society life in the late 19th century.

Paul Revere

Paul Revere's name is so firmly fastened to Boston's history that it's scarcely possible to rate one without citing the other. In many respects, he symbolizes the transition from outraged colonialism to visionary independence.

It was a lucky day for the Bay Colony when Paul's father, Apollos de Revoire, left his home in the Channel Islands and set sail for Boston. Apollos was a talented craftsman who produced goldware and silverware of exquisite and extraordinary design. And on January 1, 1735, he and Mrs de Revoire produced an extraordinary Boston baby who became Paul Revere.

Paul inherited the family business, improved on his father's craftsmanship, and, from his shop in the North End, quickly won the reputation of being the best silversmith in colonial America. That might have been sufficient distinction for the average Bostonian, but not for Revere. Early in life he took off on a career that embraced enough sidelines, specialities, diversions, adventures and excitements to satisfy a dozen men. He was an expert horseman, a skilled man-at-arms, and an authority on explosives. As a young man, he served as a worthy artillery lieutenant in the French and Indian Wars.

Through the years, Paul also excelled as an artist, inventor, merchant, mechanic, politician, engineer, orator, dispatch rider, leading bell ringer for Old North Church, share-holder in the privateer *Speedwell*, operator of a gunpowder mill, maker of copper sheathing for the U.S.S. *Constitution*, designer of whale-oil chandeliers for the Massachusetts State House, metallurgist skilled in casting cannon and bells, maker of false teeth for General Joseph Warren, participant in the Boston Tea Party, artillery colonel in defense of Boston Harbor, printer, publisher, propagandist – and assorted other occupations.

Meanwhile, he found time to marry and to sire eight children; then, when his first wife died, he re-married and fathered eight more. For relaxation, he would drive his cows all the way from the North End to Boston Common and tether them there for grazing. And, from time to time, the Committee of Safety kept him galloping in and out of Boston on inter-colonial messenger duties.

This, then, was the man the Committee of Safety summoned in haste on the night of April 18, 1775. There was work to be done and a critical message to be delivered. Somebody must mount up and ride

post-haste to Buckman's Tavern in Lexington to warn John Hancock and Sam Adams that 800 Redcoats would be moving out from Boston to arrest them, and would then march on to Concord to destroy a store of rebel guns and ammunition.

Revere galloped to Medford where he stopped at the home of Captain Isaac Hall, commanding officer of the local minutemen as well as a well-known distiller of Medford rum and a most generous host. That might account for the unproven allegation that Revere hadn't bothered to wake up anybody between Charlestown and his stop-off at Isaac's. "After that," he wrote in his journal, "I alarmed almost every house till I got to Lexington." This was around

12.30am. Perhaps history owes a nod of recognition to Isaac Hall and his midnight rum.

At Buckman's Tavern, Revere joined with the alternate dispatch rider, William Dawes, who had made the run from Boston via another route. Neither Revere nor Dawes ever got to Concord that night. En route, they joined up with Dr Samuel Prescott of Concord, heading home from Lexington. The Redcoats nabbed all three horsemen in a roadside ambush but Dawes and Prescott escaped, with Prescott managing to alert the colonial militia at Concord. The war was on.

As for Revere, the tireless old patriot was still handling enough tasks to keep 10 normal men busy when he died in 1818, aged 83. His much visited grave is in the Old Granary Burying Ground. ❑

RIGHT: Paul Revere, a man of many talents.

IMMIGRATION AND RENEWAL

*First came the Irish, then the Italians and the Jews. As the population changed,
so the city transformed itself with some remarkable architecture*

By the time Robert E. Lee surrendered at Appomatox, Bostonians were tired of war. Like most Americans, all they wanted was to return to the old way of life and to get back to the business of running their town. But Boston was no longer the city it had been a generation earlier. For one thing, the balance of national power was shifting away from New England to New York City, where an up-and-coming breed of capitalists like the Vanderbilts, Astors and Carnegies were beginning to stake their claim to the Industrial Age. The old combination of textiles and shipping, while lucrative in its day, was no match for the steel and railroad empires.

These new industrialists were more aggressive and materialistic. Unpleasant though it was, Brahmins got a whiff of their own obsolescence. The virtues of good breeding, frugality and civic-mindedness seemed a pallid anachronism in the face of the new regime of "social Darwinism" – a philosophy posited on the most "unlovely" credo, "survival of the fittest."

Metropolitan ambitions

Boston was changing physically, too. The modest port town had blossomed over 50 years into a rambling metropolis. The city had not only grown in population to 314,000 (1875), but in overall dimensions from its original 780 acres (316 hectares) to 24,000 acres (9,700 hectares).

In 1857, the most ambitious of several landfill projects was launched in the Back Bay, a development that would eventually replace Beacon Hill as the city's most prestigious neighborhood. The job took more than 30 years, and created some 450 acres (180 hectares) of "made land." But to Bostonians, the Back Bay was more than a real estate development; it was a symbol of a new age – of a modern, cosmopolitan city.

Unlike the cramped quarters of the old city, Arthur Gilman's design called for broad, Parisian-style boulevards and generous public spaces. The lavishly styled homes that went up

LEFT: focused electioneering by James Curley.
RIGHT: young Italian immigrants in 1911.

along Beacon Street and Commonwealth Avenue were complemented by the grandeur of H.H. Richardson's Trinity Church and the splendid Public Library designed by McKim, Meade and White, both on Copley Square.

The former was built because of the destruction of the first Trinity Church, the most historic

building lost in the Great Fire of 1872, which leveled more than 65 acres (26 hectares) of downtown and destroyed 765 buildings. It was mainly a commercial disaster: most buildings were crammed with raw materials and manufactured products. Bankrupted insurance companies added a melancholy postscript to the story. Impressive new buildings arose from the rubble and stricter laws encouraged safer construction methods.

The Irish invasion

The physical expansion of Boston was in some respects a reaction to the changes going on in the older parts of town. Since the late 1820s, Boston had undergone a huge increase in its immigrant population. Most newcomers were Irish, driven from their homeland by the potato blight of 1845–50. Uneducated, desperately poor, and often weak or ill after months of hunger, they came by the thousands and huddled into the tenement houses of the North, West and South Ends.

Bostonians were suspicious of the Irish not only because they were foreigners but because they were Catholics. Anti-catholicism in New England went all the way back to the Puritans, who viewed "papists" as a loathsome brand of heretic. Until the late

THE IRISH INFLUX

The tide was so overwhelming that by 1855 there were 50,000 Irish in Boston alone, nearly one-third of the total population.

in the secretive American Party – the so-called "Know-nothings" who responded to every question about the organization with the same annoying answer, "I know nothing." By 1860, the frenzy had reached such a fever pitch that almost every state office, including the governor's, was occupied by a Know-nothing candidate.

The Civil War proved to be something of a reprieve for the Irish, as Bostonians turned away from inflammatory Know-nothing rhetoric and focused their attention on the larger issues of slavery and the South. Some

1700s, anti-catholicism was part of Boston's "Pope Day," when gangs of young men from the North and South Ends brawled on the Common, the North Enders burning the Pope's effigy on Copp's Hill if they emerged victorious, the South Enders doing the honors on the Common.

By the early 1830s, local ministers were sounding the alarm against the "Catholic menace." In 1834, a mob burst into the Ursuline Convent in Charlestown and burned it to the ground. Three years later, the "Broad Street Riot" involving some 10,000 people broke out after a Yankee fire brigade accidentally collided with an Irish funeral procession. In the political arena, resistance against immigrants took shape

immigrants joined the Union army or took jobs in war-related industries, proving once and for all that they weren't conspiring against the Yankee way of life. But for the most part, the conditions of Irish neighborhoods continued to be appalling. Housing was overcrowded and unsanitary, and work places were often dangerous. Crime was notably bad in the North End, where Anne Street (now North Street) was notorious for its bordellos, gambling halls, and roving bands of sailors.

It really wasn't until the 1880s that the Irish began to break out of the slums. In part that was due to modernization of the city. The installation of electric wires, the construction of the country's first subway and the expansion of city bureaucracy created a demand for civil servants and utility workers. Just as the Irish started to move up the economic ladder a new wave of immigrants from southern and eastern Europe arrived to fill the void. By 1890 the Irish were sharing their neighborhoods with about 45,000 Italians, 4,000 East European Jews and a scattering of Poles, Portuguese and Greeks.

Once again bigotry reared its head. In 1894, three Harvard graduates founded the Immigration Restriction League of Boston and even persuaded Congressman Henry Cabot Lodge to stand behind their cause. By then, however, the tide could not be stemmed. By 1910, 30,000

under the control of homegrown bosses such as Martin "Mahatma" Lomasney and John F. Fitzgerald (*see panel below*).

The Curley years

From the same mold came James Michael Curley who dominated Boston politics from 1920 till 1950, serving now as mayor (four times), now as governor and now as congressman, and who in 1943, won an election from a jail cell. Curley was an ambitious man with poor immigrant parents and no formal education beyond grammar school. However, he devoured books on law, politics, literature and the fine arts and

Italians and 40,000 Jews were firmly entrenched in the North and West End.

And now the Irish discovered they had a flair for politics: to coax, to buy and, on occasion, to conjure votes from the grave. Hugh O'Brien, in 1884, became the first Irish mayor and, through nearly the entire 20th century Boston's mayor was of Irish origin. It was as if an invisible sign "ONLY IRISH NEED APPLY" was hung on the Mayor's door. However, unlike in New York City, there was no political machine to recruit the Irish vote. Rather, Irish neighborhoods fell

LEFT: bustling Boston Harbor in the 19th century.
ABOVE: the wharves were a major employer.

"HONEY FITZ"

John F. Fitzgerald, the charistmatic "Honey Fitz," so-called because he would sing "Sweet Adeline" at the drop of a shillelagh, became mayor in1905. A spellbinding blarney-dispenser, he proceeded to conduct one of the city's most corrupt administrations. He lost his seat in the following term, but reclaimed City Hall in 1910 after promising voters a "Bigger, Better, and Busier Boston." And, he did give them a zoo, locally established Mothers' Day, and led Red Sox rooters to New York for the World Series. His daughter Rose married Joseph P. Kennedy in 1914 and one of their nine children, John Fitzgerald Kennedy, became America's first Catholic president.

had a remarkable photographic memory. By the time he was a public figure he dressed impeccably, attended banquets, held forth on oriental jade, quoted the classics and cited appropriate passages from Shakespeare and Tennyson when he needed to display the trappings of a learned Bostonian.

With biting wit, personal charm and an uncanny ability to make political friends, Curley thumbed his nose at both Republicans and Democrats and created a city-wide patronage system, the "Curley Machine." He considered the bosses petty (the Democratic City Committee was a "collection of chowderheads") and the Brahmins "gabbing spinsters and dog-raising

matrons in federation assembled." The day after his election he sent the Yankees into fits of apoplexy by proposing to sell the Public Garden for $10 million and placing a water pumping station under the Common.

With Curley firmly at the helm, Boston endured the Great Depression and, like many American cities, was devastated. But with a healthy cut of Roosevelt's New Deal and, after 1941, a piece of the war industry, the city survived intact, if shaken. Ironically, it was Curley's success at attracting federal projects that helped lead to his downfall. With the US government supplying jobs and money, the "old pol's" patronage system – and powerbase – was destroyed.

In addition, the Boston Irish and the Boston Brahmins were beginning to discover each other. The latter, taking a good look at the former after almost half-a-century of inattention, found that not infrequently the Irish had become more Brahmin than the Brahmins themselves. Why should the two groups not combine to work together in financial and political affairs? Curley, always hated by the Brahmins, no longer needed by the Bullyboys, was eased out.

The Kennedy years

Boston politics underwent a change after World War II. The days of cigar-chomping bosses and wholesale patronage seemed to have run their course. During the war, a new electorate came of age that was more interested in economic progress than stale ethnic rivalries. Second- and third-generation immigrant families were now part of the middle-class, and they wanted leaders who represented mainstream values and good clean government. Indicative of this change is the fact that since World War II many of the Speakers of the House of Representatives have been Boston Irish and, in 1946, Bostonians sent a young man to Congress who seemed to epitomize those qualities. His name was John F. Kennedy, grandson of "Honey Fitz." He was handsome, charming and idealistic. And he came to symbolize, both for Boston and the nation, the hope of progressive politics.

In Boston itself, the search for "non-political" leaders turned up John Hynes, who handed James Curley a stunning defeat in 1949. An unassuming, soft-spoken bureaucrat, "Whispering Johnny" showed remarkable ambition as mayor, launching in 1957 the Boston Redevelopment Authority which, over the next 15 years, would carry out urban renewal projects covering 11 percent of Boston's land. This exceeded those in any city of comparable size.

Rebuilding the city

The urban renewal program was implemented mainly during the tenure of Mayor John F. Collins (1960–68). He cajoled prominent business people to help finance his revitalization plan and also brought to Boston Edward J. Logue, who had a genius for guiding projects through the rocky terrain of federal bureaucracy.

Meetings of the Vault, as the group of businessmen was called, led to the New Boston in the shape of such buildings as the Government

Center, the Prudential Complex and the Charles River Park. Private enterprise announced its presence with the John Hancock skyscraper and the Christian Science Complex. I.M. Pei, a Harvard- and MIT-trained architect, was heavily involved in several, both public and private, of these projects.

The program got off to a somewhat shaky start when, as the result of bureaucratic vandalism and insensitivity, Scollay Square was razed to the ground, a well-established community of Italian, Irish and Russian Jewish

ED THE BOMBER

Not everyone appreciated the efforts of city planner Edward J. Logue to rebuild Boston's city center. To his critics, the New Haven man became "Ed the Bomber."

has the Hall become a symbol of the recycled and revitalized Boston.

But while resources were being lavished on the city center, trouble was brewing in the neglected outer neighborhoods. Since the war, middle-class families had been moving out to the suburbs, with the city losing 100,000 residents in the 1950s, a further 56,000 in the 1960s and 78,000 in the 1970s. Population then leveled off at today's figure of approximately 550,000, which was about where it had stood at the turn of the 20th century.

immigrants was evicted and the Government Center built. However, by the 1970s, under Mayor Kevin White who held continuous office longer than any other mayor in the city (1968–84), the thrust changed from bulldozer mega-development to recycling with serious attempts to utilize the city's physical and social resources. Faneuil Hall was one of the first and most successful of these projects and just as Jiminey Cricket (the weather vane on the roof of that building) was the symbol of Boston so

LEFT: "Honey Fitz" hands out Christmas baskets.
ABOVE: John F. Collins, mayor from 1960 to 1968.
ABOVE RIGHT: Ted Kennedy, part of a political dynasty.

The school busing crisis
Poor blacks and Hispanics filled the void created by this exodus and as minority populations swelled in neighborhoods such as Roxbury, the South End and Mission Hill, a whole new set of racial tensions started bubbling to the surface. On the one hand, blacks were calling for a long overdue share in city services, housing and education. On the other, working-class whites felt themselves being pushed out of their old neighborhoods and in competition for the same limited resources.

As the civil rights movements gained momentum in the 1960s, the situation grew more volatile. In 1974 the National Association for the

Advancement of Colored People sued the Boston Board of Education, claiming it was not in compliance with anti-segregation laws. It was true that blacks and whites went to different schools, the Board replied, but that was only because blacks and whites lived in different neighborhoods. The federal court didn't agree. Intentional or not, ruled Judge Garrity, Boston was guilty of segregation, and he ordered a program of busing to integrate blacks and whites.

The riots that surrounded the busing crisis turned Boston upside-down and shocked the nation. Every day the evening news telecast images of racial hatred: school buses sur-rounded by police cars, children threatened by protestors, a crowd of whites beating a lone black man with an American flag on the steps of City Hall. Americans wondered what was happening to Boston, one of the country's most liberal cities, the birthplace of abolition, the very crucible of democracy.

Leading the anti-busing movement was school committee-woman "You Know Where I Stand" Louise Day Hicks and City Councillor Ray Flynn who, however, when elected Mayor in 1983, proved to be a friend of blacks and other minorities.

In spite of the turmoil, Boston in the 1980s

THE BIG CLEAN-UP BEGINS

Boston's most dramatic metamorphosis in the 1990s occurred just a few miles from downtown. During the 1988 presidential election George Bush shamed Michael Dukakis with a notorious campaign photo-op using the polluted waters of Boston Harbor as his backdrop. Within a decade a court-ordered clean-up costing billions of dollars transformed what had been the dirtiest harbor in the country into waters fit for swimming. Harbor porpoises, Atlantic white-sided dolphins and harbor seals were once again common sights for sailors. The Harbor Islands gained new attention and support, being designated as a national park area in 1996.

The Charles River had also suffered for decades from use as an industrial waste repository. Its noxious state was even celebrated in the 1966 pop-hit "Dirty Water" by The Standells. In an equally famous political photo-op, Governor William Weld took credit for the transformation of the Charles River when he jumped into its waters fully clothed.

Waters weren't the only thing to be purified. Within the city, the Combat Zone, once one of the East Coast's sleaziest adult entertainment districts, suffered a withering death, eradicated by social factors: the rise of adult home video, Aids, and community pride. For the nearby streets of Chinatown, this marked a welcome transition as tourists returned and businesses benefited from increased trade.

was the hub of the "Massachusetts Miracle," which was based largely on high tech and venture capital which launched the governor of the Commonwealth, Michael Dukakis, to the Democratic presidential nomination in 1988. Skycrapers and office towers began to be constructed as if there was no tomorrow. Yet the city became the victim of its own success and by the late 1980s had started to run into economic problems. The sure winners – financial services, minicomputers and armaments – all went into recession and, by the end of the decade, the Massachusetts State bond rating was the lowest in the country.

graphics. In 1972, Massachusetts had been so solidly Democratic it was the only state in the union won by George McGovern against Richard Nixon. A generation later, for the first time in the state's history, registered independent voters outnumbered registered Democrats.

A new century

After nearly 400 years, Boston is still a city of ideas – "The Athens of America." Its universities attract some of the world's best minds; its artists hail from an inventive tradition; its religious communities are vital and committed. The Puritans are long gone, but John Winthrop's

A time of growth

By the mid-1990s Boston's fortunes mirrored the robust economy throughout America, with the growing popularity of mutual funds and the evolving biotechnology businesses attracting capital into the local economy. The vigorous local health care industry continued to expand, growing at a 3 percent annual rate. New office space that went begging at the end of the 1980s rented at a premium a decade later.

The election of Governor William Weld, a Republican, signaled a subtle shift in local demo-

LEFT: school busing caused problems in the 1970s.
ABOVE: investment has brought new wealth to the city.

vision is still very much a part of what this city is still about in the 21st century. "We must love one another with a pure heart," he said aboard the *Arbella*. "We must bear one another's burdens." Over the years Bostonians have learned and re-learned how to make that idea a reality. There have been dramatic changes since Winthrop first stepped ashore, but Boston has endured.

After all, there is a reason why, in poll after poll, Boston is voted one of America's most livable cities. This is a town that refuses to give up. In the end, Bostonians will find their solutions where they always have, in "the father-hood of God, the brotherhood of man, and the neighborhood of Boston." ❑

THE BIG DIG

For years people complained about Boston's legendary traffic snarl-ups.
Then came a radical solution: if you can't beat the cars, bury them

America was booming after World War II, as GI Bill-assisted college grads bought their first homes, drove family cars and enjoyed their new TV sets. Yet Boston was still suffering the effects of an economic depression dating back to the 1929 Wall Street crash. The smart minds of the time concluded that the way

to stem the urban decline was by rolling out the red carpet to the automobile. The carpet itself was laid by the wrecking ball and bulldozer, as city blocks and whole neighborhoods disappeared in dust, replaced by an elevated ribbon of asphalt — known as the Central Artery — designed to carry 75,000 cars a day.

While critics have described the result an urban "wound" and a pedestrian no-man's-land, the smart minds were correct and Boston thrived. Despite a paucity of parking spaces downtown and the peculiar habits of Massachusetts drivers – whom many outsiders regard as homicidal or merely insane – automobiles and trucks are now everyday fixtures of downtown business and the

city's growth. So much growth, in fact, that the Central Artery's daily 75,000 vehicles increased to 190,000 by the end of the 20th century, giving the Artery vehicular "congestive heart failure" each rush hour.

Today's smart minds are urban surgeons who, rather than performing a routine bypass, have opted for a more adventurous operation: a complete circulatory replacement intended to keep the patient healthy and functioning until the day the flow is redirected to newer pathways. In the case of the Central Artery, a third harbor tunnel named for Red Sox great Ted Williams has been added, linking the city to Logan Airport. Large sections of the granny knot of bridges and ramps crossing the Charles River are being replaced with a dramatic streamlined cable-stayed bridge. But the core of the entire project is burying the old Central Artery underground while adding additional traffic lanes and simplified entrance and exit ramps. This last procedure has given rise to the more familiar name for the entire Central Artery/Tunnel Project: "The Big Dig."

The largest and most complex highway project ever undertaken in an American city has transformed Boston into a city populated by massive cranes that rise above the city like H.G. Wells's Martian tripods. Walking and driving in the city has become a continual guessing game as roads and pathways are diverted or redirected by heavy equipment. The entire project has greatly exceeded the original timelines and projections, and visitors planning to walk or drive in the city should be aware of the project's progress and prepare to encounter detours.

To sink an elevated highway underground requires excavating 13 million cubic yards of dirt, estimated to be enough to fill 13 football stadiums. Just what does one do with all that dirt? In an ironic twist of fate, more than 4,400 bargeloads are being moved to Spectacle Island in Boston Harbor. Spectacle has had the dubious distinction of being one of the city's trash dumps for 200 years; for many years it housed a foul horse-rendering plant and later suffered from underground fires that smoldered for years.

With the dirt from the Big Dig, Spectacle Island has grown 60 ft (18 meters) higher, becoming the tallest point in the Harbor. It is also being reclaimed: with the garbage of the past now buried under new urban soil, Spectacle will become the gateway to the Harbor Islands National Park area, with hiking trails, a beach and a mussel habitat area. More than 2,400 trees and 26,000 shrubs will be planted there as the projects nears conclusion. Yet another 3 million cubic yards of additional Boston clay will be made available to local cities

THE BIG SPEND

Some critics of the Big Dig painted the project as a billion-dollar boondoggle funded by American taxpayers who would never drive a mile in Massachusetts.

water on either side, has reclaimed its position as a coveted place to live. Some even project Boston may echo Vienna's rebirth following the replacement of its medieval city wall with the Ringstrasse in the 19th century.

During the early years of the Big Dig a frequent topic on local talk shows and in barbershops was the widely reported prediction of massive migrations of displaced rats disturbed from their lair within the Artery's infrastructure. Surreal images of a gray carpet of refugee rodents moving across the Boston Com-

and towns to cap exhausted landfills.

Eventually, a city that has spent the past 50 years with its back to the water will be a unified community bisected by 27 acres (11 hectares) of new parkland developed where the ugly green girders of the elevated Central Artery once stood. Plans by real estate developers hoping to exploit this new urban property were defeated when structural studies revealed that the new underground roadway could not support high-rise buildings above. The North End, which has spent nearly two generations isolated by traffic and

LEFT: the Big Dig disrupts the South Station area.
ABOVE: the expressway about to be depressed.

mon toward the homes of Beacon Hill and Bay matrons captured the city's attention. But the rats did not materialize.

One US congressman awarded the Big Dig his "Porker Award," pointing out that 85 percent of the project's expense will be paid for by federal rather than state taxes, and that funds earmarked to finance relocation of existing electric, gas, water and telecommunications lines disrupted by the construction subsidized necessary improvements and upgrades. Some urban critics even predict the Central Artery/Tunnel Project will become obsolete on the day of completion due to the constantly expanding number of cars and other vehicles entering the inner city area. ❏

THE BOSTON CHARACTER

Only Bostonians, they say, can understand Bostonians. That statement in itself says a lot about a singular psyche

Boston's self-proclaimed status as the Hub of the Universe, though it wasn't meant to be taken entirely seriously, was a red rag that has infuriated many literary bulls. "Boston prides itself on virtue and ancient lineage – it doesn't impress me in either direction," wrote the philosopher Bertrand Russell in 1914. "It is musty, like the Faubourg St Germain. I often want to ask them what constitutes the amazing virtue they are so conscious of."

In the mid-19th century, the valued virtue was culture, as the New World, a child rapidly approaching adulthood, sought to convey its maturity to the Old. Not that everyone worshipped it: "In Boston," wrote Charles Mackay in 1859, "the onus lies upon every respectable person to prove that he has not written a sonnet, preached a sermon, or delivered a lecture."

Birth of the Brahmins

Self-esteem was certainly valued even more than sonnets, and the city's establishment readily approved Oliver Wendell Holmes's description of them as "Boston Brahmins." Not only was the alliteration attractive; the term also suggested an ancient lineage, a certain austerity, unquestioned wisdom. No matter that the 19th-century businessmen who ran Boston were often closer in their intellectual interests to Donald Trump than to an Indian ascetic: "Brahmin" was accepted. No Madison Avenue copywriter could have done a better job.

The tone had been set even earlier, in 1841, by George Combe, a phrenologist who, having studied the city's inhabitants from 1838 to 1840, delivered the kind of prognosis that court physicians reserved for absolute monarchs: "Here the female head is in general beautifully developed in the moral and intellectual departments, and the natural language of the countenance is soft, affectionate and rational. In the

men, also, large moral and intellectual organs are very general, but Benevolence and Veneration are more frequently large than Conscientiousness. The cerebral organization of this people, taking them all in all, appears really to have been enlarged in the moral and intellectual regions by long cultivation, added to the

influence of a favorable stock."

But along with the superior stock came stock attitudes. The problem, for many, was that Boston, rather than creating its own distinctive culture, was slavishly imitating the discredited characteristics of its cast-off colonial parent. "The Bostonians are really, as a race, far inferior in point of anything beyond mere talent to any other set upon the continent of North America," wrote Edgar Allan Poe in 1849. "They are decidedly the most servile imitators of the English it is possible to conceive."

Even the Bostonians' speech patterns and accent came under fire as being slavish replicas of Oxford English. As an anonymous wit put it,

---

PRECEDING PAGES: detail from the Café du Barry mural on Newbury Street, Back Bay; a street vendor entertains in Faneuil Hall Marketplace.
LEFT: Boston Brahmin. **RIGHT:** Boston's finest.

if you hear an owl hoot "To whom" instead of "To who," you can be sure it was born and educated in Boston. The Brahmins were impervious to such sneers, of course, and the curious inflections and intonations have remained unmodified so that you will be invited, for instance, to *pahk yuh cah* rather than park your car.

Whether you will be able easily to accept such an invitation, however, is doubtful, since traffic congestion is one of the Hub's chronic afflictions. The city center's roads, which remain more faithful in their patterns to 17th-century cow tracks than to anything suggesting a grid, encourage local drivers to be aggressive: they race away from traffic lights, weave in and out of lanes, and tailgate alarmingly. Visitors from Europe find such behavior quite normal; people from other American cities, where driving is more sedate and courteous, think they're in a Hollywood movie. It's not just an impression either: insurers confirm that Boston's drivers are the nation's most accident-prone.

> **MUTUAL UNDERSTANDING**
>
> "Only Bostonians can understand Bostonians and thoroughly sympathize with the inconsequences of the Boston mind."
>
> – Henry Adams,
> *The Education of Henry Adams* (1907)

BOSTON ON FILM

Boston was too far away from movie production companies to allow any dramatic location street shooting during the first 60 years of cinema history. By the early 1960s the collapse of the studio system and the invention of lightweight camera and sound equipment allowed Boston to play some celluloid supporting roles. An early episode of the TV series *Route 66* guest-starring Robert Duvall as a heroin addict is notable for its record of the 1962 Boston skyline. Six years later Norman Jewison shot *The Thomas Crown Affair* (with Steve McQueen and Faye Dunaway), the first major Hollywood production to lens on the streets of Boston. *Between the Lines* (1977) captures the world of an alternative newspaper, based on Boston's *Real Paper*. *The Brinks Job* (1978) tells the saga of the notorious armed car robbery. Another TV series *Spenser For Hire*, based on Massachusetts's own Robert B. Parker's novels, was shot in and around the city. (While the stories were based in Boston, *Cheers*, *Ally McBeal* and *St. Elsewhere* were shot in California.) In 1998 Cambridge's own Matt Damon and Ben Affleck captured the heart of the city with their script, *Good Will Hunting*, featuring South Boston in all its glory. Other recent independent movies include: *Next Stop Wonderland* (an allusion to the final stop on the Blue Line), *Southie* (another South Boston saga), and *Monument Avenue* (Charlestown).

Perhaps the planners hope that placing the central expressway underground will bury the problem.

Ever adaptable, Bostonians have responded to the traffic chaos by regarding walking as a virtue. Where a New Yorker would unhesitatingly flag down a cab, the Bostonian, eschewing extravagance, will step smartly towards his or her destination. Given the jams, of course, that's sound common sense; as the joke has it: "Shall we walk or do we have time to take a cab?"

Split personality

But if walking is sometimes a necessity, it is usually a pleasure. It enables one to savor the gains they unearth among the scheduled markdowns. The city is unquestionably America's medical capital; yet in its very center sits the vast concrete bunker of the Christian Science Complex, whose occupants reject many of the tenets of modern medicine.

Academics adore such paradoxes and probably encourage them. Boston is a factory town whose product is college graduates and each new generation adds its own pinch of quirkiness to the cocktail, sustaining the legend. Also, many find jobs and stay on in the area after graduating, adding fresh blood to the population and keeping urban sclerosis at bay.

strange contradictions of this untypical town. The architecture expresses part of its split personality: the size, color and design of the carefully preserved older buildings convey class, heritage and a human scale, while the gleaming new skyscrapers and vast concrete bunkers radiate boldness, modernity and commercial confidence but can sometimes seem soulless. A spell of window-shopping will quickly indicate that Boston is an expensive place to live; yet here is Filene's Basement, where society matrons as well as secretaries boast of the bar-

LEFT: the Irish influence remains very strong.
ABOVE: showing a sisterly spirit.

And so the debate goes on. For more than two centuries, the Boston character has delighted and infuriated, almost in equal measure, and has defeated most attempts to define it. Such attempts, Bostonians will tell you, are futile in any case, unless you had the good fortune to be born and brought up in the Hub of the Universe. It's an attitude summed up by the old story of the Bostonian who dies and, with due dignity, approaches St Peter at the Pearly Gates in order to present his credentials and seek permission to enter. St Peter asks him where he is from, and on being told "BOSTON," hesitates, then says, "Well, your record is spotless, and you may come in, but I don't think you will like it here." ❏

THE VISUAL ARTS

The founding fathers had little time for frivolities such as painting and sculpture,
but their descendants determined to turn Boston into the Athens of America

The visual arts did not come easily or soon to Boston. When, about 1630, New England was born in the "howling wilderness," neither the harsh reality of survival nor the narrow path of Puritan theology lent itself to the pleasures of painting, sculpture or the decorative arts. These, if not actually proscribed, were clearly a matter of suspicion in a society that found its expression as well as its aesthetic in religion and government.

In no time, however, the founding fathers were lamenting a drift in their progeny who demanded prosperity as much as salvation from the wilderness. As the old virtues of piety, moderation, and industry conflated a warm and heady desire to succeed, Boston created an ambitious mercantile society. Its members, unafraid of the little pomps and vanities their parents had abhorred, determined to have their fair share of culture and a civilized enthusiasm for the arts.

Early artists

Eighteenth-century Boston, like any self-respecting English provincial capital, was pretty much a matter of status symbols and luxury goods – portraits and tombstone carvings, silver tea pots and coats of arms on carriage panels. There was no artistic past; even if there had been, nobody would have cared. Boston was a thoroughly modern town: everything was fashion and the latest style. The cult of the past would arrive only later.

Monumental sculpture and history painting, the touchstones of the visual arts on the continent, would not be appreciated to any real degree – and then only in a limited manner – until the early 1800s and the Federal era. Landscape painting would not truly flourish before the coming of the Victorians. Genre painting appeared with the Edwardians and the "Boston School" of 1900.

PRECEDING PAGES: *West Church* by Maurice Prendergast.
LEFT: *Mrs Fiske Warren and her Daughter* by the influential John Singer Sargent.
RIGHT: sculpture at Wellesley College Museum.

In artistic terms, however, great strides were made in the 18th century by Bostonians as gifted as John Singleton Copley and Paul Revere, and the general level of artistic achievement was unsurpassed, and quite probably unmatched, in the American colonies. Copley's portrait of Revere, now in the

Museum of Fine Arts (MFA), is the result of a fortuitous meeting of artist and sitter, and worth careful study for what it tells of 18th-century Boston – practical, proud and unafraid of a dignified opulence.

The message is writ large in Copley's great portraits of Boston's mercantile aristocracy, which are also seen at their best in the MFA. Keeping these faces in mind gives added meaning to a visit to King's Chapel, where it is easiest to find the 18th century in the modern city. The air is chill and sweet with an unmistakable New England tang.

The Revolution changed many of the players, but the game remained the same as Boston entered the 19th century and the era of its greatness. Even so, the arts remained more than a little suspect in the young republic. John Adams, with a whiff of brimstone worthy of his ancestors, still pondered whether the arts, those suspicious handmaidens of luxury and aristocracy, had any place in a democracy. "Are we not," he cautioned with fretful anxiety, "in too great a hurry in our zeal for the fine arts?"

Federal Boston, unlike earlier periods, remains very much in evidence, with Charles Bulfinch's gold dome of the State House – it was originally gray – dominating Beacon Hill. Aesthetically, the city today is its own greatest

asset, with the carefully preserved Federal townscape of the Hill blending seamlessly with the Victorian sweep of the Back Bay.

Nineteenth-century Boston took pride in its transformation of the "howling wilderness" into the "American Athens" – no mean feat in a scant 200 years when the odds are against you. Educational, charitable and cultural institutions (with "fair" Harvard generally given pride of place) were carefully nurtured as the proper sphere for a "Brahmin" aristocracy, rich beyond the wildest dreams of their immigrant ancestors and heavy with intellectual pretension.

Artists were admired and assimilated as the ornaments of that society. This high regard is sometimes said to account for the decorative rather than incisive character of much of this Brahmin culture, where the unpredictable tendency of artists to comment and to criticize was curbed with the flattery of dinner invitations and with kind words. In a few notable cases – Copley and William Morris Hunt, for example – a handsomely dowered daughter tempered the force of artistic fury.

The Athenaeum

No cultural institution was as central to the arts in Federal Boston as the Boston Athenaeum. In a series of increasingly grand homes, it mounted Boston's first public exhibitions of painting and sculpture and assembled the city's first generally accessible public collection of art. By 1850, it had taken up residence in the Italianate palazzo on Beacon Street where it remains. Some of its collection also remains, and some has gone to enrich the holdings of the MFA, whose parent the Athenaeum became in 1870 when it divided its responsibilities between literature and the visual arts. The Athenaeum was a potent force in the flowering of American painting and sculpture in the 19th century, and its grand home is redolent with that penetrating taste that marked Federal America's neoclassicism.

By the time the Athenaeum had transferred its mandate in the visual arts to the new MFA, taste itself was changing and there were new gods for the new museum age. Ruskin, the Renaissance and Florence had superseded Rome and the neoclassic ideal, and in Boston the robust graces of the ancient world had been replaced with the languid artfulness which became so much a part of the late 19th-century culture in the city. Ruskin disciples and Harvard professors succeeded in turning the American Athens into a kind of Florence on the Charles. Genteel enthusiasts, weak and well-bred as water, returned to Europe to a nostalgic reality peopled with Bostonians whose literary equivalents are familiar from the novels of Henry James and Edith Wharton.

The French influence

The terrible social and political catharsis of the Civil War brought forth a rich artistic flowering in New England. Culturally, Boston tended to define itself in terms of education and morality, but this would always he challenged, after the

1850s, by a bold and unexpected interest in modern French art. Its earliest champion was the painter William Morris Hunt, a New Englander who had studied in France with Couture and Millet, and who married so well that Bostonians paid more attention to his taste than they might otherwise have done. They patronized his French friends and acquired fine collections of French pictures into the bargain.

Hunt introduced the Barbizon painters (placing so many Millets locally that those which

with a remarkable lack of prejudice. The MFA has been heir to quite a few of these collections, and its galleries on Huntington Avenue are unsurpassed in areas as diverse as Asian and classical art and 19th-century French painting.

In the realm of plastic arts, the MFA's Egyptian Old Kingdom collection, unrivaled except at the Cairo Museum, is the result of joint Harvard-MFA expeditions which began in 1905 under the direction of Dr George A. Reisner. The glorious sculpture and the architectural pieces in the

found their way to the MFA make that museum's holdings unrivaled anywhere in the world). He created an enthusiasm that outlived him, reaching what is surely its ultimate expression in the dozens of Monets that poured into Boston. Forty of them happily also found their way to the MFA.

Most private collections formed in 19th-century Boston were smaller and generally less showy than their counterparts in New York. They were, however, often more discerning, and ranged through the entire history of taste

LEFT: Boston Athenaeum. **ABOVE:** *Boston Common at Twilight* by Ferderick Childe Hassam.

Indian Art Section owe much to joint MFA-University of Pennsylvania expeditions. Incidentally, the MFA is entirely supported by private gifts, bequests and annual subscriptions: it receives no assistance from public funds.

A number of other institutions, mainly educational, have also assumed the role of the private collector, and well repay the trouble of a visit. The Fogg Art Museum at Harvard in Cambridge houses outstanding collections. Also noteworthy are the Rose Art Museum at Brandeis University in Waltham, with its remarkable contemporary American art, and the Wellesley College Museum in Wellesley, with its distinguished historical collection (the superb ancient marble known as the "Wellesley youth" is alone worth the trip).

Collecting as a cultural pursuit began rather later than it did elsewhere in America, and the few early local collections of importance have long since been dispersed, as have those of early institutions such as the Athenaeum. Several important collections from the second half of the 19th century were embedded more or less intact in various local museums, but one – the finest of them all – has been preserved as it was created, a few hundred yards from the MFA. For many, the MFA with all its masterpieces takes emotional second place to the Isabella Stewart Gardner Museum, for where it is great, the Gardner is unique.

The Gardner Museum

Although the collection built up by Isabella Stewart Gardner (*see panel below*) is uneven, its highlights are remarkable. They include Giotto and Piero della Francesca, Degas and Sargent, and the Titian Room is stunning. But even Titian gracefully gives pride of place to the ensemble she lovingly created. In an age when museums have almost totally decontextualized their works of art, it is a pleasure to add that Mrs Gardner's context makes her Titian sing with an added reso-

How Isabella Stewart Gardner Built an Institution

Isabella Stewart, born in New York in 1840, became a Bostonian when she married the financier Jack Lowell Gardner. The Brahmin and his vivacious wife, whose actions were often frowned upon by proper Bostonians, became enthusiastic art collectors and filled their Commonwealth Avenue home with treasures from frequent trips to Europe.

When Gardner died in 1889, "Mrs Jack" set about building the Venetian palazzo of her dreams and embellishing it with her collection of spectacular paintings, sculpture, furniture and textiles. Fenway Court opened with a private party on New Year's Day, 1903. Mrs Gardner received her guests at the head of the double staircase while 50 members of the Boston Symphony Orchestra entertained. Logs burned in each room as guests indulged in two of her delights: doughnuts and champagne.

Mrs Gardner lived on the top floor of Fenway Court until her death in 1924, and she still presides there in the shape of her controversial portrait painted by Sargent in 1888. It caused a Boston scandal because Mrs Gardner appeared in what was then considered to be a revealing low-cut gown.

Fenway Court's surfeit of masterpieces has less to do with its glory than one might expect, for although masterpieces are not in short supply, most museums would consign a good part of the collection to the storeroom.

nance. There is really nothing more wonderful, or more of a piece with Boston, than the Gardner.

Fenway Court is often said to have inspired a revival of interest in local artists and revived a long tradition of local patronage, but in truth Boston, like most American cities, was (and, alas, is) conspicuously unenthusiastic about the home-grown product. A flurry of chauvinistic interest in the painters Gilbert Stuart and Washington Allston in Federal Boston was not followed by a like interest in their successors (the best, like Winslow Homer, simply left town as a result) and was soon entirely supplanted by a taste for foreign old masters. Boston patronage

taste for mural painting in the Boston Public Library, MFA and Harvard's Widener Library, the work of William Paxton and Edmund Tarbell clearly also grew out of the aesthetic shock administered by Mrs Gardner's superb Vermeer at Fenway Court. (This Vermeer and several other treasures were stolen in 1990.)

The Boston School summarized everything that Boston had come to admire in the arts: technical skill, languid sentiment, and an often maddening refinement brought to the study of a narrow, genteel world. Looks can be deceiving, because the style took root with the rude health of a roadside weed and its practitioners

of American sculptors followed the same downward curve, from brisk interest to benign neglect, although a taste for public monuments made Boston a marvelous place in which to stroll and to look at statues.

The Boston School

Painting would flourish once again around 1900 with the emergence of the "Boston School." Encouraged by the vital example of John Singer Sargent, who indulged a perhaps misguided

are still numerous and popular. Their work, in fact, fuels the success of today's Newbury Street art market.

Newbury Street, long the center of the art market and the luxury trades in Boston, has always suffered because of its proximity to New York. Madison Avenue is too close for comfort, and collectors, no less than artists, regularly fall subject to its variety and charm. Nonetheless, artists both serious and admirable remain, and the graduates of the art schools and universities continually swell the ranks. The arts in Boston still flourish with a determination worthy of the rocky soil that gave them birth. ❏

FAR LEFT: courtyard, Isabella Stewart Gardner Museum.
LEFT: *The New Necklace* (1910) by William Paxton.
ABOVE: *My Family* (1914) by Edmund Tarbell.

STRIKING THE RIGHT NOTE

Thanks to Arthur Fiedler, everyone has heard of the Boston Pops,
but they're just the tip of a large iceberg of music-making

Boston is positively awash with music. That's not surprising, given that the very first orchestra in the nation was formed here in 1810 or 1811 (records are hazy) under the baton of Johann Christian Gottlieb Braubner, who also helped to establish the Handel and Haydn Society. This, America's first organiza-

moved into today's Symphony Hall, which, although not the most handsome of buildings, has superb acoustics.

Now, about 250 concerts, attended by an audience of 1½ million, are performed annually. Millions more listen to recordings and broadcasts of the orchestra which, in 1918, under the baton

tion dedicated exclusively to music, sang Haydn's *Creation*, the first oratorio to be sung in the land, in King's Chapel in 1815.

Boston's most renowned ensemble is the Boston Symphony Orchestra (BSO) or simply Symphony; it was founded by Major Henry Lee Higginson in 1881, and tickets for its concerts are handed down from generation to generation. The BSO gave its first performance in 1881 in the Music Hall under the baton of George Henschel. This was an enormous success, and in its first year almost 85,000 attended the orchestra's 20 concerts and the same number of rehearsals. The halcyon days of the much loved orchestra begin at the start of the 20th century when they

of Karl Much, cut the world's earliest orchestral recordings and then, in 1926, under the direction of Serge Koussevitsky, made the first orchestral broadcast in the nation.

Come magnolia time, the conductor and leading performers of the BSO disappear and, with the big cats away, the mice begin to play popular music. The auditorium is filled with tables, and champagne corks pop. These are the Pops; they began in 1885 as the Promenade Concerts and most proper Bostonians find them just a little *déclassé*. Yet tickets are hard to come by during the two-month season. Some say that the word Pops is not derived from popular music nor from popping champagne corks but rather owes its origins to the fact that a march called *The Pops* was played in very first week of these concerts.

In July the orchestra transfers to the Hatch Shell, an outdoor music stand on the banks of the Charles River and there delights enormous audiences with a series of outdoor performances – the Boston Pops Esplanade Concerts – lasting for four weeks. Arthur Fiedler, who conducted from 1919 to 1979, and successors such as John Williams and Keith Lockhart have introduced

THE HATCH SHELL

The Hatch Shell was built in 1940, using $300,000 left in the will of Maria E. Hatch, who died in 1926. She had willed the cash to be used for a public work in memory of her brother, Edward Hatch.

at the biannual Boston Early Music Festival, which has a worldwide reputation.

And, all the time, the city's two major music schools (New England Conservatory and the Berklee College of Music) make music with innumerable groups and orchestras. So, to a lesser extent, do the 50 or so colleges and universities in the Greater Boston area.

Try as it will, Boston has never been a major force in opera – although when Jenny Lind, the Swedish nightingale, came to Boston in 1850,

the joys of classical music to untold thousands.

Other, lesser known ensembles bring music to devotees around town. Music is also made by the Pro Arte Chamber Orchestra, founded by a Harvard University minister, Larry Hall. It specializes in works by Boston composers and during its first 10 years offered 24 world premiers of these musicians. The Boston Camerata Chamber Orchestra, Banchetto Musicale, the Cantata Singers and the John Oliver Choral and many other groups come into their own

LEFT: concerts at the Hatch Shell, on the banks of the Charles River, draw large audiences.
ABOVE: performance at the Berklee College of Music.

she conquered and was conquered; after her marriage, she returned to live at Louisburg Square on Beacon Hill. The first Boston opera company opened in 1909 with a performance of *La Gioconda* but by 1915 was bankrupt. Sara Caldwell resurrected the company as The Opera Company of Boston in 1957 and, with many vicissitudes, kept it going for more than three decades, filling the repertoire mainly with less popular works.

It may yet rise again. Several promising new ventures have formed as Caldwell and her supporters continue to seek adequate funding. Perhaps one will emerge as the nucleus of the opera company that a cultivated city such as Boston deserves. ❏

FOOD

Seafood remains one of the New England classics, but the influence of immigrants and new traditions are making their mark

While Boston and surroundings can't claim the gustatory prominence of a Paris or Rome, native Massachusetts cuisine holds a singular position in the most famous and most often reenacted meal in American history. From Key West to Tucson, for many Americans the fourth Thursday in November is the one moment of the year they taste Cape Cod cranberry sauce or New England squash. On Thanksgiving, in what is the nation's only simultaneous universal dining experience, the Massachusetts palate is the American palate.

Whether Fanny Farmer actually enjoyed the long hours preparing a turkey dinner is unrecorded, but her place in Boston and American cooking history is celebrated. This 1889 graduate of the Boston Cooking School, and later head of her own culinary academy, profoundly advanced the preparation of American food with her emphasis on accurate recipe directions. She was known as "the mother of level measurements" and her *Boston Cooking School Cook Book* attained sales of more than 3 million copies. Sixty years later another author from across the river in Cambridge, Julia Child, popularized French cooking in the first widely-watched television cooking show, *The French Chef*, the forerunner of the hundreds of instructional programs that now flood the airways.

Bye-bye Beantown

Stereotypically, Boston is thought of as the home of the baked bean, traditionally cooked in molasses and sugar. Yet one will have to search a score or more restaurant menus – offering everything from *crème de cailles au genièvre* to *pla rad pik* – before finding a side order of Boston brick-oven baked beans.

Not so with seafood. The Pilgrims might have been a bit confounded by our mania for lobster. They considered the crustaceans fit only for pig food, or bait; well into the 19th

LEFT: formal food at an upscale Boston hotel.
RIGHT: informal eating at a Quincy Market café.

century, boatloads of lobsters sold for pennies, and prisoners rioted at the prospect of yet another lobster dinner. New England's lobster harvest is today a $150 million-a-year enterprise. And while creative preparations abound, menus still feature traditional boiled lobsters and "lobster rolls" – toasted hot dog buns

filled with chunks of lobster meat, tossed with celery and mayonnaise.

The settlers weren't quite so blind to the appeal of oysters, however. As early as 1601, Samuel de Champlain had singled out the area now known as Wellfleet, on Cape Cod for its exceptional beds of oysters.

Boston's fabled clam chowder got its name from the French settlers of Breton Canada, who simmered their soups in a *chaudière* (cauldron). Such long, slow cooking is needed to render the hard shell quahogs (pronounced "co-hogs") palatable. The small and medium-size versions – cherrystones and littlenecks – are delectable served raw, on the half shell. Soft-shell, long neck clams – commonly known as "steamers" – are a favored repast all along the coast, dipped first in brine (to wash off the grit), then melted in butter. Outside of the city clam shacks fire up their fry-o-lators to prepare another favorite: clams batter-coated and fried.

Clambakes were once a New England tradition, especially on Cape Cod. The customary procedure was to lay out a stone pit on the beach, build a driftwood fire, cover the hot stones with seaweed, add clams and their accompaniments

THE BREWING TRADITION

The prevalence of microbreweries has a long tradition. With no access to safe drinking water, the Pilgrims, both adults and children, drank beer because the alcohol content kept the microbes at bay.

now very nearly ubiquitous, usually served marinière or poached in white wine. Seasonal bay scallops have always enjoyed greater gourmet cachet than the larger, tougher sea scallop, but until recently, restaurants invariably threw away the tastiest part, serving only the adductor muscle. Bay scallops are now available year-round, and the more adventurous fine restaurants have begun serving them whole, whether on the half-shell or cooked.

Cranberries – so named by Dutch settlers

(typically lobsters, potatoes, corn on the cob), and then top it all off with more seaweed, a sail-cloth tarp, and plenty of sand, leaving the whole to bake for about an hour. Most coastal resort restaurants these days dispense with clambake *per se*, and just serve what's called a "shore dinner" – steamed.

It was the abundant cod, however, that initially lured English fishermen, and eventually settlers, to the Boston area. Fillet of young cod, called scrod (from the Dutch *schrood*, for "a piece cut off"), still graces traditional menus.

Exposure to European traditions has introduced two relatively new seafood treats. Mussels, long ignored by Boston restaurants, are

who thought the flowers resembled cranes – are one of the few fruits native to North America. Native Americans used sassamanesh – "bitter berries" – as a dye, a poultice, and as food, pounded with venison to make "pemmican" (meat cakes) or sweetened with maple sap. Long before Vitamin C was recognized, whalers would set off to sea with a barrel of cranberries to prevent scurvy.

Today, visitors can tour Massachusetts cranberry bogs and celebrate fall festivals from Plymouth to Nantucket.

With no access to safe drinking water, the Pilgrims – adults and children alike – had no choice but to drink beer (the alcohol content kept the microbes in check). Today they could travel north to visit Boston's many microbreweries, and perhaps join a Brew Pub Tour.

Apple seeds, which came to New England with the Pilgrims in 1620, contributed another popular beverage: apple cider. This fresh pressed apple juice was a favorite drink in colonial times and was also converted into "hard" or alcoholic cider. President John Adams claimed that a tankard of hard cider every morning calmed his stomach and alleviated gas. Hard cider has enjoyed a trendy revival in recent years led by a number of New England brands which even offer exotic raspberry and cinnamon varieties.

Ice cream

Like the rest of New England, Bostonians can be a mite obsessive about their ice cream, as can be observed on any warm evening when long lines form at the local ice cream parlor. Americans eat more ice cream than any other nation, and New Englanders are said to consume 14 more pints of the stuff annually than any other region. (When ordering an ice cream cone, don't be surprised if you are asked if you want it "with jimmies." This is nothing more than New England slang for what the rest of the world calls "sprinkles.")

The immigrant influence

In Boston, flavors that would previously have been considered "exotic" have entered the mainstream food vocabulary, in part due to the waves of immigration that have brought new culinary traditions to the city. The Italian immigrants who settled in the city in late 1800s and early 1900s have left an indelible stamp on the city's food, and the many North End restaurants are always a popular destination.

Since 1960, almost 80 percent of immigrants to the US have come from Asia, Latin America, and the Caribbean. Boston now boasts Chinese, Japanese, Thai, Vietnamese, Cambodian, Malaysian, Puerto Rican, Mexican, Haitian, and many other ethnic eateries, where clams in black bean sauce and lobster sautéed with ginger and scallions blend local ingredients into the classic cuisines of their home countries. The possibilities are endless.

LEFT: chefs at Locke-Ober's Restaurant, Winter Place.
RIGHT: the celebrated Warren Tavern, Charlestown.

This melting pot of flavors has also turned into more upscale fusion cuisine, where celebrity chefs are transforming Boston restaurant menus. Adventurous eaters can indulge in salad of Maine rock crab with lobster knuckles and fried taro, crispy squash risotto cakes, pumpkin ravioli with mussels marinière, lightly fried lobster with lemongrass and Thai basil, ginger barbecued skate wing served over spicy jalapeño slaw with Boston baked beans, or seared scallops in cider sauce.

But old tradition endures as well. Those boiled lobsters, that baked cod, finished with a bowl of ice cream remain on the Boston menu. ❏

A FOODIE'S HISTORY OF BOSTON

1700: Dried codfish go to Lisbon in exchange for port wine.
1795: The 39-year-old French gastronome Jean-Anthelme Brillat-Savarin comes to Boston to sample consommé.
1862: Jacob Fussell opens first Boston ice-cream plant.
1869: Boston gets fresh meat from Chicago stockyards courtesy of the first refrigerated railcars.
1889: Dunn's restaurant sells 10-course dinner for 25 cents.
1892: Boston Public Schools pioneer school hot lunches.
1917: Boston food riots due to rising costs.
1919: North End molasses explosion kills 13, injures 60.
1959: Locke-Obers restaurant switches to frozen vegetables; no one takes notice.

A PASSION FOR SPORT

Baseball, basketball, hockey and football all have their fanatical followers.

And few participatory activities can outpace the Boston Marathon

At the start of the 1978 baseball season Mark Starr, who headed the *Newsweek* bureau in Boston, was on assignment in Jerusalem. He visited the Wailing Wall whose fame – dare it be written? – is challenged only by the "Green Monster," the left field wall at Fenway Park where the Red Sox baseball team plays. After writing a supplication on a piece of paper, he inserted it between the cracks of the Wall. He begged God to let the Sox win the World Series that year. Starr still believes that it was this sacrilegious behavior which denied the Sox the American League pennant when, in the ninth inning of their decisive play-off game with the New York Yankees, Bucky Dent hammered out a three-run homer.

Such sports fanaticism among Bostonians, especially when it comes to baseball, is not unusual. Come summer and, if the Sox are on a roll, then all is well and Boston sports fans walk tall. Let the September Swoon come – as it almost invariably does – and all are dejected and life is scarcely worth living.

Infatuated fans

Many staid, cultured, educated Bostonians turn to the sports pages of the morning newspaper before checking their investments and then reading the world news. Starr believes that this is because tragedies are more enjoyable than comedies and substantiates this theory by citing the works of Shakespeare.

Still, for much of the time, Red Sox followers are presented not only tragedies but are simultaneously entertained with comedies. How else can one describe the sixth game in the World Series, in 1986, when the Sox were within a heart-beat of clinching the title until a grounder trickled through the legs of first baseman Bill Buckner?

Some suggest that Beantown's infatuation

with sport has a regional basis and results from an inferiority complex *vis à vis* New York. Others say that it is the result of immigrant groups (especially the Irish) and student groups seeking a cause to follow. But no: the reasons are arcane, abstruse and complex and the best that can be said is that Bostonians consider their

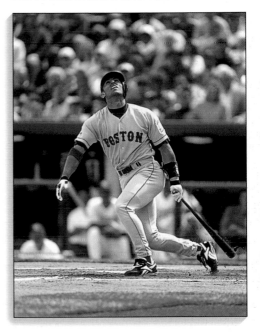

teams, especially the Sox, to be their patrimony and they simply inherit their devoted loyalty.

The latter was seen when, in 1976, the Bruins, the Boston ice hockey team, traded Bobby Orr, their star defenseman, to the Chicago Blackhawks. Many who held life-long tickets to the Boston Garden, where the Bruins once played, simply tore them up and vowed never to enter the Garden again. They kept their word until Orr retired and made peace with the team. Finally, Boston sports fans are knowledgeable, and the media, whose coverage of the teams exceeds that found anywhere else in the country, merely serve to fan the flames.

PRECEDING PAGES: Red Sox star John Valentin and coach Jim Rice at Fenway Park.
LEFT: the Boston Celtics in action. **RIGHT:** the Red Sox.

A city of firsts

Boston's infatuation with sports is reflected in – or is it the result of? – the fact that here, as in so many other fields, it has known so many firsts. A commemorative stone on the Boston Common informs that "On this field the Oneida Football Club of Boston, the first organized football club in the United States, played against all comers from 1862 to 1865. The Oneida goal was never crossed." Would that the New England Patriots, whom disillusioned fans attempt to dismiss by saying that they do not play in Boston but at Foxboro, could approach that record in a single game of consequence, such as a Super Bowl, let alone four seasons!

On the other hand, Bostonians embrace Springfield, 90 miles (145 km) to the west. There, in 1881, James A. Naismith hung peach baskets at either end of a local YMCA hall and thus gave birth to the game of basketball. This was a somewhat pedestrian affair until Naismith decided to remove the bottoms of the baskets. Then, in 1895, in neighboring Holyoke, William Morgan introduced the game of volleyball.

Before this, in 1874, the first grass tennis court in the nation was inaugurated at Nahant (part of Greater Boston). This was also the year when the nation's first football goal posts

appeared on the playing fields of Harvard. In 1875, Charles W. Waite, while playing first base in Boston, donned a baseball glove, the first of the "kid glove aristocracy." And, in 1876, F.W. Thayer, a Harvard man, astonished all by wearing a mask when catching at baseball.

The Sox

To most Bostonians, sport is synonymous with the Red Sox, their beloved baseball team which, year after year, raises them to heady heights and plunges them into stygian depths. It is as if the Puritan or Catholic blood surging through Bostonian veins insists that they have a cross to bear. The Sox – no need to bother

BABE RUTH

George Herman Ruth, born in a poor area of Baltimore in 1895, became one of baseball's most celebrated players, earning $80,000 a year, then a record, in 1930 and 1931. He played for the Boston Red Sox from 1914 until 1919, when he was sold to the New York Yankees. In 1935 he played his last season with the Boston Braves.

"The Babe." as he was universally known, had a flamboyant reputation off the field – which some believe scuppered his chances of gaining a coveted major league manager's job in later life – but he was indisputably one of baseball's best left-handed pitchers before becoming a remarkable outfielder. He died in 1948, at the age of 53.

with the adjective Red, for what other are there for Bostonians? – have homered, bunted and fumbled at small, cosy, intimate Fenway Park with its terrifying left-field wall, the Green Monster – ah, there lie a thousand stories – since 1912.

Even before that, in 1903, they had won the very first World Series. By 1918, they had been crowned world champions five times. Since then the Sox have never won another World Series, although on several occasions they have seen – even practically touched – the Promised Land. Could

ANYONE FOR TENNIS?

The US Pro Tennis Championships are played on the hard courts of the Longwood Cricket Club, 564 Hammond Street, Brookline (tel: 731 2900) in the seond week of July.

American League. This was not only because of the Babe, who, when he set his record in 1927 with 60 homers, hammered eight of them at Fenway Park, but because of the steady stream of other top Sox players whom Frazee kept trading to the Yankees.

Frazee's problem was money – or rather the lack of it. In addition to owning the Sox, he was a failed theatrical impresario who was always in debt. (In 1925, however, two years before he died, he backed the enormously successful musical *No, No, Nanette*

it be because of the curse of the Bambino, or did Harry Frazee, the owner of the Sox from 1917 until 1923, sell his soul to the devil: the damned Yankees?

The Bambino or the Babe, christened George Herman Ruth, arrived in Boston from Baltimore in 1914 and, with incomparable pitching and then superman hitting, was the toast not only of Boston but of all America. And then the unthinkable happened: in 1920, Harry Frazee sold the Bambino to the New York Yankees who, for the next half-century, dominated the

with its show-stopping "Tea for Two.")

The tormenting of the Sox by the Yankees did not cease with Frazee's death. In both 1949 and 1978, when the teams met on the final day of the season, the result would decide the American League championship. You've guessed it: on both occasions the Yankees won. Glorious retribution occurred in 1990 when Bucky Dent, the Yankee's manager, was fired after a game with the Sox at Fenway Park: Dent's ninth inning homer in the 1978 game had been the hit that destroyed the Sox. (A similar decisive game had been played in 1904 when, because of a wild pitch by the Yankee's Jack Chesboro, the Sox won.)

LEFT: Fenway Park, home of the Red Sox.
ABOVE: Little League baseball hopefuls in Newton.

In 1935, Tom "Mister" Yawkey, for whom money never was a problem, became owner of the Sox and buying rather than selling became the order of the day. The faithful were not immediately rewarded but had to wait until 1946 when the Sox won the pennant, a feat which they repeated in 1967 and 1975 and then, under the reign of Mrs Jean Yawkey, who had assumed control of the club on her husband's death, in 1986.

Four times the Sox were led toward the Promised Land, but it was not to be: each of these four World Series went the full seven games and each time the Sox left empty-

was then involved in a game that featured 10 double plays (the Sox hit into six of these). Amends soon followed when, in a game against Detroit, they had 12 two-base hits – another American League record.

In 1959, with the signing of infielder "Pumpsie" Green, the Sox became the last club in the majors to be integrated. One wonders if some Macchiavelian scheme was behind this signing for, it has been said, by signing Green the Red Sox passed on an opportunity to sign Hall of Famer Willie Mays. The club's racial history has long been an issue, but in the 1990s the team finally began to shed its lilly-white image,

handed. This, in spite of the fact that their teams included the mighty Ted Williams, six times American League batting champion and the last player in the majors to hit over 400; Carl Yastrzemski, who had more than 3,500 hits; and Most Valuable Player and two times Cy Young winner Roger Clemens, who, in a memorable 1986 game, threw 20 strike-outs.

On the other hand, Sox teams also included players who, in one game in 1990 against Minnesota, succeeded in hitting into two triple plays in one game – a major league record – and yet winning that game. Statisticians claim that one triple play in a game should occur once in every five years: two – ugh! The same team

adding a number of black and latin players, and signing Elaine Weddington – not only a black but a woman – as assistant general manager. Also, the Sox added play-by-play in Spanish to their regular broadcasts, becoming the tenth team in the majors to offer such a service.

The Celtics

The accusation of racism was also once leveled against the Celtics, Beantown's beloved basketball team, although Chuck Cooper, who was signed in 1950, was the first black player in the National Basketball Association (NBA) and, in 1966, the Celtics made history by becoming the first major league team in *any* sport to name a black head coach, Bill Russell. Yet, in the early 1990s, with the NBA dominated by black players, the Celtics were the only team fielding an all-white starting five. On the other hand, during the 1963–64 season they became the first NBA team to put five blacks on the floor at the same time.

Black or white, the green and white has been the most successful team in any major sport in the country. Unlike the Sox, who began at the top and then went into decline – will they ever win another World Series? – the Celtics started disastrously when the 11-team Basketball Association of America (later to become the NBA) was founded in 1946. Then, coached by Arnold (Red) Auerbach and with such basketball immortals on the floor as Larry Bird, Bob Cousy, Dave Cowens, John Havlicek, Tom Heinsohn, K.C. Jones, Sam Jones and Bill Russell – the list is never-ending – they started winning until the rafters at the Boston Garden had scarcely space for another banner. Beginning in 1959, the Celtics won an unprecedented eight championships on the trot, and their dominance continued throughout the 1970s and 1980s.

Auerbach, first coach, then manager and finally president of the Celtics, small in stature and a mere Lilliputian among his Brobdingnagian players, has been honored by the city to which he brought so much pleasure and such distinction with a bronze, life-sized statue, clutching his inevitable cigar. It sits in the Faneuil Hall Marketplace.

The Bruins

But the beloved Boston Garden is gone, replaced by the FleetCenter built next door in 1996. The banners commemorating those championships that once hung on the rafters of the Garden have been transferred to the new arena, where they are joined by five others honoring the Stanley Cups won by the Bruins, who, in 1924, were the first American team to receive a franchise in the National Hockey League. In terms of success and ability to frustrate fans, the Bruins occupy a position somewhere between the Sox and the Celtics. A winning record for 23 years in a row is the longest of *any* professional team and scarcely a season passes when they do not reach the play-offs. Yet, sadly, so too does scarcely a

season pass when those same Bruins are sent packing in the first or second round of the NHL's interminable play-offs, and the Stanley Cup paraded through another city.

Greatest of all Bruins was Bobby Orr, who joined the club when only 18 and who revolutionized hockey, not only in Boston but throughout the world, by showing that defensemen could attack and score goals. He was the league's MVP on three occasions and won the Norris Trophy for outstanding defenseman eight consecutive times. Other greats have been Eddie Shore, who, in the Bruins' early days, was largely responsible for giving them their

reputation as a "joy-through-brawling" team, and Phil Esposito, five times NHL scoring leader, and more recently, Ray Borque, who has thwarted the opposition since 1980, winning four Norris trophies as the league's most outstanding defenseman.

The Patriots

For much of the 20th century, football was the least successful major league sport in Boston, as the city failed to retain either the Boston Redskins of the 1930s or the Boston Yanks of the 1940s. The Patriots arrived in 1965, purchased for only $25,000 by William H. Sullivan Jr., who started his sports career as publicity man-

FAR LEFT: the Bruins in action. **LEFT:** the Celtics.
RIGHT: Red Auerbach, the famous coach, manager and president of the Celtics, still has his fans.

ager for that other Boston baseball team – the Braves – who have long since (1953) decamped Boston, first to Milwaukee and then to Atlanta.

Sullivan followed a similar route, moving his club in 1971 25 miles south of Boston to Foxboro, then dropping "Boston" from the name for the more generic "New England." Like the Red Sox, the Pats have never seemed more futile then when playing for the championship. Super Bowl appearances in both 1986 and 1996 ended in disaster as the team was mauled by first the Chicago Bears, then the Green Bay Packers. Still, the Patriots have produced such superb players as John Hannah,

football bowls. Then, on occasions, Harvard or Boston University has won the NCAA hockey championships. Four members of the United States hockey team which so dramatically overthrew the Russians to win the 1982 winter Olympics at Lake Placid were from the Boston University squad and the roster of gold medal winning U.S. women's hockey team was predominantly made up of players from Boston's college squads.

In crew, Harvard shines not only on the national but also on the international level. Indeed, the entire Harvard eight represented the US at the 1968 summer Olympics in Mexico

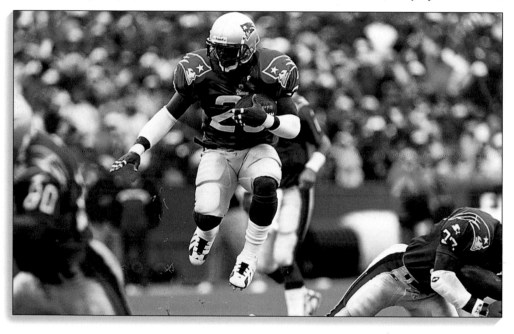

who played with them for his entire career and who was selected by *Sports Illustrated* as "the greatest lineman of all time," and Drew Bledsoe, who has emerged as one of the game's premier quarterbacks.

Collegiate endeavors

With few exceptions, those 50 colleges and universities situated within 30 miles of Boston make little impact at the national level on the college sports scene. In a word, they are parochial. One exception is Boston College, a name respected in both football and basketball and a member of the Big East Conference. The College is sometimes invited to post-season

City. Harvard, joined by Boston University, MIT and Northeastern, also does well on the national level in dinghy sailing. Back on land, Harvard, more often than not, has the country's top college squash team.

Boston has always been well represented at the Olympics. At the first modern games, held in Athens in 1896, athletes from the Boston Athletic Association and the Suffolk Athletic Club provided the nucleus of the US team and the hop, step and jump – the very first event of the modern Olympics – was won by James Brendan Connolly, who came from Boston. ❏

ABOVE: the Patriots keep football's flag flying.

The Marathon

A win at Boston "is the most important prize in the world of marathoning." So said Fred Lebow, director of the New York marathon. It all began in 1897 when 15 runners lined up in Ashland and, when the gun was fired, started to run to Boston. Thus began the world's oldest annual marathon, held on Patriot's Day (in mid-April), and drawing its inspiration from the marathon at the first modern Olympics in 1896.

Since 1907 the race has started at Hopkinton rather than Ashland and, since 1927, has been run over the official Olympic distance of 26 miles, 365 yards. The race passes through eight municipalities and is watched by about 1½ million spectators. It is mainly downhill, although those who suffer the agonies of "Heartbreak Hill" would scarcely agree.

Apart from 10 years between 1973 and 1983 when the laurel wreath crowned an American entrant seven times, foreigners have dominated since World War II. First the Finns held the limelight, winning six times between 1954 and 1962. Then Boston became a happy hunting ground for the Japanese, who have won seven times since 1953. In the 1990s, runners from Kenya took a liking to the course, dominating both the men's and women's divisions.

Few foreign winners, great as they may be, are long remembered by the public, but two American winners have become legends. Clarence DeMar won Boston for the first time in 1911 and for the seventh time in 1930. He competed until 1951, when he was 61. The legendary Mr "Boston Marathon," John A. Kelley, ran the marathon for 61 consecutive years before finally retiring from the full distance at age 84. He had won twice (1935, 1945), been second seven times and was in the top 10 a total of 19 times. "There are other good marathons," he said, "but they don't have tradition. The other marathons are all Johnnies-come-lately."

Once, runners broke records at Boston. Now, with the proliferation of such races held on flatter courses around the world, most record-breaking takes place elsewhere. Still, no other race can match either Boston's tradition or its innovations.

The first wheel-chair competitor raced unofficially in 1970, completing the course in about seven hours. Now, official wheel-chair winners have finished and showered before the first non-disabled athlete breaks the tape. Visually impaired runners also compete.

Women first began to run in 1966 but official entries weren't accepted until 1972. Bedlam broke loose in 1967 when K. Switzer, an official entrant, turned out to be Katherine Switzer. When an official tried to bar her from running, her burly boyfriend physically intervened. Katherine ran.

In the early 1980s it seemed that the marathon, despite its worldwide appeal, might have to be abandoned. Other big city marathons had become ten a penny and awarded prize money. Not so Boston; it remained an amateur event in which athletes ran for prestige and fun. And the organizers, the Boston Athletic Association, could not generate large TV revenues because the race is held in the middle of the

day on a Monday – scarcely prime viewing time.

Once again, as he had more than 200 years before, John Hancock, this time in the shape of a financial company bearing his name, came to the rescue with a multi-million-dollar sponsorship deal. Now, prize money at Boston, the only marathon to offer equal prize money in all classes to both men and women, is equal to that awarded at other major marathons and the event is assured of sound financial backing into the 21st century.

Today, about 8,000 runners who have met pre-entry time qualifications line up for the starter's gun, but thousands more manage to find their way to Hopkinton and then jog, walk, limp or drag themselves across the finish line as unofficial entrants. ❏

RIGHT: the marathon attracts 8,000 runners.

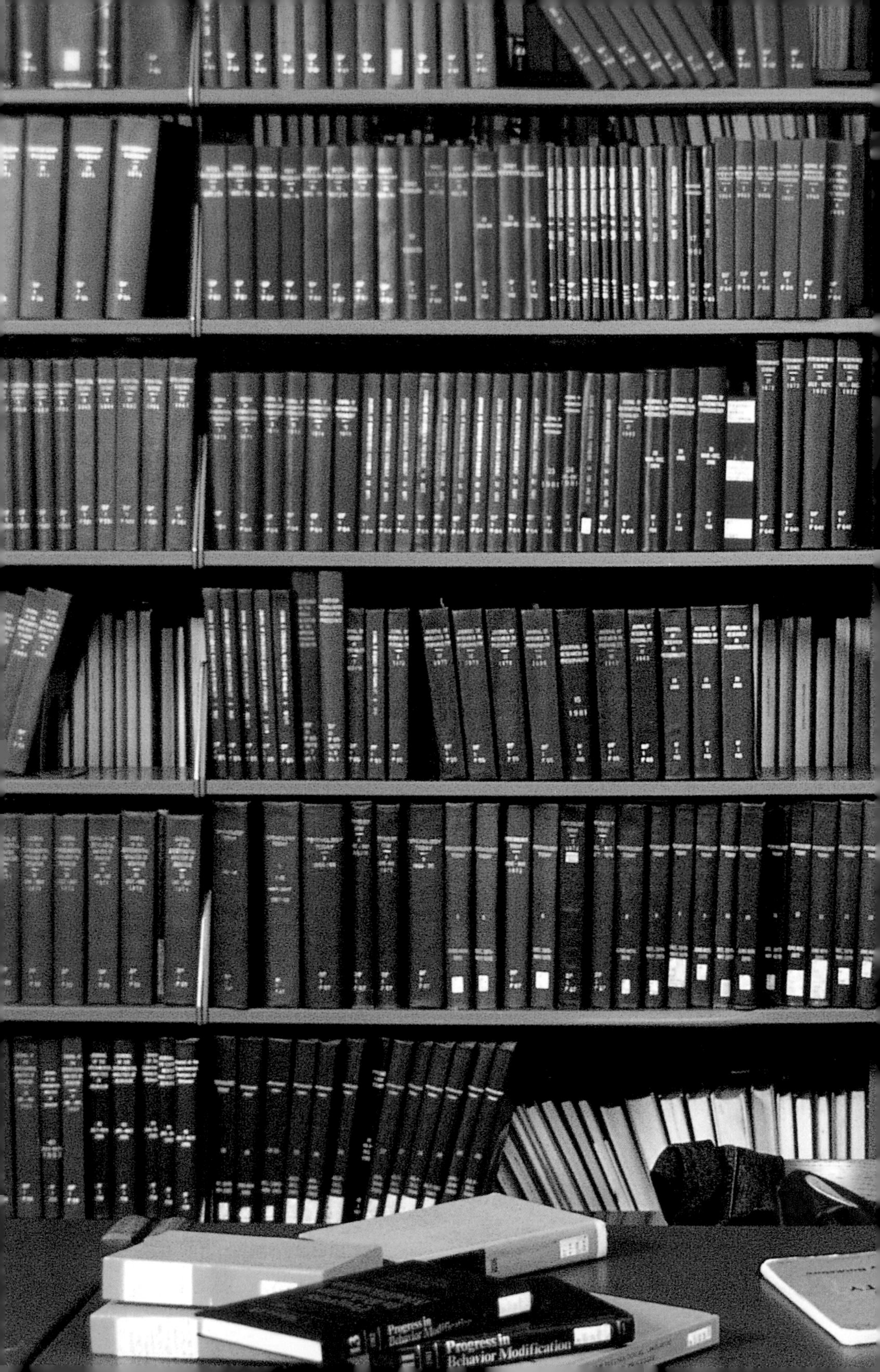
13
Progress in Behavior Modification

THE EDUCATION INDUSTRY

What cars are to Detroit, so colleges are to Boston. Not only do they help give the city its character, they also bring in billions of dollars a year

Boston has been firmly linked to learning ever since William Blackstone, the first white settler, lugged 200 books with him to the cabin where he lived alone on what is now the Boston Common. Today there are 60 colleges and universities in the Boston and its surrounding communities, the greatest concentration in the world.

The 250,000 college students at these schools comprise nearly half the city's population, something that is evident each Memorial Day when they arrive en masse in rental trucks that clog the narrow streets. Many of them stay, contributing to Boston's rich cultural and intellectual life. Almost two-thirds of the adult population has at least an undergraduate degree, and Boston leads the nation in the number of PhDs and medical doctors per capita and the total number of Nobel laureates. Collectively, the city's teaching hospitals get fully one-half of all National Institutes of Health research funding. In New York, Mark Twain once said, they ask how much money a man has; in Philadelphia, what family he's from; in Boston, how much he knows. His neighborhood abutting Harvard is "one of the intellectually best-endowed places in America," the economist John Kenneth Galbraith once said.

Presidential pedigrees

This extraordinary brainpower helps account for Boston's disproportionate role in the nation's literary, technological, political and economic life. From the New Deal to the present day, for instance, Harvard professors and alumni have occupied the upper echelons of government, business and the arts. Half a dozen US presidents have had a Harvard pedigree. Wellesley College produced the first black female judge in the United States and the first female secretary of state. Graduates of the Massachusetts Institute of Technology control

entire industries; the entrepreneurial alumni of MIT alone have founded an estimated 4,000 companies worldwide, with 1.1 million employees and annual sales of a quarter of a *trillion* dollars. Massachusetts is first in the nation in per-capita spending on university research and development. With barely 5 percent of the nation's population, New England accounts for more than 10 percent of all patents awarded to colleges and universities.

Faculty and students at Boston-area universities and colleges invented anaesthesia, the telephone, the digital computer, the instant camera, and the World Wide Web. These schools also helped make Boston the unquestioned literary capital of the United States in the 19th century, giving us Ralph Waldo Emerson, Henry Wadsworth Longfellow, and Nathaniel Hawthorne, among others; they continue to produce a lopsided share of high-profile authors including John Updike, Andre Dubus, James Carroll, Doris Kearns Goodwin,

PRECEDING PAGES: studying in Boston University Library. **LEFT:** commencement at Boston University. **RIGHT:** the Baker Library at Harvard University.

Robert W. Parker, Gish Jen, and David Mamet.

Harvard was founded only 16 years after the arrival of the Pilgrims at Plymouth, making it the nation's oldest university, but Boston also boasts the first medical school, first nursing school, first school of architecture, first music conservatory, and first football stadium – again, Harvard's. No surprise that Boston also has the oldest taxpayer-supported public library and first printing press.

While few Boston-area universities compete on the national college football stage, that doesn't stop enthusiastic crowds of students and alumni from flocking to the bleachers on

LEARNING BY THE BOOK

The Boston area can't claim America's first university press, but among the region's many book publishing houses are two of the world's leading academic presses. Harvard University Press, founded in 1913, is noted for a prestigious list of titles covering history and philosophy to natural science. Publisher of Harvard luminaries Edward O. Wilson, Stephen Jay Gould and Carol Gilligan, Harvard University Press has also had some surprise bestsellers such as Eudora Welty's *One Writer's Beginnings*. The MIT Press, opened in 1932, is no less highly regarded, with a list specializing in cognitive science, architecture and philosophy, among other disciplines.

crisp fall Saturdays under blue skies surrounded by colorful foliage. The city's annual rowing race, the Head of the Charles Regatta, is the largest in the world, and Boston College, Boston University, Harvard and Northeastern meet in the Beanpot Tournament for what is arguably the finest college hockey played.

A major employer

Its wealth of universities and colleges gives Boston more than bragging rights. Higher education pumps an estimated $10 billion a year into the area economy, and employs 125,000 people, making it one of the top four industries. It also is one of the region's biggest exports; more than a quarter of the students come from outside New England, and more than 5 percent from outside the United States. This despite the fact that Boston-area private universities and colleges are among the most expensive in the country, with tuition that is about one-third higher than the national average.

Students continue to be drawn by, among other things, the opportunity to cross-register between schools. Several small colleges in the city's Fenway section, all within a 15-minute walk of one another, have formalized this arrangement, pooling their resources to cut costs and dramatically increase their offerings to more than 2,000 courses taught by a combined 500 faculty members.

Another big lure is the variety and abundance of resources. Boston College has more Irish materials that any institution outside of Ireland, for example, and Brandeis the most comprehensive program in Judaic studies outside Israel. Boston University claims the world's largest archive of Hollywood memorabilia. And Harvard has the world's largest academic library of any kind.

Higher education remains woven tightly into the fabric of the city, and not only by paralyzing traffic on Memorial Day weekend. The Harvard Extension School offers 600 courses to the community, enrolling 14,000 people. Thousands of students volunteer to perform community service. College radio stations and newspapers, and innumerable public lectures, add to the city's cultural life.

Harvard University

Harvard clearly is at the center of this world, not only the oldest and the highest-rated university in the United States, but also the richest, with an endowment in the tens of billions. It has nearly 40 Nobel laureates on its faculty, a like number of Pulitzer Prize winners, and more U.S. presidents among its graduates that any other university. Governed by the oldest corporation in the Western Hemisphere, the school was opened in 1636 with one "master" and a dozen students. Given a boost in 1638 when a young minister named John Harvard left it half of his estate and all his books, the school was renamed in his honor. (On

BUCKLEY ON HARVARD

"William F. Buckley Jr. once remarked that he would rather be governed by the first 100 names in the Boston telephone book than by the faculty of Harvard University."

—Richard Nixon, *The Real War* (1980)

administered. Undergraduates attend Harvard College, and many of them live in one of 12 "houses" (there is a 13th house for nonresident upperclassmen) that serve as colleges-within-a-college. Each has its own master, tutors, dining room, library and an active schedule of athletic, social and cultural events. Radcliffe College, to which women once were required to apply in order to be accepted into Harvard, finally ceased to exist in that role in 1999, and became a Harvard-operated research center on gender.

the other hand, the statue of John Harvard in Harvard Yard cast by Lincoln Memorial sculptor Daniel Chester French is woefully inaccurate; Harvard was benefactor but not founder, the school was opened was 1636 and not 1638, and it is not John Harvard at all, since no likenesses of him existed. An undergraduate was enlisted to pose for the work.)

Over its long history, Harvard has maintained an odd configuration. It has 10 graduate and professional schools, some of them in Boston rather than in Cambridge and each independently

Left: Radcliffe Yard, Harvard Square.
Above: Harvard College's Eliot House.

How smart are Harvard students? More than 2,000 high school valedictorians apply every year, any only half get in. Nearly 400 have perfect scores on their SATs. And almost all the 18,000 applicants each year are in the top 10 percent of their high school class. Despite this, the chances of being admitted is only one in 10. "You can always tell a Harvard man," a 19th-century wag observed, "but you can't tell him much." (Lest anyone think Harvard students never look up from their books, however, the university claims the largest number of athletic teams of any campus in the country.)

From its original 12 students, Harvard has grown to 18,000, with 23,000 faculty and staff.

Its most prominent graduates include, among many others, 11 justices of the Supreme Court, Al Gore, Elizabeth Dole, Henry Kissinger, Norman Mailer, Pete Seeger, James Agee, Wallace Stevens, T.S. Eliot, Leonard Bernstein, William S. Burroughs, John dos Passos, Robert Frost, Henry James, Henry David Thoreau, Ralph Nader, W.E.B. Du Bois, Tommy Lee Jones, Jack Lemmon, Stockard Channing, and John Lithgow. Other notables, such as Microsoft's Bill Gates, attended, but dropped out.

Commencements are steeped in ceremony. Faculty enter according to rank, graduates compete to deliver an oration in Latin and the pres-

the Carpenter Center of the Visual Arts. Widener Library is the largest at any university in the world, with 13 million volumes that include a Shakespeare first folio and a 1520 treatise by Martin Luther. The university also owns extraordinary museums, the 265-acre (107-hectare) Arnold Arboretum and a 3,000-acre (1,200-hectare) forest in central Massachusetts.

MIT

A short distance farther along the Charles River is the Massachusetts Institute of Technology, one of the world's preeminent schools of science and engineering, and also highly regarded

ident sits in the same wobbly chair used at every such occasion since 1737. Until 1769, graduates were arranged in order of their parents' social status. Now they march into Harvard Yard in alphabetical order. Keynote speakers have used the platform of a Harvard commencement to deliver major policy pronouncements, most notably the Marshall Plan for Europe detailed in the commencement speech of General George C. Marshall on June 5, 1947.

Harvard's campus is a potpourri of architecture spanning centuries, including colonial-era red brick, Federal-style buildings by Charles Bulfinch and the lone North American commission of the Swiss-French architect Le Corbusier,

for its programs in architecture, economics, urban studies and urban planning.

Founded in 1861, MIT opened in quarters on Copley Square in Boston in 1865 and immediately found itself fending off proposals that it merge with Harvard to create, as the then-governor of Massachusetts put it, "a great university in Cambridge." Such a proposition long ago stopped being seriously considered, though students at either school today may take classes at the other. On the other hand, MIT did ultimately move to Cambridge in 1916, settling in under the now familiar Great Dome modeled after the Pantheon in Rome. A favorite target for student pranksters, the dome has been variously turned into an enormous jack-o-lantern, and covered with a giant red and white beanie. Self-described student "hackers" have managed to transport a working phone booth, fiberglass cow and intact dormitory room to the roof; in perhaps their greatest feat, they put a police car on top of it, complete with flashing lights and a box of doughnuts on the front seat.

Other structures on the mile-long campus along the Charles were designed by I.M. Pei (Class of '40) and Eero Saarinen.

More than half of MIT's 10,000 students are enrolled in graduate programs, and more than 30 of its faculty have won Nobel Prizes. Here was developed the first chemical synthesis of Vitamin A, the inertial guidance system, the World Wide Web and the magnetic core memory that made digital computers possible in the first place. The institute leads the nation in research and development funding from private industry. There are more than 1,000 MIT spin-off companies headquartered in Massachusetts alone, employing 125,000 people and representing an estimated 10 percent of the economic base. MIT also operated the Lincoln Laboratory, a federally sponsored center for research in advanced electronics for defense, communications and air traffic control. And on the Cambridge campus, the Media Lab, founded in 1980, is helping to create digital video and multimedia, funded mostly by corporate sponsors. Computers outnumber people by a significant margin at the Media Lab, which is developing such things as thinking toys, full-parallax holography, and wearable computers.

Boston University

Directly across the river, Boston University is the nation's third-largest private university, with more than 30,000 full- and part-time students, and more international students than any other U.S. university or college. Founded in 1839 as the Newbury Biblical Institute in Newbury, Vermont, BU moved to Concord, New Hampshire, before landing in Boston. It boasts the nation's oldest college of music and first school of public relations, graduated America's first black psychiatrist, and was the first university to open all of its divisions to women, producing

---

LEFT: Massachusetts Institute of Technology's Great Court and the Rogers Building.
RIGHT: continuing an old Boston tradition.

the first woman PhD and the first black woman medical doctor. Alexander Graham Bell taught at BU while he was developing the telephone, the Rev. Martin Luther King Jr., F. Lee Bailey and Faye Dunaway were graduates, and Tipper Gore met her husband, Al Gore, while she was a student at BU and he attended Harvard.

Today BU has 17 schools, including communications, medicine, law, theology and dentistry. Under its longtime strong-willed president, John Silber, who once ran unsuccessfully for governor, it attracted internationally renowned faculty and millions of dollars in grants for such projects as a center for photonics, the study of

light and ways to use it for data storage, imaging systems, medical applications, and sensors. In 1989 it took over the management of the entire school system of Chelsea, a neighboring town plagued by low funding and poor academic achievement, and in 1993 opened its own private high school called the Boston University Academy.

Its Twentieth Century Archive holds the largest collection of Hollywood memorabilia in the world and the personal papers of such figures as Angela Lansbury, Fred Astaire, Ella Fitzgerald, Bette Davis, Edward G. Robinson, Joan Fontaine, Gene Kelly, Myrna Loy, and Douglas Fairbanks Jr.

Boston College

At the other end of the trolley line that passes Boston University is rival Boston College in the Chestnut Hill section, straddling the Boston border with neighboring Newton. Founded by the Society of Jesus, BC was opened with three teachers and 48 students in Boston's South End in 1863. One of 28 Jesuit colleges in the United States, it is today the nation's largest Catholic university with an enrollment of nearly 15,000.

A university in all but name, BC has 11 schools, colleges and institutes offering 13 degree programs on the Chestnut Hill campus and a satellite law school campus a mile away

gram, linking classroom learning with practical experience. Students alternate conventional study on the campus with three- or six-month periods of paid employment related to their major. Each year, 6,000 Northeastern students work in a co-op job for one of more than 2,000 participating employers. The graduates of this program have started more companies than those of any other university except MIT.

Practical education has long been a hallmark of Northeastern, which began as a night school affiliated with the local Young Men's Christian Association – itself the first YMCA branch in the United States. Incorporated as a college in

in Newton. It also operates the Weston Observatory, headquarters of a 15-station New England seismic monitoring network. With roots deep in Boston's Irish community, BC holds the most comprehensive Yeats collection outside of Ireland and a collection of pre-Vatican II religious artifacts. It also fields by far the best major sports teams in the region, with nationally ranked football and basketball programs.

Northeastern University

Closer to the center of the city is Northeastern University, with 26,000 students another of the nation's largest private universities. Northeastern's claim to fame is its so-called co-op pro-

1915, it began to grow into a campus next to the site of the city's first major league baseball stadium, the Huntington Avenue Grounds, where the first World Series had been played. Although the stadium is gone, it is memorialized by a marker in the shape of home plate.

Today Northeastern has nine undergraduate and 10 graduate and professional schools. The best known are in law and criminal justice, many of whose graduates enter public service.

Emerson College

Emerson College, whose urban "campus" ranges from converted brownstones in the Back Bay to renovated buildings alongside the

Boston Common, is the only private four-year college in the United States devoted exclusively to the study of communication and the performing arts at the undergraduate and graduate level. Emerson likes to call itself the place where people with something to say learn how to make themselves heard, and many have taken them up on the promise; alumni include Jay Leno, Henry Winkler, Spalding Gray, Steven Wright, Bobbi Brown, and Dennis Leary. Founded in 1880 by Charles Wesley Emerson as an elocution school, Emerson today is renowned for its departments of mass communication, theater arts and communication disorders, and equally popular locally for its eclectic student-run radio station, WERS-FM.

Faced with space constraints in its original Beacon Street quarters, Emerson at one time considered moving out of Boston, but instead took a big risk and began to move its campus deeper into the city, including neighborhoods around the Common that were then considered marginal, turning an elegant but neglected 1917 office building into a dormitory for more than 700 students and restoring the breath-taking 1903 Majestic Theatre, one of the jewels of Boston's theater district but by that time facing demolition. The area is now among the most desirable in the city, thanks in great part to the presence of the college and its students.

Suffolk University

Also downtown, Suffolk University is a private institution founded to serve students otherwise denied access to college because of income, religion or social class; its fees are still about half those of competing schools. Once exclusively a law school, Suffolk now also has a college of liberal arts and sciences, a school of management, a school of art and design, and a marine biology station in Maine. Its main campus is within a stone's throw of the State House and, as part of an expansion, it has added a grand new law school building and its first dormitory, both on Tremont Street; demand for dorm rooms was previously sparse, since nearly half of Suffolk's 6,400 students are part-time.

Tufts University

Tufts University is about 5 miles (8 km) north

LEFT: in the science lab at Boston College.
RIGHT: studying in Radcliffe Yard.

of Boston in Medford. A non-sectarian university founded under the aegis of the liberal Universalist Church in 1859, Tufts became a university in 1953, and has firmly shed its one-time reputation as a safety school for students rejected by the Ivy League. With an enrollment of about 5,000 undergraduate students, it has the same number of Fulbright scholars as considerably larger Harvard.

More than 98 percent or enrolling Tufts students expect to go on to graduate or professional study, and Tufts itself may be better known for its graduate programs than its undergraduate. Its School of Veterinary Medicine in Grafton,

40 miles west of Boston, is the only one in New England and one of only two private veterinary colleges in the United States. The Fletcher School of Law and Diplomacy is America's oldest graduate school for international relations. Its medical school, at the center of the university's medical campus in Boston's Chinatown section, ranks sixth among U.S. medical schools for the impact of its clinical research. And the School of Nutrition Science and Policy, created by the late Tufts president and nutritionist Jean Mayer, is the only one of its kind in the country, and home to one of the USDA's six human nutrition research centers.

P.T. Barnum of Barnum & Bailey's Circus

was one of the founders of Tufts, and contributed its mascot, Jumbo, an elephant reputed to have been killed by a train in Canada while pushing a baby elephant off the tracks. The front of Barnum Hall had to be removed to fit the giant animal inside the building, where a fire in 1979 left nothing but the tail – still kept in the university's archives. Jumbo's ashes, on the other hand, are in a peanut butter jar in the athletic director's office.

Wellesley College

Wellesley College is about 13 miles (21 km) west of Boston, put there for a purpose: so that

of the first colleges in the country to offer political science. It is also the home of the influential National Center for Research on Women, known for its studies of school-age girls. Art is a particular strength, thanks in no small part to Wellesley's own superlative collection of works by Monet, Cezanne, van Dyck, de Kooning, Nevelson, and Calder.

The school also has an extensive complex of greenhouses, an arboretum, an observatory and a contemporary science center acclaimed by the Boston Society of Architects as "the most beautiful piece of architecture, building, monument or structure" in the area. The pastoral

its women students would not be exposed to the corrupting influence of male undergraduates. Its motto, *Non Ministrari sed Ministrare*, means, "Not to be Ministered Unto but to Minister."

Founded by Henry and Pauline Cazenove Durant in 1875, Wellesley has remained all-woman, even though some of its fellow "seven sisters," (now called the "seven siblings," and now technically six with the merger of Radcliffe into Harvard) have become co-ed. The 2,300 students choose from majors in the traditional liberal arts and in such fields as electrical engineering, psychobiology and urban psychology, and can cross-register at MIT and other schools. In 1883, Wellesley became one

500-acre (200-hectare) campus is one of the finest in America, with its own lake, a nine-hole golf course and 24 tennis courts. The 182-ft (55-meter) Galen Tower at its center has a 30-bell carillon played almost daily by student members of the Wellesley Guild of Carillonneurs.

Fiercely feminist, Wellesley nonetheless maintains some of its original genteel traditions – including the odd custom of hoop-rolling, in which students clad in graduation robes roll wooden hoops across the campus; the winner is said to be the most likely to succeed. In 1939, a Harvard man named Ned Read dressed in drag, secretly entered on a dare from his friends, and won.

Alumni include some of the leading women in business, politics and media, including Madeleine Albright, Hillary Clinton, Diane Sawyer, Judith Martin, Marjory Stoneman Douglas, the composer of *America the Beautiful* and the author of the Nancy Drew and Bobsey Twins series. Madame Chiang Kai Shek also graduated Wellesley, at a time when hers was an exotic presence; today, a quarter of the students are Asian.

Babson College

Nearby Babson College, also in Wellesley, is internationally recognized for its focus on entrepreneurial leadership. Founded in 1919 by financier and entrepreneur Roger W. Babson, it is considered to have one of the top MBA programs in North America and Europe; 2,000 of its students are in the graduate school, and most of the 1,500 undergraduates also plan careers in business.

Brandeis University

Also in the western suburbs is Brandeis University in Waltham, the nation's youngest private research university and the only nonsectarian university founded by the American Jewish community. Named for Supreme Court Justice Louis D. Brandeis, the school opened with extraordinary enthusiasm in 1948 on the former campus of the Middlesex School of Veterinary Medicine. Eleanor Roosevelt was an early member of the board of trustees, Leonard Bernstein a visiting faculty member in the music department, Aaron Copland a member of the music advisory committee, and Max Lerner a professor in American civilization. Visiting intellectuals included W.H. Auden, Dylan Thomas, e.e. cummings, Margaret Mead, Archibald MacLeish, Alfred Kinsey, and Felix Frankfurter.

Although about two-thirds of its 4,000 students are Jewish, Brandeis does not have a strong religious emphasis. Laid out by Eero Saarinen, the Brandeis campus features three chapels – one Jewish, one Protestant and one Catholic – designed by the same architect who planned the United Nations, and situated so that none ever casts its shadow on another. The university also boasts the biggest collection of con-

temporary American art in New England, and one of the best in the nation.

Brandeis is known for its Gordon Public Policy Center, the first interdisciplinary multi-university center for public policy. Its Heller School for Social Welfare is renowned. And its Judaic studies program and holdings are the largest outside Israel. The university has been ranked third in the nation – behind only Princeton and Yale – in the humanities, and sixth in the biological sciences.

Simmons College

One of the half-dozen colleges in Boston's Fen-

way section, Simmons College was established in 1899 by John Simmons as the first women's college in the nation to combine liberal arts with career preparation, a radical notion for women at the time (there are now a few men among the 2,200 students in the college's graduate divisions, but all the 1,210 undergraduates are women). Simmons has four graduate schools, including the only graduate business school for women in the world, which annually sponsors a national symposium on women and leadership; alumni include some of the nation's top female CEOs. Its graduate program in library and information science is consistently rated one of the best in the country.

LEFT: a study in studying at Brandeis University.
RIGHT: a professor at Brandeis.

Boston also is home to some of the nation's finest music conservatories.

New England Conservatory

The New England Conservatory, founded in 1867, is the oldest school of its kind in the country, and ranks as one of the top for performing and teaching musicians. The conservatory's faculty comprise more than half of the performers in the Boston Symphony Orchestra, which performs at nearby Symphony Hall, and many of the rest were trained there. With just over 800 graduate and undergraduate students, it stages 600 free concerts a year, many

graduates come from outside of the United States, the largest proportion of any higher education institution. Alumni include producer and arranger Quincy Jones and performers Melissa Etheridge, Bruce Cockburn, Paula Cole, Kevin Eubanks, Tracy Bonham, Bruce Hornsby, Patty Larkin, Aimee Mann, and Branford Marsalis.

University of Massachusetts

Across town in Columbia Point on Dorchester Bay is the modern $137 million campus of the University of Massachusetts, a public university often overlooked among the city's better known private universities. Because of the

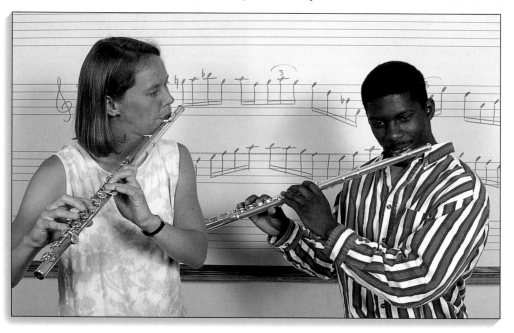

of them in the 1,000-seat Jordan Hall, owned by the conservatory and acclaimed as one of the world's most acoustically perfect performance spaces. Alumni include Sarah Caldwell, Cecil Taylor and Coretta Scott King, who met her husband, the Rev. Martin Luther King Jr., when he was studying at neighboring BU.

Berklee College of Music

Founded in 1945, the Berklee College of Music has quickly become the world's largest independent music college and the premier institution for the study of contemporary music ranging from folk to funk, swing to salsa and rock to ragtime. Forty percent of its under-

strong history of private higher education in Massachusetts, only 23 percent of students in the state are enrolled in public universities, compared to the national average of 58 percent. UMass-Boston opened in 1974 and serves about 12,000 students, all of them commuters and many of whom work full-time to subsidize their educations. The university was merged for the former Boston State College in 1982. UMass has five campuses in all, the flagship in the central Massachusetts town of Amherst and the others in Lowell, Dartmouth and Worcester. ❑

ABOVE: the New England Conservatory is the oldest school of its kind in the United States.

A Medical Trailblazer

I n 1846, Dr John Collins Warren delivered his verdict to those who had observed Mr Gilbert Abbot undergoing surgery at the Massachusetts General Hospital: "Gentlemen, this is no humbug." Mr Abbot, who was operated on for a tumor, had just told the entranced gathering that he had "suffered no pain." This was because here in Boston, for the first time in the world, ether had been used to anaesthetize the patient. Today, at the hospital (usually known as the MGH, Mass General, "Man's Greatest Hospital" or, to medical students, the "massive genital"), the visitor can see the Ether Dome, the work of Bulfinch, and the operating theater where ether was first used. (Public tours on Tuesdays and Thursdays at 2pm).

In the same way that Boston is numero uno in education, it is America's leader in medicine. Today, the hub boasts 17 major hospitals and Greater Boston has nearly 100 facilities. Harvard, Boston University and Tufts each has its medical school and the Massachusetts Institute of Technology has a medical program with Harvard. In the past 50 years more than a score of doctors and scientists working at Boston's hospitals and medical schools have won Nobel prizes in physiology and/or medicine.

Among these is John Enders who, with Frederick Robbins and Thomas Weller, won this illustrious award in 1954 for their work in developing the poliomyelitis vaccine which effectively eliminated this scourge. (Later, Jonas Salk in Pittsburgh developed the mass production of this vaccine which would wipe polio from the face of the earth.) Almost 150 years before this, Dr Benjamin Waterhouse of Harvard Medical School (HMS), who constantly lectured on the "ruinous effects of smoking tobacco," had been the first to introduce smallpox vaccination in the country.

A more recent Nobel laureate in medicine (1990) is Joseph Murray who, in 1954, at the Peter Bent Brigham Hospital, was part of a team that successfully performed the first human kidney transplant. And open-heart surgery was first performed at the Boston Children's Hospital by Professor Robert Gross in 1967. Then there was 12-year old Danny Everett who, in 1962, while hitching a ride home on a train after pitching in a Little League baseball game, had his arm shorn off. Dr Ronald Malt and his emergency room team at the MGH performed the first successful replantation of a human limb.

RIGHT: history is made at Massachusetts General Hospital when ether is used for the first time.

The list of firsts is long: abdominal surgery (1886); creation of the Drinker respirator (iron lung) in 1928; artificial kidney (1945); clinical reports on efficacy of birth control pills (1959); techniques for freezing and thawing blood (1964); abdominal electrocardiography for monitoring the fetus during labor (1973) and developing artificial skin for burn victims (1981).

Less dramatic, but just as important, Boston national medical firsts include Linda Richards, the first trained nurse; the first medical school to admit women (Boston University); the first city to establish a municipal water supply; and the first Board of Health. On an international level, the much respected, oft-quoted *New England Journal of Medi-*

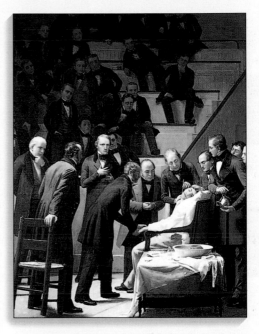

cine, founded in 1812 by Dr John Collins Warren and James Jackson, is the oldest continuously published medical journal in the world.

With the ratio of doctors to residents nearly 50 percent above the national average, is Boston a good place to fall ill? Not necessarily: many physicians are more interested in research than in everyday caring.

The greatest concentration of hospitals is in the Longwood area in Brookline. This houses not only HMS but also the Brigham and Women's Hospital which receives more funding than any other independent hospital in the US, the Children's Hospital, the Dana-Farber Cancer Institute and the Beth Israel Deaconess Hospital. The region qualifies as a mini-city, with a population of more than 20,000. ❏

ARCHITECTURE

Boston is like a museum of architecture – but it's a living museum,
still setting standards for the rest of the United States

Boston has been called the "most European city in America," owing primarily to its compact urban scale. Arguably, Chicago is its only rival as a living study of American architectural and urban planning, though due to the latter's relative youth and the catastrophic fire, Chicago can't claim a comparable rich legacy, something quite evident when one walks Boston's Beacon Hill, the North End or Back Bay.

Boston takes its architecture very seriously, acknowledging its impact upon the public setting. Its rigorous review and approval processes date back to the Boston Street System Law of 1635, which ordered the citizenry to "avoyd disorderly building to the inconvenience of streets and laynes for the more comely and commodious ordering of them."

Complementary styles

The city's exacting standards pay rich dividends in an artful juxtaposition of divergent styles that allows each structure to stand in mutually complementary relief. Notice the handsome mirrored backdrop that I.M. Pei's John Hancock Tower offers Henry Hobson Richardson's Romanesque Revival masterpiece, Trinity Church at Copley Square, or how the flourishes of the Old State House are flattered against the setting of One Boston Place's dark grid.

In the late 18th and early 19th centuries, State House architect Charles Bulfinch established Jeffersonian Classicism as the architectural vocabulary of Boston. This manner of balanced composition abounds in Bullfinch's other work on Beacon Hill and nearby: the Harrison Gray and John Phillips houses, the Central Wharf buildings, and St. Stephen's Church. Bulfinch's one-time employees Asher Benjamin and Alexander Parris carried on the tradition; Benjamin with the Charles Street Meeting House

and Parris with his Quincy Market and St. Paul's Church. Benjamin and Parris subsequently perpetuated Bulfinch's distinctive "Boston Bowfront" brick residential style, copied and recopied throughout Beacon Hill, the South End and Back Bay. The gracious residential enclave of Beacon Hill presents an exhaustive survey of the archi-

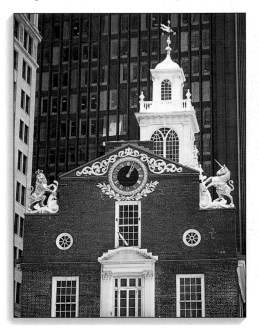

CHARLES BULFINCH

Boston-born Charles Bulfinch (1763–1844), America's first professional architect, took much of his inspiration from the classical and neoclassical traditions of Europe. After graduating from Harvard University, he traveled widely in Europe, seeking the advice of Thomas Jefferson, whom he met in Paris, and being strongly influenced in London by the style of Robert Adam.

As head of Boston's local government for many years, he played a central role in upgrading the street system and improving Boston Common. In 1818 he became the fourth architect to take responsibility for designing the US Capitol in Washington, D.C.

PRECEDING PAGES: the Christian Science complex. **LEFT:** old and new – Trinity Church reflected in the John Hancock Tower. **RIGHT:** the Old State House, built in 1748 after fires had destroyed two earlier buildings.

tecture of this period, with textbook examples of Georgian, Greek Revival, Gothic Revival Federal and Victorian styles.

While the schools of architecture at Harvard and the Massachusetts Institute of Technology were among the first in the United States, the leading mid-19th century Boston architects were primarily Paris-educated and heavily influenced by French Gothic and Italian Renaissance styles. Richardson's First Baptist Church along with his monumental Trinity composition stand in Back Bay pre-figuring the style ultimately called "Richardsonian Gothic." McKim, Mead and White's Boston Public Library and Algonquin Club buildings are executed in the grand form of Renaissance palazzos. Indeed, the entire Back Bay neighborhood, built as part of a 30-year public works landfill project, is modeled on a French residential pattern — Gallic stylistic touches predominate with Beaux Arts and French Second Empire facades and steep-banked mansard roofs. Although the nearby South End is patterned after English res-

MANAGING THE CHARLES

The Charles River Basin, north of the Back Bay, was modeled after the Alster Basin in Hamburg. Harbor tides were kept out of the river by a dam completed in 1910.

BOSTON PUBLIC LIBRARY

Contrasting architectural styles have always created controversy in Boston as fashions changed. In *My Life in Architecture*, Ralph Adam Cram favorably compared the new Boston Public Library, which opened in 1895, with its adjacent ecclesiastical neighbor: "No greater contrast could be imagined than that between Trinity Church and the new Library across the way. On the one hand an almost brutal, certainly primitive, boldness, arrogance, power; on the other a serene Classicism, reserved, scholarly, delicately conceived in all its parts, beautiful in that sense in which things have always been beautiful in periods of high human culture."

idential configurations, Winston Churchill declared Commonwealth Avenue the most beautiful residential boulevard in the world.

By the 20th century a number of European architectural titans selected Massachusetts as a site for their work in North America, some actually settling here, most notably the Bauhaus founder Walter Gropius, who joined the Harvard architecture department in the late 1930s. A prime example of the period's International Style is the Polaroid Building, prominently sited on the Cambridge side of the Charles River. In fact, Cambridge outpaced Boston with mid-century architectural landmarks: Gropius, Eero Saarinen, and Alvar Aalto designed notable structures for Harvard and MIT. Le Corbusier's only building in North America is Harvard's Carpenter Center for the Visual Arts, reportedly intended to stand alone in a large field rather than the crowded streets of Harvard Square.

Bulldozers and brutalism

Later 20th-century architecture in Boston was foreshadowed by massive leveling of old neighborhoods during the 1950s and '60s. Now recalled with nostalgia by lifetime Bostonians, Scollay Square, the squalid nexus of the city's tawdry nightlife, befell the wrecker's ball in the 1960s. The city replaced it with the controver-

tion and reuse that remains vital 30 years later, reinforced by a great many successful contemporary adaptations of existing structures. The Rouse Company's rejuvenation of Faneuil Hall Marketplace set an example copied throughout the country, as has the redevelopment of Shepley, Rutan and Coolidge's handsome 1899 South Station. The commercial Pilot House, Lewis Wharf, Custom House Block (where Nathaniel Hawthorne was an inspector), and Mercantile Wharf buildings have been converted into apartments. Graham Gund's Church Court condominium transforms the shell of a 19th-century Gothic revival church into a struc-

sial Government Center Plaza, featuring Kallman and McKinnell's "Brutalist" style City Hall at its center. Critics condemned the new City Hall structure, though its merits if not charms are recently finding appreciation. A few blocks away across from the Old Corner Bookstore at Downtown Crossing, another Kallman and McKinnell design garners more popular approval: the Borders bookstore, originally designed as a banking headquarters.

Nevertheless, the Government Center saga engendered a climate of restoration, revitaliza-

LEFT: Faneuil Hall Marketplace, ringed by high-rises.
ABOVE: the palatial Boston Public Library.

ture that blends seamlessly with the surrounding Back Bay style and scale. Frank Gehry's popular 1989 renovation of a onetime warehouse at 360 Newbury produced an office building with Tower Records occupying its ground floors. And with 125 Summer Street, Kohn, Pederson, Fox produced a winning example of "historic skirt" preservation in the financial district, retaining the facades of several 19th-century buildings at street level.

More than 7,000 buildings in Boston have been designated as historic landmarks and the number is growing each year. If the mood continues, who knows? The Custom House Tower was terribly unpopular in 1915 and it is on the list. Today one hears people talking more frequently with increased affection about the similarly reviled Prudential Tower.

Cool sophistication

None of this is to say that original designs have been lacking in Boston. While much of the country spent the 1980s clamoring for "postmodern" novelties, Boston architecture enjoyed some striking new compositions. Goody, Clancy & Associates created the splendid multi-use State Transportation Building by the Theater District and the landmark Tent City residential complex in the South End. Stylish high rises

THE JOHN HANCOCK TOWER

A photographer's favorite because of the mirrored images it provides of its more Classical neighbors, New England's tallest building was designed by I. M. Pei & Partners for the John Hancock Mutual Life Insurance Co. and was completed in 1976. Its 60 stories of gray-tinted glass framed in black aluminum reach 740 ft (226 meters) into the sky, and telescopes on the top-floor viewing deck provide incomparable views of the city.

Built over eight years, the tower had its share of construction problems. Unanticipated stresses caused some of the 10,000-plus panes of reflective glass in the irregularly shaped building to buckle and snap.

were designed by Philip Johnson at 500 Boylston and International Place, and by Jung Brannen Associates at One Financial Center. A coolly sophisticated addition was made to the Back Bay with Gwathmey, Siegel's 37 Newbury (near Louis Boston), and a handsome one by Robert Stern's 222 Berkeley Street (the Houghton Mifflin/FAO Schwarz building). Skidmore, Owings & Merrill's majestic 1987 Rowes Wharf will be seen as an even greater triumph when the Big Dig is completed, giving it acres of parkland for a front yard.

In 1630 John Winthrop said, "We must consider that we shall be as a city upon a hill. The eyes of all people are upon us." While he was speaking metaphorically about the social experiment of the new world, his words have long been taken to heart by the architectural community of Boston.

Today they're enforced locally by the Boston Redevelopment Authority and in the press by internationally-known architectural critics Robert Campbell and Jane Holtz Kay. Indeed, Winthrop was prophetic. Paul Goldberger recently wrote in the *New York Times*: "In Boston we see not only architecture but whole urban patterns work themselves out, as if on trial for the rest of the country."

New perspectives

There is so much to see in the city's often-crowded spaces, that Boston's architectural treasures continue to surprise even longtime residents. Rounding an unfamiliar corner one can see a well-known landmark in an arresting light or glimpse another from a compelling new perspective. While the old Jordan Marsh building (now Macy's) may seem merely a regimented Federalist design, should one step back from the intersection at Summer and Chauncy streets, there is an opportunity to notice a delightful arrangement of concave and convex corner windows.

With one's eyes averted from street level, a stroll through the streets of Boston may be as rewarding as a visit to a fine museum. Yet when doing so, it is well to be wary of another of Boston's notable attributes: its notoriously reckless drivers. ❏

LEFT: Commercial Wharf, the Waterfront.
RIGHT: one of Bela Pratt's two 1911 bronze statues, representing Science and Art, at Boston Public Library.

PLACES

A detailed guide to the city and surroundings, with main sites clearly cross-referenced by number to the maps

By American standards, Boston is old. Cobbled streets lit by gas-lamps can be found, and the city has dozens of National Historic Landmarks as well as more than 7,000 individual buildings locally designated as historic landmarks. Yet, because of the hundreds of thousands of students who flock here (and the many who remain after graduation), Boston is a young city well endowed with comedy clubs and restaurants and a vibrant musical and theatrical life. It also boasts superb museums and outstanding modern architecture. Boston is also a small city. Its population is 580,000 and its area 46 sq. miles (119 sq. km). Greater or Metropolitan Boston, with nearly 100 towns, encompasses 3 million people and covers 1,100 sq. miles (2,850 sq. km).

The city proper consists of 14 tight little neighborhoods, each of which believes in territorial imperative. Thus, those who reside in Dorchester, Charlestown or South Boston (all part of the city) scarcely ever admit to being from Boston: rather, they belong to Dorchester, Charlestown or South Boston. On the other hand, those who live in Newton or Quincy, both within the metropolitan area, are perfectly content to be called Bostonians.

The city's two major attractions are the Freedom Trail and Faneuil Hall Marketplace. The former consists of 16 sites, many of which played a seminal part in the history of the nation and all of which played a major role in the development of Boston. The Marketplace, revived in the 1970s, is the prototype for all such enterprises in and beyond the United States and is said to attract even more visitors than Disneyland.

The harbor – which has always been Boston's and Massachusetts' greatest natural asset – has been resurrected and the waterfront is now a joy. Then there is the river. Paris may have the Seine and Cairo the Nile, but locals exalt the glorious Charles River, which separates Boston and Cambridge. The latter, home of both Harvard University and the Massachusetts Institute of Technology, is not part of Boston but is a city in its own right with a population of about 100,000 and more than a dozen National Historic Landmarks.

Boston is also an excellent base for half- and full-day excursions, either to the coast or inland. To the south, Cape Cod and its magnificent sand dunes beckon; to the north, Cape Ann is much more rugged yet still boasts delightful beaches. History is never far away. Concord and Lexington, Plymouth and Provincetown, Salem and Newburyport, all of which played their part in the birth of the nation, await the traveler, and are covered in the following pages. ❑

PRECEDING PAGES: Commonwealth Avenue bursts into bloom; Copley Square's Trinity Church reflected in the John Hancock Tower; swan boats in the Public Garden.
LEFT: the rotunda at Quincy Marketplace.

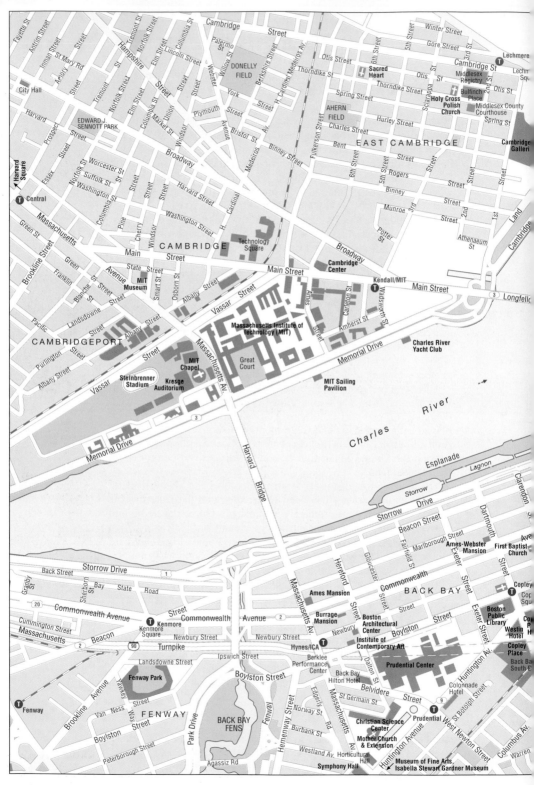

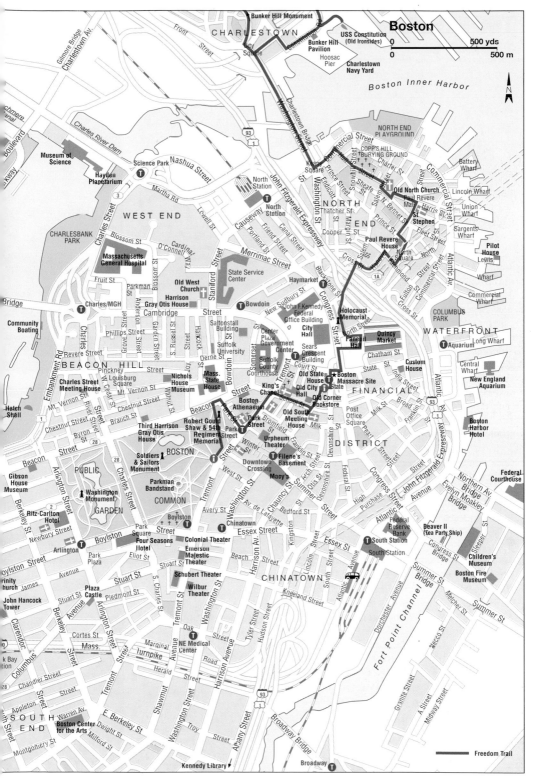

Boston

0		500 yds
0		500 m

CHARLESTOWN

Bunker Hill Monument

Bunker Hill Pavilion

USS Constitution
(Old Ironsides)

Hoosac Pier

Charlestown
Navy Yard

Boston Inner Harbor

Gilmore Bridge

Charlestown AV.

Front Street

City Square

Washington Street

Charlestown Bridge

NORTH END
PLAYGROUND

COPP'S HILL
BURYING GROUND

Battery
Wharf

Lincoln Wharf

Union
Wharf

Sargents
Wharf

Pilot
House

Lewis
Wharf

Commercial
Wharf

Charles River Dam

Museum of
Science

Hayden
Planetarium

Science Park

Nashua Street

North
Station

North
Station

Martha Rd

Lowell St

Causeway

Portland St

Friend St

Canal Street

Merrimac Street

State Service
Center

Haymarket

New Sudbury St

John F. Kennedy
Federal
Office Building

Blackstone St

Holocaust
Memorial

Quincy
Market

Faneuil
Hall

WATERFRONT

Aquarium

Long Wharf

Central
Wharf

New England
Aquarium

Columbus
Park

WEST END

CHARLESBANK
PARK

Massachusetts
General Hospital

Blossom St

Fruit St

Parkman St

Cardinal
O'Connell Way

Cambridge Street

Old West
Church

Harrison
Gray Otis House

Bowdoin

Stanford Street

Center
Plaza
Government
Center

Suffolk
University

Saltonstall
Building

City
Hall

Sears
Crescent
Building

Custom
House

FINANCIAL
DISTRICT

Community
Boating

Charles/MGH

Phillips Street

Garden St

Revere Street

Russel St

Hancock St

Derne St

Court St

State

Chatham St

Hatch
Shell

BEACON HILL

Pinckney St

Mt. Vernon St

Cedar St

Chestnut Street

Branch St

Myrtle St

Joy St

Walnut St

Bowdoin
Street

Beacon Street

Nichols
House
Museum

Mass.
State
House

Boston
Athenaeum

King's
Chapel

Old State
House

Old City
Hall

Boston
Massacre Site

State
Street

Old Corner
Bookstore

Post
Office
Square

Milk St

Broad St

India Street

Boston
Harbor
Hotel

Chestnut Street

Byron St

Third Harrison
Gray Otis
House

Robert Gould
Shaw & 54th
Regiment
Memorial

Park
Street

Old South
Meeting
House

Milk

Devonshire St

Franklin St

Federal

High

Purchase Street

Atlantic

Northern Av
Bridge

Federal
Courthouse

Gibson
House
Museum

Ritz-Carlton
Hotel

Newbury Street

Arlington Street

Charles Street

Soldiers &
Sailors
Monument

Parkman
Bandstand

PUBLIC
GARDEN

Washington
Monument

Boston
Common

Dark
Street

Winter
St

Orpheum
Theater

Filene's
Basement

Arch St

Summer Street

Otis St

Congress Street

John Fitzgerald Expressway

Evelyn Moakley
Bridge

Boylston

Four Seasons
Hotel

Colonial Theater

Emerson
Majestic
Theater

Downtown
Crossing

Macy's

Chinatown

Essex Street

Chauncy St

Bedford St

Kingston St

Federal
Reserve
Bank

South Station

South Station

Beaver II
(Tea Party Ship)

Children's
Museum

Boston Fire
Museum

Trinity
Church

John Hancock
Tower

Plaza
Castle

Stuart St

Piedmont St

Schubert Theater

Wilbur
Theater

CHINATOWN

Beach St

Harrison Ave.

Kneeland Street

Atlantic Avenue

Congress St
Bridge

Summer St
Bridge

Sleeper St

Melcher St

Summer St

Fort Point Channel

Clarendon

Cortes St

Mass.
Turnpike

Marginal
Road

Herald St

NE Medical
Center

Tyler Street

Hudson Street

Broadway Bridge

Neco St

A Street

Midway Street

Back Bay
Station

Columbus
Av

Chandler Street

Appleton St

SOUTH
END

Warren Av.

Boston Center
for the Arts

Dwight St

Milford St

Montgomery St

E. Berkeley St

Shawmut Av

Washington Street

Troy St

Albany Street

Dorchester Avenue

Broadway

Kennedy Library ▶

—— Freedom Trail

THE FREEDOM TRAIL

Boston is both rich in history and small enough to navigate on foot. The Freedom Trail is a convenient way for visitors to take in the most important sites

The Freedom Trail, which is a 3-mile (5-km) painted path linking 16 historic locations that all played a part in Boston's Colonial and Revolutionary history, was born in 1951 and, in 1974, part of it became Boston's National Historical Park. Although its individual attractions are several centuries old, it was only in 1951 that William Greenough Schofield, a newspaperman and author, suggested that the sites that make up the trail be linked in a numbered sequence. Until then, according to Schofield, "tourists were going berserk, bumbling around and frothing at the mouth because they couldn't find what they were looking for. Nobody knew where anything was or how to get there."

A LEISURELY PACE

It may be tempting to see the city by tour bus, sightseer trolley or the amphibious vehicles called duck boats. All provide quick introductions to some of the major sites, but only by walking on foot can you choose your own pace, decide when to eat, or explore that interesting looking building around the corner that isn't on the tour guide's itinerary. Good walking shoes and a map are a necessity. (Free Freedom Trail maps are available at the National Park Visitor Center at 15 State Street next to the Old State House.) The entire trail can be walked in one day, but it's probably wiser to do it more leisurely over two days.

The red line of paint or brick runs from the Boston Common to the Bunker Hill monument in Charlestown. In some locations – leaving the Old South Meeting House, navigating the streets of the North End or crossing over into Charlestown – it's fairly easy to lose the trail if you aren't watching it carefully. So have that map handy.

These four pages give a broad overview of the Freedom Trail. The individual attractions are covered in detail in the appropriate chapters of the Places section; cross-references are given.

▷ **RELIVING THE PAST**
An actor impersonates Benjamin Franklin at Faneuil Hall *(page 141)*, adjacent to Quincy Market's shops and restaurants.

△ **COLONIAL MYTHS**
Tourist 1: "Why did the settlers have to follow a red line?". Tourist 2: "The British made them do it."

△ **THE STATE HOUSE**
Charles Bulfinch designed the magnificent red brick and domed structure *(page 118)* when he was only 24 years old. A guided tour is available.

▷ **PARK STREET CHURCH**
The church *(page 119)* is known for its architecture and its place in abolitionist history. It was here that the hymn *America* was first sung on July 4, 1831.

△ KING'S CHAPEL BURYING GROUND

The 1630 cemetery was the town's first. A chapel joined it in 1689. *Page 138.*

▽ THE OLD CORNER BOOKSTORE

Books by Stowe, Emerson, Hawthorne and Thoreau were edited and first printed here. *Page 139.*

◁ OLD GRANARY BURYING GROUND

John Hancock, Paul Revere, Samuel Adams, and Mother Goose are all interred here. *Page 119.*

▷ OLD SOUTH MEETING HOUSE

This building *(page 139)* witnessed many of the incendiary debates, including a famous rally against the hated tea tax.

▷ **U.S.S. CONSTITUTION**
"Old Ironsides" is the oldest commissioned ship in the United States Navy and is consistently the most visited site on the Freedom Trail. An adjacent museum details the navy's early history. *Page 180.*

△ **OLD STATE HOUSE**
Inside are many historic artifacts, from ship models to a vial from the Boston Tea Party. Outside, a star within a circle of cobble-stones marks the site of the Boston Massacre of March 5, 1770. *Page 140.*

▷ **FANEUIL HALL**
The second-floor assembly room of this magnificent building is still used for debates, lectures and readings. *Page 141.*

◁ **COSTUME DRAMA**
Expect to encounter actors on the Freedom Trail. This one is filling in some of the background to the Boston Tea Party.

◁ PAUL REVERE HOUSE
This is the oldest house in downtown Boston. Its frame is mostly authentic, but the interior is a recreation of a colonial household. *Page 155.*

▽ FIGHT FOR FREEDOM
The colonists pinned down the British in Boston for nearly a year in 1775–76 by bombarding them from Dorchester Heights.

PAUL REVERE RIDES AGAIN

Boston misses few opportunities to relive its stirring history.

● On March 5, Boston Massacre Day, the Charlestown Militia leads a parade from the Old State House to City Hall Plaza.

● Patriots' Day, on the third Monday in April, is the year's biggest celebration. Paul Revere's and William Dawes' rides are re-enacted the previous evening. On the day itself, after a parade in Back Bay, the first two battles of the Revolution are staged at Lexington Green and Concord. The Boston Marathon *(see page 77)* is also run.

● On the first Monday in June, the Ancient and Honorable Artillery Company gathers at Faneuil Hall and parades to Copley Square.

● On June 17, following a parade from Charlestown, the Battle of Bunker Hill is re-enacted at the Monument.

● On July 4, the Declaration of Independence is read from the balcony of the Old State House.

● On December 10, the Boston Tea party is re-enacted.

▽ OLD NORTH CHURCH
Boston's oldest church (1723) housed the signal lanterns that told Revere the British were heading for Concord. *Page 156.*

▽ COPP'S HILL BURYING GROUND
Once a Native American cemetery, it now offers an eclectic assortment of old colonial gravestones and great views. *Page 158.*

▷ BUNKER HILL MONUMENT
A statue of Colonel William Prescott, who led the troops at the Battle of Bunker Hill, in front of the 221-ft (67-meter) obelisk. *Page 182.*

BEACON HILL AND BOSTON COMMON

*Here the Freedom Trail links with the Black Heritage Trail.
Architectural gems include the State House, Park Street Church
and many of Charles Bulfinch's finest houses*

In many ways, Beacon Hill and the Boston Common make an unlikely pair. Beacon Hill is an essentially residential neighborhood. It's reserved, quiet, and as dignified as the old Boston families who have traditionally chosen to live there. The Common, on the other hand, is loud and lively, with all kinds of characters passing through. It's the nation's first public park and the democratic heart of Boston, a place where anyone with a soapbox is welcome to hold forth. Together, the two areas have a dynamic but balanced relationship, and it's safe to say that neither would be the same without the other.

Hub of the Solar System

Beacon Hill rises from the northern border of the Common at Beacon Street, peaks at the crest of old Mt Vernon, and then slopes down to the Charles River and the West End. Located within this small, protected enclave is one of the city's loveliest quarters. The streets are relatively long and narrow, the sidewalks are lit by gaslamps, and the tidy rows of Federalist houses still reflect the air of gentility so highly valued by their 19th-century inhabitants.

By accidents of history and geography, Beacon Hill is divided into three distinct sections. The South Slope, generally recognized as classical Beacon Hill, is bordered by Beacon, Pinckney, Bowdoin and Charles streets. The less exclusive North Slope runs down the opposite side of the Hill from Pinckney to Cambridge Streets. And the Flat Side, which is built entirely on landfill, occupies the broad area of level ground west of Charles Street and bordering the Charles River.

Beacon Hill isn't the oldest neighborhood in Boston, nor is it the wealthiest or necessarily the most interesting. Its importance to the city is based on the class of people who lived there. From 1800 to about 1870, Beacon Hill was the home of Boston's oldest, wealthiest and most distinguished families, the so-called Brahmins. Appleton, Cabot, Lodge, Lowell – the list includes several hundred, all of them related to early Boston settlers and many of them enriched by the China trade.

The relatively modest homes of Beacon Hill were perfectly suited to the Brahmins' peculiar blend of wealth and self-restraint. As a member of one of its most important families put it, Beacon Hill was the kingdom of the "cold roast" Bostonians, wealthy enough to buy good meat but too frugal to warm it up. Which is not to say that there was a lack of *noblesse oblige*. What Brahmin families withheld for personal fastidiousness they often gave away in the name of civic responsibility. Many of Boston's

LEFT: cobblestoned Acorn Street in Beacon Hill.
BELOW: statue of the Quaker, Mary Dyer, State House.

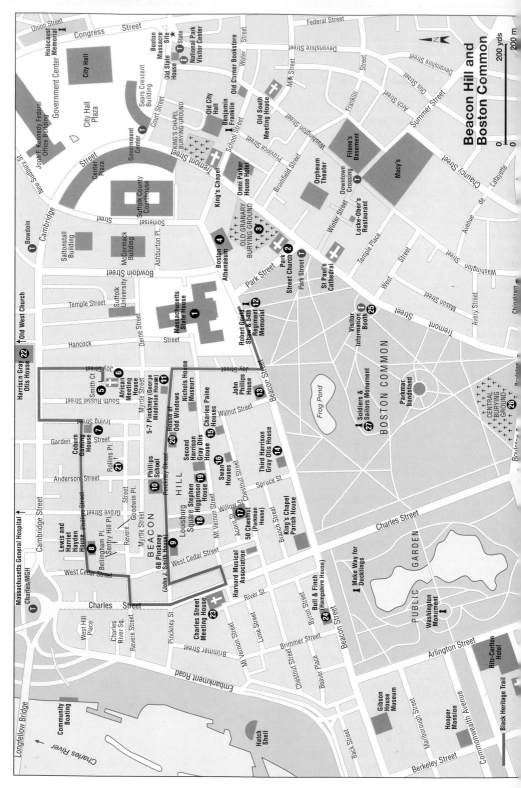

Beacon Hill and Boston Common

Holocaust Memorial

Union Street

Congress Street

Federal Street

City Hall

City Hall Plaza

Government Center

Sears Crescent Building

John F. Kennedy Federal Office Building

Government Center Plaza

Suffolk County Courthouse

Saltonstall Building

McCormack Building

Ashburton Pl.

Boston Massacre Site

Old State House

National Park Visitor Center

State Street

Water Street

Old Corner Bookstore

M.K. Street

Devonshire Street

Devonshire Street

Otis Street

Arch Street

Summer Street

Old City Hall

Benjamin Franklin

Old South Meeting House

Washington Street

Franklin Street

KING'S CHAPEL BURYING GROUND

School Street

Province Street

Bromfield Street

Orpheum Theater

Filene's Basement

Macy's

Chauncy Street

Lafayette Avenue

Bowdoin

Cambridge Street

Center Street

Tremont Street

Somerset Street

King's Chapel

OLD GRANARY BURYING GROUND

Park Street Church

St Paul's Cathedral

Omni Parker House Hotel

Downtown Crossing

Locke-Ober's Restaurant

Winter Street

Temple Place

West Street

Mason Street

Avery Street

Washington Street

Chinatown

Boston Athenaeum

Massachusetts State House

Temple Street

Hancock Street

Robert Gould Shaw & 54th Regiment Memorial

Park Street

Beacon Street

John Phillips House

Tremont Street

Visitor Information Booth

Soldiers & Sailors Monument

BOSTON COMMON

Parkman Bandstand

Frog Pond

CENTRAL BURYING GROUND

Boylston Street

Old West Church

Harrison Gray Otis House

Joy Street

Smith Ct

African Meeting House

5-7 Pinckney (George Middleton House)

Nichols House Museum

House of Odd Windows

Charles Paine Houses

Walnut Street

Second Harrison Gray Otis House

Third Harrison Gray Otis House

Spruce St

Massachusetts General Hospital

Charles/MGH

Coburn Gaming House

Garden Street

Rollins Pl.

Phillips School

Louisburg Square

Stephen Higginson House

Swan Houses

50 Chestnut (Parkman House)

King's Chapel Parish House

Charles Street

PUBLIC GARDEN

Make Way for Ducklings

Washington Monument

Lewis and Harriet Hayden House

Bellingham Pl.

Grove Street

Phillips Street

Revere Street

Myrtle Street

Goodwin Pl.

Anderson Street

Sentry Hill Pl.

BEACON HILL

68 Pinckney (John J. Smith House)

West Cedar Street

Mt Vernon Street

Acorn Street

Willow Street

Chestnut Street

Branch Street

Byron Street

Bull & Finch (Hampshire House)

Beacon Street

Arlington Street

West Hill Place

Charles River Sq.

Revere Street

Pinckney St.

Charles Street Meeting House

Brimmer Street

River St.

Lime Street

Mt Vernon Street

Chestnut Street

Beaver Place

Gibson House Museum

Ritz-Carlton Hotel

Longfellow Bridge

Community Boating

Embankment Road

Charles River

Hatch Shell

Hooper Mansion

Black Heritage Trail

Marlborough Street

Commonwealth Avenue

Berkeley Street

Back Street

Harvard Musical Association

Charles Street

West Cedar Street

Grove Street

200 yds

200 m

Map
on page
116

finest institutions (including the Common) have benefited from the Brahmins' "wholesale charity."

Beacon Hill was a fitting home for the Brahmins in another respect: the new neighborhood fulfilled an old Puritan myth. It really was John Winthrop's "city upon a hill," and in a new country dedicated to individual achievement, it was the perfect place for the Elect to survey the world around them.

By about 1870, many of the old families began leaving Beacon Hill for more spacious homes in the Back Bay, which was then being developed. The Hill fell on relatively hard times for some years until its charms were re-discovered by a new generation of residents in the mid-1900s. Today, many single-family homes have been made into apartments or condominiums, but externally the Hill still represents a remarkably complete picture of 19th-century architecture and urban planning.

It seems ironic, but the history of Beacon Hill isn't nearly as exciting as that of other Boston neighborhoods which figured more prominently in the colonial and revolutionary periods. You'll undoubtedly hear about the Hill's illustrious residents (Henry James, Louisa May Alcott, Charles Sumner and Oliver Wendell Holmes, to name just a few), and there are plenty of stories about Charles Dickens hanging around with Henry Wadsworth Longfellow and "Jamie" Fields, and about Edgar Allen Poe getting kicked out of parties for drunkenness.

Beacon Hill charm.

Yet, for a neighborhood so rich in historic associations, the history of Beacon Hill is most distinguished by its lack of weighty events. There were no battles here, no catastrophes and no world-shaking discoveries. In fact, considering the number of scholars who have populated the neighborhood over the years, more history was probably written in Beacon Hill parlors than ever transpired on the Hill itself.

There are a few exceptions, of course. A murder, for example. In 1849, an upper level Brahmin, George Parkman, was killed and dismembered by Dr John Webster, a Harvard Medical School professor, and then stashed in the basement of his laboratory. The event caused a sensation, and Brahmin society, always mortified by excessive attention, was doubly mortified by the sordid nature of the crime.

A community of free blacks gathered on the North Slope of Beacon Hill in the early 1800s, and many of its members were leaders in the anti-slavery movement preceding the Civil War.

BELOW:
window boxes are
carefully tended.

A sense of separation

But there's more to Beacon Hill than its past. Of all the neighborhoods in Boston, this is the most insulated and self-contained. It's as if the architects designed it as an answer to the old Puritan dilemma – how to be in the world but not of it – because Beacon Hill is both a part of, and apart from, the surrounding city.

The first thing you notice on entering Beacon Hill is exactly this sense of separation. It feels as if you've left modern Boston behind and stepped into a 19th-century village. Traffic thins out, the streets narrow and city noises begin to fade. This is the Boston of another age. It's a town of red brick and cobblestone, of hidden gardens and graceful bay windows. Flower boxes brim with color. Elm trees shade the sidewalk. Aside from a few other tourists, there's almost no one on the street.

The effect is created by a number of factors, but the

John F. Kennedy statue outside the State House.

BELOW:
the State House.
RIGHT: window in
the State House.

most important element is stylistic homogeneity. Aside from the parked cars, there are few intrusions from the modern world, and thanks to an aggressive program of historic preservation, an abundance of original details survives. But above all, Beacon Hill owes its special ambience to its original developers and to the native talents of the untrained housewrights who designed and built most of the homes.

The State House

The first European resident of Beacon Hill was the Rev. William Blackstone, an English hermit who settled on the Shawmut Peninsula several years before the Puritans. After selling most of his land to John Winthrop, Blackstone retired to a small, 6-acre (2.4-hectare) estate at the foot of the South Slope. At the time, the area was called Trimount after the three distinct peaks (Sentry Hill, Mt Vernon and Cotton Hill) that rose above the Common. Over the years that followed, all three summits were gradually flattened by as much as 60 ft (18 meters) and the excess soil and rock were used to fill in the tidal flats where Charles Street is today.

In 1737 Beacon Hill got its first building of any true substance and Boston got its finest "mansion-house." The house was built by Thomas Hancock, a wealthy merchant and the uncle of John Hancock, who inherited both house and fortune after his uncle's death. The landmark stood on Beacon Street overlooking the northeast corner of the Common until 1863. Today, the site is marked by a plaque.

In 1803, the Hancock mansion was joined by a building that continues to dominate Beacon Hill: the **Massachusetts State House ❶** (Mon–Fri 8.45am– 5pm; tel: 727 3676; frequent tours). The State House is the masterpiece of Charles Bulfinch, the most important American architect of his day (*see page 95*).

Today, the State House's appearance is the result of several significant

changes. The original red brick structure is now backed by an ungainly rear extension and flanked on either side by marble wings. Although clumsy, the new additions haven't detracted from Bulfinch's dignified facade, whose grand two-story portico is surmounted by the famous gold dome. In Bulfinch's original design the dome was covered with white shingles. Paul Revere sheathed it in copper and later, in 1861, it was gilded with gold leaf. It was also changed during World War II, when it was painted black in case of an air attack.

Inside the State House, the most impressive rooms are the few that survived the building's alterations. Especially notable are the **Senate Chamber**, the **Reception Room**, the **House of Representatives** (home of the beloved Sacred Cod) and **Doric Hall**, a vaulted, columned, marble chamber that rises beneath the dome.

From the front steps of the State House one can cross Beacon Street and stroll the short length of Park Street which terminates below the sturdy Georgian steeple of the **Park Street Church ❷** (Jul–Aug Tues–Sat 9am–3pm; Sept–Jun by appointment; tel: 523 3383). The church was designed by Peter Banner and completed in 1810. The renowned abolitionist William Lloyd Garrison launched his public crusade against slavery from the pulpit in 1829, and Henry James described the church as "the most interesting mass of brick and mortar in America," That may be true from a historian's point of view, but architecturally the interior is not especially interesting. A film recounting its history is shown in the basement.

The Old Granary Burying Ground

Although it's now surrounded by modern buildings, the **Old Granary Burying Ground ❸** (daily 8am–4pm; tel: 536 4100), located near the corner of Park and Tremont streets, was originally a part of the Common and took its name from an

Map on page 116

Park Street Church is responsible for giving this part of the Common its nickname – "Brimstone Corner" – after the fiery sermons delivered by its Congregationalist ministers and the barrels of gunpowder which were stored in the basement during the War of 1812.

BELOW: House of Representatives, the State House.

Joy Street bikers.

BELOW:
Park Street Church.
RIGHT: Paul
Revere's tomb in
the Old Granary
Burying Ground.

old granary that once stood where the Park Street Church is now situated. The first body was committed in 1660, making it one of the oldest cemeteries in Boston. Among the historic figures buried here are Samuel Adams, Peter Faneuil, Paul Revere, John Hancock, Elizabeth "Mother" Goose and the victims of the Boston Massacre. An obelisk in the middle of the graveyard marks the resting place of Benjamin Franklin's parents. Unfortunately, the headstones have been moved so many times, they no longer correspond to the actual graves, some of which are four bodies deep. Believe it or not, the neat rows we see today are an accommodation to the lawnmower. Still, the icons and inscriptions carved into the stones are absolutely fascinating, and, considering the nature of the place, more than a little chilling.

Taking the longer route back to the State House, walk down Tremont away from the Boston Common and take a left on Beacon Street. The unobtrusive entrance at 10½ Beacon Street is that of the **Athenaeum** ❹ (tel: 227-0270), a private library and Brahmin stronghold. Casual visitors are only allowed limited access to the first and second floors. Founded in 1807, the Athenaeum, whose barrel-vaulted fifth floor is nirvana for the book lover, contains the library of George Washington and also houses a notable collection of American portrait paintings. (So impressive is the Athenaeum's superb Italian palazzo inspired interior that Hollywood movie crews have used it to double for Harvard's libraries.) From here it is a very short walk up Beacon Street back to the State House.

The Black Heritage Trail

Begin exploring Beacon Hill history with the short **Black Heritage Trail**, a second Freedom Trail confined to a few blocks overseen by the National Park Service. (Guided tours are available.) When Massachusetts declared slavery ille-

gal in 1783, the migration of runaway slaves to Boston grew enormously. Free blacks settled in the North End but later moved to the North Slope of **Beacon Hill.**

Just off **Joy Street** is tiny **Smith Court ❺**, where, at one time, all the houses were occupied by blacks. Facing these is the **African Meeting House ❻**, the oldest black church in the nation still standing. Dedicated in 1806, it was called "the haven from the loft" because of the practice in Old North Church of relegating black worshippers to the loft. It was also known as "Black Faneuil Hall" because of fiery anti-slave meetings held here. These culminated in 1832 when William Lloyd Garrison founded the New England Anti-Slavery Society. In his words: "Faneuil Hall shall ere long echo with the principles we have set forth. We shall shake the nation by their mighty power."

Next door, at the corner of Joy Street, stood the **Abiel Smith School**, dedicated in 1834 to the education of the city's black children. Yet voices of integration were already being heard, for, although the black community had fought hard for this school, some were opposed, arguing that it would crystallize segregation. Led by William C. Neill, who lived in Smith Court and who was the first published black historian, they formed the Equal Schools Association (separates are not equals), which called for the school to be boycotted.

In 1850 the State's highest court ruled that the school provided an education equal to that of other public schools in the city and so blacks need not be admitted to the public system. However, in 1855 the State Legislature outlawed segregation and the Smith School was closed.

Near here, at the corner of **Phillips** and **Irving streets** was the **Coburn Gaming House ❼**, a "private palace… the resort of the upper ten who had acquired a taste for gambling." Also on Phillips Street (No. 66) is the **Lewis and Harriet**

The New England Anti-Slavery Society started here in 1832.

BELOW:
classic doorways.

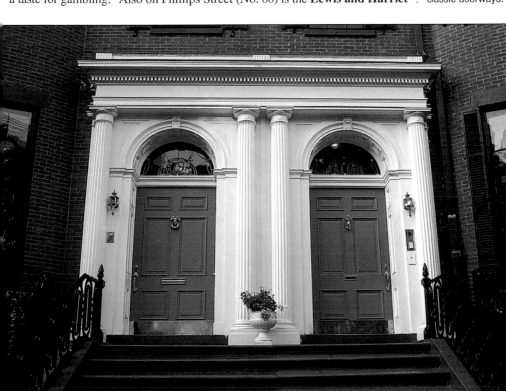

TIP

For full Information on
the Black Heritage
Trail and Boston's
black history, visit the
Museum of Afro-
American History at
the African Meeting
House, 46 Joy Street.
(Mon–Fri 10am–4pm;
also same hours on
Sat and Sun in Jun–
Aug; tel: 739-1200).

Hayden House ❽. This was one of the most important of the many "underground railway" stops on the Hill which sheltered fugitive slaves on their way to freedom in Canada. In 1853 the Haydens were visited by Harriet Beecher Stowe, who was researching for her book *Keys to Uncle Tom's Cabin*. She was astonished that the house was a haven for 13 slaves. It is said that Hayden kept two kegs of gunpowder in the basement so that the house could be blown up if searched.

And so to **Charles Street**, where the **Meeting House** of that name was built in 1807 for the Third Baptist Church. In the mid-1830s the Church's segregationist traditions were challenged by Timothy Gilbert, who invited black friends to his pew. He was expelled and, with other white abolitionist baptists, founded the First Baptist Free Church. It became Tremont Temple, "the first integrated church in America." In 1876 the Meeting House was bought by the African Methodist Episcopalian Church and, in 1939, was the last black institution to leave the Hill.

Further up the Hill, at **68 Pinckney** ❾, is a handsome home that belonged to John J. Smith, a distinguished black statesman who migrated to Boston from Virginia in 1848. Stationed in Washington during the Civil War, he was a recruiting officer for the all-black Fifth Cavalry. Subsequently, he was thrice appointed to the Massachusetts House of Representatives, and then to the Boston Common Council.

The large red-brick building at the corner of Pinckney and Anderson streets is the **Phillips School** ❿, which, when opened to blacks in 1855, became the city's first inter-racial school. The clapboard house at **Nos. 5–7 Pinckney** ⓫ is the oldest (1791) existing home on the Hill built by a black person. The lot was bought by G. Middleton, a black equestrian, and Lewis Glapion, a mulatto barber. Middleton, a colonel in the Revolutionary War, led the all-black company "Bucks of America."

End the tour across from the State House at Augustus Saint-Gaudens's famous

BELOW:
Pinckney Street.

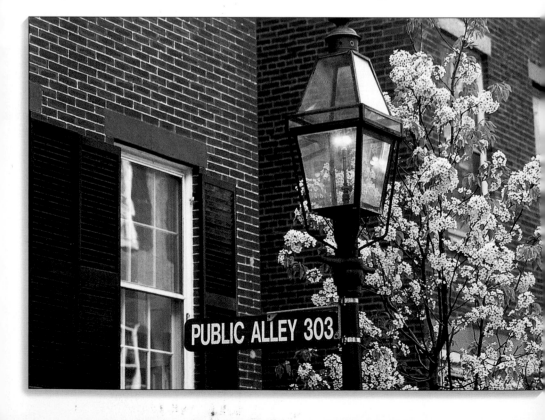

PUBLIC ALLEY 303

bas-relief that honors **Robert Gould Shaw and the 54th Regiment** ⓬. This, the first black regiment in the North, was recruited in Massachusetts. Shaw, a young white officer from Boston, volunteered for the command. He and many members of the company were killed during the assault on Fort Wagner, South Carolina, an event recreated in the 1989 Hollywood movie *Glory*. The Saint-Gaudens memorial is considered by many the sculptor's finest work and was later celebrated by Robert Lowell in his poem *For the Union Dead*.

The South Slope

At about the same time that the State House was being completed, Bulfinch became involved in another large-scale project on Beacon Hill. Together with several other enterprising townsmen (including Harrison Gray Otis, Joseph Woodward, Jonathan Mason and William Scollay), Bulfinch became a member of the Mt Vernon Proprietors which bought about 19 acres (7.7 hectares) of pasture on the South Slope. Plans were drawn to level the summit, lay out streets and subdivide house lots.

The Proprietors originally intended to build free-standing homes surrounded by gardens, but the economics of development soon dictated a more efficient plan – joining homes at a common wall. At first, two or three houses were built together, and then, as the pace of development quickened, entire streets were lined with single unbroken rows. Although Bulfinch designed several of Beacon Hill's grandest estates, most of the buildings were erected by untrained builders. Their instincts for proportion, sturdiness and modest ornamentation still define the neighborhood's essential character.

A tour of the old Mt Vernon properties is limited entirely to the **South Slope**. The best place to start is on the northeast corner of the Common, directly in front

Map on page 116

Harrison Gray Otis, a US Congressman and mayor of Boston, played a central role in buying land to facilitate the development of Beacon Hill. Bulfinch designed a succession of three homes for him on Cambridge Street (1796), Mt Vernon Street (1800) and Beacon Street (1805), all of which survive.

BELOW: pooches meet up on Pinckney Street.

Traditional knocker.

RIGHT:
Louisburg Square.

of the State House. From here, proceed straight down Beacon Street until you reach the corner of Charles Street.

Fronting the Common along its northern border, **Beacon Street** is the Hill's public face. This is Oliver Wendell Holmes's "sunny street that holds the sifted few." The buildings here are among the oldest on Beacon Hill, and boast a level of grandeur and ornamentation largely unmatched by the rest of the neighborhood.

As you stroll down the hill, be sure to take note of the **John Phillips House ⑬** (1 Walnut St.) and the **Third Harrison Gray Otis House ⑭** (45 Beacon St.), both designed by Bulfinch between 1804 and 1808. "Purple panes" still hang in the window frames of **King's Chapel Parish House** (63–64 Beacon St.) and of **39** and **40 Beacon Street**. The unusual color is caused by a chemical defect, and the purple panes, installed in the early 1800s, have become a part of Beacon Hill folklore.

Take a right at the corner of Charles Street and then turn right again at one of the narrow cross streets that lead up the slope. The first and most intimate one is **Chestnut Street**. The combination of simple structures, modest scale and artful detailing make this one of the most pleasing streets on the Hill. The buildings are especially notable for the delicate use of ornamentation, including wrought-iron balconies, bootscrapers, Greek Revival porticos and fan lights, all of which tend to vary and lighten the plain brick facades.

Again, there are far too many distinguished homes to list, but a few highlights include the **Charles Paine Houses ⑮** (6–8 Chestnut St.), the **Swan Houses ⑯** (13, 15 and 17) and **No. 29A**, all attributed to Bulfinch. The home of historian Francis Parkman is located at **No. 50 ⑰**, and the **Harvard Musical Association**, the country's oldest music library, is at No. 57A.

Take time to explore the narrow lanes that intersect Chestnut Street. Many of the smaller houses on **Willow**, **West Cedar** and **Acorn streets** were originally servants' quarters and kitchens that serviced the wealthier households. Today, these slender byways are among the most private locations on the Hill. Acorn Street, the steep cobbled alley lined with gas lamps and flower boxes, is not to be missed.

Following Willow Street uphill, you immediately come to **Mt Vernon Street**. Here the houses are larger, the street wider, and the families more distinguished. In one of his more snobbish moments, Henry James called it "the only respectable street in America."

Louisburg Square

The highlight of Mt Vernon Street, and the crown of Beacon Hill, is **Louisburg Square ⑱**, a small rectangle of grass and trees surrounded by a cobblestone plaza and stately homes. The gently rippling bowfront houses on the west side of the square (**numbers 8 to 22**) have been called the finest rowhouses in Boston, and possibly in the United States. Louisa May Alcott lived at **No. 10** and, at **No. 20**, the singer Jenny Lind married her accompanist Otto Goldschmidt.

Just beyond Louisburg Square, in the direction of the State House (to the southeast), is an impressive series of freestanding mansions. The **Stephen Higginson House ⑲** at No. 87 and its much-altered neighbor at **No. 89** were both built by Charles Bulfinch between 1804 and 1809. The **Second Harrison Gray Otis House**, next door at No. 85, was built by Bulfinch several years earlier.

The brownstone mansions across the street were constructed in 1850; their Gothic touches are a striking counterpoint to the other buildings on the street. The **Nichols House Museum** at 55 Mt Vernon St is also a Bulfinch creation, and guided tours are offered on varying days (tel: 227 6993).

At the opposite end of Louisburg Square, **Pinckney Street** runs along the crest of Beacon Hill, separating the South Slope from the less affluent North Slope. Noteworthy homes in this area include **No. 24**, the **House of Odd Windows** ㉕, which has the most eccentric design on the Hill.

"The Rim of Decency"

Beyond Pinckney, the **North Slope** pitches toward Cambridge Street and the West End. Nowadays, this is the bohemian half of Beacon Hill, one of the few places where artists, writers and students can still find tiny yet affordable apartments. Socially, the North Slope was never the equal of the South.

From the very beginning, it was considered the "bad side" of the Hill, and according to some of the South Slope's high-minded residents, the label still applies. It is only since the most recent wave of gentrification that the social gap has really begun to narrow.

Although the North Slope doesn't share the same architectural pedigree as the South, it tends to be somewhat friendlier and more relaxed. Unlike its southern neighbor, the North Slope's social life is fairly visible, and neighborhood business often spills over into the streets. On **Myrtle Street**, for example, there's a pizzeria, a café, a corner grocer and an old-fashioned, two-chair barber shop

Map on page 116

Hanging out on Pinckney Street.

LEFT: winter in Louisburg Square.
BELOW: Acorn Street.

Old West Church.

BELOW:
daffodils bloom
on Beacon Hill.

where people meet and have the sort of casual conversations that make the place feel like a living neighborhood rather than just a collection of interesting buildings.

The students bustling up and down **Temple Street** near **Suffolk University** further animate the neighborhood, and you can sometimes hear music blasting from an apartment window or car horns honking on Cambridge Street.

The North Slope was the site of Beacon Hill's earliest development, a small huddle of buildings along the Charles River established about 1725. Almost immediately, the North Slope Village began to take on an unsavory character. Its proximity to the river and its detachment from town made it a perfect spot for sailors who were more interested in taverns and bordellos than the rigors of Puritan life. North Slope entrepreneurs were only too glad to oblige them, and within a few years Boston had its first red-light district. Among sailors, the village became known as Mount Whoredom, and for nearly 100 years it rankled the morals of god-fearing citizens everywhere in Boston.

In the early 1820s a crackdown forced the last of Mount Whoredom's "bawdy houses" to shut down, and the area started to change. By then, the city's substantial black population had begun to move in, and in a few short years the North Slope became a black community center and a hotbed of abolitionist activity.

Elsewhere on the North Slope, be sure to stroll past the four, quiet, charming cul-de-sacs that run off Revere Street. **Rollins Place ㉑** is especially interesting because the classical two-story portico at the end is a mere facade. There's nothing behind it but a 20-ft (6-meter) cliff dropping down to Phillips Street. The other alleyways – **Goodwin Place**, **Sentry Hill Place** and **Bellingham Place** – are equally enchanting, each paved with red brick and lined by compact rowhouses. Branching off from opposite sides of Phillips Street (near the corner of

West Cedar) are **Primus Avenue** and a very narrow passage known as **Flower Lane**, two other alleyways well worth investigating.

The North side of the Hill ends in wide, busy **Cambridge Street**, on whose far side are several interesting buildings. At the west end of this street is the **Old West Church**, a handsome red-brick federal building from 1806. The original church was razed in 1775 when the British thought that the Americans were using it as a steeple from which to signal to their compatriots in Cambridge.

The current building, a Methodist church, is an oblong meeting house fronted by a rectangular block rising in several stages to a square cupola beneath which are swag-ornamented clocks. The large, empty interior has a balcony, supported by delicate columns with attenuated acanthus-leaf capitals, running around three sides.

Next door is the **First Harrison Gray Otis House** ❷ (Wed–Sun 11am–5pm; tel: 227 3956), designed by Bulfinch in 1796 and now owned by the Society for the Preservation of New England Antiquities. This, the most distinguished old mansion still standing in Boston, is a completely symmetrical three-story rectangular block of red bricks, with each story defined by a brownstone string course. The interior has been meticulously restored with furniture and portraits, canary-yellow wallpaper and mirror-panelled doors which would reflect candlelight. The basement contains an architectural museum.

Massachusetts General Hospital

Further to the east on Cambridge Street is the sprawling **Massachusetts General Hospital**, possibly America's greatest hospital. Its very first building, the Bulfinch Pavilion and Ether Dome, was designed by Bulfinch just before he departed for Washington to work on the United States capitol. Enquire at the

Map on page 116

First Harrison Gray Otis House.

BELOW: sightseeing trolleys, a source of income for students who are often hired as commentators.

*One of the many
antiques shops
in the area.*

hospital's main entrance for directions to this building which is an historic land-mark twice over: once because of its architecture and once because here ether was used as an anaesthetic for the first time *(see page 91)*. The Federal-style building stands on a high podium, and the main entrance is approached by two stairways that lead to the sides of a portico formed by 10 unfluted Ionic columns.

The Flat Side and Charles Street

The remaining part of Beacon Hill, a broad area of level ground built entirely on landfill, is known as the **Flat Side**. Its outstanding feature is **Charles Street**, Beacon Hill's only commercial street, while its most distinguished building is the **Charles Street Meeting House ㉓**, located on the corner of Mt Vernon Street.

Relative to the other two sections of Beacon Hill, the Flat Side occupies a neutral position. It has few of the grand associations boasted by the South Slope and almost none of the negative ones tagged on the North. As a result, people tend to overlook the residential areas, although here, as elsewhere on the Hill, the overall effect is of a quaint 19th-century town located in the middle of a modern city.

Most people come to the Flat Side to shop on Charles Street, which tends to be less hectic than downtown and more casual than the boutiques on Newbury Street. Antiques are a local specialty and there are several good restaurants and cafés where one can buy Italian pastries, *gelato* and a stiff cup of espresso.

Elsewhere on the Flat Side, the finest homes tend to be gathered on **Brimmer**, **Lime** and **Mt Vernon Streets**. There are also two very interesting courtyards tucked into the block immediately off Embankment Road. **Charles River Square** is a hidden enclave of tidy rowhouses surrounding a rectangular plaza. About a half-block away, the rowhouses at **West Hill Place** use concave facades

BELOW:
a Paul Revere bust
catches the eye in
an antiques store.

to define a circular courtyard; there's a tunnel in the back that opens to Charles Street. Unfortunately, with the intersection of three major highways only a few hundred feet away, the sound of traffic often penetrates the superb isolation these lovely courtyards must have enjoyed in the past.

Although the architecture of the Flat Side isn't as old or interesting as the rest of the Hill, there is an exceptionally handsome row of granite houses on Beacon Street directly across from the Public Garden. When they were built in 1828, most of the Flat Side was still underwater. The houses actually stood on the Mill Dam, which started at the edge of the Common and arched across the Back Bay.

Probably the most popular attraction on the Flat Side is still the **Hampshire House** with the **Bull & Finch** ㉔, a neighborhood bar located on the corner of Beacon and Brimmer streets that was reputed to have been the inspiration for the popular television series *Cheers*. During the 1980s and 1990s the success of the show transformed the place into a major tourist attraction, and people waited at the door both day and night. If it's a couple of cold ones you're after, walk midway up Charles Street to the **Sevens Pub**, where you can still belly up to the bar without being crushed by curiosity-seekers.

A geographical crossroads

The **Boston Common** is such an integral part of Beacon Hill that it's impossible to talk about one without mentioning the other. Although the two areas represent different aspects of Boston, they are linked by history and should be thought of as elements of a larger whole.

Most activity occurs on the fringe of the Common, near the **Park Street subway station** at Tremont Street's northern end. Here, vendors sell ice-cream,

Boston Common was described in 1674 by John Josselyn as "a small, but pleasant Common, where the Gallants a little before Sun-set walk with their Marmalet-Madams... till the nine o'clock bells rings them home to their habitations [and] the Constables walk their rounds to see good order kept, and to take up loose people."

BELOW: a romantic restaurant in Charles Street.

Keeping cool on the Common.

hot-dogs, T-shirts and other souvenirs, and, on occasions, religious fanatics vent their wrath. Opened with a trolley service in 1897, Park Street was the first subway station in the nation and is now a Historic Landmark.

The Common, a pentagon covering about 50 acres (20 hectares), is bounded by Beacon, Boylston, Charles, Park and Tremont streets. It is both a geographical and social crossroads, and for those unfamiliar with the city is probably the best place to start a visit. There is a **Visitor Information Booth ㉕** on the Common situated just a couple blocks south of the Park Street subway station, where one can pick up free maps and which also serves at the beginning of the Freedom Trail (*see pages 110–113*).

Taking a trolley

Several privately operated sightseeing "trolleys" (in reality, conventional wheeled vehicles with trolley-like bodywork) that run every 10 or 15 minutes set off on their city tours from here. Although some guides seem to be more interested in auditioning for comedy clubs than giving useful information, the trolleys are a good way to become acquainted with the city, especially if time is limited. Best of all, one can hop off the trolley wherever one likes, explore on foot for a while and then re-board a later trolley. There's hot competition between look-alike trolley companies; it can be a problem to ensure that you re-board the right vehicle.

BELOW: a ranger gives directions on the Common.

The people one sees on the Common represent a cross section of the city: Chinese women practicing *tai chi* in the shade of an ancient elm tree, Italian men taking a walk with their grandchildren, kids playing, and office workers soaking up the sun while enjoying their lunch.

Most people don't realize that the Common is probably the oldest and least changed section of Boston. It was established more than 350 years ago, when John Winthrop and his neighbors bought the original 50 acres from the Rev. William Blackstone. In 1640, the townsmen agreed to preserve the land as a "Comon Field" (*sic*) on which sheep and cattle were to be grazed, and it soon became a popular spot for sermons, promenades and, in the years before the Revolution, political protest. Militias used the land as a mustering ground, and public hangings were conducted at the Great Elm, which stood on the Common until 1876. Among the heretics who met a cruel end here was Mary Dyer, the heroic Quaker who insisted on the right to worship freely.

During the American Revolution, the Common was transformed into a British military center. As many as 2,000 Redcoats were quartered here during the occupation of Boston, and several dozen British soldiers killed at the Battle of Bunker Hill were interred at the **Central Burying Ground** ㉖ in the southeast corner. It is the fourth oldest cemetery in Boston, but few of note are buried here.

The west part of the common is devoted to athletic endeavor – baseball, tennis, volley ball and frisbee are all popular – and to large public meetings.

Elsewhere on the Common are several works of public art. Outstanding is the 70-ft (21-meter) **Soldiers and Sailors Monument** ㉗ which is located atop Telegraph Hill on the western side of the park. It is dedicated to the Union forces who were killed during the American Civil War.

Street musicians entertain and, during the summer, children cool off under the fountain in the **Frog Pond**. In colonial times sheep and cows slaked their thirst at the pond. Later, proper Bostonians fished in it for minnows in the summer and ice-skated on it in the winter. ❏

Map on page 116

The Soldiers and Sailors Monument.

BELOW: winter fun on the Common.

DOWNTOWN

*The Old Corner Bookstore, Old City Hall, Old South Meeting
House, Ye Olde Oyster House – everything seems ancient.
But then there's Quincy Market and Chinatown*

Map
on page
136

To walk the streets of Downtown Boston today is to walk with the ghosts of colonial settlers upon ground now shadowed by modern skyscrapers. As the centuries have passed, many street names have changed. But the streets themselves follow much the same design as they did back in the 1630s when Anne Hutchinson, the feminist leader of her day, was ousted from her home on what is now School Street, or in October 1746, when the Rev. Thomas Prince of Old South Meeting House "prayed up" a hurricane that wrecked an invading force of French warships.

There's nowhere more appropriate for beginning such a walk than at **Downtown Crossing ❶**, where **Summer** and **Washington Streets** intersect. At this spot, you are standing at the very hub of Downtown Boston – a huge bronze disc embedded in the sidewalk assures you of the fact. What the bronze plaque doesn't tell you is that South Boston is east of Downtown Boston, that East Boston is north of where you stand, and that the North End just north of Downtown Boston is south of East Boston. Also, as you stand at the center of Downtown Boston, if you move your feet a few paces to the west, Summer Street becomes Winter Street without changing its face or its direction.

Those who love the city are generally indifferent to Downtown's directional peculiarities. They are more concerned with the unique aspects of its personality, such as the assured presence of the friendly horses of the city's mounted police during snowy Christmas holidays at Downtown Crossing.

Bargain basement

As for other things unique – well, right there at Downtown Crossing, just at your elbow, is the entrance to the internationally popular **Filene's Basement ❷**. Its clientele has ranged from royalty to rag ladies, from Presidents to punks, all drawn by its system of bargain-slashing, each hoping to outwit, outwait or outgrab the other at the correct instant for a sensational bargain. An $800 Brooks Brothers suit goes on sale in the Basement at, say, $400; if unsold after 14 days, it's $300; after 21 days, $200; after 28 days, $100. Find one unsold for 35 days and your check goes to charity. Fun shopping? Sometimes it's a riot.

Sharing Summer Street with Filene's is **Macy's ❸**, formerly the flagship store of the Jordan Marsh chain. This outfit had its beginning on a frosty morning in 1851 when young Eben Dyer Jordan made his first sale in his newly-opened shop – one yard of red silk ribbon, sold to a little girl for two cents. This was a big deal for a man who had sailed down from Maine five years earlier with just $1.25 in his pocket. It was also to become a big deal for the evolution of American

PRECEDING PAGES:
Quincy Market.
LEFT: the
Palladian style.
BELOW: bargain
hunter in Filene's
Basement.

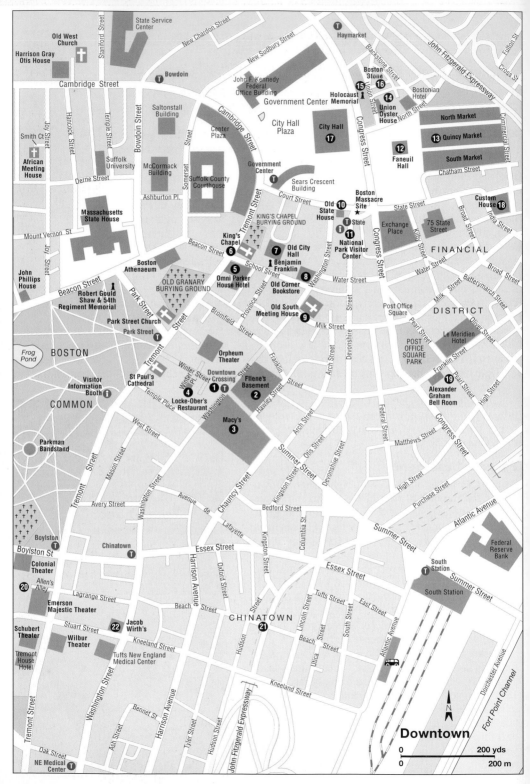

136 ◆ **PLACES**

State Service Center

Old West Church

Harrison Gray Otis House

Cambridge Street

Bowdoin

Stanford Street

New Chardon Street

New Sudbury Street

John Fitzgerald Expressway

Cross St

Fulton St

Haymarket

Blackstone Street

Boston Stone

Bostonian Hotel

Commercial Street

Smith Ct Street
Joy Street
Hancock Street
Temple Street

African Meeting House

Saltonstall Building

Bowdoin Street

John F. Kennedy Federal Office Building

Government Center

Holocaust Memorial

Union Street

15

16

14

Union Oyster House

North Market

North Street

Derne Street

Suffolk University

McCormack Building

Center Plaza

City Hall Plaza

City Hall

Quincy Market

13

Chatham Street

Massachusetts State House

Ashburton Pl.

Suffolk County Courthouse

Government Center

Sears Crescent Building

17

12

Faneuil Hall

South Market

Mount Vernon St

Court Street

KING'S CHAPEL BURYING GROUND

Old State House

Boston Massacre Site

10

State

Exchange Place

State Street

Custom House

18

India Street

Broad Street

Beacon Street

John Phillips House

Boston Athenaeum

King's Chapel

5

6

Old City Hall

7

National Park Visitor Center

11

75 State Street

FINANCIAL

Robert Gould Shaw & 54th Regiment Memorial

OLD GRANARY BURYING GROUND

Omni Parker House Hotel

Benjamin Franklin

8

Old Corner Bookstore

Washington Street

Water Street

Post Office Square

Milk Street

Batterymarch Street

Oliver Street

DISTRICT

Park Street Church

Park Street

Bromfield Street

Province Street

School Street

Old South Meeting House

9

Milk Street

Devonshire Street

Pearl Street

POST OFFICE SQUARE PARK

Le Meridien Hotel

Frog Pond

BOSTON

Visitor Information Booth

St Paul's Cathedral

Orpheum Theater

Downtown Crossing

1

Filene's Basement

2

Franklin Street

Arch Street

High Street

Congress Street

Franklin Street

19

Alexander Graham Bell Room

COMMON

Locke-Ober's Restaurant

4

Winter Street

Winter Pl.

Temple Place

Washington Street

Macy's

3

Haxley Street

Summer Street

Otis Street

Kingston Street

High Street

Purchase Street

Atlantic Avenue

Parkman Bandstand

West Street

Mason Street

Chauncy Street

Avenue de Lafayette

Bedford Street

Columbia St

Summer Street

Federal Reserve Bank

Avery Street

Avenue

Essex Street

South Station

Summer Street

Boylston

Boylston St

Tremont Street

Chinatown

Essex Street

Harrison Avenue

Oxford Street

Kingston Street

Federal Street

Atlantic Avenue

Dorchester Avenue

South Station

Colonial Theater

Allen's Alley

20

Emerson Majestic Theater

Lagrange Street

Beach Street

CHINATOWN

Tufts Street

Lincoln Street

East Street

Fort Point Channel

Schubert Theater

Stuart Street

Jacob Wirth's

22

Wilbur Theater

Kneeland Street

21

Hudson

Beach Street

South Street

Utica Street

Tremont House Hotel

Tufts New England Medical Center

Bennet St

Tyler Street

Hudson Street

Kneeland Street

John Fitzgerald Expressway

Oak Street

Ash Street

South Street

Harrison Avenue

NE Medical Center

N

Downtown

0 ——— 200 yds
0 ——— 200 m

department stores, many of which followed the Jordan Marsh formula to success.

By contrast with that commercial coup, Boston's financiers today handle transactions of mega-millions. Although not nearly as important as New York in general financial transactions, Boston has carved out for itself some special niches. Mutual funds, in which it still leads the field, began here in 1925 and, nearly a century earlier, the concept of venture capital, which still thrives here, was introduced in Boston. Many families and institutions throughout the nation depend on conservative Boston firms, hidden in unobtrusive offices, to handle their trust funds.

Some business is done over lunch or dinner. Just off Winter Street lies **Winter Place**, a narrow alley leading to the elegant and perennially popular **Locke-Ober's Restaurant ❹**, home of delightful servings of scrod and lobster, and of many a clandestine or power dinner in the small dining rooms upstairs.

Head toward the Boston Common on Winter and take a right on Tremont Street, passing the Park Street Church and the Old Granary Burial Ground arriving at School Street. At the corner of School and Tremont is the venerable **Omni Parker House Hotel ❺**, where Charles Dickens conducted literary seminars, where Ho Chi Minh waited on tables and Malcolm X toiled in the kitchen.

Across from the Parker House on School and Tremont is **King's Chapel ❻** (Mon, Tues, Fri and Sat 9am-4pm; Sun 1pm-4pm), an early stop on Boston's Freedom Trail. The Chapel had its origins in the 1680s when Britain's King James II made a colossal political blunder by sending to Boston a clergyman whose job was to install in the town the very thing the Puritans had hated and fled: a branch of the Church of England.

The Rev. Robert Ratcliffe's arrival in Boston was greeted with a roar of protest. This bothered him not one whit, and since he had no church in which to hold

They're not joking.

BELOW: Locke-Ober's Restaurant.

services he teamed with the royal colonial governor, Sir Edmund Andros, to usurp the church the Puritan-Congregationalists were using, the Old South Meeting House. Finally in 1688, Andros seized a piece of land belonging to a Sir Isaac Johnson, and there the original King's Chapel, a wooden structure, was built in 1689. This was replaced in 1754 by the present structure, built of granite blocks ferried from Quincy, 8 miles (13 km) to the south. The dedication was attended by hundreds of crown-hating locals who hurled garbage, manure and dead animals at the presiding Anglicans.

Paul Revere's largest bell is housed in King's Chapel. He called it "the sweetest bell we ever made."

Next to the Chapel, on Tremont Street, is Boston's first cemetery, **King's Chapel Burying Ground**, in use from 1630 to 1796. The Bay Colony's first Governor, John Winthrop, was buried here in 1649. The monument at the corner of the burying ground honors a French naval adjutant, Chevalier de St Sauveur, chamberlain to the French king's brother, Count d'Artois. St Sauveur was killed by a Boston mob in September 1778 while ashore buying food for his shipmates.

Moving a few yards down School Street, on the left we come to the site of the **first school in America**. This was the original Boston Latin School, which opened in 1635, and accounts for the naming of School Street when it was laid out in 1640.

Old City Hall ❼ rises in the immediate background here, a massive pile of Second Empire granite architecture. Built for politics, it now features a restaurant and office space; in its forecourt is a bronze statue of Benjamin Franklin, with pedestal tablets chronicling the important events of his life.

BELOW:
King's Chapel
Burying Ground.
RIGHT: bookshop
with a tale to tell.

A few more yards down the slope is the intersection of School and Washington streets. And here on the left is one of Downtown Boston's most loved and best preserved colonial structures, the **Old Corner Bookstore ❽** (Mon–Sat 9am–9pm, Sun noon–6pm; tel: 367-4000). Originally on this site stood the home

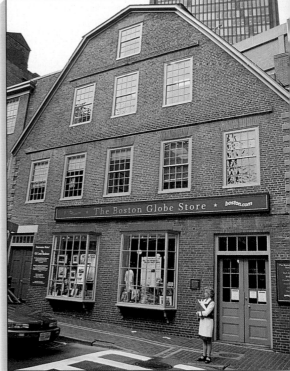

of the celebrated and courageous Anne Hutchinson. She lived here from 1634 to 1638, when she was banished from town by colonials who objected to her principles of free speech. In exile, she was killed by Mohawk Indians.

The big Boston fire of October 3, l711, destroyed Anne's cottage. It was replaced by the present structure in 1712, which through the years has served as an apothecary shop, a dry goods store, and private residence; in 1828 it became the home of a book store and publishing house – with printing press driven by teams of Canadian horses. In the Golden Age of American literature this was a popular browsing place for the likes of Whittier, Emerson, Stowe, Alcott and other distinguished writers. By the 1960s it had become a pizza parlor, from which fate it was rescued and restored by its present owners, the Boston Globe company.

Old South Meeting House

At this point we cross Washington Street to the juncture of **Spring Lane** and turn right. A walk of only a few yards brings us to one of the most important forum locations in the growth of American independence, **Old South Meeting House** ❾ (Apr–Oct daily 9.30am–5pm; Nov–Mar 10am–4pm; tel: 482 6439). The land on which Old South was built was originally a sloping cornfield and potato patch owned and tilled by Governor Winthrop. When he died, it was taken over by a preacher, John Norton, whose widow Mary offered it to her neighbors in 1663 as a church site. The grateful parishioners quickly built themselves a Meeting House of oak and cedar-board which served them for over 60 years.

One of the more important events that took place at Old South occurred on a bitterly cold, blizzardy, midwinter morning. This was the baptism of a squawking baby named Benjamin Franklin, born just around the corner on Milk Street.

Map on page 136

The venerable independent publisher Houghton Mifflin traces its origins to the Old Corner Bookstore.

BELOW: Old South Meeting House.

As a parish pastor later described it: "This little quivering mass of flesh, hardly a day old, was carried across the wintry street to be baptized on January 6, 1706, the parents evidently thinking that the midwinter climate here was less to be dreaded than the climate in the other world."

In March of 1727, the old wooden structure was replaced by a beautiful new church of brick and mortar, styled after the graceful London churches of Sir Christopher Wren. "New" Old South, dedicated on April 26, 1730, figured in American annals as the most important Meeting House in American colonial history. It was the scene of scores of protest meetings denouncing British taxation, the Stamp Act, the presence of British troops, the Townshend Acts. Ultimately, on December 16, 1773, it was the launching pad for a band of enraged Bostonians who converged on Griffin's Wharf to stage the Boston Tea Party. Early in the Revolution, the Redcoats turned Old South into a stable and riding school for the horses of the Queen's Light Dragoons. George Washington corrected that situation in March 1776.

The Old State House has what has been called "the most interesting staircase in the city." Designed like an unfurled deck of cards, it hangs unsupported between floors.

The Old State House

Turning back now on Washington Street, we pass Spring Lane and Water Street on the right and arrive at the intersection with State Street. There stands the **Old State House** ❿ (daily 9am–5pm; tel: 720-3292), the seat of colonial government.

Since 1632, in the Pudding Lane–King Street–Crooked Lane area (now Congress Street) there had been stocks and pillory, a whipping post and a thatched-roof church of sorts. And here in 1658 the Bostonians built their first official Town House, headquarters for royal rulings and for demonstrations for and against hanging Captain Kidd for piracy. The great fire of 1711 burned the place flat, but within two years the colonists rebuilt with a larger brick structure. On

BELOW: the
Old State House.

THE BOSTON MASSACRE

It was in the Old State House on December 16, 1761, that James Otis delivered his impassioned outburst against the Writs of Assistance. And it was here on the night of March 5, 1770, that a group of citizens got into a hostile shouting match with British soldiers on King Street, just outside the east wall.

Belligerent colonists swelled the crowd on one side, Redcoat reinforcements rushed in on the other. Rocks and snowballs filled the air, bayonets clanged, somebody fired a shot, and thus was born the Boston Massacre. Five colonists were killed. The only one to be widely remembered was the first to die, Crispus Attucks, a black sailor and former slave, aged around 47. His body lay in state for three days in Faneuil Hall, after which it was buried with the other victims in a common grave. Samuel Adams, the leading advocate for independence from Britain, turned the incident, which was the most serious of a number of brawls between locals and British soldiers, into effective propaganda, presenting it as a battle for American liberty. From that moment, revolution became inevitable.

Today, alongside the Old State House wall, a ring of cobblestones marks the site where the five men fell, in the very shadow of the courtyard.

December 9, 1747, another great fire gutted the building and destroyed valuable town records (plus thousands of bottles of wine) but left the brick walls standing, as they are today. The walls even survived the horrendous conflagration of 1872, which leveled most of Downtown Boston's center.

Bostonians hold a warm affection for this storied old building. It still displays the Lion and Unicorn symbols of British dominion. It still features the white balcony where the Declaration of Independence was first read to the citizens of Boston. Across the road at 15 State Street is the **National Park Visitor Center** ⓫, which offers guided walking tours of the Freedom Trail.

From the rear of the Old State House, going north on Congress Street, an open turn to the right leads to the Faneuil Hall–Quincy Market complex. Here, fronted by a statue of Sam Adams, stands **Faneuil Hall** ⓬ (daily 9am–5pm), designated by James Otis as "The Cradle of Liberty."

Faneuil Hall, built for the commercial benefit of Boston's merchants, was personally financed by young Peter Faneuil, whom John Hancock labeled "the topmost merchant in all the town." It was dedicated on September 10, 1742, in the hurly-burly action of Dock Square, which had market stalls on all four sides – waterfront, fish market, hay market and sheep market. From the day it opened, it served as a forum for the raw opinions of rebels and patriots, from Sam Adams to Paul Revere. In 1806 the hall was expanded by the architect Charles Bulfinch. It is still in demand as a forum for oratory and opinion.

Quincy Market

Adjacent to Faneuil Hall is the marketplace of that name, a vibrant, contemporary urban spot redolent with history. **Quincy Market** ⓭, as it is often called, was con-

Map on page 136

The Freedom Trail is clearly signed.

BELOW: Faneuil Hall.

As it once was:

"To reach [Durgin Park] you go through vegetable crates, plucked chickens, sides of beef, and the incredible clamor of the buying and selling of food... it is as unattractive a spot as you will encounter.".

– INVITATION TO BOSTON

(a 1947 guidebook)

BELOW: Durgin Park has a reputation.
RIGHT: "Benjamin Franklin" greets the shoppers.

structed in 1826 and served for almost 150 years as a retail and wholesale distribution center for meat and produce. By the mid-1950s the entire area had become extremely seedy and plans were afoot for its demolition. Fortunately, recycling came to be the word and the market was renovated to its former glory – leading, it is claimed, to the resurgence of urban marketplaces throughout the nation.

The market consists of three long buildings. The center one is of granite with a Doric colonnade at either end and a dome and rotunda in the center. Tree-lined malls separate this building from two longitudinal side buildings which are built mainly of brick. The ground floor of the main building bulges with more than 40 foodstalls while the upper floor has a few somewhat more formal restaurants. More than 100 retail stores compete for your money in the lateral buildings, which also house a number of restaurants. These include **Durgin Park**, which has been here since the 1830s. Its waitresses are famed for harassing and insulting patrons, who appear to love the treatment.

A lively flower market adds further color, as do many charming wooden push-carts from which peddlers sell their wares, most of which are geared to tourists. Entertainers – jugglers and clowns, musicians and magicians – perform regularly. Little wonder that Faneuil Hall Market is now one of the major tourist attractions, not only in Boston but throughout the entire nation, attracting more than 10 million visitors a year.

Just to the west of the north building, a tiny park contains two bronze life-size likenesses – one seated, one standing – of James Michael Curley *(see page 39)*. The shine on the seated statue's knee suggests that many visitors like to perch there.

North from here on Union Street leads immediately to the **Union Oyster House ⑭**, or **Ye Olde Oyster House** – whichever you prefer to call it. This may

date back to the origin of the street itself in 1636, and was specifically mentioned in a plan of 1708.

Map on page 136

The building housed the *Massachusetts Spy* newspaper from 1771 to 1775. It then became the headquarters for Ebenezer Hancock, brother of John Hancock and paymaster for the Continental Army. It was the temporary home of Louis Philippe, later ruler of France (1830–48). He eked out his exile in Boston by teaching French to students in his second-floor bedroom. As for the oyster angle, one legend is that the place sometimes served up 35 barrels of Cape Cod oysters a day, with Daniel Webster regularly downing six oysters per glass of brandy – and he drank several of the latter.

Ebenezer Hancock lived in the neighboring house owned by his brother John; it is just a few steps along and to the right, on **Salt Lane**. The city's oldest brick house, it dates back to 1660, when it was owned by Boston's first Town Crier, William Courser.

Nearby is a slender line of glass and steel towers that constitute one of Boston's most recent public monuments, **The Holocaust Memorial ⑮**.

Oyster haven.

The Boston Stone

Where Marsh Lane, Salt Lane and Creek Square intermingle is the **Blackstone Block**, where three centuries of architecture can be found. And here, at Salt Lane corner, sits the **Boston Stone ⑯**, a huge stone ball and a stone trough, shipped from England in 1700 to serve as a paint mill. While grinding out oil and pigment, it also was established for more lasting use as the Zero Stone – that point from which all distances from Boston were measured. The Downtown Crossing market notwithstanding, this humble but historic monument still stands as the hub of "The Hub."

BELOW: the Holocaust Memorial.

From burlesque to bureaucracy

Return to Congress Street and climb the many stairs leading up to the new **City Hall** ⓱, a controversial pile of niches, grottoes, squares and holes, described by much of the Boston press as "the ugliest pigeon coop in the world."

Now we are standing in what used to be **Scollay Square**. Here used to stand the Old Howard burlesque theater, the stage-home of such show-stoppers as Ann Corio, Jimmy Durante and Sliding Billy Watson. Where now the city conducts its business stood the Crawford House, in which dancer Sally Keith nightly twirled her two top tassels in opposite directions, openly defying the laws of physics. Helter-skelter, here and there across this once-grimy and magnetic acreage, were tattoo parlors, fortune tellers, gypsy palmists, cheap gin mills, snap-photo joints, hash houses, Joe & Nemo hot dogs, and whatnot.

A striking Robert Motherwell mural hangs in the John F. Kennedy Federal Office Building.

All this is remembered with nostalgia by generations of college students, traveling salesmen, suburban sightseers, vacationing Walter Mittys, and especially by sailors from the ships of all the world's great navies, who ganged into Scollay Square to start many a rousing conflict of their own.

But then, by 1960, along came urban renewal. In rumbled the bulldozers to level not only Scollay Square but the entire residential West End. Scollay Square suddenly became the new squeaky-clean Government Center. The planners wiped out almost every physical vestige of the past. They created an emptiness fanning out from Court Street and called it **City Hall Plaza** – a delightful place for those who like acres of dull bricks unrelieved by shrubbery or trees.

BELOW: shopping at Downtown Crossing.

Just beyond the brick-laid plaza rises the **John F. Kennedy Federal Office Building**, ready to provide help on income taxes, Social Security and assorted other problems. But you don't have to be a local Presidential product to get a

Boston building named after you. Former Speaker of the House John McCormack of South Boston, for example, was honored in the naming of the Center's Post Office and Custom House Building. Another former Speaker, Thomas "Tip" O'Neill of neighboring Cambridge, has his name on a **Federal Office Building**, across the way on **Causeway Street**.

Map on page 136

Marbled halls and obelisks

The financial neighborhood reaches roughly from Federal and High streets near the waterfront to Franklin and State streets near Post Office Square on the north. This part of Downtown, especially State Street, is a superb architectural sampler where the visitor can observe a wide variety of styles. Step into **Exchange Place**, **Church Green Building**, **One International Place** and **75 State Street**, and gawk at their glorious marble halls.

Back in the early 1900s, the architectural symbol of Boston's Financial District was the then-new 495-ft (151-meter) **Custom House Tower** 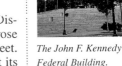; it rose like an obelisk in **McKinley Square** where **India Street** intersects State Street. In those days, not only did the tower dominate the waterfront skyline but its presence also sparked and dominated considerable hot argument among style-conscious financiers, some of whom applauded the tower, some of whom loathed it. The original Custom House, at its base, had been a thing of true beauty, designed by the architect Ammi B. Young. When dedicated in 1847, it was a superlative example of Greek Revival architecture, featuring Doric granite columns and a graceful dome – a building of classic lines and proportion.

But then, in 1913–15, along came the firm of Peabody & Stearns with a commission to reshape the structure with a fresh and more practical design. They

The John F. Kennedy Federal Building.

BELOW:
Quincy Market and the Custom House Tower.

proceeded to top the columns and the dome with an additional 30 floors of office (now hotel) space crowned by decorations that included winged beasts, scrolls and a huge clock face. The result still provokes occasional architectural disputes, but whether for good or ill, the old structure has lost its mission and is dwarfed by towering new buildings. Meanwhile, the top of the tower has become a favorite nesting place for peregrine falcons. They do some of their best swooping over the deep canyons of the tall counting houses.

Visit, in this part of town, the **Alexander Graham Bell Room** ⓭ (tel: 743 4747) at 185 Franklin Street to view the re-assembled attic from nearby Court Street where, on June 3, 1875, the inventor sent speech sounds over a wire electrically. The telephone was born. On display here are the world's first telephone switchboard – it connected six lines in 1877 – and the world's first commercial telephone.

Elsewhere, much of downtown Boston has changed or disappeared during the past half-century. The famed Boston Wool District, with its firm links to Australia and to New England textile mills, has dwindled to a mere shadow, nearly wiped out in the Depression of the 1930s. The same applies to the downtown Leather District, crippled by the emigration and death of the New England shoe industry but recently revived by chic shops and eateries.

Return to Downtown Crossing, walking south along Washington Street toward Kneeland, you soon pass on the right the site of the old **Adams House** and restaurant of the same name. This was once a terminal stop on the early Boston–Hartford–New York stage coach route. This section of the city has been in limbo for years. On Washington you can see the remains of what were once the movie palaces of the 1930s and 1940s. Little remains of what was once the **Combat Zone**, one of the sleaziest and most notorious enclaves of commercial

BELOW: gateway to Chinatown at Beach and Hudson streets.
RIGHT: Chinatown's attractions.

vice on the East Coast. Thanks to prolonged public outrage and the demands of civic leaders, it has been politically garroted to extinction. The topless bars and sex pockets have been wiped out, with only a few traces remaining.

With Emerson College's purchase of many buildings on Tremont in the 1990s this area began to transform itself. Pride of place on Emerson's urban campus goes to the College's glorious 800-seat **Majestic Theater** in Boston's Theater District. Nearby is **Allen's Alley ⑳**, honoring Boston's wry comedian Fred Allen, who left his imprint on most aspects of show business, from burlesque to musical revue, and from New York radio to Hollywood television. Allen loved his Boston. As he once remarked: "California is a great place to live – if you're an orange."

The New England Medical Center grew out of the Boston Dispensary, set up in 1796 to provide health care for the poor. Today it is the city's first full-service private hospital and is the principal teaching hospital for Tufts University School of Medicine.

Chinatown

Alongside the former Combat Zone (and gradually absorbing its streets and alleys) is Boston's colorful **Chinatown ㉑**, guarded at its eastern gateway, diagonally across **Atlantic Avenue** from **South Station**, by a looping arch and an ornate pair of stone dragon dogs. Chinatown, whose main drag is **Beach Street**, is not very large but is packed with Asian restaurants and exotic stores that draw thousands of tourists and regulars nightly from the abutting Theater District on Tremont Street and the hotels to the west. It's great fun to visit.

On leaving Chinatown and turning right on Kneeland, look for **Jacob Wirth's ㉒** old-time dark-and-sudsy restaurant on the right (tel: 338 8586). Since 1868, generations of newsmen, theater people and artists have relished the dark brew and brauschweitz, served by white-aproned waiters. It's a place that never changes. On the left are the **New England Medical Center** and the **Wilbur** and **Schubert theaters,** where for years many Broadway-bound productions had their first performances. ❏

LEFT: mural in Chinatown.
BELOW: Jacob Wirth's.

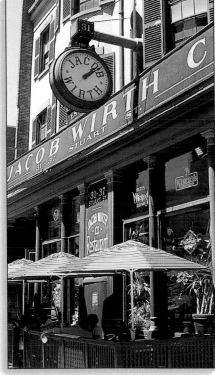

THE NORTH END

Paul Revere lived here, and so did successive waves of European immigrants. Old North, Boston's oldest church, is a major stop on the Freedom Trail

Map on page 152

An angel flies over the **North End**. It happens every year during the Feast of the Assumption. She is the messenger of the Madonna del Soccorso, protector of the fishing fleet and patron saint of Sicilian immigrants. She floats above the street, her arms outstretched to the crowd below, and then releases a basket of white doves. The birds fly into the night, and the angel disappears.

This particular year, the little girl who plays the role of the angel looks somewhat hesitant as she dangles from a pulley three stories above the street. Yet, although not more than nine years old, she plays the part flawlessly. Her satin robe shimmers against the night sky as she is lowered to a statue of the Madonna. When the crowd begins to cheer, a smile lights up her face.

Earlier that day, the men of the Fishermen's Club carried the Madonna through the streets in a day-long procession of brass bands and traditional Sicilian music. As they passed from one block to another, people threw money from the windows or pinned it to the Madonna's gown. At every stop the men lowered the platform and then hoisted it back onto their shoulders with a great show of effort. A cry went out: "*Viva la Madonna!*" And the crowd answered back: "*Viva !*"

PRECEDING PAGES: reenacting Paul Revere's ride past Old North Church. **LEFT** and **BELOW:** Italian traditions are carried on in colorful parades.

Little Italy

Three hundred years ago, the North End was known as the "island of North Boston." On colonial maps it looks like an irregular thumb jutting into the Atlantic Ocean with a canal, called the Mill Stream, cutting it off from the larger Shawmut Peninsula. In recent years the **Southeast Expressway** following the same course as the old canal cut off the neighborhood even more abruptly. While water no longer surrounds the North End, it has remained set apart from the rest of the city – a cultural island, Boston's Little Italy. All this is about to change as a thin strip of green parkland welcomes visitors to the North End.

Sociologists describe the North End as an "urban village." Old-world attitudes are still very much a part of life here. They are enacted in public rituals like the Feast of the Assumption as well as in day-to-day life. Italian is spoken in the streets, family is the center of social activity, and in general, community is valued over privacy.

The neighborhood also looks and sounds like an Italian *quartiere*. Many streets are narrow and crooked, laundry flaps on outdoor clotheslines, and produce is sold at open-air stands. The sense of community is so thick you can almost feel it in the air, and it's not unusual to find three or even four generations sharing the same small space – children playing

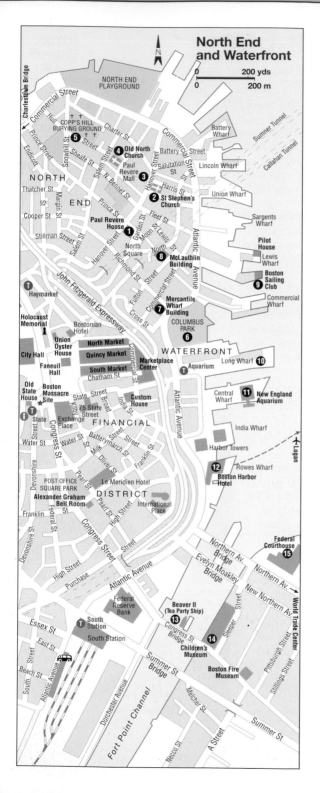

in the street, young couples talking in cafés, and old folks watching from the stoops. If there is a prevailing sound in the neighborhood, it's the buzz of conversation. Talk is like glue here: it holds everything together, making this one of the few Boston neighborhoods where people are still actively involved in one another's lives.

In fact, the community is so tightly knit that it is often difficult for outsiders to gain anything but a superficial impression. The best that most visitors can hope for is a fragmented view – a collection of tiny insights into the way North Enders think and feel. Inevitably, the most compelling images are drawn from the neighborhood's social life. It might be a Saturday with its raucous open-air market, or an early morning mass at St Leonard's Church when old women dressed in black come to light candles and say the rosary. It might be a group of slick young immigrants arguing about soccer in the middle of Hanover Street, or old men playing cards at a social club tucked away in a quiet alley.

Whatever you find, the scenes are likely to be strange, affecting and oddly varied. Put them all together, and you'll begin to understand what makes life in the North End so special.

Economic vicissitudes

Historically, the North End has had its ups and downs. When the Puritans arrived in 1630, it was a marshy finger of land with few apparent virtues, although, as one member of the party wrote, it was well-protected from the "Woolves, Rattle-snakes and Musketos" [sic] that they found so troublesome at their Charlestown camp. By the late colonial period, the small cluster of timber houses had become one of Boston's most fashionable quarters, with several fine homes and some of the richest families in town.

Unfortunately, most of the prominent residents were Tories who, when the British evacuated in 1776, hightailed it to Canada and took their money with them. Rich Yankees pulled out too, preferring the more genteel atmosphere of Beacon Hill, which was just then being developed. Artisans, sailors and trades-men filled the empty houses, and for the remainder of the 19th century the North End was a workingman's quarter dominated by the shipping industry.

In the mid-1800s, the North End was overrun by European immigrants, and the neighborhood became a slum notorious for its bordellos, street crime and squalid conditions. The Irish were the first to settle in any great numbers, pour-ing into the neighborhood after the Potato Famine of 1846. Under the leadership of political bosses like John "Honey Fitz" Fitzgerald *(see page 39)*, they dom-inated the area for well over 35 years, muscling their way into mainstream soci-ety by way of hard work and the Democratic political machine.

East European Jews followed the Irish, and by 1890 they had established a thriving residential and business district along Salem Street. The Italians – most of them originating in the southern provinces – were the last group to arrive in substantial numbers; but by the 1920s they had established an overwhelming majority. By then, most of the other groups had begun to move out, and the Italians have dominated the neighborhood ever since.

In recent years, the North End's well-earned reputation for neighborliness has made it a prime target for gentrification, especially along the waterfront. Rents have skyrocketed, condo conversions have run rampant, and some old-time residents are getting priced right out of their homes. With the old guard aging and the new generation moving out, some dyed-in-the-wool North Enders worry that the old neighborhood is slipping away. But, although it's true that the Italian population isn't as large as it used to be, the spirit of the community is no less persistent.

Map on page 152

Strolling in Hanover Street.

BELOW: neighborhood shops are friendly places.

Good food and colorful history

Most people come to the North End for one of two reasons. During the day they visit historic sites, and at night they come to eat. Both activities are certainly worthwhile, but there's much more here than the Freedom Trail and the customary bowl of linguine.

The speed of tenement building can be gauged by the fact that, between 1850 and 1855, the number of Irish in Boston soared from 35,000 to 50,000. Most of them settled in the North End.

By and large, the North End isn't much to look at. Unlike Beacon Hill or the Back Bay, it isn't a planned community. There isn't a uniform architectural style or much interest in large-scale historical preservation: in fact, quite the opposite. The North End has an improvisational quality, as if the neighborhood was built piecemeal without the benefit of an overall plan. What evolved is a hodgepodge of buildings, some quite attractive, others downright ugly. Many were built in the late 1800s as tenement houses for European immigrants. The concern at that time wasn't how pretty a building looked but how many people could be crammed inside.

The archaic street plan makes things even more confusing. The North End is one of those places where it's easy to get lost and probably best that you do. With alleyways and sidestreets running off in every direction, all kinds of unconventional spaces can be discovered in the neighborhood's less-traveled areas. Turn a corner, and you're likely to bump into anything from a vegetable garden to a street festival.

When you tire of walking around the neighborhood, head for one of the cafés and watch the neighborhood walk around you. Chances are you'll be in good company. At any given time, in any given café, at least a handful of North Enders are doing the same thing.

BELOW:
the Italian influence.
RIGHT:
summer festival.

The best place for people-watching is **Hanover Street**, the neighborhood's

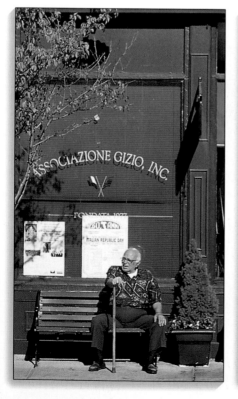

central thoroughfare and the heart of its business district. Restaurants and cafés stretch from one end to the other, and a steady stream of tourists walk the Freedom Trail. If you're looking for a place to eat, you can't go far wrong here, or for that matter, anywhere else in the neighborhood. Making a selection is more a question of style than of quality.

From Hanover Street, turn right on Richmond Street and then left to enter **North Square**, where the **Pierce-Hichborn** and **Paul Revere houses** stand side by side. The former, which belonged to Nathaniel Hichborn, Paul Revere's cousin, is an asymmetrical, three-story brick building built between 1711 and 1715 in the new English Renaissance style. This was a radical departure from the Tudor-style wooden dwellings built in the previous century. It was restored in 1949.

Paul Revere's home

Paul Revere's house ❶ at 19 North Square (Nov to mid-Apr daily 9.15am–4.15pm; mid-Apr to Oct daily 9.30am–5.15pm; tel: 523 1676) is a two-story dwelling with an overhanging second floor. It was built in 1676 and is the oldest house in downtown Boston. When Revere purchased the house in 1770, the third floor had been added, but in the early 20th century this was removed to "restore" the building to its original appearance. It is furnished today much as it was when it was home to Paul and the first Mrs Revere, who bore him eight children, and then, when she died, to the second Mrs Revere, who bore him a similar brood.

One of the upstairs rooms is covered with wallpaper which is a reproduction of paper made in Boston towards the end of the 18th century. It also contains

Revere remembered.

BELOW: the home of Paul Revere.

several pieces of the furniture that belonged to the Reveres. A cabinet displays attractive silver, some made by Revere. Outside, in the courtyard, is a 931-pound (422-kg) bronze bell cast by Revere, generally acknowledged to have been the best bell-maker of his time. (*For a profile of Paul Revere, see page 35.*)

Return to Hanover Street via Fleet Street and, after 150 yards, reach **St Stephen's Church ❷** with its white steeple. Built in 1804 as a Congregationalist Meeting House, this simple, dignified structure is the only one of five Boston churches designed by Bulfinch that still stands. It has had a checkered history. In 1813 it became a Unitarian Church and in 1862 it was acquired by the Roman Catholic archbishopric. Eight years later, when Hanover Street had to be widened to accommodate traffic, the church was moved back 12 ft (3.7 meters) and raised 6 ft (1.8 meters); then, in 1965, it was restored to its original level and to its Bulfinch stark simplicity.

The **Paul Revere Mall ❸**, known locally as the **Prado**, faces St Stephen's Church. Built in 1933, this generous brick courtyard is the liveliest public space in the North End – a sort of Americanized piazza where kids run around, old folks play cards, and footsore tourists take a breather from the Freedom Trail. In addition to the traditional Italian fountain, the Prado features a magnificent equestrian statue of Paul Revere, modeled in 1885 by Cyrus Dallin and cast in 1940. On the south (left) wall, bronze panels recall the history of Boston and its people.

Old North Church

At the far end of the Prado a small gate opens to the rear of **Christ Church**, also known as **Old North ❹**. To the left of the gate is the three-story (originally it was two) brick home of Ebenezer Clough, built in 1712.

Paul Revere was also a dentist and made false teeth for General Joseph Warren, who was killed at Bunker Hill. Revere later identified the skull from the dental work.

BELOW:
business beckons.
RIGHT: Paul
Revere statue at
Old North Church.

The Old North, Boston's oldest church, is one of its most treasured historical monuments. Built in 1723 to house the town's second Anglican parish, the
Old North is most famous for its part in Paul Revere's ride to Lexington. On
April 18, 1775, Robert Newman snuck out of his home and placed two
lanterns in the belfry as a signal to Revere – "one, if by land, and two, if by
sea" – that the British army was advancing to Concord. Ironically, General
Gage is said to have watched the Battle of Bunker Hill from the very same belfry only a few months later.

Old North's steeple, 191 ft (58 meters) high, has always been Boston's
tallest and a major landmark. Twice, in 1804 and again in 1854, it was blown
over by hurricanes and subsequently restored. America's first peal of eight
bells hangs in the belfry; it was first rung in 1745 and has tolled for every
departed President of the nation since George Washington died in 1799. The
bells were cast in England and range in weight from 620 to 2,545 pounds
(281–1,155 kg), with a total mass of 7,272 pounds (3,300 kg). They are a
"maiden peal" (because each bell has a perfect tone without having been
filed down or machined). Reputed to be the sweetest in the nation, they bear
the inscription "We are the first ring of bells cast for the British Empire in
North America." Paul Revere, at 15, came to this church and, with some
other young men, signed a contract to ring the peal.

Enter the church, whose interior has been painted white since 1912. High
pew boxes, designed to keep in the warmth of hot coal or bricks which were
placed on the floor on wintery days, are still intact, with the names of the family owners engraved on bronze plates. The clock at the rear of the church and the
four baroque Belgian cherubs which surround it date back to the opening of

Map on page 152

The four 18th-century Belgian baroque cherubim with trumpets which stand in front of the organ in Old North Church were booty captured by a privateer owned by members of the congregation. They were probably destined for a French church in Canada.

LEFT: St Francis statue and, **BELOW**, angel in Old North Church.

Map on page 152

the church. So does the organ case, although the actual instrument dates only from 1759. The bust of George Washington, in a niche to the left of the apse, was the first public memorial to the great man and was said by General Lafayette in 1824 to be "more like him than any other portrait." The church has 37 crypts, containing, it is claimed, 1,100 bodies.

Immediately to the north of the church is a small garden with markers recounting historic events and distinguished persons of the parish. One of these informs that "Here on 13 Sept. 1757, John Childs, who had given public notice of his intention to fly from the steeple of Dr Cutler's church, performed it to the satisfaction of a great number of spectators." Childs made three flights, once firing a pistol in mid-air: alas, nobody knows how he flew.

Next to the church is a gift shop, at the rear of which is a tiny museum. The museum's major treasure is the *Vinegar Bible*, sent by King George II to Christ Church in 1733. It derives its name because of a typographical error on one of its page headings in which "Parable of the Vinegar" appears instead of "Parable of the Vineyard."

BELOW: Copp's Hill Burying Ground.
RIGHT:
the box pews in Old North Church are laid out as they were in colonial times, although they are not as tall.

A postscript must be added. Nobody is absolutely certain that Old North Church is actually the church where the lanterns were hung: in 1775, several churches stood in the North End.

Copp's Hill Burying Ground

On exiting from the church, walk up Hull Street for about 150 yards to **Copp's Hill Burying Ground ❺** (summer 8am–5pm; in other months 9am–4pm), Boston's second-oldest cemetery (after King's Chapel) and the North End's quietest corner. Its present name comes from that of William Copp, who farmed

on the hill's southeast slope in the mid-17th century. In the colonial period, the base of the hill, known pejoratively as New Guinea, was occupied by the city's first black community and about 1,000 blacks are buried in the cemetery's northwest corner.

A tall black monument commemorates Prince Hall, who helped found Boston's first school for black children. However, his main claim to fame is that he was the founder, in 1784, of the African Grand Lodge of Massachusetts, the world's first black Masonic Lodge. Near here is the tombstone of "Capt. Daniel Malcolm, Mercht," who is remembered for smuggling 60 casks of wine into port without paying the duty. He asked to be buried "in a Stone Grave 10 feet deep," safe from British bullets. His body may have been safe, but his tombstone was not: on it are scars made by the Redcoats who singled out this patriot's gravemarker for their target practice. In the southeast corner of the cemetery is the Mathers' family tomb, where Increase, Cotton and Samuel may be buried.

Weekend processions

If you visit the North End in summer, be sure to catch one of the local feasts. They are held almost every weekend in July and August, with Sundays being by far the most exciting days, and usually involve street fairs, entertainment, processions and, at least once a year, the famous flying angel. ❏

THE WATERFRONT

History was made here and is relived in the Boston Tea Party Exhibit. The New England Aquarium and the Children's Museum combine education with entertainment

Map on page 152

From its earliest days Boston was a busy seaport and, indeed, until the second half of the 19th century was the busiest port in the nation. Its apogee was reached in the middle of that century when, it was said, 15 vessels entered and left the harbor every day of the year. Then, warehouses and counting houses occupied a dozen wharves at which clippers, "the highest creation of artistic genius in the Commonwealth," unloaded and loaded their cargoes.

These included baubles for Native Americans on the Pacific coast who traded sea otter pelts with the Chinese in return for silk. Tea was dispatched all over the world. Sugar and molasses from Barbados and Jamaica were made into rum, then bartered for slaves in Africa.

In the second half of the 19th century the port went into decline, a process hastened when, in 1878, the construction of Atlantic Avenue severed the finger-like piers from the rest of the city. With the building in the 1950s of the Expressway, which, mile for mile, was then the most expensive stretch of road ever built in the country, Boston finally turned its back on its patrimony.

Then, in the 1960s, with the restoration of Quincy Market and Faneuil Hall and the building of City Hall Plaza, the resurrection began. Abandoned warehouses on dilapidated, rickety wharves were transformed into condominiums. Berths once occupied by barques and brigantines became home to elegant cabin cruisers and sleek sloops, many belonging to those living in the condominiums. Offices and hotels, restaurants and museums were also built and the population of longshoremen, truckers and Irish laborers was replaced with realtors, lawyers and tourists. The waterfront has regained its excitement.

PRECEDING PAGES: the waterfront. **LEFT:** boat watching at Long Wharf. **BELOW:** splashing out at Columbus Park.

Recycled warehouses

If you leave the Quincy-Faneuil carnival and head towards the water, you will immediately encounter **Columbus Park ❻**, a small grassy sward with the **Rose Kennedy Rose Garden** and a children's playground. A trellised walkway leads to the waterfront which, at this point, has been landscaped into a romantic area of cobblestones, bollards and anchor chains.

On the left stretches **Commercial Wharf** with a granite warehouse in which the second set of sails for the *U.S.S. Constitution* was made. It has been recycled into a condominium complex with a mansard roof, for which Bostonians have such a predilection.

The best example of a recycled warehouse stands behind you on the far side of Atlantic Avenue. The **Mercantile Wharf Building ❼**, originally twice its present length, is constructed of rough Quincy granite ashlar blocks and is the masterpiece of Boston Granite Style. Those interested in architecture will

The view from Columbus Park.

wish to continue along Richmond Street, at the north side of this building, and then immediately turn right onto Fulton Street to see the **McLauthlin Building 8**, the first cast-iron building in New England. This five-story 19th-century jewel has delicate rounded arched windows separated by subtle pilasters, and each level is separated by a string course. Its perfect, repetitive rhythm is marred only by the upper level.

From here, a right turn on Lewis leads back to Atlantic Avenue, which very soon becomes Commercial Street. Proceed northward past **Lewis** and **Union wharves**, both of which have gentrified granite warehouses.

Enthusiastic sailors might wish to make for the **Boston Sailing Club 9** at the end of Lewis Wharf, where an excellent fleet of boats awaits them. (Minimum membership is one month.)

When the **Pilot House**, on the north side of this wharf, was being renovated in 1972, a false floor was discovered, fueling speculation that the building was used not only by pilots but also by opium smugglers. More grisly was the finding of two embracing skeletons in the basement of **Usher House**, which stood on this wharf and which was demolished in 1880. This prompted the claim that the skeletons were those of the sailor and the young wife of an elderly man about whom Edgar Alan Poe wrote in his macabre 1839 novel *The Fall of the House of Usher*.

Granite is replaced by red brick on **Lincoln Wharf**, where a massive red building with magnificent rounded, arched windows covering five stories has been recycled into apartments.

The north side of Lincoln Wharf is bounded by **Battery Street**, whose name gives the clue to the fact that here, in 1646, the North Battery was built in order to command the entrance to the inner harbor and the Charles River. It was from

BELOW: the condos come with a berth for your boat.

Map
on page
152

here that, in 1776, British troops were ferried to Charlestown to take up their positions in the battle of Bunker Hill. Immediately beyond this, on the site now occupied by the **Coast Guard**, once stood **Hartt's Naval Yard**, where the *U.S.S. Constitution* was built and launched in 1797.

A free outdoor swimming pool just beyond this, the northern extremity of wharfland, awaits those who are hot and tired. Others might wish to proceed on an immaculate waterfront esplanade to the **Charlestown Bridge**, which, after about a mile, leads to Charlestown and the *U.S.S. Constitution* and the Bunker Hill monument. To continue an exploration of the waterfront, return to Columbus Park.

Long Wharf

Immediately to the south of Columbus Park is **Long Wharf ❿**. When built in 1710, it was, if not one of the wonders of the world, at least the wonder of the region. The wharf, which had roots near the Customs House, stretched out into the harbor for almost 2,000 ft (600 meters). It was here, in 1790, that the *Columbia Rediviva*, the first American ship to sail around the world and the first to participate in the China trade, berthed after her 35-month, almost 50,000-mile (80,000-km) voyage. From here, in 1819, the first missionaries for Hawaii departed and, in 1895, Joshua Slocum set off aboard the *Spray* on the first one-man voyage around the world, which lasted 38 months. Would Nathaniel Hawthorne – who, in his capacity as a customs officer, often visited the wharf – still write: "Long Wharf is devoted to ponderous, evil-smelling, inelegant necessaries of life"?

Gaze out from the beautiful esplanade at the end of the wharf to North Boston and to the planes taking off from Logan Airport. These are the successors to the flying clippers which Donald McKay built on land now occupied by the airport.

BELOW:
seeing the city
from a cruise boat.

Mackay's clippers, epitomized by the *Flying Cloud*, were the fastest and most beautiful sailing ships ever to fly the stars and stripes. Boats for Provincetown, the Charlestown Navy Yard and the Harbor Islands depart from Long Wharf.

Fish, chips and tea

The Aquarium's logo.

Long Wharf on its south side joins with the vestigial remains of **Central Wharf**, built according to Bulfinch's plans in order to accommodate the overflow of the China trade. The wharf is now home to the **New England Aquarium** ⓫ (Sept–Jun Mon–Fri 9am–5pm, Sat, Sun and holidays 9am–6pm; Jul–Aug Mon, Tues and Fri 9am–6pm, Wed and Thur 9am–8pm, Sat and Sun 9am–7pm; tel: 973 5200). It's impossible to miss the aquarium for, in the plaza, high in the air, a bright red sculpture, *Echo of the Waves*, slowly rotates. In the center of the plaza water flows through a large basin, at the bottom of which stands a bronze sculpture, *Dolphins of the Sea*. Immediately to the left of the aquarium entrance, harbor seals frolic and provide free entertainment for those too impecunious to enter the aquarium.

Nobody has told the rockhopper penguins in the enormous **Ocean Tray**, which covers most of the floor of the Aquarium, that the cold water section is their territory and that the warmer water is for the jackass penguins – and so they swim from island to island and the two groups freely intermingle.

Soaring skyward from the floor of the Ocean Tray is the **giant ocean tank**, the world's largest cylindrical salt-water tank, in which giant turtles, sharks, moray eels and a multitude of other fish swim in and out of a spectacular man-made coral reef. At set times, a diver enters to feed the tank's occupants. A ramp gradually winds around the tank, ascending for four stories and providing a view of more than 70 small tanks containing thousands of fish from through-

BELOW: New England Aquarium.

out the world. A hands-on tidal pool enables small fry to become acquainted with the marine world.

Map
on page
152

The *Discovery*, a floating pavilion whose design is evocative of a Mississippi river steamer, is moored alongside the main building and contains a large theater where dolphins and sea lions show how intelligent they are. Shows are not devoted to tricks but rather, this being Boston, are educational. However, they are also entertaining. The *Voyager II,* which belongs to the Aquarium, makes whale-watching cruises (see pages 174–75; rain checks if whales not seen) with a naturalist aboard who also lectures on the harbor and its islands.

Immediately south of the Aquarium, on the stump of **India Wharf**, the horizontal has been replaced by the vertical. On the site of a four-story Bulfinch building that stretched for hundreds of feet, two rather unattractive 40-story towers, built by I. M. Pei in 1971, soar skyward. It says much for Boston that the giant minimal stainless-steel sculpture by David von Schlegell, which occupies the space in the angle formed by the towers, has not been vandalized.

Next comes **Rowes Wharf**, entered through a monumental, gold and russett post-modern six-story arch. The **Boston Harbor Hotel** ⓬ stands where formerly stood the South Battery, built in 1666, and then warehouses. The wharf, no longer busy with clippers and barques, is now the terminal for sleek commuter craft that serve the South Shore and Logan Airport. Some harbor cruises also depart from here.

The Tea Party Exhibit

Fort Point Channel now intersects the waterfront. This area was the bustling transfer point for many New England industries during the latter years of the

BELOW: snacking at the Boston Harbor Hotel, Rowes Wharf.

Arthur, a familiar TV character and regular guest at the Children's Museum.

BELOW: the Boston Tea Party reenacted. **RIGHT:** giant lobster, Children's Museum.

19th century. On a short wharf in the Channel at Congress Street Bridge stands the **Boston Tea Party Exhibit**, which consists of a small museum (9am–dusk; 9am–5pm spring and fall; tel: 338 1773) and the replica *Beaver II* ⓭, moored alongside the museum. The *Beaver II*, a Danish brig built in 1908, has similar lines to the *Beaver*, the smallest of the three tea ships moored at Griffins Wharf on that fateful December evening in 1773 when a band of patriots disguised as Mohawk Indians boarded the ships and threw all their tea – 340 chests containing 90,000 pounds of the leaf – into the harbor. This was the famous act of defiance against the British Crown for having imposed taxes without granting representation. (**Griffins Wharf** stood about 300 yards northwest of the current exhibit and is marked by a plaque set in the walls of a commercial building at the foot of **Pearl Street**.)

The Children's Museum

On leaving the Tea Party Exhibit, turn left and make for a giant, 40-ft (12-meter) milk bottle, a vintage lunch stand from the 1930s. It marks the entrance to the **Children's Museum** ⓮ at 300 Congress Street (10am–5pm, with extended hours until 9pm on Friday; tel: 426 6500), the third oldest such attraction in the world. There's nothing elegant about this museum; occupying a former warehouse, it is a place where, apart from some dolls and their houses in glass display cases, the visitor is encouraged to touch, push, twist and shove the exhibits, to blow bubbles and to clamber on suspended sculpture.

The museum also attempts to instill visitors with social conscience. A major exhibit is the Kids' Bridge, which helps children learn about other cultures and racial diversity. This learning process is furthered by a complete two-story Japanese silk merchant's home, a gift from Kyoto, with which Boston is twinned. A full-size wigwam and contemporary American Indian house show the past lifestyles and present traditions of the region's Native Americans, and a Grandparents' House re-creates home life *circa* 1959, complete with old board games and black-and-white TV programs. Exposure to Latin-American food and culture is given by Super-mercado, based on a real Latino supermarket in Boston. New England's maritime traditions are reflected in hands-on boating exhibits and an environmental exhibit, Under the Dock, which simulates the underwater landscape of Fort Point Channel and includes a 14-ft (4-meter) fiberglass lobster. Youngsters are given easy-to-digest information about bodily functions in a popular section of the museum, and toddlers have their own safe play space.

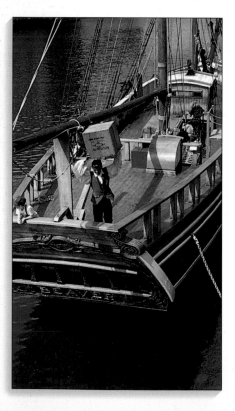

On exiting from the museum, the visitor cannot but admire the view of the densely packed new soaring skyscrapers of the **Financial District**. Turn right and reach, after 200 yards, **Northern Avenue**. Across the road is **Fan Pier**, site of the new **Federal Courthouse** ⓯ part of Boston's waterfront restoration and development. Proceed westward along this avenue for the **World Trade Center** and for some of the city's most popular seafood restaurants. Early risers might like to show up on **Pier 4** around 6.30 a.m. when a daily fish auction is held. ❑

Map on page 152

Map below

THE HARBOR ISLANDS

After years of being largely ignored, the islands have been designated as a national park area and recreational facilities look set to expand

The 30 Boston Harbor Islands were added to the National Park system by the federal government in November 1996, calling them the **Boston Harbor Islands National Recreation Area**. This designation as a national park area followed 24 years as a state park and has inaugurated a new era in island assessment, renovation, and development.

Perhaps the most powerful symbols of the harbor islands' renaissance are the 12 egg-shaped sludge digesters, 170 ft (52 meters) high, on the horizon just beyond Logan Airport. The digesters are on **Deer Island ❶**, once a true island refuge for mainland deer and a summer hunting ground for native Americans hundreds of years ago, today a peninsula connected to the town of Winthrop and home to the Massachusetts Water Resources Authority Deer Island sewage treatment plant. Thanks to the massive sludge treatment project on Deer Island, much has changed since presidential candidate George Bush scored political points in 1988 against his rival, Massachusetts governor Michael Dukakis, proclaiming Boston Harbor the dirtiest in the nation.

The Massachusetts Water Resources Authority is a public authority created in 1984 to provide water and sewer services to 2½ million people. Visitors who want to see just how Boston Harbor's waters are cleaned can get tours by

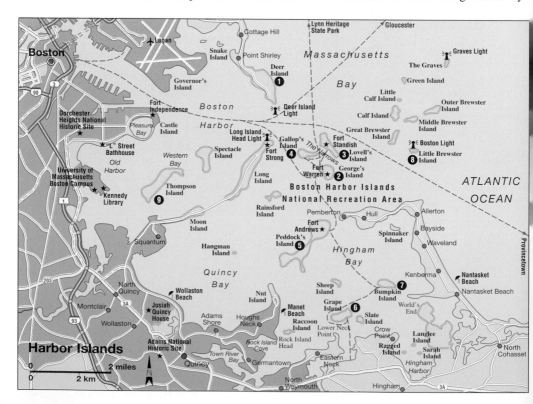

special arrangement. A secondary treatment plant was added in the late 1990s as was a 10-mile (16-km) sewage outlet pipe that carries outflow far from Boston Harbor. The beneficiaries are harbor wildlife, which can be seen from the return of harbor porpoises, and improved health for edible fish such as winter flounder. More dramatically, the cleaner, more inviting beaches along the harbor and the islands ensure their future role as a recreational area.

Glaciers created the islands as they retreated from North America 16,000 years ago, leaving a Boston basin punctuated by drumlins – sand and gravel hills – that became islands when the sea level rose around 5,200 years ago. Some are now connected by bridges or causeways to the mainland, and three (**Governor's**, **Apple** and the aptly named **Bird**) have become one and are now Logan Airport.

The farthest Boston Harbor island is **Graves**, a rocky outcrop with a lighthouse, 10 miles (16 km) from downtown Boston, and the biggest is the 214-acre (87-hectare) **Long Island** connected by a bridge to **Moon Island**, Quincy, and the south shore.

A switchback history

The Boston Harbor Islands have played an important role in Boston's cultural and economic history. Their first visitors, native Americans (the Massachuset and others) used them as hunting grounds. They became farming lands for early colonial settlers, and later battlefields and internment camps.

As the strategic importance of these islands as guardians of the city was appreciated forts were constructed on Peddock's (Fort Andrews), Lovell's (Fort Standish) and George's (Fort Warren) which remained active from King Philip's War of 1675 to the 20th century. Some of the islands served as hospitals, almshouses, quarantine facilities, prisons, and reformatory schools. During the 18th century, they were popular resorts for Bostonians who would visit to enjoy not only the sea air but also the illicit pleasures of gambling and boxing matches. Others hosted summer homes for the wealthy, lighthouses, and makeshift encampments for local fishermen, while some islands were used for the disposal of sewage and waste as they slowly fell into desuetude. And as one would expect of any decent archipelago, the Islands are said to harbor buried pirate treasure (Lovell's) and ghosts (George's).

Although much of the islands' future remains to be defined, six islands are currently the focus of visitor activity: George's, Peddock's, Grape, Bumpkin, Lovell's, and Gallop's. Trips to the islands embark from Long Wharf, as well as from Lynn Heritage State Park north of the city and Hewitt's Cove in Hingham to the south.

George's Island ❷ has always been, in state and National Park history, the island gateway to the other harbor islands, a 45-minute boat ride (7 miles/11 km) from downtown Boston. Among its amenities, George's offers recreational fishing along its shores for blues and stripers, and a chance to learn about the harbor's military history through its Fort Warren (built in 1833), a training ground for Union soldiers and a prison for confederate captives. George's has a refreshment stand, picnic areas, guided tours, and magnificent views of the Boston skyline, Boston Light, and nearby Gallop's and Lovell's islands. From June to October there is

TIP

For a brief sample of the islands, take the 10am ferry from Long Wharf in Boston for the 45-minute trip to George's, stay an hour, then catch the next hourly ferry back. In a full day, you can take in up to three islands by boarding one of the water taxis on George's Island that make circuits of the other islands.

BELOW: Fort Warren on George's Island.

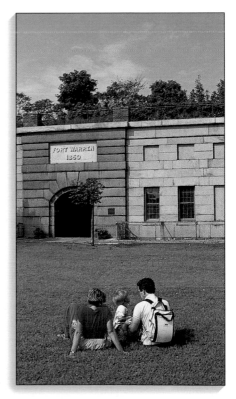

daily ferryboat service from George's to Gallop's, Lovell's, Peddock's, Grape, and Bumpkin islands, with weekend service in spring and fall.

Lovell's Island ❸ was runner-up to New York as the site for the Statue of Liberty. It offers the opportunity for overnight camping by special permit near the ruins of Fort Standish, built in 1900, and has one of the island's few beaches.

The adjacent **Gallop's Island ❹** is dominated by the remains of a large drumlin, surrounded by trails. During World War II, Gallop's was the site of a U.S. Maritime Radio Training School and a hospital. Its main inhabitants are now rabbits.

A little more than a mile south of George's lies **Peddock's Island ❺**, which consists of four drumlins connected by sand or gravel bars. On it were discovered 4,100-year-old human bones, the oldest archeological find in New England. This third largest harbor island has a brackish pond, a marsh, many walking trails, and the remains of Fort Andrews built under the shadow of the Spanish American War and garrisoned during World Wars I and II.

Grape and Bumpkin islands

These are the final two islands accessible by daily ferryboat in the spring and summer. They are located in Hingham Bay and are protected by the long arm of Nantasket Beach and the town of Hull. **Grape Island ❻** is one of the finest camping islands in the harbor offering a wealth of trails for inquisitive visitors who may encounter skunks, rabbits, and lots of birds among the wild berry trees. **Bumpkin ❼** lies close to the Hull peninsula, hosts the remains of a children's hospital and a farmhouse now overgrown with local vegetation including bayberries and wild raspberries. There are a choice of camp sites among its walking trails.

Great Brewster, the most rugged of the four Brewsters, offers magnificent

TIP

There is no drinking water on the islands, so bring plenty of water as well as food. Only George's Island has a concessions stand. All the islands have toilet facilities.

BELOW:
George's Island

Map on page 170

panoramas of the inner harbor, the Atlantic and the **Boston Light**, which stands on **Little Brewster** ❽. The lighthouse, built in 1716, was the first in the nation, but the building was constructed only in 1782 after the British had blown up the original before departing Boston in 1776. The lighthouse, a National Historic Landmark, is the only one in the nation still manned by keepers. The war of 1812 again found the British in the harbor and, near the light, the British ship *Shannon* engaged the American frigate *Chesapeake*. The British won the battle but not immortality: that went to Captain James Lawrence of the *Chesapeake* with his command: "Don't give up the ship!"

Access to many of the other harbor islands is possible by private boat or from tours organized by organizations including the Friends of Boston Harbor and the New England Aquarium. Both groups organize annual lighthouse visits to Little Brewster to see Boston Light. Friends takes visitors to **Thompson Island** ❾, owned and managed by private, non-profit Thompson Island Outward Bound Education Center. The island has a large salt marsh and rolling fields.

Besides hiking and camping, the islands are often used for a variety of other activities: there are apple festivals, cruises to experience nature in winter, Civil War reenactments on George's Island, and an Edgar Rowe Snow Day to celebrate the memory and works of Boston Harbor's consummate Harbor Islands storyteller. For the more adventurous, the outlying Brewster Island offers some of the best scuba diving in New England and wildlife cruises to the islands offer a chance to see sea ducks, barn owls, redwing blackbirds, double crested cormorants, harbor seals, and a variety of seashore life in easily accessible tidepools. There is recreational fishing throughout the islands for striped bass, winter flounder, and bluefish. ❑

Free overnight camping is available on the islands. Telephone (617) 223-8666 for a schedule and to obtain a permit.

BELOW:
Boston Light on Little Brewster.

WHALE WATCHING

One of the world's greatest gatherings of humpback whales takes place every summer off the coast of Massachusetts. Today their hunters carry cameras

Pegasus and Pepper, Batik and Gemini, Petrel and Ishtar make a great spectacle as they lunge, breach and flipper. You can see them by boarding one of the large white whale-watching boats which, each day from Easter until early October, leave Boston and Provincetown on a three-hour sightseeing voyage.

Their destination is Stellwagen Bank, a shallow underwater deposit of sand and gravel, to which, year after year, Pegasus and her friends, who are hump-backed whales, return after spending the winter in their West Indies breeding grounds. Experts recognize the different humpbacks, which often reach lengths of 40–50 feet (15 meters) and weights of 30 tons, by their distinctive body markings, especially those on their tail flukes.

Huge quantities of plankton and an infinite number of small sand eels are the magnets that attract to Stellwagen Bank the world's largest concentration of whales. The vast majority of the 500 or so who visit each year are humpbacks, but there are minkes, finbacks and a few right whales.

AN EATING MACHINE

The humpback is basically a bulk feeder who dives deep below the schools of sand eels and then lunges upward through the school with its mouth open to engulf large quantities of fish and water. Its rorquals (folds of skin that begin at the chin and stretch to the whale's navel) balloon up and probably double the capacity of the mouth. This allows the animals to capture hundreds, if not thousands, of fish with every lunge they make.

▽ **WHAT TO BRING**
The waters can be rough, so bring anti-seasickness tablets. Rainwear is useful in April and May. A 35mm SLR is more effective than an automatic camera.

▷ **DOLPHIN DELIGHTS**
Visitors are often fortunate enough to be entertained by scores of frolicking dolphins, which seem more curious than fearful of their human observers.

▷ **WHEN TO SEE THEM**
The season lasts about six months. Humpbacks and minkies begin arriving in April and May and the numbers peak from June to October.

◁ **FREQUENT SIGHTINGS**
It's fairly rare for a visitor not to see a whale during a trip. More often than not, the whale-watching boats approach within 50 feet (15 meters) of at least half a dozen humpbacks.

△ **LURING THE WHALES**
Some whale-watching operators feed gulls, hoping that their presence, usually a good indicator that there are fish close by, will help attract whales.

◁ **SUMMER GATHERINGS**
Stellwagen Bank National Marine Sanctuary attracts 17 species of whales, dolphins and porpoises.

▷ **TAKING A PEEK**
A humpback pokes its head out of the water (spy-hopping, as it's called), revealing its pleated throat.

THE HEYDAY OF YANKEE WHALING

The above dramatic painting by Robert Walker Weir, Jr., on show at the Kendall Whaling Museum in Sharon, Massachusetts, is a reminder that whales as a source of income are not new to New England. Nor is their annual visit to Stellwagen Bank. In the 1770s local fishermen hunted the right whales which populated Stell-wagen and started the decline in their numbers from 50,000 to the 250 or so which now survive. (Right whales are so-called because they were the right whales to hunt: they swim slowly, enabling the hunters to keep abreast of them in row-boats. Once harpooned, right whales float on the surface rather than sink.)

Whale oil lit the lamps of the world, and New England vessels – 735 of them at their peak – prowled the globe. Then petroleum-based kero-sene was discovered in Pennsylvania in 1859. Whaling began to decline and soon the opening up of the West offered more alluring opportunities to the adventurous than a hazardous life at sea.

CHARLESTOWN

The U.S.S. Constitution and the Bunker Hill Monument attract the Freedom Trail trekkers and the Warren Tavern allows you to combine historical research with having a drink

Map on page 180

Charlestown, which today is a northern neighborhood of Boston, was founded in 1629, one year before Boston, when 10 men with their families and servants were sent by the Massachusetts Bay Company to inhabit the company's New England holdings. One year later this scant band was joined by John Winthrop, who would become the colony's first governor, and his shipload of 800 Puritans.

Conditions were difficult, disease was rife, the water was foul and fear of Indians was ever-present. In 1631 Winthrop and many of his followers crossed the Charles River estuary and settled in Boston. However, the doughty few who remained prospered and by the end of the 17th century had established a democratic town meeting, founded a church and school, built a mill and even hanged Massachusetts' first witch. The town thrived and became the fourth busiest port in the country. However, in 1776 it was razed by the British and consequently none of the buildings bordering its tree-lined streets pre-dates 1800.

Charlestown is usually reached via the **Charlestown Bridge**, although a more pleasant and exciting approach is to board the ferry at **Long Wharf** for a short voyage to the U.S.S. *Constitution* National Park. Alternatively, the Orange line of the "T" can be ridden to the **Community College** stop.

Charlestown's **City Square ❶** is entered from the bridge. Immediately to the northwest is small, leafy **John Harvard Mall**, in the center of which stands a solid, granite memorial to this Charlestown man who "was sometimes minister of God's word" and who, when he died in 1638 aged 27, bequeathed his library of 300 books and half his estate to the struggling New-towne College which thereupon assumed his name. Harvard Mall is where the first settlers built their fort. Eight plaques embedded in the walls recount the subsequent early history of the settlement.

Immediately to the right of the mall is tiny **Harvard Square**, where No. 27, built *circa* 1800, is one of the very few stone houses in Charlestown. It originally served as the town dispensary. Above the mall is **Harvard Street**, a dignified curving street where many notables lived in still-standing, handsome mid-19th-century houses with mansards and bow windows. Turn left and return to City Square, passing No. 16, which was occupied by Edward Everett, governor of the state and president of Harvard.

Old Ironsides

Diagonally across the square is the **Charlestown Navy Yard ❷** which, during its heyday (1825–68 and World War II) employed thousands of men. Now, after years of desuetude, it is enjoying a resurrection not only because of the U.S.S. *Constitution* and other

PRECEDING PAGES: remembering Bunker Hill. **LEFT:** housing in Charlestown. **BELOW:** service with a smile.

U.S.S. Constitution.

tourist attractions but because many buildings have been recycled into handsome apartments and hi-tech laboratories. The towering masts of the *Constitution*, which can be seen from afar, dominate the yard and are the magnet that attracts visitors to the Park (daily 9.30am–3.50pm; expect long lines; tel: 242 5670).

"Old Ironsides," whose copper sheathing, bolts and fittings were made by Paul Revere, was built in Boston and first sailed from the harbor in 1778 in a shakedown cruise. Thirty years later she was decommissioned after being involved in 40 victorious engagements, including the sinking of the British warship *Guerrière* in 1812. During this battle the *Constitution* earned the nickname "Old Ironsides" when a sailor, on seeing the enemy's cannon balls apparently bouncing off her side, exclaimed "Her sides are made of iron!" The *Constitution* had been constructed of "live oak," which is found only in the sea islands of Georgia and which is said to have five times the durability of common white oak.

The fact that the *Constitution* is moored in Boston and has not long since been scrapped is the result of several land battles. In 1830 she earned a reprieve when the young Oliver Wendell Holmes penned a poem "Ay! pull her tattered ensign down,/Long has it waved on high," which touched the nation's heartstrings. Holmes, portrayed by an actor, can be seen in stove hat wandering about the Navy Yard, often accompanied by Captain Isaac Hull, who commanded the *Constitution* in her engagement with the *Guerrière*.

In 1905, when she was to be used for target practice by the Navy, a group of concerned citizens intervened, and finally, in the 1920s, when she was in need of restoration, Boston schoolchildren contributed their pennies to a drive which spread throughout the land. In 1954, legislation was enacted making Boston

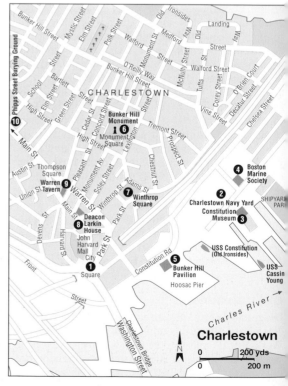

Charlestown

the permanent home port of the *Constitution,* and here she proudly sits, the oldest commissioned warship in the world and liable – in theory, anyway – to be called into active service. It's unlikely, though: since 1897, apart from a 22,000-mile (35,000-km) voyage in 1921 and a short overnight trip to Marblehead in 1997, she has left her berth only on July 4, when tugs pull her into the harbor for her annual "turnaround." Then she fires her cannons in joy rather than in anger.

Naval insights

Further insight into the *Constitution* and life aboard her can be gained by visiting the **Constitution Museum** ❸, about 600 yards east of the mooring. Between the two, and a couple of hundred yards to the south, the sleek, grey World War II destroyer U.S.S. *Cassin Young DD-793* can also be visited. Although she was built in California, 14 sister-ships were launched in the Charlestown Yard during World War II; at that time, it employed 50,000 workers who constructed 141 ships and serviced 5,000 others.

Rest those weary feet in the ward-room of the **Boston Marine Society** ❹, just beyond the Constitution Museum. The two main purposes of this Society, formed in 1742 by Boston sea captains, was to start a collection box – it can still be seen and still functions – to provide assistance to members and their families in times of distress, and "to make navigations more safe." Even today, the Society appoints the Pilot Commissioners who, in turn, appoint the Boston Harbor pilots. The Museum's two rooms are rich in paintings, models of ships (including those great clippers built across the harbor in East Boston at the yard of Donald McKay) and much nautical memorabilia.

Outside the Navy Yard, at its west end, stands the **Bunker Hill Pavilion** ❺.

The wheel of the U.S.S. Constitution.

BELOW: actors portray Oliver Wendell Holmes and Captain Isaac Hull at Navy Yard.

It presents an excellent wrap-around show, "The Whites of Their Eyes," which owes its title to the command given to the American army at the battle of Bunker Hill not to shoot "'til you see the whites of their eyes."

The Bunker Hill Monument

The Battle of Bunker Hill, the Revolution's first major clash, was fought on June 17, 1775. Although the British outnumbered the Americans by 2,500 to 1,500, around 1,000 of them were killed or wounded, compared with 440 Americans. The British victory enabled them to hold Boston – temporarily.

And so to Breed's Hill where, in Monument Square, a 221-foot (67-meter) high granite obelisk, the **Bunker Hill Monument ❻** (daily 9am–4.30pm; tel: 242 5641), soars upwards from the heart of an immaculate sward the size of three or four football fields, which is surrounded by iron rails and pierced by four gates. This is where, on an area probably twice as large, was fought the Battle of Bunker Hill; the hill itself actually lies about 300 yards to the north.

The cornerstone for the Monument was laid on the 50th anniversary of the battle and the Monument was dedicated in 1843. Its construction resulted in the first commercial railroad (horse-drawn) in the nation. This was required to haul the massive granite blocks from their Quincy quarry to the Neponset River, from where they were barged to Charlestown. Alongside the Monument is a small museum with several exhibits including an excellent diorama of the battle. A strenuous climb of 294 stone stairs leads the visitor to the top of the Monument, but some find the views a little disappointing.

At the south part of the park, between the obelisk and the main entrance gate, the Massachusetts Gate, stands a bronze statue of Colonel William Prescott who commanded the American forces at the battle.

Leave Monument Square via **Winthrop Street** and immediately enter **Winthrop Square ❼** which, for a century, was the **Training Field** where Charlestown boys learned the art of war. From here, soldiers were sent to fight

BELOW: historic Charlestown.
RIGHT: the Bunker Hill Monument.

in the Revolution, the War of 1812 and the Civil War. Monuments and plaques at the north of the Square remember those who did not return. The **Old Training Field School** from 1827 at the south border of the square is now a handsome private residence.

Descend Winthrop Street for a couple of hundred yards and turn right onto **Main Street**. At Nos. 55–61 is the post-revolutionary **home of Deacon Larkin ❽**, who lent Paul Revere a horse for his famous ride to Lexington. Incidentally, the horse was not returned.

The Warren Tavern

Continue along Main Street. The immaculately restored three-story **Warren Tavern ❾** at No. 105 was one of the first buildings erected after the burning of Charlestown by the British and is the oldest tavern in continuous use in Boston. It is also probably the oldest extant building in Charlestown.

Continue further on Main Street, passing handsome three-decker clapboard houses painted in a variety of hues and be surprised by an incongruous imposing French château, formerly the Charlestown Savings Bank.

Beyond this and across the road is the **Phipps Street Burying Ground ❿**, where at least 100 graves are pre-1700 burials and about 10 times that number are pre-1800 burials. This, one of the three oldest cemeteries in Boston, provides the best historical record of pre-revolutionary Charlestown. This is because of a unique layout: families were buried in rectangular plots which were arranged to correspond to the locations of their homes. Although John Harvard is not buried here, a monument to the preacher was erected by Harvard graduates in 1828. From here, it is just a couple of hundred yards to the Community College stop of the "T". ❏

BELOW:
the Warren Tavern.

BACK BAY AND FENWAY

Map on page 188

This varied area encompasses grand houses, the Public Garden, the Boston Public Library, the John Hancock Tower, the Christian Science Complex, and the Museum of Fine Arts

The **Back Bay** has been likened to so many different places that it's difficult to know which comparison is closest to the truth. Depending on whom you ask, it is Boston's Champs Elysées, Fifth Avenue or Nob Hill. All have an element of truth, but none captures the whole. Here are grand boulevards, stately mansions and inspiring Victorian churches. But here too are glass-plated modernism, condominium conversions and brash consumerism.

Perhaps the most accurate thing you can say about the Back Bay is that it is a product of vision. Unlike Downtown or the North End, where streets and buildings grow according to their own organic logic, the Back Bay is the result of meticulous urban planning. It is a deliberate creation, literally manufactured from the ground up. And, although unified in style and proportion, it doesn't feel regimented or artificial. There always was enough room for personal whimsy to give the neighborhood a human touch.

PRECEDING PAGES: Back Bay with, in background, the Charles River Basin and Cambridge. **LEFT:** the John Hancock Tower. **BELOW:** one of Boston's finest.

Taming the tide

Originally the Back Bay was exactly that – a shallow estuary that reached well beyond Columbus Avenue. In 1814, a developer, Uriah Cotting, built a dam across the bay from the Boston Common to Sewall's Point, near today's Kenmore Square. His plan was to harness the bay's tidal currents in order to power some 80 mills. Unfortunately, Cotting died before his mill dam was finished. In the end, there was far less tidal power than he had expected, and only a handful of mills were built.

With the tides now obstructed by the dam, the estuary became stagnant, and the sewage that, until then, had always been channeled into the Back Bay began to present a problem, especially when the wind shifted east. In 1849 the mayor declared the Back Bay "offensive and injurious to the large and growing population," and after eight years of political wrangling a plan was finally approved to fill it in.

The first trainload of gravel was dumped into the fetid water in 1857, and for more than 30 years a new load arrived every 45 minutes, 24 hours a day. When the project was finally completed, 450 acres of new land had been created.

Fortunately, the rush of speculation that accompanied the project was tempered with respect for quality and a concern for the public good. From the very beginning, the Back Bay was looked upon as an opportunity for Boston to take its place among the world's great cities, and there was enough public interest – and private capital – to ensure that it measured up to the proper standards.

Most people accepted that the city needed more space for parks and civic institutions, and a remarkable 40

Back Bay

200 yds

200 m

percent of the new land was reserved specifically for these purposes. Generous though it was, there were definite limits to public beneficence. With so much at stake, there was never any question about who was in control. The Back Bay would ultimately bear the stamp of society's upper crust.

By the mid-19th century, Boston's upper class was beginning to pull away from its Puritan moorings. The Brahmins' inclination for thrift was being challenged by a new spirit of self-indulgence and the rise of the *nouveaux riches*.

The change in attitude had a clear impact on urban planning. Unlike Beacon Hill, styled on the old English model, the Back Bay was influenced by the more cosmopolitan French approach. Its inspiration was the sweeping boulevards and elaborate architecture of Paris. By the time construction started, the eclectic phase of American architecture was in full swing. Architects began integrating Classical, Gothic and Renaissance motifs into their designs as each stylistic revival came in and fell out of fashion.

By 1900, construction of the Back Bay was virtually complete, and apart from a few isolated structures, it remains essentially unchanged. Today, it is perhaps the finest cache of Victorian architecture in the US and it also boasts a unique historical element. Because construction was started in the east and gradually moved west, the long streets are like a timeline chronicling the progression of styles during the latter half of the 19th century.

Mapping out the territory

Geographically, the Back Bay falls into two distinct areas. North of Boylston Street, the neighborhood is criss-crossed by a perfect grid. The cross streets are even organized in alphabetical order from Arlington to Hereford. Other than

Map on page 188

Back Bay blooms.

BELOW:
Victorian tea dance on a swan boat.

The Public Garden.

BELOW: *Make Way for Ducklings.*

Newbury and Boylston Streets, this area is almost exclusively residential. The northern border is marked by the busy traffic of Storrow Drive, although foot-bridges provide access to the **Esplanade**, **Hatch Shell ❶** and **Union Boat Club** (*see pages 223–4 of the chapter on the Charles River*).

South of Boylston, the tidy grid gives way to the logic of public spaces. This is where the Back Bay gets "lumpy", each lump defined by a large, self-contained development. Altogether there are four: Copley Square, Copley Place, the Prudential Center and the Christian Science Headquarters. Although several large apartment buildings stand here, the area is predominantly occupied by department stores, hotels, shops and offices.

The Public Garden

One other section of the Back Bay stands alone: the **Public Garden**. Adjacent to the Common, it was built of landfill in 1859, some 200 years after the Common was established. Its designer was George Meacham. This lush 24-acre (10-hectare) rectangle, probably Boston's prettiest, most relaxing park and a perfect spot to begin a Back Bay tour, has flower beds, exotic trees and several splendid works of sculpture, including the magnificent equestrian statue of George Washington facing the Arlington Street gate.

The Garden's central attraction is the **Lagoon ❷**, surrounded by enormous willow trees. Inspired by *Lohengrin*, the swan boats that make lazy figure eights in the water have been operated by the same family, the Pagets, for three generations. A picturesque suspension bridge, supposedly the world's shortest, crosses the pond at its center.

Just inside the park's entrance at the corner of Charles and Beacon streets is

Map on page 188

a set of bronze statues depicting the Mallard family of *Make Way For Duck-lings* ❸, Robert McCloskey's classic children's book. Small children adore clambering over the eight ducklings or riding on Mrs Mallard's back. Elsewhere in the park, statues of interest include that of Edward Everett Hale, author of *The Man Without a Country* (at the Charles Street entrance opposite the Boston Common), and Charles Sumner, who led abolitionist forces in the US Senate before the Civil War (on the Public Garden's Boylston Street perimeter).

The Public Garden is fronted by an impressive line of buildings, including the **Arlington Street Church** ❹, the **Ritz-Carlton Hotel** ❺ and **Harbridge House**. The Arlington Street Church is the most impressive. It was the first building to be constructed in the Back Bay, and its elaborate spire and brownstone facade are a departure from the comely meeting houses favored by the previous generation of Bostonians. The Ritz-Carlton shares honors with the nearby Four Seasons as the city's most prestigious hotel.

The Back Bay grid is immediately west of the Public Garden and connected to it by the **Commonwealth Avenue mall**. Originally, the four main streets in this section of the Back Bay corresponded to different levels in the social hierarchy, with the wealthiest old families residing on Beacon Street, the less affluent old families on Marlborough, the *nouveaux riches* on Commonwealth Avenue and the social climbers on Newbury Street. Homes were originally designed for single families and their corps of servants, but after the Great Depression of the 1930s many were subdivided into apartments or rooming houses. In the 1970s and 1980s, condominium conversions gutted the interiors even further. Recently, with a new generation of wealth moving in, more care is being taken to preserve historic details.

Commonwealth Avenue Mall.

BELOW: swan boats have been operated by the same family for three generations.

BELOW:
Newbury Street
shops and galleries.

Today, although Commonwealth Avenue is still one of the most pleasant strolls in the city, it is the smart shops on **Newbury Street** that grab most attention. Unfortunately, **Beacon Street** attracts too much traffic to carry off its traditional reserve. **Marlborough Street**, on the other hand, in spite of a lively contingent of students, is still quiet and shady. With its excellent stores and sidewalk cafés, **Boylston Street** lacks the ambience of the rest of the Back Bay.

A long but rewarding stroll through Back Bay requires moving up and down the grid of streets. Start on Beacon Street near the Garden and finish at the corner of Boylston Street and Massachusetts Avenue. En route, there are many great old houses and a host of architectural styles.

The **Gibson House Museum** ❻ at 137 Beacon Street (hourly tours Wed–Sun 1–4pm; tel: 267 6338) is a historic Back Bay home with original Victorian furnishings. The sumptuously furnished dining room is set with a Rockingham service and English Regency chairs.

Commonwealth Avenue

The Back Bay comes gloriously into its own on **Commonwealth Avenue**. A shady mall which contains a handful of interesting statues runs down the middle of this French-inspired almost 100-yard-wide boulevard, whose openness would have been impossible in the tight quarters of old Boston. Although the houses tend to be uniform in proportion and ambience, the play of styles on "Comm Ave" covers more architectural ground than elsewhere in the Back Bay and gives the street an almost whimsical quality. Exemplifying this is No. 176–178; it has a Romanesque rusticated stone porch which supports a bay window and a bowfront tower topped by a conical roof. The mansard on the top floor with dormer pediments is Flemish.

The parade of spectacular buildings continues on Newbury Street, but for most visitors, the architecture is secondary to the galleries and boutiques that make this a haven for Boston's "beautiful people." Outdoor cafés add a Continental élan to Newbury Street and provide the best vantage for the chic to see and be seen.

Map on page 188

Between Arlington and Berkeley Streets on Newbury can be seen the first Gothic Revival Church in the Back Bay, **Emmanuel Church**. Since 1970 it has been dedicated to "a special ministry through art," and is famed for its cycle of Bach cantatas performed every Sunday between September and May.

Nearby on Newbury is Ralph Adams Cram's **New England Life Building ❼**, built on the original site of MIT. Evoking both corporate power and a mausoleum, the building, begun in 1939, inspired Harvard poet David McCord to write: *Ralph Adams Cram / One morning said damn, / And designed the Urn Burial / For a concern actuarial.*

Some of the chill has disappeared in recent years as the ground floor has been converted into shops on Newbury and Bolyston. Its plain granite face is offset by the 236-ft (72-meter) spire of the **Church of the Covenant**, a stirring Gothic structure with original Tiffany windows and a bristling crown of peaks and gables.

The magisterial structure across the street, which now houses **Louis Boston ❽** was completed in 1864 as the Museum of Natural History, the forerunner of Boston's Museum of Science. Its serene classical design is by William Gibbons Preston. Across the street on the corner of Boylston and Berkeley is a FAO Schwarz store with a huge statue of a bronze **teddy bear ❾**, which is both popular with children and a favorite rendezvous location. FAO Schwarz resides in Robert A. M. Stern's design for 222 Berkeley Street, an office complex that is attached to the far more controversial **500 Boylston ❿**, designed by

LEFT:
FAO Schwarz's big bear.
BELOW: the massive New England Life headquarters on Newbury Street was built between 1932 and 1942

First Baptist Church.

Philip Johnson and John Burgee in 1988. The designers apparently took an ironic approach to the problem of relating a modern skyscraper to its old neighbors. They transformed the simple elegance of a Palladian window – a common feature in old Boston houses – into an enormous, looming black-glass facade. The building is fronted by an equally monstrous colonnade which, again, gives it a certain ironic continuity with the classical 19th-century revival.

It may be enough to make one want to return to some of Back Bay's other grand old mansions. The **Hooper Mansion** ⑪ on Commonwealth Avenue (No. 25–27) is one of the many fine houses in this area.

Soaring above Commonwealth Avenue (at Clarendon) is the tower of Richardson's Romanesque **First Baptist Church**. The tower's frieze was modeled by Bartholdi (sculptor of the Statue of Liberty) in Paris and was carved by Italian workmen. The faces in it are said to be likenesses of noted Bostonians, including Longfellow, Emerson, Hawthorne and Sumner. The trumpeting angels on the corners looking down on the Back Bay have earned the building the sobriquet of "Church of the Holy Bean Blowers."

John Hancock Tower

Between the east and west sections of Boylston is **Copley Square**, one of America's most celebrated public spaces. The plaza itself is not that inviting: a late 1980s rehabilitation was a bit pallid though it left the space greener and somewhat more congenial. The boldest coupling around the square is **Trinity Church** ⑫ and the 1976 **John Hancock Tower** ⑬. When I. M. Pei's plan for the Hancock Tower was unveiled, there was a fear that the giant, rhombus-shaped skyscraper would overpower Trinity Church. At 790 ft (241 meters), it is the tallest building in New

England, but Pei's design has an intriguing twist. Because the building is sheathed with reflective glass, it acts like an enormous mirror. In a sense, it is both conspicuous and invisible. It steals Trinity's glory but reflects it right back.

The best way to experience the Hancock Tower is from the 60th-floor observatory (9am–10pm; tel: 247 1977). The views are spectacular, and a "Boston 1775" exhibit shows what the city looked like before the Back Bay was landfilled.

The Hancock Tower is an eye-catcher, but by rights Copley Square belongs to Trinity Church. With Trinity, Henry Hobson Richardson's adaptation of the Romanesque style came into full blossom. The ingenious arrangement of large-scale structures, coupled with an artful use of masonry and ornamentation, make this one of the great ecclesiastical buildings in the US. Richardson continually altered the plans while the church was being constructed, and said of his winning plans: "I really don't see why the Trinity people liked them, or, if they liked them, why they let me do what I afterwards did." Visit the interior, resplendent with intricate woodwork, stained-glass windows and frescoes by John La Farge. A bronze statue of the Rev. Phillips Brooks standing outside the north transept of the church is inscribed with the Bostonian's concept of the cardinal virtues: "Preacher of the Word of God/Lover of Mankind/Born in Boston/Died in Boston."

Across the Square from Trinity Church is the **Boston Public Library** ⓮, a Renaissance Revival palace designed by Charles Follen McKim, and built between 1887 and 1895 (*see page 96*). A 1971 addition by Philip Johnson, as dignified as the original building but more modern in style, fronts Boylston Street.

Explore the sumptuous interior of the old library. The **John Singer Sargent Gallery** features a series of murals that some critics rank among his most powerful work. **Bates Hall** is a cavernous barrel-vaulted reading room wrapped in

Map
on page
188

*In the courtyard of
the Public Library.*

BELOW: this bronze
outside Boston
Public Library
represents Art.

marble, oak and sandstone. And the lovely Italian courtyard cloistered in the center of the building is one of the city's most peaceful retreats and a joy for anyone who enjoys thumbing through a book in the open air.

The third side of Copley Square is occupied by the **Copley Plaza Hotel** , an elegant Renaissance-style palace where society ladies enjoy afternoon tea. Designed by Clarence Hardenbergh, who is famed for the Plaza in New York and the Willard Hotel in Washington DC, the Copley Plaza suffers from being the wallflower, overlooked because it stands next to three of the most famous buildings in America.

Poised at the corner of Copley Square, **Copley Place** is the most recent "lump" in this section of the Back Bay. Controversial since its opening in the early 1980s, the sprawling, 9-acre (3.6-hectare) development combines retail space, offices, hotels and parking facilities. Reactions have been mixed. The exterior is neither especially offensive nor attractive, although as far as shopping malls go, the interior is quite plush. The gleaming glass canopies and criss-crossing superstructure are visually exciting, and there's an interesting stone waterfall in the central atrium that adds a surprisingly restful quality. The shops – including Tiffany, Gucci, Sharper Image, and Neiman Marcus – are clearly targeted for the high end of the market. A glass footbridge connects Copley Place with the Prudential Center.

New Old South Church

The beautifully ornamented, polychromatic **New Old South Church** is an 1875 Gothic gem that sits across from the Boston Public Library on Boylston Street. Anywhere else, it would be the center of attention, but here it is something of an afterthought. The tower, dating from 1938, is not the original but retains much of its predecessor's stones. That tower turned out to be Boston's

When Old South Church moved to the Back Bay in 1875, its former Washington Street building, Old South Meeting House, was slated for demolition. A corporation was founded to raise funds to preserve it as an historic monument – Boston's first example of heritage defeating commerce.

BELOW: the Copley Plaza Hotel.

Map on page 188

Leaning Tower of Pisa, tilting at the rate of about an inch a year; when dismantled in 1931, it had already tilted almost 3 ft (1 meter).

Back on Commonwealth Avenue observe the former **Hotel Vendôme** (No. 160), designed in the French Second Empire style in 1871. Once the most prestigious hotel in the Back Bay, the Vendôme was the one at which Presidents Grant, Harrison, Cleveland and McKinley stayed. Diagonally across from the hotel on the Commonwealth Mall is one of Boston's newest memorials to the firefighters who died battling a blaze at the Vendôme in 1973.

Facing Commonwealth with an entrance on Dartmouth is the **Ames-Webster Mansion** (306 Dartmouth Street), built in 1872 for railroad tycoon and congressman Frederick L. Ames. Now converted into a handsome office building, this is home to the most palatial space in all of the Back Bay mansions and features stained-glass windows by John La Farge.

Around the corner, Marlborough Street has a number of charming Queen Anne houses including numbers 276, 257 and 245, all built between 1883 and 1884. Although Marlborough is generally more modest than the rest of the neighborhood, there are a few exceptions. The **Hunnewell Mansion** (315 Dartmouth Street) and the **Cushing-Endicott House** (No.165 Marlborough Street) represent two very different styles but are equally grand in size and bearing. Bainbridge Bunting, in his authoritative book *Houses of Boston's Back Bay*, suggests that the latter is perhaps the most handsome house in the district.

Back on Commonwealth, note the unusual statue of sailor and historian **Samuel Eliot Morison** *(see margin note)* dressed in foul weather gear and seated on a rock. The statue sits outside the **St Botolph Club**, of which Morison was a member.

On Newbury, the old **Exeter Street Theater** dominates its corner like a

Admiral Samuel Eliot Morison (1887–1976), won Pulitzer Prizes for his biographies of Columbus and John Paul Jones. His 1962 book "One Boy's Boston" recalls life in the city at the end of the 19th century.

BELOW: spring blooms on Marlborough Street.

The Algonquin Club.

medieval fortress. The massive Romanesque structure was built in 1884 for a group of psychics known as the Working Union of Progressive Spiritualists. An account of the temple's dedication informs that an astral spirit materialized for the occasion, appearing out of nowhere in the darkened auditorium "like a column of phosphorescent light." The Temple was converted into a movie theater in 1913 and in recent years has served as furniture department store and bookstore.

Moving west, the **Algonquin Club** ⓴ (217 Commonwealth Avenue) with its self-important Italian Renaissance Revival facade was a McKim, Mead & White design of 1887.

Looking south one sees Back Bay's skyline dominated by the 52-story **Prudential Tower** ㉑, a monument to 1960s urban renewal and the international style. Below the tower, set somewhat back from the south side of Boylston Street is the **Prudential Center**, or "Pru," a mixed project built in the late 1950s and early 1960s. At the time it was built the *Boston Globe* said: "All the daring and imagination in this country today is not being spent on launching space missiles. Boston and Prudential are shooting for their own moon." The Tower Skywalk has stunning views of the city, and the renovated shopping mall in the Center has proven popular.

The Christian Science complex

Adjacent to the Pru is Boston's most monumental space, the **Christian Science Center** ㉒. It was created in the early 1970s by the Christian Science Church, a worldwide movement which had its beginnings in 1866 when Mary Baker – she was not yet Eddy – a religious, yet scarcely conforming, Calvinist, slipped on an icy sidewalk in Lynn, near Boston, and suffered serious internal

injuries. Three days later, while reading about the healings of Jesus (Matthew 9, 1–8), she completely recovered.

Mary Baker devoted her next nine years to a thorough study of the scriptures so as to better understand the divine law underlying spiritual healing. She became convinced that healing is not miraculous but a natural result of speaking and thinking in accord with God's law.

These studies resulted in a metaphysical system which she named Christ Science and set forth in a booklet, published in 1875, *Science and Health, with Key to the Scriptures*. She repeatedly revised this text to make it more effective as the "textbook" for the study and practice of Christian Science. Mary Baker hoped that the Christian church would accept her "discovery" but was rebuffed. In 1879 she and 15 followers founded the Church of Christ, Scientist, with the aim of reinstating "primitive Christianity and its lost element for healing." Not until the church moved from Lynn to Boston in 1882 did the movement take off.

In 1889, Mary Baker Eddy suspended all operations in order to reconstruct the church completely, and in 1892 she founded the First Church of Christ, Scientist, in Boston as the "mother" church of Christian Science (*see page 200*).

The centerpiece of the modern building is a 670-ft (204-meter) long reflecting pool – a welcome venue for Bostonians on hot summer days. It also serves as part of the center's air-conditioning and beneath it is a garage. Its south side in summer is ablaze with flowers which border a stately row of linden trees. Dominating the other long side of the pool is a basilica-like structure which is a mixture of Byzantine and Italian Renaissance and a long five-story colonnaded building.

Tucked in between the two and engulfed by the basilica is the original Mother

Map on page 188

BELOW:
the Christian
Science complex.

Christian Science's Empire on Earth

Mary Baker Eddy (1821–1910) opened her first church in 1894 and the next year she published the *Church Manual*, often called the "denomination's constitution," which she continued to revise until her death. The movement which she had first conceived in 1875 now has more than 2,600 churches in 67 countries.

At Christian Science Sunday services a lesson-sermon, which members are expected to have studied during the previous week, is preached from the pulpit by two elected readers. These have as their theme 26 rotating subjects, such as "God," "Man," "Reality," and consist of related passages from the Bible and from *Science and Health*. These two books constitute the impersonal dual pastor of the church. At Wednesday evening services, congregants share healing and other experiences. Those engaged in full-time healing are called Christian Science practitioners and usually charge a nominal fee.

Eddy believed that numbers are not a measure of spiritual vitality and stated in the *Manual* that statistics should not be made public. However, what is known is that this very wealthy church is an aging organization which has failed to attract many new members, especially among the young, and is currently running in the red.

The Christian Science Publishing Society, the media arm of the church, is not so coy and is proud that each week it reaches through print, radio and television more than 9 million people. It all began in 1908 when Mary Baker Eddy founded a newspaper, the *Christian Science Monitor*. The paper, which does not have a religious bias, is highly respected and its writers have won six Pulitzer Prizes; yet it has not posted a profit since 1961. It circulates to 174 countries.

Circulation peaked in 1970 at around 150,000 but over the next 20 years it fell to about half that figure. In 1988 the paper was completely revamped in the hope of reviving circulation. Also launched was a glossy monthly, the *World Monitor*. In 1996 the Publishing Society embraced cyberspace, unveiling an electronic edition of the *Christian Science Monitor* on the World Wide Web.

The Mother Church became involved in radio in 1920, and today its programs are carried on more than 200 public radio stations in the US. Short-wave radio, beamed worldwide, broadcasts 20 hours a day to 219 countries. Monitor Television began in 1985 and appeared on cable for several years. Programs tended to be relentlessly international in content and viewpoint, although the audience consisted mainly of Americans with a limited appetite for foreign news.

The Christian Science Publishing Society needed deep pockets, as annual losses reached tens of millions of dollars. How long, observers wondered, could a nonprofit institution with a public service philosophy ignore the unforgiving laws of the marketplace? The church's answer was to retreat from television back to radio and print, and to seek new ways, such as the World Wide Web, of achieving an "outreach to mankind." ❏

LEFT: founder Mary Baker Eddy.

Church, built in 1893–94 as a Romanesque affair with a square bell-tower and a rough granite facade. A five-story elliptical Sunday school at the southwest corner of the pool and a 28-story administrative building at the southeast complete the ensemble.

Map on page 188

The interior of the basilica – the church annex, entered through a handsome portico of 10 limestone columns – is a glorious column-free affair which can seat 5,000 people on three levels. The impressive organ is the largest pipe-organ in the Western hemisphere.

The Christian Science media organization is housed in the classically inspired **Publishing Society Building**, which contains a comfortably appointed reading room and the **Mapparium**, a remarkable walk-in stained-glass globe of the world, 30 ft (9 meters) in diameter and with fascinating acoustic properties. Entry to the reading room and Mapparium is free, as are the regular tours of the Christian Science Center, details of which are posted in the lobby of the Publishing Society Building.

Close by, at the corner of Massachusetts Avenue and Huntington Avenue, is **Horticultural Hall**, a handsome baroque building dating from 1900–01 and housing the venerable Massachusetts Horticultural Society, founded in 1829.

New art, old mansions

Back on Boylston merging with the Prudential is the spacious **Hynes Convention Center**. Across the road is the **Institute of Contemporary Art ㉓** (ICA), housed in a 19th-century Romanesque former police station. The ICA, a laboratory for new ideas in the visual arts, hosts many new exhibitions each year, but it has no permanent collection.

LEFT: entrance and, **BELOW**, a stained-glass window at the Mother Church of Christian Science.

Back Bay entertainer.

Nearby are the **Charles Francis Adams House** (20 Gloucester Street) and the **John F. Andrew House** (32 Hereford Street). (Not unexpectedly, some of the grandest houses occupy the corners of blocks.)

Further toward the river are some other unusual houses that shouldn't be missed. The **Ames Mansion** (No. 355) on Commonwealth Avenue and Massachusetts Avenue informally welcomes visitors. A few blocks away, at the corner of Massachusetts Avenue and Beacon, Graham Gund's **Church Court** ㉔ development integrates the facade of a 19th-century church into a lively condominium complex. And, if living in a church is too elevated, the **Burrage Mansion** (314 Commonwealth Avenue) bristles with turrets, towers and Gothic ornamentation, suggesting a French château on the Loire.

The modern concrete structure at the corner of Hereford Street and Newbury is the **Boston Architectural Center**. The Richard Haas *trompe-l'oeil* mural on its rear wall is a cross-section of a Renaissance duomo. The two-story buildings on the rest of the block are converted stables where Back Bay families originally kept their horses and carriages. Be sure to take a look at the surrealist "Tramount" mural near the end of the block. Beyond this, **Tower Records** ㉕ and the Hynes/ICA subway station at 360 Newbury are housed in a dramatic modern recycled building designed by Frank Gehry.

Fenway

BELOW:
Burrage Mansion.

A few steps past the Christian Science Center, **Symphony Hall** ㉖ puts the finishing touches to the Back Bay. The modest Renaissance-style exterior isn't nearly as impressive as the magnificent interior. A young professor of physics was hired to guarantee that the hall would be acoustically perfect, and it's no exag-

geration to say that there isn't a bad seat in the house. You can catch the Boston Symphony from October to April; the Boston Pops play in May and June.

Beyond the Christian Science complex, the densely packed Back Bay yields to the **Fenway**, a loose collection of institutions and apartment buildings joined by the meandering path of the Back Bay Fens. These islands of activity form a sort of urban archipelago that drifts out to Brookline without any real focus or organizing theme.

The Fenway first became fashionable in the early 1900s, when the Back Bay was nearing completion. The area was especially attractive to civic and to educational institutions that had outgrown downtown quarters and were looking for a place to expand. The **Massachusetts Historical Society** (founded in 1791) moved into a grand new mansion at 1154 Boylston Street in 1899 and **Harvard Medical School** followed its lead in 1906. Today, the Fenway is home to several important museums and theaters, a number of major hospitals and 14 colleges, including part of the sprawling campus of Northeastern University.

The geographical focus of the area is the **Back Bay Fens**, a major link in Frederick Law Olmsted's Emerald Necklace. Unfortunately, a busy road encircles the Fens and isolates it from the neighborhood. Joggers and community gardeners still make good use of the area, but it could do with more attention.

Moving away from the Christian Science Church and Symphony Hall on Huntington Avenue are some of Boston's most beloved arts institutions. **The Boston University Theater** ㉗ is home to the Huntington Theater Company, a professional residing company noted for performing classic and contemporay drama. Nearby is **Jordan Hall** at the **New England Conservatory of Music** ㉘, internationally renowned for both its acoustics and the music performed there.

Maps on pages 188, 203

BELOW: a student conducts at the New England Conservatory of Music.

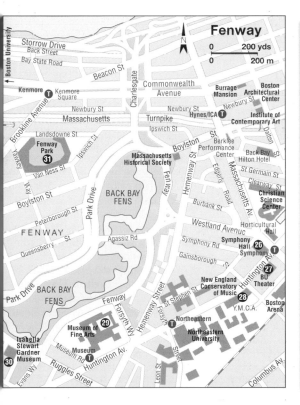

Map on page 203

Isabella Stewart Gardner engaged many performers, such as Paderewski and Nellie Melba, for private concerts, and her museum still presents more than 125 concerts a year.

BELOW: the Museum of Fine Arts. **RIGHT:** the Isabella Stewart Gardner Museum.

Huntington Avenue opens up somewhat with the buildings of the **Northeastern University** campus, but what attracts most visitors to the Fenway are the **Museum of Fine Arts** (MFA) ❷ and the Isabella Stewart Gardner Museum. The former's collection, one of the world's greatest, is housed in a massive classical structure completed in 1909 and in I. M. Pei's West Wing, built in 1981. Visitors pressed for time might concentrate on the Old Kingdom Egyptian treasures; the Asiatic collection, especially the Japanese items; Impressionist paintings, especially those of Monet; the Boston school of painters (Stuart, Sargent and Copley); and the early American silver collection, including pieces by Paul Revere. In the **Japanese Garden**, an attempt has been made to recapture the spirit of the 18th-century New England coastline. *(See also pages 206–7.)*

The **Isabella Stewart Gardner Museum** ❸ is within easy walking distance of the Museum of Fine Arts. The Venetian palace in which the museum is housed was built by Gardner for the specific purpose of displaying her art collection. A native New Yorker of clearly extravagant means, Isabella Stewart married John Lowell Gardner of an equally wealthy Boston family in 1860. Until her death in 1924, "Mrs Jack" cultivated a reputation for unconventional behavior in the primly conventional society of Victorian Boston. Although she apparently did not keep lions in her cellar or walk them on a leash down Beacon Street (as legend has it), Mrs Gardner had wide-ranging interests, from Oriental philosophy to the Boston Red Sox.

Her will stipulated that everything be preserved exactly as she left it – and so it was until March 1990, when thieves disguised as policemen made off with works of art valued at $300 million, including Vermeer's *The Concert*, three Rembrandts, five by Degas and a Manet. To date, they're still missing.

The museum still has enough eclectic European and American items to satisfy everyone, however. Exceptional works include paintings and drawings by Titian, Bellini, Matisse, Botticelli, Whistler and Sargent. In the center of the palace is a glorious courtyard with a Roman mosaic pavement, a skylight and, throughout the year, an abundance of flowers. *(Also see page 60.)*

Fenway Park

Just north of the Fens is an institution closer to the hearts of most Bostonians: **Fenway Park** ❸. Built in 1912, this is the smallest stadium in the major leagues and one of the oldest. Baseball legends like Ted Williams and Carl Yastrzemski played their entire careers at Fenway, but Red Sox fans have been heartbroken since 1918, the last year Boston won a World Series.

Kenmore Square is two blocks away from Fenway Park. The intersection is a major link for commuter lines and is usually choked with traffic and pedestrians. Most of the square is devoted to fast-food joints and convenience stores. **Boston University** stretches along Commonwealth Avenue at the western end of the square and also spills into Bay State Road, a quiet strip of ivy-covered townhouses.

Kenmore Square's real claim to fame is the giant "**Citgo**" sign flashing from a nearby rooftop. It's Boston's unlikeliest landmark, but local devotees convinced the city to give the sign protected status. ❏

THE MUSEUM OF FINE ARTS

Few museums in the world rival the MFA for the quality and scope of its decorative and fine art collections. Every one has something exceptional

One of the first museums in America, the MFA opened in 1870 and in 1909 moved into the present building. Cyrus Edwin Dallin's bronze equestrian statue *Appeal to the Great Spirit* (left) was placed in the forecourt in 1913.

The highly cultured citizens of 19th-century Boston were keen collectors. Many were passionate about things Asian, and their treasures in due course came to the MFA, forming the nucleus of an outstanding collection. Others travelled to Europe, and the museum acquired one of the foremost holdings outside Paris of Impressionist painting, in particular works by Monet, Pissaro, Sisley, Renoir and Manet. It has nearly 70 works by Jean-François Millet. The American art collection is one of the best in the US; the European and American decorative arts rooms display superb silver, porcelain, furniture and musical instruments. The Nubian and Egyptian collections are unrivalled in the world.

There is so much to see, the first-time visitor would be well advised either to pick out just one collection, or take a (free) tour that highlights the best from all the collections. *Also see page 204.*

▽ AMERICAN DECORATIVE ARTS
The museum is strong in decorative arts from pre-Civil War New England. Below: a Paul Revere teapot, *c.*1760–5.

△ THE JAPANESE GARDEN
Tenshin-en, "The Garden of the Heart of Heaven," is one of three gardens in which visitors may draw breath (beside the West Wing; open spring through early fall).

▷ THE IMPRESSIONISTS
Renoir's *Dance at Bougival* (1883) shares wall space with equally important works by such European painters as van Gogh, Degas, and Gauguin.

◁ LANDSCAPE ART

The New England landscape is captured in works by such American artists as Winslow Homer and Edward Hopper. Left: Edward Hopper's watercolour *Lighthouse and Buildings, Portland Head, Cape Elizabeth* (1927)

△ AMERICAN ART

The Letter by Mary Cassatt (1890). More formal are the portraits by colonial painters Gilbert Stuart and John Singleton Copley, and society portraitist John Singer Sargent.

▽ THE ASIAN COLLECTION

A highlight of the excellent Asian collection is this little 12th-century AD (Jin Dynasty) Chinese buddha, made of lacquered wood with painting and gilding.

THE ANCIENT WORLD

For 40 years from 1905, Harvard University and the Museum of Fine Arts collaborated on an archeological excavation in Egypt, based at the Great Pyramids at Giza. From this, the museum acquired a world-famous collection of Egyptian treasures. Among many Old Kingdom sculptures is this beautiful statue of King Mycerinus, who built the Third Pyramid at Giza, and his queen, dated to *circa* 2548–30BC.

Other treasures include gilded and painted mummy masks, and some amazingly well preserved hieroglyphic inscriptions. The Giza expedition's director, Dr Reisner, also worked in the Sudan and brought home a dazzling collection of Nubian artifacts, the best in the world outside Khartoum. Particularly awe-inspiring is the exquisite gold jewelry, inlaid with enamel and precious stones, and the sculptures, varying in size from huge statues of Nubian kings to tiny shawabtis.

THE SOUTH END

Map
on page
212

*This area, an ethnic cocktail of more than 40 nationalities,
includes the massive Cathedral of the Holy Cross
and some of Boston's most distinguished residential areas*

The **South End**, not to be confused with South Boston, is that area adjacent to and to the south of the Back Bay. It is delineated by the Southwest Corridor, Berkeley Street and Harrison and Massachusetts Avenues. This area, where landfill and building began in the 1830s, was originally called Shawmut Neck. By the middle of the 19th century its layout was very similar to that seen today, and by the 1870s the area was fully developed into a grid pattern with blocks of homogeneous red-brick three- and four-story stooped rowhouses. These lined short, often discontinuous, streets running perpendicular to the main thoroughfares. It has often been said that, if the Back Bay is French-inspired, the South End is English, with more park-centred squares and a rather more florid style of architecture.

Most thoroughfares were unattractive wide swathes along which traffic passed as quickly as possible. Some houses had mansard roofs. Indeed, the first such roof – now so much part of the Boston architectural scene – appeared in the South End in the free-standing Deacon House, which was acclaimed as "one of the wonders of the mid-century."

The South End enjoyed a fleeting decade of prosperity. But when its wealthier residents abandoned it for the new and fashionable Back Bay, it became home to the *nouveaux riches*, the working class and the latest immigrants. Among the first group was the eponymous hero of Dean Howells' novel *The Rise of Silas Lapham* who "bought very cheap of a terrified gentleman of good extraction who discovered too late that the South End was not the thing, and who in the eagerness of his flight to the Back Bay threw in his carpets and shades for almost nothing."

However, some, such as Walbridge A. Field, who had been Chief Justice of Massachusetts, remained loyal and still resided in the South End at the turn of the century. Many private homes were turned into lodging houses. By the end of the century only seven of the 53 houses in elegant Union Park (*see page 214*) remained private. Desuetude engulfed the district.

A polyglot hodgepodge

The rebirth of the South End began in the 1960s. Today, it boasts an ethnic mix as varied as its architecture is homogeneous. More than 40 nationalities – mainly Puerto Ricans, Greeks, Syrians and Lebanese – reside in the district, as do blacks, young white professionals and gays. What, one wonders, would be the reaction of George Apley's Brahmin father, whom J.P. Marquand created and who, in the 1870s, left the South End the day after coming out of his home and saying: "Thunderation, there is a man in shirt sleeves on those steps."

PRECEDING PAGES:
Boston's popular
rock station.
LEFT: on parade in
the South End.
BELOW: the South
End in winter.

Leave Copley Square and stroll south on **Dartmouth Street** for about 300 yards to **Back Bay Station ❶**. Facing the Station is the **Southwest Corridor**, a landscaped 50-yard wide park under which the railway tracks run. This park, built in the 1980s, is a bridge linking the Back Bay and the South End: formerly, the railway track was a barrier which separated the two.

Enter the Southwest Corridor and immediately turn left onto **Yarmouth Street** and appreciate the attempts that have been made to retain the integrity of the South End. The right side of the street is lined with 19th-century red-brick rowhouses; the left side consists of modern, low-rent, red-brick apartments. The rounded bows, so characteristic of the older South End houses, are echoed in the new apartments by much more linear bays.

While a doctoral student at Boston University's School of Divinity, the Rev. Martin Luther King Jr. lived on St Botolph Street.

Return to the Southwest Corridor and, before turning into Braddock Park, which parallels Yarmouth Street, make a brief diversion via **Follon Street**, on the right side of the park, into **St Botolph Street**. This street is named after the sainted monk for whom England's Boston (a contraction of St Botolph's town) was named. **Braddock Park ❷** is typical – but probably the least known – of half a dozen leafy residential squares which pepper the South End. All are handsome but none has the social cachet of Louisburg Square – or indeed of anywhere on the South Slope of Beacon Hill.

These areas all have a long, narrow garden, with a splashing fountain or two, enclosed by wrought-iron railings. Each red-brick, three- or four-story rowhouse that lines the long axes of the square is entered by a steep stoop which often rises a full story to the second floor (in which case a door beneath the stairway enters directly into the lower first floor). All have a regular cornice line; some are topped by a mansard roof. Adding attraction is wrought-iron orna-

BELOW: the leafy residential squares attract professionals.

The South End

mentation in the form of balustrades and railings around small gardens and sometimes over windows and balconies.

Leave Braddock Park and turn right on Columbus Avenue, immediately reaching the intersection of that street and Warren Avenue. Here stands the red-brick **Concord Baptist Church**, readily recognizable by its large octagonal clerestory. It was built in the 1870s, when many Baptist congregations moved to the South End, but most of its members now live in other parts of metropolitan Boston. Tiny **Harriet Tubman Park ❸**, which stands in the lee of the church, remembers the "Moses of the South," a runaway slave who organized the "underground railway," a network of abolitionists who helped thousands of slaves escape to freedom. They built secret passageways in their homes and held huge parties to cover the flight of their transient guests who were en route to freedom in Canada. Many slaves remained in Boston.

Continue on Warren Avenue for about 500 yards, turn left onto Clarendon Street and enter an enclave known as **Clarendon Park**. Its streets carry the names – Appleton, Warren, Chandler, Lawrence – of prominent Beacon Hill residents. These streets are lined by attractive small versions of Beacon Hill houses which were built, it has been suggested, to accommodate the servants of those whose names they bear.

From Cyclorama to arts center

A right, rather than a left, turn from Warren onto Clarendon takes the visitor to the unusual **Cyclorama Building**, recognizable by the kiosk, a salvaged lantern, which stands outside it. The Cyclorama was built in 1884 to house a gigantic circular painting (400 by 50 feet) of the Battle of Gettysburg by Paul Philippoteaux.

Map on page 212

LEFT: gentrification adds primary colors.
BELOW: on the move.

Subsequently, it was used for revivalist meetings, dare-devil bicycle stunts and sporting events, including boxing contests which featured John L. Sullivan, a favorite South End son. It was here in 1907, when it was used as a garage, that Alfred Champion pioneered the spark plug.

Since 1970 the building has been part of the **Boston Center for the Arts** ❹, which has attracted some excellent restaurants to its immediate neighborhood. The lively complex encompasses artists' studios, galleries and small experimental theaters. Proceed southwest on **Tremont Street** for a couple of hundred yards and turn left into **Union Park** ❺, since 1859 the South End's most distinguished residential area. Facing one another and separated by a garden with two splashing fountains are rows of red-brick houses with swells (not the occupants but the bays which protrude from the facades), oriel windows and steep stoops.

The Lebanese poet, essayist, novelist and artist Khalil Gibran (1883–1931) came to Boston in 1885 with his parents and grew up in the South End.

Since gentrification began, the cost of homes here and in other parts of the South End has rocketed; at the end of the 1970s it was still possible to buy an old rooming house for just $40,000. This rush for bargains resulted initially in some friction between the incoming yuppies and the indigenous population, many of whom had been living here for only a decade or so themselves, but the area has since become a fairly harmonious melting pot of many ethnic groups plus a substantial gay population.

A great cathedral

Exit from Union Park, cross Shawmut Avenue and continue to Washington Street to be greeted by the imposing towering facade of the **Cathedral of the Holy Cross** ❻. This, one of the world's largest Gothic cathedrals, can seat 3,500 and accommodate double that number. The puddingstone exterior with granite and

BELOW:
sports enthusiasts.

Map on page 212

sandstone trim has an assymetrical facade. (Even if the spires had been added, it would still be assymetrical.) Since comparatively few Irish Catholics are left in the area, the cathedral is now used largely on special occasions.

The exterior belies a truly Gothic interior, which has a vast clear space interrupted only by two rows of columns extending along the nave and supporting the central roof. Light enters through innumerable undistinguished stained-glass windows. The largest of these line the transept and tell the story of the exaltation of the cross by the Emperor Heraclitus and the miracle by which the cross was verified.

Until the 1980s the Washington Street "El," the elevated train line built in the early 20th century, passed within yards of the Cathedral's entrance. The noise was deafening, and it is claimed that the Yankees routed the line this way in order to disturb the Irish congregants. The Puritans' fortified gate and the town's gallows stood just a few hundred yards to the northeast on Washington Street, the original road to Boston over the neck of the peninsula.

Proceed southwest on Washington Street for three blocks. There, lying side by side, are **Blackstone** and **Franklin squares**, two geometrical, flat, grassy areas, each about the size of four football fields and each having a splashing fountain as a centerpiece. Although not built until the 1860s, the squares had already been planned by Bulfinch at the start of that century.

Each square, on its south side, is backed by a stately building. One can readily believe that the elaborate French Second Empire edifice which graces Franklin Square was one of the city's most elegant hotels, the St James, where General Grant once lodged when he was President *(see margin note)*. The building, which became familiar to many through the television series *St Elsewhere*, now houses the elderly. The Blackstone building, less flamboyant and more severe, consists of brownstone rowhouses with handsome pedimented formal windows and doors enclosed by pilasters.

The St James, on Franklin Square, had a short life as a hotel. It opened in 1868 with more than 400 rooms but was taken over in 1882 by the New England Conservatory of Music.

BELOW:
adding color to the neighborhood.

Continue on Washington Street for half a dozen blocks. Turn right onto Massachusetts Avenue and enter **Chester Square** ➐, which, until 40 years ago, was the grandest residential square in all Boston and indeed could begin to be compared to the great London squares. Then "MassAve" was realigned. It now pierces the heart of the oval park which separates the two crescents of 70 opulent rowhouses.

Chester Square debouches into Tremont Street. A left turn immediately leads to the **Pickering Piano Factory** ➑, which, when opened in 1850, was the largest building in the nation, other than the Capitol. It was saved from extinction by being converted into artists' studios and apartments. The dominating feature of this handsome six-story building is an octagonal tower, half of which projects forward from the middle of the main facade and which, above the cornice line, supports a lantern.

A right, rather than a left, turn onto Tremont leads first to **Concord Square** and then to **Rutland Square**, two more handsome residential squares. Further down Tremont Street, on the right, the square-campanile red-brick Romanesque revival tower of the **Church of the Lord Jesus Christ of the Apostolic**

Map on page 212

Faith beckons. It is now part of the very successful **Villa Victoria Housing Project**, most of whose inhabitants are Puerto Rican and most of whose architecture is somewhat at odds with the rest of the South End.

If, at the Cyclorama, instead of continuing your explorations of the South End you had turned left onto Berkeley Street, proceeded for 400 yards and then turned right onto Columbus Avenue and proceeded a further 200 yards, you would have arrived at Bay Village, a tiny, delightful oasis which makes the South Slope of Beacon Hill look like a bustling metropolis.

(An alternative way to enter this haven is from the intersection of Columbus, Arlington and Stuart streets, which is dominated by a massive rusticated granite Italian Renaissance fortress whose hexagonal tower is a landmark. This building, now the **Plaza Castle 9**, was once the armory of the First Corps of Cadets.)

The name Bay Village is a relatively modern one, conjured up by real-estate developers.

Village in a city

Bay Village 10, where Edgar Allan Poe once lived, has been described as Beacon Hill on mud-flats. It was developed in the 1820s when the Back Bay was still a tidal basin and a quarter of a century would elapse before the first buildings appeared in the South End. Today, the neighborhood, consisting of half a dozen short, gas-lit streets lined by uniform red-brick rowhouses, still has a 19th-century ambience. Many of the painters, housewrights and cabinet makers who created the grand homes on Beacon Hill built and lived in these, their much more modest homes, in Bay Village, and in recent decades a number of these houses have been sensitively renovated by people who can't quite afford a Beacon Hill property.

Enter the Village by **Piedmont Street**, which faces the Plaza Castle's Arlington Street facade. There's nothing too attractive here, but at Number 52 stood the

BELOW: many artists live in the South End.
RIGHT: row after row of brownstones.

"Napoleon Club," reputed to be America's first gay bar. It owes its location to the fact that Bay Village is close to the city's Theater District and, during Prohibiton, was filled with speakeasies. Piedmont Street is soon crossed by **Church Street** – its church is long since gone – which is the start of a more tranquil area.

A half-block down Piedmont is a plaque in the sidewalk commemorating one of Boston's – and America's – worst disasters. Here stood the **Coconut Grove** nightclub where on the evening of November 28, 1942, 492 people died when a fire spread throughout the building. The tragedy brought about major fire prevention laws requiring sprinklers, clearly marked exits and doors that open outward in all public buildings.

Turn right onto Church Street and, proceeding along it, wander into Winchester and Melrose streets, before arriving at **Fayette Street**, the oldest street in the district. It is all quite lovely, with immaculate window-boxes filled with colorful blooms. At the end of Fayette Street is **Bay Street**, Boston's shortest street; it contains just one house – the smallest house in Boston.

Incidentally, the streets you tread and the homes you admire were originally 12–18 ft (3.7–5.5 meters) lower. When Back Bay was filled in, the Bay Village (then called the Church Street district) flooded and, in a mammoth undertaking, about 500 buildings were raised. From Fayette Street, turn onto Arlington Street and resume the hurly-burly of life in Boston. ❏

THE CHARLES RIVER

There's the expected rowing and sailing, of course, but by the river you can also find the astonishing Museum of Science and the Hatch Shell, home to the Boston Pops

Nature, with a hefty nudge from man, has blessed Boston with the Charles River – or, more specifically, the **Charles River Basin**, which stretches upstream for about 9 miles (14 km) from the mouth of the river. The basin, whose width is between 200 and 2,000 ft (60–600 meters) and which covers a moderately sinuous course, has been designated as a National Historic Civil Engineering Landmark and is on the National Register of Historic Places.

This basin, especially that part in the heart of the city, provides pleasure both on the water and on the banks, especially the south bank. In fall and spring, skiffs and larger shells skim the surface, pursued by launches from which demanding coaches shout their exhortations. Boston crews, usually collegiate, invariably win medals at both national and international level; indeed, the entire Harvard eight who rowed on these waters represented the US at the 1968 Olympics.

In winter, the basin typically freezes over – not reliably enough, unfortunately, to permit safe skating, though the banks become a great cross-country ski path. For most of the year dozens of sailboats from several sailing clubs, again mostly collegiate, tack to and fro and give a joyous appearance to the scene. And then there are marinas, home to elegant white power-boats. The scene was not always such: before the Charles River Basin came into existence in 1908, the stench from tidal mud flats filled the air.

Not only does the Charles, christened by the 15-year-old Prince Charles who, 10 years later in 1625, became Charles I of England, bring enormous pleasure to Bostonians and to visitors but it has also played an important role in history. Paul Revere rowed across its waters before taking to horse, the U.S.S. *Constitution* was built at its mouth and the first telephone conversation in the world spanned the river.

The estuary

Start a river safari at the **Charlestown Bridge** at the mouth of the river. A forerunner of this bridge was the very first bridge across the river, which opened 11 years to the day after the Battle of Bunker Hill with mighty cannon salutes and shouts of:

> *You Charlestown pigs,*
> *Put on your wigs,*
> *And come over to Boston town.*

The Bridge, with an enormous span of 1,053 ft (321 meters) and a width of 423 ft (129 meters), was considered the greatest feat of engineering ever undertaken in America. Within 15 years a further three privately funded bridges had firmly linked Boston to the mainland; until then, the city had been a peninsula with something of the character of a tight little island.

Immediately upstream from the Charlestown Bridge is the **New Charles River Dam ❶**, which controls

PRECEDING PAGES: a tranquil moment at the Charles River Basin. **LEFT:** July 4 fireworks at a Hatch Shell concert. **BELOW:** watching the rowing.

*An exhibit in the
Museum of Science.*

BELOW:
a dinosaur in the
Museum of Science.

the water level in the river basin. An observation window overlooks three locks. The two for pleasure boats can be extremely busy, with more than 1,000 craft passing through in a day; only a rare commercial vessel ventures into the basin via the third lock. Just beyond this, on the Cambridge (north) side, is the **Charlesgate Yacht Club**, one of four power-boat marinas on the river.

A little further upstream, atop an older dam, is the **Museum of Science ❷** (Sat–Thur 9am–5pm, Fri 9am–9pm; extended evening hours Sat–Thur in July and Aug; tel: 723-2500). It began life in 1830 as the Boston Society of Natural History and moved here in 1951. Even before entering the museum, observe the garden bordered by rock samples, some quite beautiful, from throughout the world. These include pieces from the Giant's Causeway in Northern Ireland, the Rock of Gibraltar and Mont Blanc. The world-class museum is very much a hands-on affair and contains hundreds of exhibits in six major fields: astronomy, computing, energy, anthropology, industry and nature. Visitors can determine their weight on the moon, listen to a transparent talking woman, see bolts of lightning, watch chickens hatching, and much, much more. Computing exhibits include the Virtual Fish Tank, a computer-simulated model, and the Best Software for Kids Gallery. An exhibit tracing the computer revolution from the 1940s into the future is planned.

The **Hayden Planetarium's ❸** projector and multi-image system offer excellent programs on astronomical discoveries, plus exciting laser light shows incorporating computer animation.

Those who suffer from motion sickness may want to skip the **Mugar Omni Theater**, where wrap-around state-of-the-art movies are projected onto a 76-ft (23-meter) high domed screen, with sound blasting from 84 speakers; but for the strong of stomach it's well worth a visit. There are late shows at weekends.

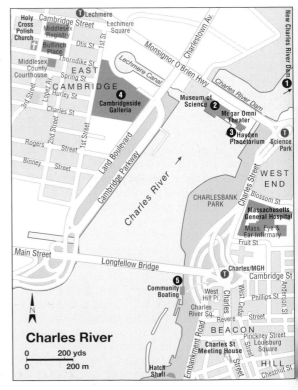

Charles River

0   200 yds

0   200 m

A further half-mile upstream is the **Longfellow Bridge**, completed in 1900 and the oldest and most ornate bridge across the river. Its four readily recognizable towers have led to the nickname **Salt and Pepper Bridge**. Originally called the Cambridge Bridge, it was given its present name in honor of Henry Wadsworth Longfellow, who used it when going to visit his friends on Beacon Hill. The surroundings have been enhanced by the cleaning and greening of the basin, the activity of white wings and the oft-colorful garb of oarspeople.

At the northwest corner of the bridge the **Lechmere Canal** runs for about 200 yards to end in a circular basin at whose center is a soaring fountain. Bordering this basin is **Cambridgeside Galleria ❹**, an upscale shopping mall. River boats leave from here for short cruises on the Charles.

The river basin

Tucked into the southwest corner of the bridge is the clubhouse of **Community Boating ❺**, which is believed to organize the world's oldest and largest public sailing program. Many an Olympic and America's Cup sailor first put to sea here on the embankment of the Charles River.

However, not all the scudding white sails of traditional center-boards and psychedelic sails of wind-surfers have set off from the Community Boating quay. Some belong to the Massachusetts Institute of Technology Sailing Club whose clubhouse is somewhat upriver and across from the Community Boating. Others belong to the Emerson College Sailing Club, whose headquarters building is just a few yards upstream from the Community Boating quay.

Immediately beyond this is the boathouse of the **Union Boat Club**, founded in 1851 by gentlemen interested in rowing who were also admirers of Daniel

Map on page 222

TIP

If you feel inclined to join the scullers, Charles River Canoe & Kayak (617-965 5110) rents single and two-person kayaks. Duck Tours (617-723 3825) offers a less strenuous ride on the river in military-surplus amphibious vehicles.

BELOW: the Salt and Pepper Bridge.

*Bust of Arthur
Fiedler near the
Hatch Shell.*

BELOW: Community
Boating close to
the Hatch Shell.

Webster's *Union Forever* speeches. In order to maintain the integrity of the riparian banks, they built their clubhouse, not on the river, but diagonally across Embankment Road, at the foot of Chestnut Street.

Nowhere are the river banks as busy as here on the Esplanade. Many come to sun, to laze or to feed the ducks while others, more energetic, jog, cycle or roller-skate. Here, too, is the **Hatch Shell** which is home to the Pops and other concerts during summer. Near the Shell is a large bust of Arthur Fiedler (1894–1979), who founded the Boston Sinfonietta in 1924 and went on to conduct the Boston Pops Orchestra for 49 years from 1930 until his death. The atmosphere is informal: many concertgoers come equipped with blanket and picnic basket. Immediately south of the river an idyllic lagoon, spanned by four small arched stone bridges, stretches for about a mile.

Seeing Boston at its best

The most lively part of the Esplanade is demarcated at its western end by the **Harvard Bridge**, also called the **Massachusetts Avenue Bridge** but referred to, more often than not, as the **MIT Bridge** because its northern end leads directly to that institute's campus. This is where the river is at its widest. Look back (eastward) from here: the vista is immense – a sheer joy to behold. To the left is the MIT campus; to the right is the Back Bay and then Beacon Hill with the glistening dome of the State House and behind that the downtown skyscrapers. And the river is vibrant with sailing boats and shells. This is Boston at its very best. Is this vista superior to that looking west from Longfellow Bridge? It's an open question.

Casual strollers practically take their life in their hands on crossing the MIT bridge, for it invariably teems with a seemingly infinite number of joggers, bikers and bladers, all looking very competitive. No question as to the length of the bridge – it is painted on the sidewalk: 364.4 smoots + one ear. Oliver R. Smoot, a 1958 Lambda Chi Alpha pledge at MIT, was required to measure the length of the bridge using himself as a yardstick. Every spring and fall his successors refresh the information. He must have been rather small: a *smoot* works out at about 62 inches (158 cm).

Proceed upstream past the **Boston University**, sometimes called the **Cottage Farm Bridge**, then the graceful curving red-brick **John W. Weeks** pedestrian bridge. Harvard University buildings now line both grassy shores, and the next bridge, the **Larz Anderson**, links the college buildings with the playing fields and the Business School as well as joining Cambridge to the suburbs of Allston and Brighton. The Larz Anderson replaced an older bridge which became so congested at football games that it prompted the *Harvard Lampoon* to parody Longfellow's *The Bridge*: "I stood on the bridge at midnight/I had left the field at five."

Beyond Harvard, the river now twists through a pleasant landscape, passing boathouses and marinas, playgrounds and parks. At Christian A. Herter Park, the **Publick Theatre** has been putting on low-cost professional productions in summer – Shakespeare, Gilbert and Sullivan *et al* – for a quarter of a century in a charming little open-air amphitheater. The suburb of **Watertown** is about 3 miles farther up, across the river. ❑

Head of The Charles Regatta

Fragile wooden craft skim the surface of the water, some with a single oarsperson, others with several occupants. Tens of thousands of spectators throng the river banks while others prefer the vantage point provided by half a dozen bridges. The rich fall colors of the leaves on the trees bordering the river are complemented, rather than shamed, by the vivid singlets worn by some of the crews and the brilliant colors of their oar blades.

This is the scene at the Head of the Charles regatta, the world's largest one-day regatta for oarspeople in the world, held on the second to last Sunday in October. In an era when prize money in sport has reached astronomical proportions, the Head of the Charles Regatta – colloquially "The Head" – is a breath of fresh air. There is no prize money: participants pay their own expenses and no one really cares – and many spectators do not even know – who wins. That insistent American maxim that winning is all that counts is abandoned, at least for one day.

The first regatta was held in 1965. Since then the event has grown until now more than 4,000 oarsmen and women and almost 1,000 boats appear. Invariably, most participants are from New England, but Canada is always well represented. Also, each year sees increasing numbers of crews from California and Texas and foreign crews from Peru and Puerto Rico, Australia and the Soviet Union, plus England, France and Switzerland.

But exactly what is a head of the river race? It works like this: competing boats set off one after the other, at brief intervals – rather than together – and are timed over the length of the course. In other words, a head of the river race is a procession of boats. On the Charles, boats start at intervals of 15–20 seconds and all timing is electronic. It is difficult for spectators to determine which boat is in the lead but there are moments of intense excitement when a crew, faster than that ahead of it, tries to pass another shell – and sometimes succeeds.

The river is narrow and tortuous over part of the 3-mile (5-km) course and crews that hog the center of the channel can prevent a faster boat from overtaking them. At all but the last of the six bridges the rules compel crews to use the center span of the bridge: at the last bridge, however, crews may take either the center or starboard arch. But the starboard channel is narrow, and, unless a sharp turn to port is made under the arch, the crew will find themselves aground.

All are catered for at "The Head." Octagenarians and Olympians compete, as do men and women, grandparents and grandchildren. An unusual twist is men coxing all-women crews. Eighteen events are held, catering to singles, doubles, fours and eights and for youths, masters, grand-masters and veterans. Between 40 and 80 shells compete in each race.

The racing day is long, starting at 9.30 a.m. and finishing about seven hours later. Barbecues abound and liquor, officially banned, flows. The regatta is a great occasion for reunions of schools, colleges and clubs – of groups who have not met, perhaps, for half a century. As one Olympic coxswain remarked: "This is not a regatta: it's a convocation." ❏

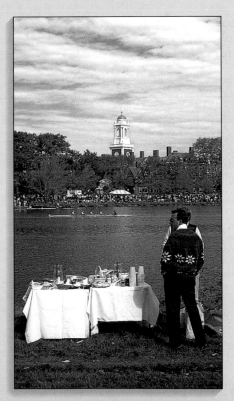

RIGHT: North America's oldest river regatta.

THE EMERALD NECKLACE

*After exploring the parks and boulevards known as the Emerald
Necklace, this chapter goes on to seek out the jewels
to be found in Boston's lesser-known suburbs*

Map
on page
230

The **Emerald Necklace** is not an heirloom but rather a 6-mile (10-km) series of parks and boulevards which begins at the Public Garden *(see page 190)* and ends in Franklin Park in Roxbury. Frederick Law Olmsted, arguably the first landscape architect in America, and renowned as the designer of New York's Central Park, was responsible for the final master plan. Olmsted was a visionary and an idealist who found many kindred spirits who agreed with his theory that city parks should be rustic and informal and thus provide the greatest possible contrast to a brick and stone, man-made urban environment. His designs reflect a deeply thought-out approach to life and a concern for the well-being of his fellow man.

Olmsted had traveled in Europe and as a young man had walked with his brother from Liverpool to London. He found the quiet English countryside with its hedgerows, pastures and splendid trees preferable to the geometric, formal gardens favored by Continental aristocracies. Unpretentious, pastoral landscapes seemed most conducive to soothing the troubled urban spirit and would, he felt, return a sense of the poetry of nature to urban life. They would be the visual equivalents of democracy, whereas fountains, *grandes allées* and monumental sculpture would only reinforce the idea of an elite, breeding resentment and envy.

The landscapes of the Emerald Necklace are man-made and contrived, but the intention was to make them appear as if they had stood for centuries. Trees, including copper beeches, stately elms, great stands of oaks and groves of pine, all of which are indigenous to the area, were planted among native undergrowth and flowering shrubs. Land was graded and sculpted to enhance views and to increase beauty in the same way that "natural" parks were created by "Capability" Brown, the 18th-century English landscape architect.

A Necklace like no other

The best place to begin an exploration of the Emerald Necklace is at the beginning of **Commonwealth Avenue**, Boston's grandest street *(see page 191)* across from the Public Garden. Follow this to Massachusetts Avenue, beyond which is a confluence of over-hanging expressways. Olmsted intended this area to be a dramatic transition from city to country, and at one time it was. To the right the **Charles River** would be visible and to the left the beginning of the marsh-lands of the Fenway, extending beyond H.H. Richardson's puddingstone Boylston Street Bridge. Sadly, these views are no longer possible.

At **Boylston Street Bridge** one looks out over the Fenway through which flows the Muddy River. Here begins the Olmsted-designed portions of the Necklace that exist today. The name "Fenway" evokes images of

PRECEDING PAGES:
the view from
Dorchester Heights
National Monument.
LEFT: fall at the
Arboretum.
BELOW: winter at
the Arboretum.

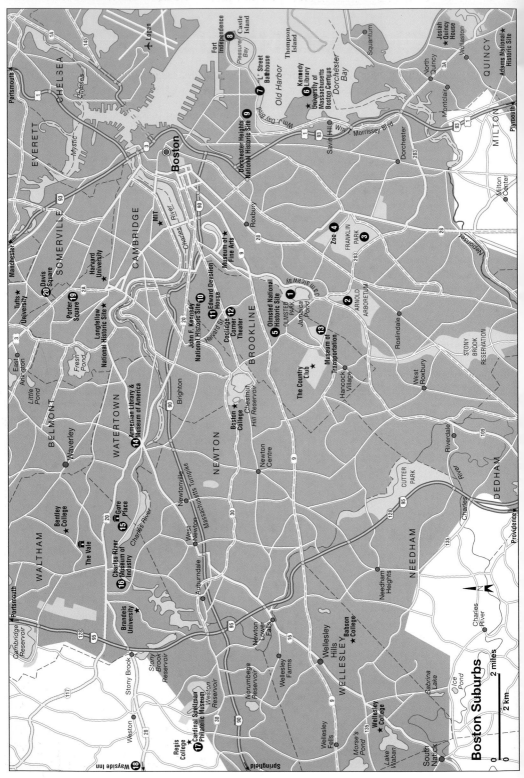

Boston Suburbs

East Anglia in England (a fen is land reclaimed from salt-water marshes for farming) and announces Olmsted's intentions of imitating the English countryside. This area was originally intended to be a salt-water inlet and to provide a nesting ground and habitat for shore birds. However, when the Charles Basin was dammed in 1910, fresh-water reeds took over. Although not part of the original plan, they provide a picturesque rural effect.

The **Fenway Victory Gardens**, dating from World War II, are colorful throughout spring and summer and benefit from friendly competition among their green-thumbed tenders. Further along is the glorious, in summer, **City Rose Garden**. Although the area is not the untamed wilderness for which Olmsted aimed, it does offer visual relief after a day of sightseeing.

Continue along the Riverway, which soon becomes the Jamaicaway, passing on the right **Olmsted Park ❶**. Observe on the left the shamrock shutters at **350 Riverway**, which was once the home of "Hizhonner" James Michael Curley (*see page 39*). This section of the Emerald Necklace retains much of its original character. Soon **Jamaica Pond**, a small jewel ringed by tree-lined paths, is reached. Sailboats and rowboats can be rented at a half-timbered boathouse.

On the Jamaicaway, turn right and after a short distance stop at the **Arnold Arboretum ❷**, designed by Olmsted and a Brookline neighbor, Charles Sprague Sargent. Harvard University maintains the 265 acres (107 hectares), open throughout the year. The Arboretum is home to many rare trees and shrubs, including 300-year-old bonsai trees and the world's largest collection of lilacs which, every June, during Lilac Week, parade their colors.

The Arboretum, built for the study of plants, has always been splendidly maintained. Not so **Franklin Park ❸**, a couple of miles farther along the Arbor-

Landscape architect and noted travel writer Frederick Law Olmsted (1822–1903).

BELOW:
hanging out at the Arnold Arboretum.

JFK at the helm.

BELOW:
John F. Kennedy's
birthplace.
RIGHT: the John F.
Kennedy Library.

way. Olmsted intended this to be the culmination of his chain of parks, a bucolic escape for the city dweller, accessible by streetcar or by foot. (The Orange line terminus of the "T" is within a mile of the park's entrance.)

Originally, flocks of sheep kept the grasses down and Bostonians played lawn tennis and croquet on Franklin Park's large pastures. Urban buildings, other than inconspicuous puddingstone structures for utilitarian purposes, did not exist. Trees were planted in the manner of an English country house park, and early photographs show the realization of Olmsted's ideal. He placed Franklin alongside Central and Prospect Parks in Brooklyn as his favorite and most important designs.

Years of neglect left Franklin Park a hostile wilderness, but recent efforts have returned it to something of its intended beauty. The **Zoo ❹** has been revived and a handsome addition is the African Tropical Forest, a 3-acre (1.2-hectare) environmental building where more than a 100 free-flying birds dart among gorillas, hippos and thousands of plants. Other attractions are the aviary (Birds' World) and the Children's Zoo. The 18-hole public **golf course** has also been refurbished.

Nearby in **Brookline** at 43 Warren Street is the **Olmsted National Historic Site ❺**, where Frederick Law Olmsted had his office and home during and after the construction of the Emerald Necklace. Drawings, plans and papers can be seen. Olmsted did not intend his necklace to stop here. Rather it was meant to cut a broad swathe to the northeast, toward Castle Island in Boston Harbor, 3 miles (5 km) distant along urban rather than rural Columbia Avenue to Columbia Circle.

JFK and the Brownies

Abandon Olmsted temporarily and travel south on Morrissey Boulevard for slightly less than a mile. A left turn past the fortress-like modern **University of**

Map on page 230

Massachusetts Boston Campus, occupying a splendid piece of land jutting into Boston harbor, leads to the striking **Kennedy Library ❻**, designed by I. M. Pei. This contains the president's papers and, of more interest, exhibits covering JFK's life. Personal items on display include the president's desk and the coconut shell on which he carved a cry for help after his PT boat was sunk during World War II. A 30-minute film is part of the tour. *The Ventura*, the president's sailboat, sits behind the library.

Back at Columbia Circle, skirt the waterfront on the **William J. Day Boulevard**, Olmsted's intended Strandway, passing three early 20th-century yacht clubs and the **"L" Street Bathhouse ❼**, used by hardy Brownies for ocean swims year-round. After 3 miles (5 km), you reach **Castle Island**, which since 1891 has been linked to the mainland.

Here stands **Fort Independence ❽**, whose only military involvement was during the last days of the siege of Boston in 1776 when British artillery unsuccessfully bombarded the Americans on Dorchester Heights. A promenade encircles the massive fort, whose antecedents date back to 1634. The park surrounding the fort offers splendid views of the outer harbor and islands; it has a fishing pier jutting into the water and is a popular summer picnic spot. An obelisk commemorates Donald McKay, the East Boston shipbuilder who was renowned for his China trade clippers. The most famous, the *Flying Cloud*, held the record for sailing from New York to San Francisco around the Cape of Good Hope.

Return for about 1 mile to the intersection of East Sixth Avenue and the boulevard. Drive uphill through "Southie" for slightly more than a mile to **South Boston High School**, passing on the way immaculate triple-decker clapboard houses which sometimes fly the Irish tricolor.

Behind the school, in Thomas Park, is the **Dorchester Heights National Historical Site ❾** which marks where, "out of Aladdin's lamp," American engineers built the fortifications that forced the besieged British to depart from Boston in 1776. A 215-ft (65-meter) white marble Georgian Revival style monument (irregular opening hours) commemorates the victory.

Brookline

Southie, although technically part of the City of Boston, is only one of many colorful surrounding communities. Nestled by Boston's outlying neighborhoods to the north and south, **Brookline** asserted its independence from Boston early, and by the 19th century was Boston's wealthiest suburban enclave. Several interesting sites may be visited here. The heart of Brookline is **Coolidge Corner**, easily reached by a short ride on the Green line "T." A 10-minute walk northwest on Harvard Street takes one to **Beals Street** where at Number 83 is the **John F. Kennedy National Historic Site ❿**, birthplace of the president. His parents lived in this modest, two-story house from 1914 to 1921, but a growing family resulted in a move to larger quarters.

Closer to Coolidge Corner on Harvard Street is the tiny **Edward Devotion House ⓫** built in 1680 which sits on the grounds of the Devotion School. At the center of Coolidge Corner is the beloved **Coolidge Corner Theater ⓬**, a 1930s Art Deco movie house

TIP

Trips west on the Green Line once it travels above ground are free. Trips east (intown) are standard fare.

BELOW: Dorchester Heights National Monument.

TIP

To go from the center of Brookline (Coolidge Corner) to Harvard Square, avoid going into Boston by taking the number 66 bus – a 30-minute trip.

saved from the wrecking ball by its devoted fans. Surrounding the theater are a number of smart shops and exotic restaurants.

Away from the bustle of Coolidge Corner, the **Museum of Transportation** at 15 Newton Street has a superb collection of early automobiles housed in the carriage house of the former estate of the diplomat Larz Anderson. An excellent view of the Boston skyline is offered from the hilltop behind the museum. Across the road is *the* **Country Club**, founded in 1881 and the forerunner of hundreds of such establishments throughout the nation.

Watertown

North of Brookline on the other side of the Charles is **Watertown**. Near California Street one can see a ladder used by herring returning from the open sea to spawn in sheltered waters. Just west of Watertown Square is the small but interesting **Armenian Library and Museum of America**, which houses a diverse collection of Armenian textiles, ceramics, coins and religious art. Continue on Route 20 for 2 miles (3 km) and then turn left on Gore Street to reach **Gore Place**. This 22-room, red-brick mansion was designed by Rebecca Payne Gore – one of the first women to design a great home – and built in 1805 by her husband, Christopher Gore, after they had returned from Europe, where Mrs Gore had obtained many ideas from the French architect J-G. Legrand. Mrs Gore enjoyed her comforts, and the home has some of America's first flush toilets and showers. A later innovation is the flying staircase that spirals three full flights upwards.

The house, with its oval rooms and stunning wallpaper, was originally a country estate for the Gores, but in later years they occupied it more frequently and were known to invite 450 people for breakfast. Today, it is a treasure trove of early 19th-century European and American decorative arts; about 100 items, including paintings by Trumbull and Sargent, belonged to the Gores. The grounds, which run down to the river, cover an area of 40 acres (16 hectares).

On leaving Gore Place, turn right and then immediately left onto Route 20. After about 2 miles (3 km), turn right onto **Lyman Street** for a visit to the grounds of the Lyman House, **The Vale** (1793). This long, low house (by appointment only, tel: 617-893 7232) was greatly altered in 1882, and all that remains of the original is the oval salon and ballroom. The Vale is renowned for its landscape (open to the public), based on broad vistas dotted with clumps of trees and contains three 19th-century greenhouses, in which grow a grapevine from London's Hampton Court and a century-old camellia tree.

Charles River Museum of Industry

Back on Route 20, pass through the center of Waltham and immediately turn left on Moody Street and continue until the river. Here is the **Charles River Museum of Industry**, an Historic Landmark. The Boston Manufacturing Company textile mill, in whose power plant the museum is located, was a significant site in the Industrial Revolution. It was the first integrated textile mill – raw material went in one end and the finished product came out the other – and was the site of the first known strike in American industry when the company announced a retroactive pay cut. The museum not only

BELOW: studying outside Fort Independence at Castle Island.

Map on page 230

tells the story of the mill but also exhibits products such as precision metal-working instruments, watches, bicycles and automobiles – aficionados will love the Stanley Steamer – which were manufactured in and around Waltham.

Continue south on Moody Street, which becomes Lexington and, after about 2 miles (3 km), turn right on Commonwealth Avenue. This route skirts the **Lakes District** where the Charles, dammed at the mill, meanders among islands and peninsulas and is beautified by lily ponds. Until the 1950s this was the site of two extremely popular recreation areas. Two steamboats sailed on the river, and one would see literally thousands of canoes in this region.

Philatelists will continue from the boathouse on Route 30 West for nearly 3 miles (5 km) and then turn right onto Wellesley Street to reach **Regis College.** Ignore the main entrance and enter at the sign Postal Museum to reach the **Cardinal Spellman Philatelic Museum ⓱**, the only museum in the country custom-built for the display of stamps. The nucleus of the collection – which, with 300,000 items, is one of the world's largest – was started by Cardinal Spellman. To this have been added the Dwight D. Eisenhower collection and Papal States stamps.

Mills were a major employer in the 19th century.

Longfellow's Wayside Inn

On leaving the college, turn left and, after a couple of miles, regain Route 20. Here, turn left and after 10 miles (16 km) – 20 miles (32 km) from Boston – and, beyond the small town of **Sudbury**, arrive at Longfellow's **Wayside Inn ⓰** which, although not on the river, stands in a bucolic setting. It claims to be the country's oldest operating inn. Known as John How's Black Horse when built in 1661, the tavern became inexorably linked with Henry Wadsworth Longfellow when *Tales of a Wayside Inn* appeared in 1863. The inn, whose rooms can be explored, still offers "Food, Drink and Lodging for Man, Woman and Beast." It was restored by motor mogul Henry Ford in the 1920s. In its grounds stand the **Red Schoolhouse** supposedly attended by Mary and her little lamb, and a working reproduction of an **18th-century gristmill**.

BELOW: the gristmill at Longfellow's Wayside Inn.

Refugees from Harvard Square

Returning to some of Boston's inner rings, it's worth noting some recent changes just north of Harvard Square. The extension of the Red line of the "T" north of Harvard Square in the early 1980s sparked life into fairly undistinguished neighborhoods. Cambridge's **Porter Square ⓳** became a reasonable alternative to more expensive housing closer to Harvard. Even more dramatic changes occurred in **Somerville**. In the early 20th century Somerville was one of Boston's industrial spokes, with a major railroad yard, meat-packing houses, bakeries and machine shops. As these industries died out, students from nearby campuses flocked here.

Later the Red line extension acted like an urban blood transfusion with **Davis Square ⓴** now one of the live-liest places around Boston. Here are unusual and award-winning restaurants, funky coffee houses, alternative bookstores and used CD shops, many driven out of Harvard Square by high rents. Luckily Somerville retains much of its past identity, and it is not unusual to find blue-collar families, Harvard grad students and young Boston money managers living side-by-side.❏

CAMBRIDGE

Being as old as Boston, the former New Towne has its share of history and cemeteries. But these days it's a one-industry town – and the industry is education

Map on page 240

Cambridge, separated from Boston by the Charles River and linked to it by half a dozen bridges, was founded in the same year as Boston. Originally called New Towne, it was the Bay Colony's first capital. It is still a city in its own right: its population of more than 100,000 makes it the second largest city in Massachusetts. Each fall this number is swollen by about 25 percent by students attending Harvard University or Massachusetts Institute of Technology (MIT), both of which also attract many tourists to the city.

Harvard Square, the focal point of Cambridge for the visitor, can be reached readily from Boston on the Red line of the "T". The square and its immediate surroundings have many restaurants and stores, including a notable concentration of bookshops. Papers from throughout the world can be purchased at the large kiosk in the middle of the square.

A tall, abstract, granite sculpture entitled *Omphalos* stands next to the kiosk. If the sculpture had been commissioned by Harvard rather than by the Metropolitan Transport Authority, one would have cried hubris, knowing that it was the intent of the sculptor's patron to indicate that Cambridge and not Delphi was the navel of the world. In the square pierced and tattooed skateboarders mingle with undergraduates and tourists, and music fills the air as street musicians play at every corner. (There are more than four because the square is amorphous.)

PRECEDING PAGES: Widener Memorial Room at Harvard's Widener Library. **LEFT:** Harvard Yard. **BELOW:** Harvard Square.

Colonial memories

Cambridge has a long and proud colonial history which is as rewarding as exploring the Harvard campus. Head north from the square on **Massachusetts Avenue**, leaving Harvard College to the right and immediately pass on the left the **First Unitarian Church ❶** where "Fair Harvard" was sung for the very first time on the occasion of the college's 200th anniversary.

Next to the First Unitarian Church is the **Old Burying Ground,** known as "God's Acre," in which Harvard's first eight presidents are interred, as well as 19th-century American painter Washington Allston. Several veterans of the Revolution, including two black soldiers, also lie here. Bear left onto **Garden Street** where, on the left, is **Christ Church ❷**, Cambridge's oldest house of worship (1761), which fulfilled the congregants' request to Peter Harrison, America's first architect (Harrison also designed Boston's King's Chapel), for "no steeple, only a tower with a belfry." When most of the Tory congregation fled in 1774, the church was used as a barracks and the organ pipes were melted down for bullets. A bullet hole in the vestibule is said to be from the rifle of a Redcoat as he marched toward Lexington. The

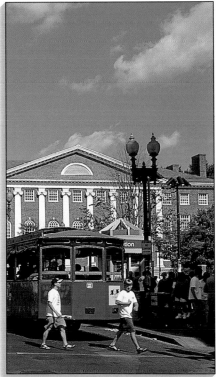

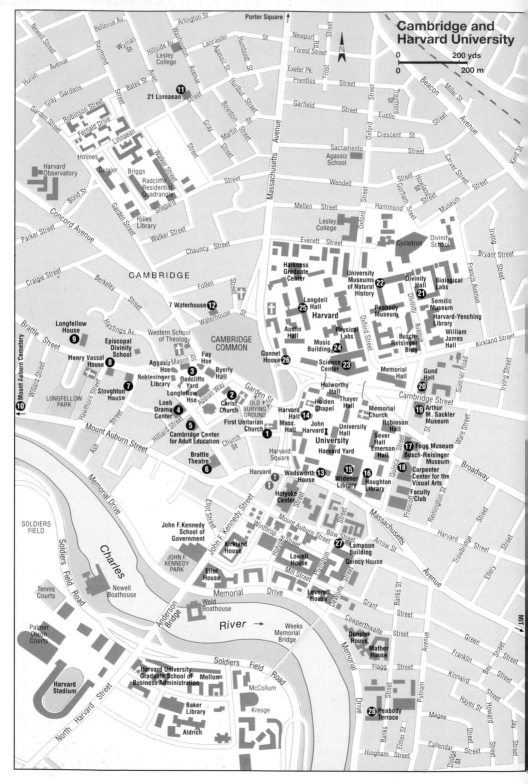

Cambridge and Harvard University

Porter Square

N

0   200 yds
0   200 m

Bellevue Av.
Arlington St
Newport Street
Forest Street
Exeter Pk
Prentiss
Garfield Street
Beacon Street
Miller St
Traymore
Eustis
Wyman St
Washington Avenue
Lancaster St
Agassiz St
Humboldt St
Frost Street
Street

Gray Gardens
Raymond Street
Hillside Av.
Lesley College
Avon St
Bates Av.
Bowdoin Street
Hurlbut Street
Martin Street
Gray Street

11 21 Linnaean

Robinson Street
Fernald Drive
Garden Street
Linnaean Street
Walker Street
Holmes
Currier
Briggs
Radcliffe Residential Quadrangle
Shepard
Hilles Library
Walker Street

Harvard Observatory
Bond St
Concord Avenue
Parker Street
Garden Street
Chauncy Street

Sacramento Street
Agassiz School
Wendell Street
Mellen Street
Oxford Street
Crescent St
Carver Street
Howard St
Gorham St
Hammond Street
Museum
Irving Street
Bryant Street
Francis Avenue

Massachusetts Avenue

Lesley College
Everett Street
Cyclotron
Divinity School

Craigie Street
Berkeley Street
Follen Street
Waterhouse St

CAMBRIDGE

12 7 Waterhouse

Harkness Graduate Center
University Museums of Natural History **22**
Divinity Hall **21**
Biological Labs

Brattle Street
Hastings Av.
Longfellow House **9**
Western School of Theology

Langdell Hall
25 Harvard
Peabody Museum
Divinity Avenue
Semitic Museum
Harvard-Yenching Library
William James Hall
Oxford Street
Kirkland Street

Episcopal Divinity School
Henry Vassal House **8**
Mason St
Fay Hse
Austin Hall
Physical Labs
Busch Reisinger Bldg
Gund Hall **20**

CAMBRIDGE COMMON
Agassiz Hse
Schlesinger Library
Radcliffe Yard
Longfellow Hse
Byerly Hall
Music Building **24**
Memorial Hall
Cambridge Street

Willard St
Hawthorn Street
7
Stoughton House
LONGFELLOW PARK
Loeb Drama Center **4**
5
Appian Way
Christ Church **2**
Garden St
OLD BURYING GROUND
Gannet House **26**
Science Center **23**
Holworthy Hall
Holden Chapel
Thayer Hall
Arthur M. Sackler Museum **19**

10
Ash Street
Hilliard Street
First Unitarian Church
Cambridge Center for Adult Education
Harvard Hall
Mass. Hall **14**
John Harvard
University Hall
Memorial Church
Robinson Hall
Sever Hall
Emerson Hall
Fogg Museum **17**
Busch-Reisinger Museum

Mount Auburn Street
Church St
University
1
University Yard
Brattle Theatre **6**
Harvard Square
18
Carpenter Center for the Visual Arts
Faculty Club
Broadway

Memorial Drive
Harvard **i**
Wadsworth House **13**
Widener Library **15**
16
Houghton Library
Prescott St
Remington St
Harvard Street

SOLDIERS FIELD
Holyoke Center
Winthrop Street
Mount Auburn Street
Bow Street
Arrow St

Charles
Soldiers Field Road
John F. Kennedy School of Government
Kirkland House
Eliot Street
John F. Kennedy Street
Holyoke Street
Plympton St
DeWolfe Street
Lampoon Building **27**
Lowell House
Quincy House
Massachusetts Avenue
Trowbridge Street
Ellery Street

Tennis Courts
JOHN F. KENNEDY PARK
Newell Boathouse
Eliot House
Weld Boathouse
Mill Street
Leverett House
Grant Street
Banks St
Green Street
Franklin Street

Palmer Dixon Courts
Anderson Bridge
Memorial Drive
River →
Weeks Memorial Bridge
Cowperthwaite Street
Dunster House
Mather House
Flagg Street
MIT

Harvard Stadium
North Harvard Street
Soldiers Field Road
Harvard University Graduate School of Business Administration
Mellon
McCollum
Memorial Drive
Banks Street
Elmer St
Putnam Avenue
Hayes St
Magee
Callendar Street

Baker Library
Kresge
Aldrich
28 Peabody Terrace
Hingham Street
Dodge Street
Jay Street

church was reopened on New Year's Eve, 1775, when George and Martha Washington attended worship.

Immediately across the road from Christ Church is a traffic island with a granite lectern topped by a bronze plaque honoring **William Dawes**, the other messenger sent to warn the patriots of the coming of the British. Footprints of his galloping horse are simulated in brass on the pavement.

North of this is **Cambridge Common**, a veritable treasure trove of markers, memorials and monuments and a place inexorably associated with George Washington, for it was here on July 4, 1775, that he assumed command of the Continental Army. Make for the flagpole and the cluster of three cannons, abandoned when the British left Boston on March 17, 1776, placed about cobblestones on the west side of the Common. A bronze relief shows Washington on horseback under an elm tree, assuming command. On the reverse side is the text of Washington's orders given here on July 4, 1775, the Congressional document that officially melded the colonial militias into a unified Continental Army. A smaller stone, adjacent to an elm which is enclosed by an iron fence, commemorates Washington's famous elm, cut down in 1923 because it impeded traffic.

Education for women

Cross Garden Street and enter the old **Radcliffe Yard** ❸, where this renowned women's college began life in 1879. Until recent years, women who attended Harvard were required to apply to Radcliffe, but in 1999 Radcliffe College as such was fully integrated with Harvard, with the Radcliffe name retained by the Harvard operated research center. To the right and left are **Byerly Hall** and **Fay House**. The latter, a Federal-style building from 1806, is the oldest structure in the Yard and once housed the entire college apart from student rooms. Byerly, with its innumerable chimneys, originally was a warren of science laboratories and was described as having "the most modern equipment for the study of chemistry, physics and astronomy."

Across the Yard is striking **Aggasiz House** with its Ionic portico. Named after the founder of Radcliffe, it contains a 350-seat theater where Eugene O'Neill's first play opened and failed and where Jack Lemmon got his start. On either side are the **Radcliffe Gymnasium** and the **Schlesinger Library**. The **Murray Research Center**, which studies the impact of social changes on lives, especially those of women, now occupies the ground floor of the gymnasium. Upstairs is the **Radcliffe Dance Center**. The Schlesinger Library has an outstanding collection of literature on the history of women in America and is the country's top research center devoted to women's studies. The library, open to the public, includes a Culinary Collection with more than 2,300 cookbooks.

Buckingham House and **Putnam House**, the two intrusive, low, grey, clapboard buildings in the Yard – or is it really the brick buildings which are intrusive? – are respectively a Child Care Center and a Career Services Office. On the other side of the Yard is **Longfellow House**, a long red-brick neo-Georgian affair with paired entrances framed by pilasters. It houses the **Graduate School of Education**.

Map on page 240

An early settler, John Bridge (1578–1665), ran the first public school in Cambridge.

BELOW: students with benefactor John Harvard.

Loeb Drama Center.

Tory Row

Exit from Radcliffe Yard onto **Brattle Street**, once known as Tory Row because in the 18th century most of its houses were owned by loyalists. It was also called Church Row, because its residents both built and worshipped at Christ's Church.

A left turn and a 300-yard stroll through the madding crowd and the hustle and bustle of commerce to Brattle Square might cast some doubt that this is the most prestigious street in Cambridge, famous for both history and architecture, but a right turn and a walk of about three-quarters of a mile fully justifies these claims. Here, all the hubbub is gone and the leafy, tranquil street is lined by splendid large clapboard houses fronted by elegant porticoes, most from the 19th century but some from the 18th, each the same yet different and each standing in its own spacious grounds. Many bear blue plaques commemorating the greats who have lived in them.

Stroll first to **Brattle Square**. En route, on the right stands Harvard's handsome, modern **Loeb Drama Center ❹**. Nearby, an outdoor café fronts **No. 56**, a simple two-story, hip-roofed, Federal-style building, home to Longfellow's "village blacksmith." But don't search for the chestnut tree under which Longfellow met Dexter Pratt: it suffered the fate of Washington's elm and was chopped down in 1870 when Brattle Street was widened.

Further along, at **No. 42**, stands the first of the famous mansions which line the length of the street. Aside from the projecting entrance this three-story gambrel-roofed clapboard house is true to its 1727 origins. It was built by the future Major General William Brattle, doctor, lawyer and minister, commander of all the militia of the province and one of the wealthiest men in

Cambridge. He fled to England in 1774. The mansion is now the **Cambridge Center for Adult Education ❺**.

Next door is the **Brattle Theatre ❻** where you might find Bogie and Bergman playing in *Casablanca*, the great Cambridge evergreen. Paul Robeson and T.S. Eliot trod the theater's boards, as did Jessica Tandy and Hume Cronyn, Hermione Gingold and Zero Mostel. In 1953 it began showing foreign film classics.

Return along Brattle Street past Radcliffe Yard. **Stoughton House ❼**, the dark building on the left at No. 90, was designed by H.H. Richardson of Boston's Trinity Church fame, and is renowned as one of the first and best examples of domestic American shingle style.

Next door at No. 94 stands the 20-room **Henry Vassal House ❽**, originally built in the 17th century; its eponymous owner gambled away his fortune. It was medical headquarters for the first American Army during the Revolution.

Across the road is the red puddingstone **Episcopal Divinity School**, whose faculty house (No. 101) with its curved central bay has all the graces of an English Regency villa. And so to the **Longfellow House ❾** (No. 105), a yellow clapboard building which is the most historic house on Tory Row. The mansion, started in 1759, originally stood amid 116 acres (47 hectares); it was one of seven Tory estates occupying the area between Brattle Square and Elmwood Avenue whose lands stretched down to the river. The house was abandoned by its owner, John Vassal Jr, in 1774, when patriots made life difficult for loyalists in Cambridge, and it was George Washington's headquarters for nine months during the siege of Boston.

Longfellow first arrived here as a lodger in 1837. After receiving the house as a wedding gift from his father-in-law, he remained until 1882. Tragically, his young wife Fanny was fatally burned here in 1861. The gardens, old carriage house and

Map on page 240

Henry Wadsworth Longfellow (1807–82) devoted his life to writing after he retired in 1854 from teaching at Harvard. His myth-creating poems include "The Village Blacksmith," "The Wreck of the Hesperus" and " The Song of Hiawatha." His best-known later work, "Tales of a Wayside Inn," was published in 1863.

BELOW: the Longfellow House on Brattle Street.

BELOW: Mount Auburn Cemetery.

the house – virtually as it was in Longfellow's time, with myriad memorabilia including a chair made from the "spreading chestnut tree" – can be visited.

Across the street is **Longfellow Park**, through which the poet would walk on his way to bathe in the river. **The Mormon Center** occupies the northeast corner of the park; the **Friends Meeting House** stands on the west side. Continue on Brattle Street, passing the large white-brick **Holy Trinity Armenian Church** with its strong eastern influence, and many distinguished homes. These include the houses (Nos. 113, 115) which Longfellow built for his two daughters, and the **Lee-Nichols House** (No. 159), built in the 1680s and now owned by the **Cambridge Historical Society** (open to the public on occasion).

Then, across **Kennedy Road** (named after a Cambridge cookie manufacturer and not the President), there is **No. 163**, former home of Edwin Land, inventor of the Polaroid camera, and **No. 165**, built in 1870 by John Bartlett, the Cambridge bookseller with whose "Quotations" the reader is undoubtedly familiar.

Turn left onto short **Elmwood Avenue** and proceed to the end, where stands **No. 33**, a splendid three-story Georgian affair from 1767. It was used as a hospital for Americans during the Revolutionary War and has since been occupied by an illustrious line of owners. Today, it is owned by Harvard and occupied by its president.

Intrepid explorers may want to cross the major intersection with Fresh Pond Parkway and arrive at **Mount Auburn Street**, where a plaque announces: "Here at the river's edge the settlers of Watertown led by Sir Richard Saltonstall landed in June 1630. Later the spot became known as Gerry's Landing for Elbridge Gerry, signatory of the Declaration of Independence and Governor of Massachusetts who lived in Elmwood nearby." (It was he who gave his name to the word "gerrymandering.")

Mount Auburn Cemetery

Continue west along Mount Auburn Street for about 600 yards to the main entrance to the **Mount Auburn Cemetery ⑩**. This bucolic Westminster, whose grounds are planted with a glorious collection of foreign and native trees and shrubs, is America's oldest (consecrated 1831) and most beautiful garden cemetery. Among more than 70,000 people interred here are Charles Bulfinch, Winslow Homer, Oliver Wendell Holmes, Henry Longfellow and Mary Baker Eddy (whose tomb is rumored to contain a telephone with an unlisted number). In recent years novelist Bernard Malamud, inventor Edward Land and architect and engineer R. Buckminster Fuller have all been laid to rest here. Fuller's grave displays an image of his geodesic dome and the cryptic epitaph, "Call me trimtab" and lies near his relative, American 19th-century transcendentalist Margaret Fuller. Although most tombs in this non-sectarian cemetery are small and modest, others are grand and the cemetery has been a showpiece of American funerary art for the past 150 years.

A climb to the top of the **George Washington Tower** situated at the cemetery's center affords wonderful views of the surrounding landscape.

One can either return to Harvard Square by walking or taking a bus along Mount Auburn Street or explore some other sights in the north part of Cambridge.

Walking back toward Harvard Square on Brattle Street take Craigie Street to Garden Street and stroll northward for about 600 yards to the old **Radcliffe Residential Quadrangle**, a pleasant affair of neo-Georgian buildings, some with cupolas. The handsome, modern **Hilles Library**, which stands in the southwest corner of the quadrangle, is much more than a library *(see margin note)* and is the site of the quadrennial Music-Listening Orgy during which hundreds of classical tapes are played from beginning to end without interruption.

Exit from the north of the quadrangle onto **Linnaean Street**. Turn right and, after 600 yards, you will reach **No. 21 ⓫**, a simple white two-story structure which dates back to the second half of the 17th century; it is the oldest entire dwelling place in Cambridge.

Linnaean Street now intersects with **Massachusetts Avenue**, which in recent years has seen an increase of exotic restaurants and boutiques, many of which recall the atmosphere of Harvard Square in the 1960s and 1970s. From here it is a stroll of about three-quarters of a mile down the avenue to Harvard Square, with **Lesley College** and Harvard Law School on the left. (The Porter Square subway station is also only a few blocks north of Linnaean, and the T will make the return trip to Harvard Square in five minutes.)

Walking down Massachusetts Avenue, spare a glance on the north side of the Cambridge Common for the two-story, gray, clapboard house at **No. 7 Waterhouse Street ⓬**. It was here that Dr Benjamin Waterhouse lived and "cut the claws and wings of smallpox" by introducing into the US, in 1800, vaccination with "vaccine threads" that he had received from Dr Edward Jenner. Waterhouse first vaccinated his own children and then sent threads to President Jefferson, who similarly treated his own children.

Map on page 240

Hilles Library, opened in 1966 and designed to act as a focus for the university's community life, includes group study rooms, a cinema named after the pioneer documentary maker Robert Flaherty, and an art gallery exhibiting the work of students, staff and faculty.

BELOW:
Harvard Square.

BELOW:
the entrance to Harvard Yard.

Harvard Yard

An exploration of the heart of Harvard is best begun by crossing to the north side of the east-west arm of Massachusetts Avenue and entering the gate to Harvard Yard. **Wadsworth House** ⓭, the yellow clapboard building to the right of this entrance, was built in 1727 and was the home of Harvard presidents until 1849. It was George Washington's headquarters for a few nights when he arrived in Cambridge. Today it houses the Alumni Office and other university officers.

The Yard is a delightful shady oasis rather than the "unkempt sheep-commons" which John Kirkland saw when he became president of the college in 1810. Then it was cluttered with a brewery and sundry privies. Kirkland is responsible for the trees, the footpaths and that tradition of care which still prevails.

In the center of the Yard and separating the Old from the New Yard, is **University Hall**, an 1816 granite building designed by Bulfinch. It now houses university offices but originally had dining rooms, classrooms, a chapel and the president's office. Fortunately, the architect anticipated the future, for, when constructed, the rear of this building was almost as handsome as the front. And it is this rear which is now the western side of the New Yard or Tercentenary Quadrangle.

The larger than life-sized bronze statue of **John Harvard** which sits below the American flag in front of University Hall is often referred to as "the Statue of Three Lies." The statue is not of John Harvard but an idealized representation, modeled by an undergraduate in 1884, the year that the figure was sculpted by Daniel Chester French. The inscription on the base refers to John Harvard as the founder of Harvard College. He was not: he was the first major benefactor. The inscription also says that the College was founded in 1638, the year of the John Harvard bequest. It was not: the correct date of its founding is 1636.

To the west of University Hall, and facing one another, are **Massachusetts** and **Harvard halls**. The former, erected in 1720, is the oldest Harvard building still standing, and the College Clock, part of the original structure on the western gable, has been painted to resemble its 18th-century appearance. During the Revolutionary War, Continental Army soldiers were billeted here.

The north side of the **Old Yard** is occupied by four freshmen dormitories. To the west are the twin dormitories of **Hollis** and **Stoughton**. The former, Harvard's fourth oldest building (1763), was home, at different times, to President John Quincy Adams, Ralph Waldo Emerson, Henry Thoreau and Charles Bulfinch. During the war 600 Colonial troops were quartered here. The wooden pump outside Hollis is a replica of the pump at which students would perform their ablutions.

Harvard Hall ⓮ (1766) is the third college building to stand on this site. Its predecessor was razed by a fire in 1764 which was called "the greatest disaster in the history of the College," destroying as it did the largest library in the colonies, including John Harvard's books. One of the latter was saved because, on the night of the fire, an undergraduate had removed it from the library. Next day, realizing the treasure he possessed, he took the book to President Holyoke who thanked him graciously, accepted the volume and expelled the student for removing it without permission.

Standing between and slightly back from Hollis and Stoughton is **Holden Chapel** (1742), Harvard's third oldest building. The chapel, built in glorious high Georgian style, with its pediments decorated with the elaborate crest of the Holdens, was called "a solitary English daisy in a field of Yankee dandelions." Even though Harvard was founded as a ministerial school, Holden was its first

The College Clock on Massachusetts Hall.

BELOW:
John Harvard.

JOHN HARVARD

John Harvard, a butcher's son, was born in the London borough of Southwark, in a house close to London Bridge, in 1607. Most of his family died in the plague of 1625, but his mother survived and, having remarried, was able to send John to Cambridge University. He graduated in 1631 and, shortly after he was married in 1637, he sold the Queen's Head inn in Southwark beqeathed to him by his mother and set sail for the New World.

Although he was never formally ordained as a minister, he served for a time as assistant pastor in the First Church of Charlestown, and had the reputation of being a learned and pious man. But, within a year of his arriving in New England, he was dead, the victim of tuberculosis.

Little more might have been heard of the young Puritan minister had he not left in his will half of his wealth, together with his library of classical and theological literature, to a school opened two years previously in New Towne, soon to be renamed Cambridge. As he had inherited property in England, his estate was worth £1,600, then a considerable sum, and his 260 books formed the core of a collection that now exceeds 10 million volumes.

The future of the school was assured, and in 1639 the Massachusetts General Court named it Harvard College.

Reading in the sun at the Widener Library.

BELOW:
the Widener
Library in winter.

chapel – more than a century after the college was founded. Later, it was the home of the Medical School; it now houses offices of choral groups.

At the north end of the Yard is the granite **Holworthy Hall** (1812). To the east is **Thayer Hall**, a stripling which first housed students in 1870.

Grander by far than the Old Yard is the **Tercentenary Quadrangle** or **New Yard**, which, on the first Monday of each June, is the scene of Commencement. This Yard is dominated on the south by the Widener Library's massive Corinthian colonnade standing atop a monumental flight of stairs and on the north by the soaring, delicate, white spire of **Memorial Church**, which honors the Harvard dead in both world wars. The rear of University Hall is on the west side, and facing this is Richardson's **Sever Hall**, its entrance flanked by turreted towers and the entire building rich in decorative brickwork. Built in 1880, it has been called "a turning point in the course of American architecture."

Widener ⓯, the third largest library in the US and the largest university library in the world, contains more than 3 million volumes stacked on 50 miles (80 km) of shelves. It is the administrative center of the university network of nearly 100 libraries which house 11 million books. The library is a memorial to Harry Elkins Widener, a young bibliophile who drowned in the sinking of the *Titanic*. As he had already indicated that he would donate his library to Harvard, his mother gave the university his books and the money to build space for millions more. Mrs Widener believed that if Harry had been able to swim he would have survived the sinking, and so, as part of her bequest, she stipulated that all Harvard students pass a swimming test before graduation.

Three interesting Cambridge dioramas (1677, 1755 and 1936) can be seen in the library, whose **Widener Memorial Room**, a glorious affair of wood paneling

and stained-glass windows, contains Harry's original private library, which includes a copy of the Gutenberg Bible and a first folio of Shakespeare. Some claim that John Singer Sargent's murals in the anteroom to the Memorial Room "are the worst works of public art ever done by a major American painter." The adjacent **Houghton Library** ⑯ has a brilliant collection of incunabula and the libraries of, among others, Cotton Mather and John Masefield. The John Harvard collection has the one book which survived the 1764 fire and "sisters" of many other works which were destroyed.

The rear of **Sever Hall**, just as handsome as the front, is flanked on the south by **Emerson Hall** and on the north by **Robinson Hall**. These three buildings, sometimes called **Sever Quadrangle**, form a unifying structure pulled together by the common use of brick and simple rectangular shapes. If it appears uncertain whether Emerson should be of stone or brick, as evidenced by the massive engaged columns of brick with Ionic stone capitals, it is because stone, which was originally to be used, was found to be too expensive.

Philosophy is taught at Emerson Hall, and legend has it that, when Gertrude Stein took her final examination here in a course given by William James, she left the building after writing in her examination book, "I don't want to take this exam: it's too nice out." Professor James returned her book with "Miss Stein, you truly understand the meaning of philosophy, 'A'."

The first school of architecture and the first school of city planning in the nation were originally located in Robinson Hall, which has classical bas reliefs flanking the entrance and the names of celebrated architects, sculptors and philosophers embossed below the upper windows.

Exhibit at the Fogg Museum.

An art and architectural hodgepodge

On exiting onto **Quincy Street** from Sever Quadrangle, one is immediately faced by the **Fogg Museum** ⑰, with the **Arthur M. Sackler Museum** to the north on Broadway and the striking modern **Carpenter Center for the Visual Arts** ⑱ on the Fogg's right.

BELOW:
the Fogg Museum.

The Fogg and the Sacker art museums contain collections any provincial city in the world would love to own. Their purpose is not to entertain the casual visitor but rather to educate students; however, they are open to the general public. Since 1991, the **Busch-Reisinger collection** has been displayed in the **Werner Otto Hall**, a large extension of the Fogg.

Collectively, these three museums boast nearly 150,000 objects; the great majority are bequests, some on long-term loan although occasional items have been purchased.

The annual budget for the Arts Museums, which include North America's largest fine arts library, is about $7 million, of which just $500,000 is spent on acquisitions. Not infrequently, Harvard alumni approach the Arts Museums for assistance in making purchases which will, when they die, go to the museums.

Outstanding in the Fogg are the Ingres canvases, the best collection outside France; a splendid assembly of pre-Raphaelite works and French impressionists; 27 Rodins; a Fra Angelico crucifixion; 54 Blake

TIP

A single admission fee covers the Fogg, Busch-Reisinger and Sackler museums. Opening hours: Mon–Sat 10am–5pm and Sun 1–5pm. Guided tours: the Fogg, Sept–Jun Mon–Fri 11am, Jul–Aug Wed 11am; the Busch-Reisinger Sept–Jun Mon–Fri 11am, Jul–Aug Wed 1pm; the Sackler, Sept–Jun Mon–Fri 2pm, Jul–Aug Wed 2pm.

BELOW:
commencement at Harvard University.

watercolors; and a print room with 300 Durers and 200 Rembrandts. The Fogg also has an excellent collection of western sculpture featuring Romanesque works from the late 11th and 12th centuries and a dazzling display of silver.

The Busch-Reisinger collection is devoted to the art of Germany, with some works from other North European countries. Outstanding is the 20th-century Expressionism, with canvases by Klee and Kandinsky and Max Beckman's *Self Portrait in Tuxedo*. Here, too, a wonderful *Pear Tree* by Gustav Klimt and the largest collection outside Germany of Bauhaus material, including the archives of Gropius and Feininger. Among older paintings the collection is especially strong in 15th- and 16th-century items from the German, Dutch and Flemish schools. Romanesque and Gothic ecclesiastical sculpture, 18th-century rococo porcelain, jewelry, textiles, furniture and metalcraft are also on display.

The Carpenter Center is the only Le Corbusier building in North America, and just one of a variety of modern buildings on the Harvard campus. When James Stirling, the English architect and designer of the Sackler Museum, was severely criticized for his design, he was reported to have exclaimed: "Doesn't fit in! I've simply created another animal for the Harvard architectural zoo!" And, indeed, the Carpenter is incongruous among the conventional buildings to its north and south and facing it from across the road – the Fogg Museum, the **Faculty Club** and the **President's House** respectively. (The President no longer lives in the house which bears his name: it is now used by the governing body.)

The most striking features of the Carpenter Center, which proper Bostonians have compared to two rhinos wrestling, is the sweeping ramp which leads from the street to the heart of the building on the upper level, the Corbusier trademarks of tall pillars, upon which the building appears to float, and concrete sun

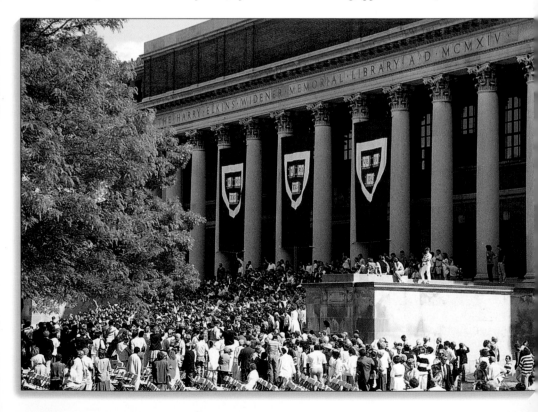

breakers which admit natural light while blocking out the sun's direct rays. Ascend the ramp and look down into the studios where artists are at work, or visit one of the many temporary exhibitions the Carpenter hosts. In the basement of the building is the **Harvard Film Archive**, dedicated to screenings of both new and classic films.

Head north across Broadway to be immediately faced by Stirling's zebra, the **Sackler Museum ⓳**, a somewhat geometrical building with orange and gray striations. The two plastic-covered windows were to be the entrance (neighbors balked) to a bridge linking the Sackler and the Fogg. Its collection is devoted to works of Ancient, Oriental and Islamic art. Here is what many agree is the most magnificent collection in the world of Chinese jades. Also on show are Japanese prints and woodblocks, Persian miniatures and Greek and Roman statues and vases.

Further north, across **Cambridge Street**, is the slender-pillared **Gund Hall ⓴**, home of the **Graduate School of Design**. The vast studio area, which is four levels high and devoid of interior walls, is a stunning highlight of this 1972 design by John Andrews. Gund is home to the Frances Loeb Library, specializing in books about architecture and urban design.

Memorial Hall

Across from Gund is **Memorial Hall**, a huge Gothic-Ruskinian pile which, like nearly all great Harvard buildings, has its admirers and detractors. Among the latter is G.E. Kidder Smith, the architectural historian: "Though not lively [it] is loved, a mammoth ugly duckling, an almost fantastic statement of the taste of its time." Memorial Hall was built in the last quarter of the 19th century to honor those Harvard dead who fell in the Civil War. Its steep polychromatic roofs were at one time topped by a soaring clock-tower whose bells called and dismissed classes. The tower was destroyed in 1956 in a spectacular conflagration.

Although from the outside Memorial Hall looks like a cathedral and although its interior is tripartite, one has only to enter to realize that this is a secular building. The vast, oblong nave was used for commencement exercises and as an undergraduate dining hall. (It has recently been restored to serve that purpose.) The transept, in ecclesiastical terms, is the memorial part of the hall, and its 17 stained-glass windows are a veritable museum of American stained glass: note especially the "Battle Window" by John la Farge. The apse, again in ecclesiastical terms, is **Sanders Theater**, which, with seating for 1,200, is still the largest auditorium in the university. It has superb acoustics and sightlines.

Continue northward, crossing **Kirkland Street**, and enter **Divinity Avenue**. At the corner stands a building that might look more at home in Bavaria than New England: the **Busch-Reisinger** building, which, pre-Sackler, housed the university's collection of German art. On the other side of Divinity Avenue stands the 15-story **William James Hall** skyscraper which houses the university's behavioral sciences department and which was designed by Minoru Yamasaki.

Homogeneity is the keynote to the other buildings on 300-yard-long Divinity Avenue even though they

Keeping cool in Cambridge.

BELOW: Memorial Hall.

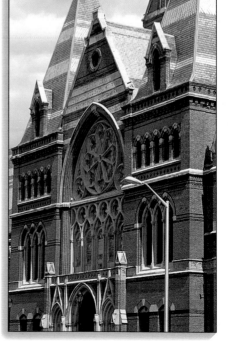

were built over a span of 150 years and serve a wide variety of purposes. To the right are the **Harvard-Yenching Library** and the **Semitic Museum**. The Semitic Museum lacks the mass appeal of its neighbors; its main attraction is a collection, changed from time to time, of old photographs of the Middle East.

Divinity Hall ㉑ is the last building on the east of Divinity Avenue, and is the oldest Harvard building (1816) devoted to its original purpose: a dormitory for divinity students. It was built because President Kirkland believed that divinity students should be isolated from the rest of the university in case they adopted "more of the spirit of the University than of their profession."

One wonders how successful his ploy was: a quarter of a century later, Ralph Waldo Emerson in his famous "Divinity School address" claimed that the atmosphere of the school was so literary that theological students were apt to regard the ministry "as an occasion of intellectual exercise and display rather than as a means of doing good to all classes in the community."

At the end of Divinity Avenue is the vast **Biological Laboratories**. Enter the courtyard of the last and observe Bessie and Victoria, two monster rhinos who guard the main entrance. The red and green doors are covered with intricate grillework representing the flora and fauna of sea, air and earth.

On the left of Divinity Avenue are the **Sherman Fairchild Biochemical Laboratories** and the University Museums. Closing the avenue at its northern end is the **Farlow Herbarium**, which contains the world's largest orchid collection.

The Museums of Natural History

With its primary entrance on Oxford Street, the **University Museums of Natural History ㉒** are comprised of the **Peabody Museum of Archaeology and**

The Farlow Herbarium, founded by William G. Farlow who held the first chair of cryptogamic botany in the US in 1879, contains more than 1.3 million specimens of lichens, fungi, algae and bryophytes. It also has a large library of associated books and manuscripts.

BELOW:
Harvard as seen from across the Charles River.

Ethnology, the **Museum of Comparative Zoology**, the **Geological and Mineralogical Museum** and the **Botanical Museum**.

Giant totem poles, Navaho blankets, Hopi ceramics and African masks are just a few of the items on display at the Peabody Museum of Archaeology and Ethnology, the oldest such museum in the Americas and the most important of the four museums. Outstanding is the **Hall of the North American Indian**, which focuses on the interaction between native Americans and newcomers. Other, less exciting, galleries cover the Indians of Central and South America, especially the Maya. The **Tozzer Library**, is said to contain America's best anthropological collection.

The greatest attraction in the Museums of Natural History is the glass flower collection in the Botanical Museum. These 847 remarkably accurate models are a unique collection made near Dresden, Germany by the Blaschkas between 1877 and 1936. The Museum of Comparative Zoology contains such treasures as Kronosaurus, a 42-ft (13-meter) long fossil sea-serpent from Australia, the Harvard mastodon, a 25,000-year-old elephant, a 65-million-year-old dinosaur egg, extinct birds such as the great auk and the passenger pigeon and hundreds of stuffed birds and animals. Rounding off this quartet of museums is the Geological and Mineralogical Museum which exhibits a large collection of gems, minerals, ores and over 500 meteorites.

Farther down **Oxford Street** toward Memorial Hall, is the airy, light and white, glass and concrete **Science Center** ㉓, the largest of all Harvard buildings and winner of an American Institute of Architecture award for its architect, Josef Louis Sert, once dean of the Graduate School of Design. A mini-museum in the Science Center houses a permanent exhibition of fascinating early sci-

Map on page 240

Harvard Yard Science Center.

BELOW: the Science Center, Harvard's largest building.

entific instruments dating back to around 1550. The collection illustrates the history of instrumentation in a broad range of subjects, from astronomy to navigation, and includes telescopes and early computing devices.

At the western end of the building five massive setbacks form a giant stairway to the stars. Despite rumors, it is not true that when trunk and tusks are put in place the Science Center will become the world's largest white elephant and will be honored with the Harvard White Elephant award, which has been held for 50 years by the Widener Library!

Law School students, when in Harvard Square, will gleefully point out to you the joke window above the Curious George bookstore advertising the law firm of Dewey, Cheetam and Howe (try saying it out loud).

Walk down Oxford Street on the eastern flank of the Science Center and turn left to see three entirely disparate buildings. To the west is the discrete, almost genteel, **Music Building** ㉔. Inscribed above its entrance are the words: "To Charm, To Strengthen and To Teach, These are the Three Great Chords of Might." To the east is the all glass **Gordon McKay Building of Engineering and Applied Physics** and the **Jefferson Physical Laboratory**, a large red-brick Victorian monster. Here, in the 1920s, a laboratory was made available to Edwin Land, a bright young undergraduate who subsequently made his fortune by inventing the Polaroid camera.

The Law School

Walk westward and immediately enter an irregular yard, part of which, deplorably, is a parking lot. It is flanked by a variety of buildings. Prominent is the white limestone **Langdell Hall** ㉕, which is the heart of the **Law School** and delineates the west side of **Law School Yard**. Because of the great length of Langdell Hall and the lack of depth of the yard, it is impossible to appreciate fully the glory of the grand ivy-covered portico of this building with its Ionic columns and pilasters. It houses part of the largest (1.4 million volumes) law library of any university in the world. The Law School, established in 1817 with six students, is now attended by 1,800 students: it is America's oldest law school.

BELOW: at work in the Music Building.

The back of Langdell Hall, almost as handsome as the front, forms the east side of a small, leafy quadrangle, around which, and spreading out from, are the 17 other buildings which constitute the Law School. Much appreciated in winter are the tunnels that connect some of these to Langdell Hall.

The Law School's polychromatic **Austin Hall** is somewhat evocative of Sever Hall and bears the characteristic Richardson imprint. The portico of this Romanesque building, completed in 1881, has three glorious round arches supported by groups of intricate colonettes and a conical-capped asymmetrical turret.

To the west, and unsuccessfully attempting to close this pseudo-yard from Massachusetts Avenue, is the somewhat incongruous **Gannet House** ㉖, a small white Greek-Revival building from 1838, home of the renowned *Harvard Law Review*.

Facing Austin Hall is the back of **Littauer Center**, which is now occupied by the university's government and economic departments.

The north side of the Law School Yard is enclosed by the modern buildings of the **Harkness Graduate Center**, opened in 1949 and designed by Architects

Map on page 240

Collaborative under the leadership of Walter Gropius. All the buildings are dormitories except the **Harkness Commons**; it contains dining areas, public rooms and some unusual works of art. The Commons faces a sunken quadrangle which is frozen in winter and used for ice-skating: during the rest of the year it is the scene of football and softball games.

The central work of art and the focal point of the entire complex is the 27-ft (8.2-meter) high stainless steel *World Tree* by the sculptor Richard Lippold. Nicknamed "Jungle Gym," "Clothes Rack" and "Plumbing," it represents a primitive religious symbol common among such people as the Australian aborigines who believed that their sacred World Tree is the hub of the universe. To welcome the spring, law students have been known to indulge in strange fertility rites around this tree.

Closer to the Charles

Harvard's domain also extends south of the Square. At the rear of a wide triangular area on **Mount Auburn Street**, the whimsical building with a gaudy door and topped by an ibis is the headquarters of the ***Lampoon*** ㉗, Harvard's famous humor magazine. To the left of this once stretched Harvard's **Gold Coast**, so-called because of the opulent lifestyle of the students who lived in these buildings, which were, at the start of the 20th century, luxurious private apartments.

Also on Mount Auburn Street, next to **Lowell House**, note a red-brick building with a six-pillared entry. This is the **Fly Club**, one of eight once snooty Harvard social clubs which have shed much of their exclusivity in recent years. Theodore and Franklin Roosevelt were members here, as were two other presidents, Lowell and Eliot.

Walk south on **John F. Kennedy Street** for 600 yards to the river. The first half of this street is occupied by stores and restaurants while the right side of the lower half is occupied by the **John F. Kennedy School of Government**, which, like most of Harvard, just grows and grows. A small attractive public park lies between this school and the river.

On the left side of John F. Kennedy Street are **Kirkland** and then **Eliot**, two of Harvard's seven original neo-Georgian residential houses, distinguished by their graceful cupolas, enclosed courtyards and mellow red-brick walls. The houses, together with newer, more modern fellows, stretch to the left along the river, ending in the contemporary **Peabody Terrace** ㉘, a 21-floor, three-towered complex for married students; the building came from the drawing board of Josef Luis Sert.

Devotees of Mercury will cross the river by the **Larz Anderson Bridge** and visit, on the left, the **Business School** campus and, on the right, Harvard's vast Elysian **playing fields**, which are both in Brighton, a suburb of Boston. (The boathouse on the left of the bridge is used by women's crews while that on the right is used by Harvard men.) The Business School is a sizeable village of relatively modest neo-Georgian buildings which display a consistent rhythm of green doors, white window frames and red-brick walls. Worth seeking out is the **Class of 1953 Chapel** designed by Moshe Safdie. From the exterior it may look a bit like a greenish oil tank, however once past

Harvard has two celebrated student publications. The "Harvard Crimson" is the undergraduate newspaper, located at 14 Plympton Street, and the "Harvard Lampoon" is a humor magazine, housed in castle-like offices on Mount Auburn Street built on land donated by William Randolph Hearst, once its business manager.

BELOW:
Lowell House.

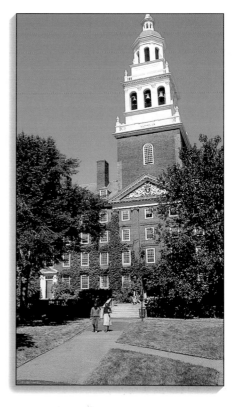

the tall weighty doors, one finds an oasis for quiet contemplation complete with a small Zen garden stocked with Japanese goldfish.

Back in Harvard Square, exit to the southeast on Massachusetts Avenue. On several blocks leading to **Sullivan Square**, and continuing beyond, there are more stores and restaurants similar to those found around the square.

About a quarter of a mile further, immediately before Central Square, stands the imposing Romanesque **Cambridge Town Hall** with its campanile. The large rusticated building with cupolated tower facing the Town Hall is an office building. **Central Square** is in flux: in and around it are several inexpensive ethnic (especially Indian) restaurants.

Massachusetts Institute of Technology

Half a mile beyond Central Square, you reach the first MIT buildings. A thoroughly unprepossessing building on the left houses the **MIT Museum Ⓐ**, founded in 1971 and containing treasures that have made MIT a leader in computer, electronic and nuclear technologies and in the atomic and space age.

Two other MIT museums are open to the public. In the **Hart Nautical Museum** in the main building are model craft ranging from Donald McKay's great Yankee clipper *Flying Cloud* to modern guided missile warships by way of America's Cup defenders. Temporary exhibits of outstanding contemporary art can be savored in the **List Visual Arts Center** in the Wiesner Building at the eastern end of the campus.

Continue from the MIT Museum along Massachusetts Avenue, cross the railroad tracks and reach the main campus. The west campus, on the right, is devoted to the students' social life; the larger east campus, to the left, is the workplace of MIT.

BELOW: Cambridge Town Hall.

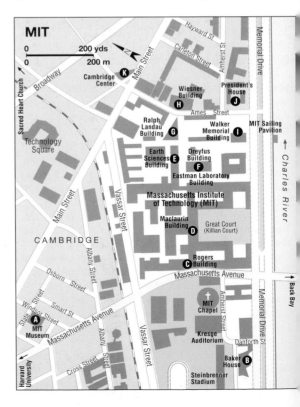

Map
on page
256

Kresge Auditorium and the **Chapel** are two outstanding buildings designed by a Finnish architect, Eero Saarinen. The former, completed in 1953, is an enormous tent-like structure rising out of a circular brick terrace; its roof appears to be supported at only three points by delicate metal rods, and it is enclosed by thin-mullioned curtains of glass. It is very much an outward-looking building. The oak-paneled auditorium seats 1,238 and a small theater accommodates 200.

The much smaller chapel, a windowless, brick cylinder set in a moat and adorned with a sculptural bell tower, is inward-looking. Light reflected from the moat illuminates the interior, where a delicate bronze-toned screen hangs behind the white marble altar block. Slightly further west is **Baker House B**, an undulating dormitory designed by the Finnish architect Alvar Aalto so that all its rooms have a view of the river.

The Rogers Building.

Back on Massachusetts Avenue is the imposing domed neoclassical facade of the **Rogers Building C** (completed in 1937 and named after William Barton Rogers, who founded MIT in 1861). Its steep stairway and four pairs of Ionic columns provides the main entrance to the teaching buildings of the School of Architecture and Planning and leads to an extensive system of tunnels claimed to be the third largest in the world. These link many of the east campus buildings.

Rather than entering here, continue on Massachusetts Avenue for a further couple of hundred yards to the **Charles River**. Turn left onto **Memorial Drive** and immediately on the left is the aptly named **Great Court** (also called **Killian Court**) in front of the monumental **Maclaurin Building D** with its Pantheon-like dome and broad Ionic portico. (Richard C. Maclaurin, a Scot, was the president of MIT who moved the institute from Boston to Cambridge.) Inscribed on the buildings enclosing the court are the names of great scientists, including Darwin

LEFT: MIT's eastern campus.
BELOW: MIT's circular chapel.

Henry Moore sculpture at MIT.

and da Vinci, Faraday and Franklin and two MIT benefactors, DuPont and Lowell.

A large Henry Moore sculpture adorns the courtyard. Until the 1950s MIT did not acquire works of art, but it now has an active Council for the Arts and major pieces of sculpture by, among others, Picasso, Nevelsohn, Lipchitz and Calder dot the campus.

Farther eastward is **McDermott Court**, dominated by the **Earth Sciences Building** , the tallest structure on campus and readily recognized by the large white sphere on its roof. In front of it stands Calder's *Big Sail*, a giant free-form metal sculpture. The Earth Sciences Building is just one of four on campus designed by I.M. Pei, a Harvard graduate who also studied at MIT. The others are the **Dreyfus Building** and the **Ralph Landau Building** which flank Earth Sciences, and, somewhat farther east, the **Wiesner Building**.

Farther along Memorial Drive it is back to neo-classicism with the **Walker Memorial Building** which is used for a variety of purposes. Facing this is the MIT **Sailing Pavilion**. And then, still on Memorial Drive, is the austere, limestone, ivy-covered **President's House**.

Main Street and **Kendall Square**, to the east of Wiesner, are today tree-bordered areas lined by handsome, soaring buildings, most of which are of red brick. A few years ago they were a desolation. Visit the landscaped garden atop the parking lot in the heart of the **Cambridge Center**, a modern hotel, laboratory and office complex. Further west, across the rail tracks, is more of the same in **Technology Square**, an urban redevelopment project in which MIT joined with the city to clear away old factories and tenements.

The name Polaroid on some of these buildings reflects the birth of the instant camera in Cambridge. Polaroid's rival, Eastman Kodak, is well represented on

BELOW:
East Cambridge's
Bulfinch Place
cupola.
RIGHT: East
Cambridge mall.

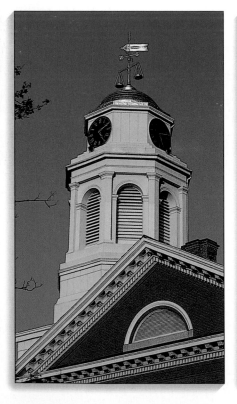

the MIT campus with the **Eastman Laboratory Building** and **Eastman Court**. George Eastman, a great MIT benefactor, believed that "the progress of the world depends almost entirely upon education" and left much of his not inconsiderable estate to MIT – "the greatest institution of its kind."

East Cambridge

Proceed north from Technology Square for about half a mile on Fulkerson Street. Turn right onto **Otis Street** where, on the right, stands the **Sacred Heart Church**, a Victorian Gothic edifice in blue trimmed with granite and built between 1874 and 1883 to serve East Cambridge's ever-increasing number of Irish immigrants.

Map on page 256

A large, terracotta and brick building 300 yards farther along Otis Street now houses the elderly and stands on the site of **Fort Putnam**. It was from here that, in March 1776, the Patriots bombarded the British during the final days of the siege of Boston.

Continue along Otis Street, lined with trim, wooden Greek Revival houses representative of the decorous vernacular architecture of 1820–70, until the corner of **Third Street**. Here stands the simple, Federal-style **Holy Cross Polish Church** sans cupola. Originally built for a Unitarian congregation in 1827, this is the oldest church in East Cambridge. It testifies to the many Polish who, together with Portuguese, Italian and Lithuanians, arrived in East Cambridge following the Civil War. They joined, in the city's factories, the Irish and Germans who had begun to arrive half a century earlier. The handsome 19th-century red-brick apartments on the same side of Third Street led to the sobriquet Quality Street.

The Cambridgeside Galleria.

The red-brick building across the road with Georgian cupola and modest Italianate campanile is **Bulfinch Place**, a former courthouse which has been brilliantly rehabilitated by Graham Gund into offices and the **Cambridge Center for the Performing Arts**. The original structure, built to Bulfinch's plans in 1812, was poorly constructed and in 1848 was redesigned as a courthouse by Ammi Young. The proud eagle which stands in the central courtyard formerly crowned the main Boston Post Office. A stele at the northeast corner of this block marks where 800 British Redcoats landed on April 19, 1775, to begin their march on Lexington and Concord.

BELOW:
Lechmere Canal.

North of Bulfinch Court is the monumental redbrick 19th-century **Middlesex Registry** with four brick porticoes, two of which stand at the head of impressive stairways. On the Second Street side are some superb wrought-iron lantern-holders. In the early part of the 20th century Cambridge was the third most important manufacturing city in New England.

Industry has been replaced by commerce. Walk a few blocks down **First Street** to reach the **Cambridgeside Galleria**, an upscale shopping mall. It stands alongside a circular basin in the center of which is a soaring fountain whose waters join the 200-yard long **Lechmere Canal** which enters the Charles River. River-boat excursions leave from the basin. East Cambridge (Lechmere) can be reached on the Green line of the "T". ❑

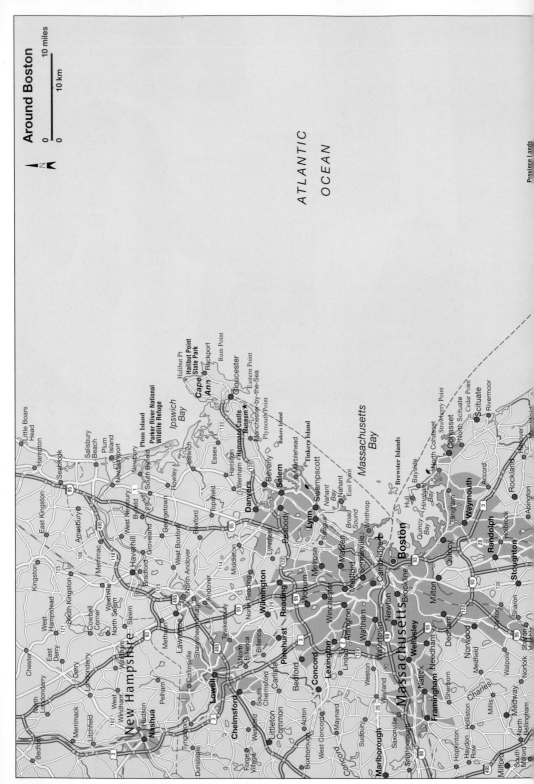

Around Boston

0   10 miles
0   10 km

N

ATLANTIC
OCEAN

Massachusetts
Bay

Cape
Ann

Ipswich
Bay

New Hampshire

Massachusetts

Little Boars
Head

Hampton
Seabrook
Salisbury
Beach
Plum
Island
Newburyport
Plum Island
Newbury
Parker River National
Wildlife Refuge
South Byfield
Byfield
Rowley
Ipswich
Georgetown
Essex
Hamilton
Wenham
Rockport
Halibut Pt
Halibut Point
State Park
Rum Point
Gloucester
Eastern Point
Manchester-by-the-Sea
Hammond Castle
Museum
Plymouth Point
Bakers Island
Marblehead
Tinkers Island
Swampscott
Nahant
Nahant
Bay
East Point
Broad
Sound
Winthrop
Brewster Islands
Bayside
Hull
Hingham
Bay
Quincy
Bay
North Cohasset
Strawberry Point
Cohasset
North Scituate
Cedar Point
Scituate
Rivermoor

East Kingston
Amesbury
Merrimac
Kingston
West
Kingston
South Kingston
Woodville
North Salem
Salem
Haverhill
West Newbury
Bradford
Groveland
West Boxford
North Andover
Boxford
Middleton
Topsfield
Lynnfield
Danvers
Beverly
Salem
Peabody
Lynn
Saugus
Revere

Chester
West
Hampstead
Cowbell
Corner
Derry
East
Derry
Windham
Londonderry
North
Londonderry
Merrimack
Litchfield
Hudson
Nashua
Pelham
Methuen
Lawrence
Andover
Shawsheen Village
Tewksbury
North
Billerica
Billerica
North Reading
Wilmington
Reading
Woburn
Melrose
Stoneham
Medford
Winchester
Arlington
Somerville
Cambridge
Boston
Lincoln
Lexington
Waltham
Watertown
Newton
Brookline
Milton

Bedford
Dunstable
Tyngsboro
Lowell
Chelmsford
South
Chelmsford
Westford
Littleton
Common
Carlisle
Bedford
Concord
West Concord
Pinehurst
Concord
Maynard
Sudbury
Weston
Wayland

Forge
Village
Boxborough
Acton
Saxonville
Framingham
Southborough
Marlborough
Hopkinton
Hopkinton
Haydon
Row
South
Milford
Milford
North
Bellingham
Medway
North Medway
Holliston
Mills
Medfield
Sherborn
Millis
Norfolk
Walpole
Sharon
Norwood
Dedham
Needham
Wellesley
Natick

Quincy
Weymouth
Randolph
Stoughton
Holbrook
Abington
Rockland
Hanover
Accord
Canton
Sharon

Province Lands

EXCURSIONS WEST

Map on page 268–9

Within easy reach of Boston are the Revolutionary sites of Lexington and Concord, the literary shrine of Walden Pond, and the historical reconstruction of Old Sturbridge Village

Lovers of history and those smitten with nostalgia will wish to "Go West" and to visit, among other places, Lexington and Concord, Harvard Village and Sturbridge. To reach **Lexington ❶**, site of the first battle of the Revolution, leave Boston on Route 2 and, after 10 miles (16 km), turn right onto Route 4–225. Immediately on the left is a contemporary building which houses the **Museum of Our National Heritage** (33 Marrett Road; Mon–Sat 10am–5pm, Sun noon–5pm; tel: 781-861 6559) featuring changing exhibits of Americana. Soon after, still on the left, is the russet-colored 1635 **Munroe Tavern** (1332 Massachusetts Avenue; mid-Apr–Oct Mon–Sat 10am–5pm, Sun 1–5pm; tel: 781-862 1703), which served as headquarters for the Redcoats and as a hospital on their retreat from Concord. Another mile and **Battle Green ❷**, a triangular affair in the heart of Lexington, is reached. Here, on April 19, 1775, Captain Parker told his men: "Stand your ground, don't fire unless fired upon, but if they mean to have a war, let it begin here!" And it did.

Atop a heap of boulders, taken from the wall behind which the minutemen shot at the British, is the **Minuteman Statue**. To the right (east) is **Buckman's Tavern**, (1 Bedford Street; mid-Apr to Nov Mon–Sat 10am–5pm, Sun 1–5pm; tel: 781-862 5598), a yellow clapboard building which dates from 1690, where 77 minutemen gathered to await the British. Following the battle, the minutemen who had been wounded were carried into this tavern, where they were given medical attention. It has been restored to its original appearance. Visitors, on guided tours through seven rooms, are shown a bullet hole in the door, muskets, cooking equipment and furniture.

A quarter of a mile to the north of the Green is the mocha-colored 1698 **Hancock-Clarke House** (35 Hancock Street; tel: 781-861 0928); it has been moved hither and thither but has now been returned to its original site. Here, on April 18, John Hancock and Samuel Adams were roused from their sleep by Paul Revere and warned of the coming of the British.

Battle Road

Leave Lexington on Route 2A from the northwest corner of Battle Green – the **Battle Road** – to travel alongside the **Minuteman National Historical Park**. Stop at the **Battle Road Visitor Center ❸** (daily 9am–5pm; tel: 781-862 7753). It's *the* best place for those interested in the Revolution to start their Lexington-Concord exploration; a film shows the events that led to that fateful April 19, 1775, and there's an animated map of British and American troop movements. Visit also the partly uncovered **Ebenezer Fiske farmhouse**, where, after refreshing himself with a drink from a well, a minuteman found himself facing

PRECEDING PAGES:
old coastguard
station, Eastham;
traditional costume.
LEFT: Patriot's Day
at Concord.
BELOW: Minuteman
Statue, Lexington.

*Memorial Day
in Concord.*

a Redcoat. "You are a dead man," announced the minuteman. "And so are you," was the reply. Both leveled their muskets; both fired; both were killed. Concord is 8 miles (13 km) away, after several stops.

Concord ❹, a handsome small town, is twice blessed, for here is where the second engagement of the Revolution took place and here, during the first half of the 19th century, lived a handful of renowned literati. **Monument Square ❺**, the center of the town, is where, on April 19, 1775, a British sergeant burning a cache of captured supplies inadvertently set fire to a building. The Americans massing on the opposite side of the river saw the smoke and, assuming that the British were burning the town, decided to march to its defense "or die in the attempt." Their advance was blocked by a British detachment guarding the bridge. Several roads radiate from Monument Square: all should be explored.

Begin by driving north on **Monument Street** for a little over 1 mile and then turning left to reach immediately the **National Historical Park North Bridge Visitor Center ❻**. Here, dioramas and a somewhat basic 12-minute audio-visual presentation explain the confluence of events that led to the battle. Visitors are invited to don colonial costume in one of the rooms. The gardens overlooking the Concord River with their view of **Old North Bridge** are quite beautiful.

You could backtrack to the Bridge parking lot, but you would be denying yourself a walk through history. Better to stroll the half-mile downhill past the **Muster Field ❼** (to the right), along roughly the route of the militia until you reach the bronze statue of the **Minuteman**, rifle in one hand and the other dragging a plowshare. On the plinth are Ralph Waldo Emerson's immortal words "the shot heard round the world." And so to "the rude bridge that spanned the flood." Today's bridge, with its "genuine antique look," was built in 1956.

BELOW:
Old North Bridge.

The idyllic setting belies the bloody skirmish. To enjoy a couple of hours of sheer bliss, paddle a canoe along the winding river and under the bridge. (Canoes can be rented at South Bridge on **Main Street**: the river at this point is the Sudbury rather than the Concord.)

The simple, clapboard **Old Manse**, 200 yards south of North Bridge, was built in 1770 and was first occupied by the Rev. William Emerson, who watched the battle for the bridge from here. Subsequently, his grandson, Ralph Waldo Emerson, lived here for two short periods. Then, after their marriage, the Hawthornes moved in and remained for three years. During this period Nathaniel wrote *Mosses from an Old Manse*, a collection of stories that secured a literary place for both house and writer. Meanwhile, Sophia was painting and scratching the study and dining room windows with her wedding ring. The longest and most charming of her inscriptions states: "Una Hawthorne stood on this window-sill January 22, 1845, while the trees were all glass chandeliers – a goodly show which she liked much though only 10 months old."

Old Manse, where Ralph Waldo Emerson lived briefly.

Literary giants

Back in Monument Square, drive northeast on **Bedford Street** (Route 62) for 200 yards to **Sleepy Hollow Cemetery ❺**. Author's Ridge, in the northeast corner, is the final resting place of Hawthorne, the Alcotts, Margaret Sidney, Emerson and Thoreau. Among the less lofty tributes are the sentiments engraved over Ephraim Wales Bull's final resting place – "He sowed, others reaped" (the developer of the Concord grape had failed to profit from his work).

Should one want to escape all the history and just commune with nature, continue on Bedford Street for another mile and watch for a small sign noting the entrance

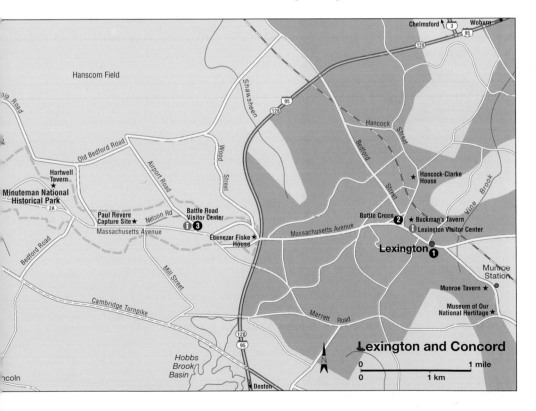

Lexington and Concord

To get to Great
Meadows, head east
on Bedford Street for
about 2 miles (3 km)
and look for a small
sign pointing to
Monsen Road. There's
a parking lot at the
end of Monsen Road.

BELOW:
young Redcoat
displays his medal.

to the **Great Meadows National Wildlife Refuge ❾**. Here serious birdwatchers mix with those wanting only a lengthy stroll amongst muskrats, otters and frogs.

Backtrack from the square for less than a mile on the Lexington Road to the junction with the **Cambridge Turnpike**. Here stands the **home of Ralph Waldo Emerson** and the **Concord Museum ❿** (200 Lexington Road; Mon–Sat 9am–5pm, Sun 11am–5pm; tel: 978-369 9763). In the former, Emerson wrote his celebrated essays ("A foolish consistency is the hobgoblin of little minds, adored by little statesmen, philosophers and divines") while in the latter, a brick building, is Emerson's study, which, apart from one round table, was transferred in its entirety from the wooden Emerson home because of fear of fire. The excellent museum consists mainly of a series of beautifully furnished reconstructed rooms from the 18th and 19th centuries. Its Thoreau Gallery boasts the largest collection of artifacts associated with Thoreau, including furnishings from his Walden Pond abode.

One mile farther along, at 399 Lexington Road, stands the shaded brown clapboard **Orchard House ⓫** (Apr–Oct Mon–Sat 10am–4.30pm, Sun 1–4.30pm; Nov–Mar Mon–Fri 11am–3pm, Sat 10am–4.30pm, Sun 1.30–4.30pm; tel: 978-369 4118), where the Alcott family lived from 1858 to 1877. Here Louisa wrote *Little Women* and *Little Men* and her father, Bronson, founded his school of philosophy. Much memorabilia is on display.

Just beyond, at No. 455, is **The Wayside** (not to be confused with Longfellow's Inn of that name in Sudbury), the home of the Concord Muster Man on the day of the battle (Mar–Dec Mon–Sat 10am–5pm, Sun 2–5pm; tel: 978-369 5912). In the next century the Alcotts resided here before moving to Orchard House. Observe the Alcotts' piano and explore a tower study where Hawthorne, who bought the house in 1851, lived and attempted to write, eventually turning

HENRY DAVID THOREAU (1817–62)

Thoreau was born in Concord, the third child of a pencil maker. He graduated without great distinction from Harvard in 1837 and tried his hand at teaching – also without distinction. Under the influence of his mentor, Ralph Waldo Emerson, who had settled in Concord, he decided that his true vocation was that of a poet and philosopher.

The two men became the focus of New England Transcendentalism, a literary movement which emphasized emotion, intuition and nature, and above all valued the individual above society. Striving for self-sufficiency, the 27-year-old Thoreau built his own home on the shores of Walden Pond, on land owned by Emerson. He lived there from 1845 to 1847, growing his own food, fishing and meditating. He later published *Walden; or, Life in the Woods*, 18 essays describing his experience.

During his stay at Walden, he spent a night in jail after refusing to pay his poll tax to a government which supported slavery. Out of this experience came his most influential essay, *Civil Disobedience*, published in 1849.

When he died, probably of tuberculosis, at the age of 44, most of his contemporaries would have regarded him as a failure. But the power of his ideas and the lucidity of his prose endured, and he is now one of America's cultural icons.

in desperation to travel writing and saying he would be happy if the house just burned down. It did not and was occupied by Margaret Sidney, author of the *Five Little Pepper* books.

Map on pages 268–9

Walden Pond

And so to **Walden Pond** ⓬, reached by returning toward Concord and then traveling south on **Walden Street**, which crosses Route 2, for 1½ miles (2.5 km). The pond is relatively small and one can take a gentle stroll around it in about an hour. The best time to visit is in the fall. During summer, when the pond becomes a giant swimming hole, Thoreau would have been unable to separate himself from "the mass of men [who] lead quiet lives of desperation." A cairn of stones stands alongside the site where Thoreau lived between 1845 and 1847.

Thoreau enthusiasts will wish to visit the **Thoreau Lyceum** ⓭ in Concord (156 Belknap Street; Mar–Dec Mon–Sat 10am–5pm, Sun 2–5pm; tel: 978-369 5912), which houses much memorabilia. There's a replica of his Walden Pond cabin.

(Concord can quickly "be done" in a couple of hours, but to explore any house usually necessitates joining a guided tour. This often requires a short wait. Most tours take about 40 minutes.)

Continue south from Walden Pond and, after half a mile, turn left. Immediately to the right is the prefabricated **Gropius House** ⓮, which expresses the Bauhaus principles of function and simplicity (68 Baker Bridge Road, Lincoln. Jun–Oct 15 Wed–Sun 11am–5pm; rest of year Sat and Sun 11am–5pm; tel: 781-259 8098). This was the first building that the great German architect designed when he arrived in the US in 1937. Another mile leads to the attractive **DeCordova and Dana Museum and Park** (Sandy Pond Road, Lincoln,

Transcendentalist thinker Henry David Thoreau.

BELOW: on a lazy river at Concord.

tel: 781-259 8355. Tues–Sun 11am–5pm), where temporary exhibitions of modern art can be viewed. The 30 acres (12 hectares) of grounds, high above **Sandy Point Pond**, are a splendid setting for sculpture. During summer, outdoor concerts are held in the amphitheater.

Also in Lincoln is a gem of a three-story blue clapboard house with an Ionic portico. The **Codman House ⓰**, its grounds landscaped like an English country estate, is a treasure trove of 18th- and 19th-century furniture and decorative arts.

Shakers and visionaries

To reach **Harvard Village** and the **Fruitlands Museums**, return to Concord and drive west on Route 2. After 13 miles (21 km), turn south on Route 110 and then immediately right onto Old Shirley Road. This crosses Depot Road to become **Prospect Hill**, where the entrance to Fruitlands is located about 2 miles (3 km) after leaving Route 2. Fruitlands, at an altitude of about 600 ft (180 meters) and with magnificent views across the Nashau River Valley to Mount Wachusett and Mount Monadnock, is immaculately maintained and its four museums (102 Prospect Hill Road; mid-May–mid-Oct 10am–5pm; tel: 978-456 3924) are a pleasure to visit.

An 18th-century farmhouse where, for some months, Bronson Alcott and his family, an English friend, Charles Lane, and others attempted an experiment in communal living is now a **Transcendentalist Museum**. One reason for the group's break-up was that Lane wished Alcott to abandon his family and to join him at Harvard's Shaker Village. Not surprisingly, Mrs Alcott did not approve. And then who could be an Adamite, as was Samuel Bower, in the harsh Massachusetts winter? (An Adamite is a nudist: perhaps an Evite is a female nudist.)

The **Shaker House**, built in the 1790s, was an office for the Harvard Shak-

Shakers, who broke away from the Society of Friends, were called Shaking Quakers, then simply Shakers, because of the way they trembled during their meetings. In their heyday in the US, between 1820 and 1860, they had a membershop of 6,000.

BELOW: in the Indian Museum, Fruitlands Museums. **RIGHT:** interpreting the past at Old Sturbridge Village.

ers Society, which flourished until 1918. Shaker handicrafts are displayed, and a variety of exhibits offer insight into the Shaker way of life – celibacy, communal ownership of property and worship joyfully expressed in dance.

Map on pages 268–9

The other two museums are the **American Indian** and the **Picture Gallery**. The former houses a selection of North American (not New England) Indian relics, historic Indian arts and dioramas. The west gallery of the latter displays delightful "primitive" portraits by early 19th-century itinerant artists, while the east gallery showcases the works of landscape painters associated with the Hudson River School.

At **Old Sturbridge Village** (Apr–Oct daily 9am–5pm; Nov–mid-Feb Sat and Sun 10am–4pm; mid-Feb–Mar daily 10am–4pm; tel: 508-347 3362), say "Good morning" or "Good afternoon" to the actors dressed in 19th-century garb and they will counter with a "G'day" and explain that, 200 years ago, that was the acceptable greeting. The village, a living history museum 55 miles (88 km) west of Boston on the Massachusetts Turnpike near exit 9, is a reconstructed village and farm from the 1830s. (It can be reached by bus from Boston.)

Traditional dress, Old Sturbridge Village.

More than 40 original buildings, from 1730 to 1840, have been collected from New England and placed here to create a village and a 70-acre (28-hectare) farm. Many stand around a central green, and a lake is spanned by a covered bridge. The blacksmith and the potter work as they would have in the 1830s. A pair of oxen harnessed to a plow are used to turn the sod. Rural life is authentically re-created, with a variety of religious and political events punctuating the daily and seasonal rhythm of village life and farm work.

BELOW: school party at Fruitlands Museums.

Two small but superb museums, one devoted to clocks and the other to glass, round off a splendid destination. ❏

SOUTH SHORE AND CAPE COD

*There's yet more history to be found at Quincy and Plymouth.
But the real attractions are the long sandy beaches and
well-preserved communities of Cape Cod*

Map
on page
282

South of Boston is Cape Cod with its glorious beaches. But, even before reaching the canal that separates the Cape from the rest of Massachusetts, several historic towns, some with not-to-be-ignored beaches, await. Mention Pilgrims, and Plymouth and Provincetown are Pavlovian responses.

Start your southern safari by leaving Boston on Route 3 (the Southeast Expressway). Observe the colorfully painted gas tank to the left. The work of a nun, Sister Corita Kent, is rumored to conceal the image of Ho Chi Minh. Take Exit 12 and join the **Quincy Shore Drive** which crosses the **Neponset River** by a drawbridge, and, 9 miles (14 km) after leaving Boston, arrive at **Quincy ❶**, which bears the honorific "city of presidents" because here both John Adams and John Quincy Adams were born. (Quincy can also be reached on the Red line of the "T".)

Home of the Adamses

Antiquarians and historians will delight in half a dozen buildings associated with the name Quincy. First to be reached on entering the city is the 1770 mid-Georgian **Josiah Quincy House** (20 Muirhead Street) which is furnished with Quincy family heirlooms. Half a mile farther south is the **Quincy Homestead** (34 Butler Road), whose handsome country mansion dates to the early 19th century.

Half a mile to the west, at 135 Adams Street, is the splendid **Adams National Historic Site** (tel: 508-773 1177), home to four generations of the Adams family for 140 years and now decorated with their furnishings and memorabilia. The delightful **Stone Library** in the immaculately maintained grounds contains John Quincy Adams's Library of 14,000 books. The **United Parish First Church** (1306 Hancock Street), a few hundred yards south of the Josiah Quincy House, is known as the **Church of the Presidents** and contains the remains of the two presidents and their wives. About a mile south of here, at 131 and 141 **Franklin Street**, are the modest salt-box houses in which the presidents were born. Simple though these dwellings may be, Abigail, wife of John, wrote that she preferred the charms of "my little cottage" to the grandeur of the London court.

But Quincy has more to offer than gracious living. Here the **Granite Railway**, the country's first commercial railway, was built in order to transport granite to Charlestown for the Bunker Hill Monument. The Metropolitan District Commission offers tours of the **railway incline** (Mullin Avenue in West Quincy), the **railway terminus** (Bunker Hill Lane), **a quarry** (Ricciuti Drive) and a **turning mill**.

On leaving town on **Washington Street** (Route 3A), observe on the right, as you cross the Weymouth Fore River drawbridge, the now defunct **Bethlehem Shipyards**. Here the *Thomas W. Lawson*, the only

PRECEDING PAGES:
beach huts at
Provincetown.
LEFT: blessing of
the fleet at
Provincetown.
BELOW: the Adams
homestead, Quincy.

seven-masted schooner ever built, was launched, as was the first atomic-powered surface ship.

Continue south on Route 3A to the **Hingham Rotary**. Exit on **Summer Street**, then turn left at **Martin's Lane** for a 1-mile drive to **World's End**, an idyllic 248-acre (100-hectare) oasis designed by Frederick Law Olmsted. At different – fortunately not at the same – times, it was proposed as a site for the United Nations and as a nuclear waste disposal site, much to the dismay of the artists and nature lovers who frequent it. Stroll on paths lined with oak, hickory and cedar trees and through rolling fields where prize Jersey cattle formerly grazed and which are now home to pheasant, quail, foxes and rabbits. Herons and egrets populate the rugged 5-mile (8-km) shoreline, and all the while the impressive Boston skyline can be seen in the distance.

Return to Summer Street, turn left and follow the road to **Washington Boulevard**. This leads to **Nantasket Beach**, the best beach close to Boston (16 miles/24 km) and to **Hull**, which offers views of the Atlantic and the harbor islands. These islands include the buffeted **Brewsters**, on which stands the Boston Light, the nation's first lighthouse *(see page 173)*.

Backtrack from Hull to peaceful **Hingham**, where the numbers on the handsome, usually white, clapboard houses on **Main Street** are not to assist mail deliveries but to announce with pride when the houses were built: this was, more often than not, in the 19th century and, occasionally, in the 18th. The town has several inspiring churches, including the **Old Ship Church** on Main Street, the oldest building in the nation in continuous ecclesiastical service. The interior of its roof echoes an inverted ship's hull, reflecting the fact that its builders were ships' carpenters.

The Hull Lifesaving Museum at 1117 Nantasket Avenue (open Jun–Sept Wed–Sun, Oct–May Fri–Sun) gives a good idea of the heroic measures needed when warnings from the Boston Light could not avert disaster.

BELOW: Plymouth Rock Monument.

Continue south on Route 3A through **Cohasset**, where **Jerusalem Road** winds past stately homes overlooking a rocky coast reminiscent of Cape Ann. Fourteen miles (22 km) farther south is **Marshfield**, where the **Daniel Webster Law Office** is located in the grounds of the 18th-century **Winslow House**; the great orator spent the last 20 years of his life here. Immediately past this, **Duxbury**, with its beautiful homes and 9-mile (14-km) long barrier beach, is a birdwatcher's paradise. The energetic might wish to ascend the 130-ft (40-meter) high **Myles Standish Monument** for a bird's-eye view of the region.

Maps:
Area 282
Town 279

Plymouth: birthplace of a nation

And so, 40 miles (64 km) after leaving Boston, to **Plymouth ❷**, the site of the first permanent American settlement north of Virginia. It was in 1620 that the Pilgrims set foot – or so legend goes – on Plymouth Rock.

Much can be seen at Plymouth relating to the Pilgrims; a trolley runs between the different sights. A stone's throw from the monument over the **Rock** (claimed to be the stone the Pilgrims first stepped on when they came ashore) is the *Mayflower II* ❹. This is a replica of the original *Mayflower*, built in England and sailed to Plymouth in 1957. The 104-ft (32-meter) long vessel, peopled with interpreters of its history, vividly conveys the hardships that its 102 passengers undoubtedly suffered on their 66-day voyage.

Statue of Massosoit at Plymouth.

Across the road from the Rock is **Coles Hill**, where, during their first winter, the Pilgrims secretly buried their dead at night to hide the truth about their fast dwindling numbers from the hostile Indians. Nearby is the site of the original settlement. Here, too, at 16 Carver Street, is the **Plymouth National Wax Museum ❸** (Mar–Nov 9am–5pm; tel: 508-746 6468) with 26 life-size diora-

BELOW: *Mayflower II* at Plymouth.

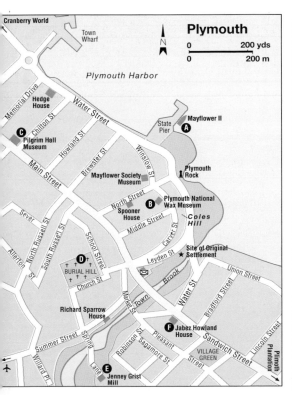

*Acting the part at
Plimoth Plantation.*

mas illustrating the Pilgrims' story from the emigration of the Separatists from
England to Holland in 1607 to the first Thanksgiving celebration in 1621. An
imposing statue of **Massasoit**, the Indian chief who helped the Pilgrims survive
their first spring, stands in front of the Museum.

Pilgrim Hall Museum ◉ (75 Court Street; daily 9.30am–4.30pm, closed
in Jan; tel: 508-746 1620), a Greek Revival building designed by Alexander
Parris and the oldest public museum in the nation – the Salem Museum is older
but began life as a private institution – has the country's largest collection of Pilgrim memorabilia, including John Alden's halbred, Myles Standish's Bible and
the cradle of Peregrine White, who was born aboard the *Mayflower*.

Farther east, beyond Main Street, is **Burial Hill** ◉, with gravestones dating
back to the colony's founding. "Under this stone rests the ashes of Willm Bradford,
a zealous Puritan and sincere Christian, Governor of Plymouth Colony from April
1621–57 [the year he died, aged 69] except 5 years which he declined." The hill
was the site of the Pilgrims' first meeting house, fort and watch-tower, where
friends and foes arriving by sea could be observed. South of Burial Hill is the
replica **Jenney Grist Mill** ◉, where corn is still ground as in the days of the Pilgrims. One can also visit several old houses, including the **Jabez Howland House**
◉ at 33 Sandwich Street (late-May–mid-Oct; call 508-746 9590 for times), the
only surviving house in Plymouth in which a Mayflower Pilgrim actually lived.

Plimoth Plantation

The year is always 1627 at **Plimoth Plantation**, 3 miles (5 km) south of the
Rock, where interpreters dressed in authentic Pilgrim costumes and speaking in
old English dialects assume the roles of specific historical residents of the

Maps:
Area 282
Town 279

colony. Query Mistress Alden about Captain Standish and she may well respond: "Oh, he lives next door and there are some, sir, who feel he is not the easiest man with whom to deal." Question the same Mistress Alden or Captain Standish about Paul Revere or George Washington and they will look at you with incomprehension. The interpreters do not simply stand around waiting for questions but go about their 1627 work and interact with one another. Even the livestock is painstakingly backbred to approximate 17th-century barnyard beasts.

Another part of the site is a reconstructed **Wampanoag village**, which recaptures Indian life in Massachusetts in the 1620s. The incongruously handsome visitor's building has audio-visual presentations and excellent changing exhibitions.

Conclude a visit to Plymouth at **Cranberry World**, on the waterfront at the north end of town. This modern museum includes cooking demonstrations and displays illustrating the history, lore and commercial development of cranberries.

Cape Cod

Seventeen miles (27 km) after leaving Plymouth on State 3, the soaring **Sagamore Bridge**, spanning the **Cape Cod Canal**, comes into view. Across it is a land of marshes and meadows, of pines and of cranberry bogs and, above all, of beaches. The region is nirvana for many Bostonians and New Englanders, New Yorkers and Canadians.

First, a word on the geography of Cape Cod, which Thoreau called "the bared and bended arm of Massachusetts." The **Upper Cape**, comprising the towns of Sandwich, Barnstable, Falmouth and Woods Hole, is the part just beyond the canal; the **Mid-Cape**, which stretches from Hyannis to Orleans and which includes the towns of Chatham, Harwich, Brewster, Dennis, Yarmouth and

The Cape Cod Canal, opened in 1914, is the world's widest sea-level canal, at 480 ft (146 meters). It is 17½ miles (28 km) long, and carries 30,000 vessels a year. A bicycle path follows the length of the canal on both banks.

BELOW: harvesting cranberries.

*The Cape Cod
Rail Trail.*

Barnstable, is at the base of the concavity; while the **Lower Cape** – that part generally likened to the forearm, stretching northwards to end with the "sandy fist" of Provincetown – includes the towns of Eastham, Wellfleet and Truro.

The Sagamore Bridge opens onto Interstate 6 (the Mid-Cape Highway), which runs first east and then north and ends, after 60 miles (100 km), at Provincetown. This is the route to take to reach a destination, but much more intriguing is Route 6A (the old King's Highway). It parallels, more or less, Highway 6 and passes through many of the Cape's 15 towns and 70 villages, most with salt-box architecture and a classical white painted church.

Distances between communities are short, and one can travel the entire Cape, with frequent stops, in a day. But it's better take several days or even several weeks. Most visitors make one township their base, though some prefer to mosey around, driving from town to town. The towns and villages are similar in many ways, yet each has its own distinctive character and its devotees who insist that their place on the Cape is far superior to all others. All are close to superb beaches.

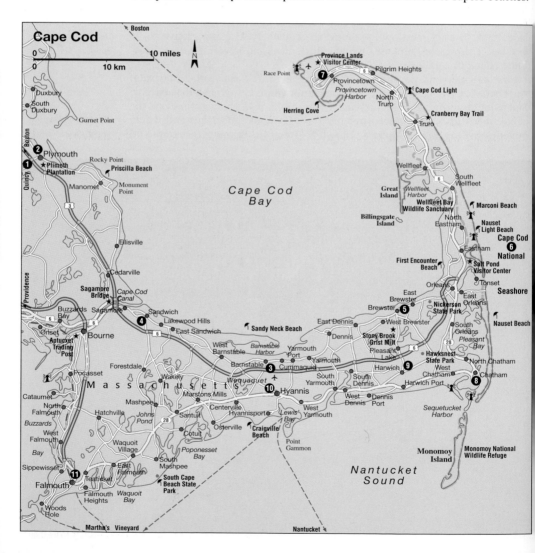

The Cape boasts about 300 miles (500 km) of sandy beaches, some backed by glorious, almost 100-ft (30-meter) high dunes. Thunderous surf is found on the **Outer Cape**, washed by the Atlantic, while gentler waters prevail in the concavity of **Cape Cod Bay**. Slightly rougher are the waters in **Buzzards Bay**, to the southwest of the Upper Cape, and **Nantucket Sound**, to the south of the Mid-Cape.

Because the Cape is exceptionally narrow, it is possible to spend the morning in roaring surf and, half an hour later, loll in placid, shallow waters. If none of this appeals, then innumerable ponds and lakes invite swimming, sailing and wind-surfing, undisturbed by ocean waves. The only snag is that resident parking permits are required at some of the better beaches.

Permits are much more readily obtained for fishing in those 20 percent of the Cape's 365 ponds which are home to, among others, brown, rainbow and brook trout, white and yellow perch, black bass and land-locked salmon. Extensive opportunities for salt-water fishing are also available.

Nearly 40 golf courses dot the Cape. The greatest concentration of greens are in the largest two towns of **Barnstable ❸** (seven courses) and **Falmouth** (five courses). Only about a dozen courses are strictly private.

Each community has set aside special areas for bicycling, but cyclists really come into their own on the **Cape Cod Rail Trail**, a paved recreational trail that runs on an abandoned railroad bed for 26 miles (42 km) from Route 134 in Dennis to Wellfleet. Its route passes quintessential Cape scenery and several cultural and historical sites. The **Salt Pond Visitor Center** of the **Cape Cod National Seashore** is right off the trail in Eastham.

Sandwich ❹, the town that glass built and the first community reached after crossing the Canal, is an especially good place to be if the weather is inclement. Not

Carousels such as this one at Heritage Plantation are a New England favorite.

BELOW: testing the water at Truro.

Sandwich Glass Museum display.

that it doesn't have its quota of good beaches, but it also has more museums than anywhere else on the Cape. Glass lamps, candlesticks and many other items exhibiting a characteristic lacy pattern popular in the second half of the 19th century can be seen in the **Sandwich Glass Museum** (129 Main Street; tel: 508-888 0251).

Several interesting historic sites border **Shawme Pond**. These include the **Hoxie House**, which, with its 17th-century furnishings, is believed to be the oldest (1637) house on the Cape. At **Dexter's Grist Mill**, in use since the 1650s, demonstrations of old milling skills may be enjoyed. **Yesteryear's Doll and Miniature Museum** (seasonal, call 508-888 1711 for times) fills two floors of the **First Parish Meeting House** with delightful memories.

Best of all is the **Heritage Plantation** (130 Grove Street; mid-May–mid-Oct daily 10am–5pm; tel: 508-888 3300), located in 76 acres (31 hectares) of gardens rich in rhododendrons and day-lilies. It houses an eclectic collection of Americana in several buildings. A replica of the round Shaker Barn at Hancock Shaker Village contains a magnificent collection of antique cars dating from 1899 to 1937. Another replica, this time of the "Publick House," a recreation hall for the Continental Army (1783), is filled with antique firearms, flags, Indian artifacts and 2,000 miniature soldiers. The Art Museum houses a glorious collection of folk art, including more than 100 Currier and Ives prints. And, for rambunctious children, there is an 1912 working carousel.

Twenty-eight miles (45 km) farther along Route 6A, at the eastern end of the Mid-Cape, is **Brewster ⑤**, another good place to spend a rainy day. The **Stony Brook Grist Mill** still grinds corn as it did in 1663. During April and May, schools of alewives (herring) returning from the Atlantic struggle in the mill-stream to leap up ladders that will lead them to the tranquil mill ponds where they spawn.

BELOW: New England Fire and History Museum.

Those fascinated by conflagrations will enjoy the town's **New England Fire and History Museum** (tel: 508-896 5711), which has one of the world's largest collections of antique fire equipment and memorabilia; more than 30 of the engines still work. There are also some period buildings, including an apothecary, on the site.

The **Dillingham House** is probably the Cape's second oldest (1660) house, and the **Sydenstricker Glass Factory** provides the opportunity to observe handsome items made in an ingenious manner. Children will enjoy a visit to the touristy **Brewster General Store**, with its musical nickelodeon; built in 1852 as a Universalist Church, it was sold for $1 in 1886 to William Knowles, who turned it into a general store.

The Lower Cape

In 1961, in order to preserve the beauty of the Cape and to highlight a number of natural and historic sights, the ocean shorelines of six towns – Chatham, Orleans, Eastham, Wellfleet, Truro and Provincetown – were dedicated as the **Cape Cod National Seashore ❻** (CCNS) under the aegis of the National Parks Services of the Department of the Interior. Visitor Centers, offering displays and interpretative programs, are located at Eastham (**Salt Pond**) and at Provincetown (**Province Lands**). Both are disappointing, although the view of sand dunes and ocean from the upper deck of the latter is spectacular.

Close to a glorious beach is the **Marconi Area** (**South Wellfleet**), where Guglielmo Marconi built his radio towers and from where, in 1903, he sent the first radio signal across the Atlantic. At Race Point in Provincetown, visit the **Life Saving Museum**, which displays the crude equipment used to rescue mariners from the thousands of vessels that were wrecked on this part of the coast.

Map on page 282

TIP

Although 117 miles (188 km) from Boston by road, Provincetown is just 57 miles (92 km) by sea. In July and August, many use the ferry which leaves Boston at 9.30am and reaches Provincetown soon after noon. There's also a regular air service; flying time is 20 minutes.

BELOW:
Old Coast Guard Station, Eastham.

Painting by Michael McGuire at the Provincetown Art Association.

What attracts most people to the CCNS, however, are its magnificent beaches and glorious desert-like dunes. They are at their best at **Nauset Beach (Orleans)**, **Nauset Light Beach (Eastham)**, **Marconi Beach (South Wellfleet)**, **Head of the Meadow Beach (Truro)**, **Provincetown** and, above all, at **Longnook Beach (Truro)** where, unfortunately, parking is almost impossible.

Provincetown's popular beaches are **Herring Cove**, about a mile from town and whose southeast section, by far the best part, is predominantly gay, and **Race Point**, a few miles north of town. It was at Race Point that Thoreau, after strolling, wrote: "Here a man may stand, and put all America behind him." Then there is **Long Point**, gained by walking across a mile-long causeway at the west end of the town. Near the start of the causeway a commemorative stone notes that it was "somewhere near here" that the Pilgrims first landed.

Provincetown

Provincetown ❼, at the very tip of the Cape, is a three-ring, often raucous circus. It has many arts and crafts stores, art galleries, shops (both elegant and tawdry), and restaurants, all of which cater to a large gay population, an indigenous colony of Portuguese fishing folk and, during the summer, hordes of tourists. And yet serious artists maintain a tradition which started in 1899 with the founding of the Cape Cod School of Art.

Commercial Street, usually referred to as **Front Street**, parallels the shore and is where most activity occurs. Paralleling Front Street is **Back Street** (properly **Bradford Street**). Near Back Street is the **Pilgrim Monument**, which commemorates the Pilgrims' stop in Provincetown in 1620 for six weeks before they moved on to Plymouth because of its more protected harbor and more

BELOW: nightlife in Provincetown.
RIGHT: drag queens on Commercial Street, Provincetown.

arable soil. The monument, a slim and stately affair adapted from the Torre del Mangia in Siena and built in the early 1900s, is the tallest granite structure in the country. It towers 352 ft (107 meters) above the town and can be ascended (it is a pleasant climb) to enjoy a grand view of the Lower Cape.

The museum at the base of the monument is splendid, with excellent dioramas showing the arrival of the Pilgrims, a fascinating whaling section and eclectic exhibits of the region's culture. The **Heritage Museum** (356 Commercial Street; tel: 508-847 7098), housed in the old **Methodist Church**, displays local artifacts and memorabilia. Works of local artists are on show in the **Provincetown Art Association & Museum** (460 Commercial Street; tel: 508-487 1750).

Leave Provincetown, return for 28 miles (45 km) on Interstate 6 to the traffic circle at **Orleans** and take State 28 for 9 miles (14 km) south to **Chatham ❽**, situated at the Cape's elbow. With its large cedar-shingled summer homes, this is the Newport of the Cape. The observation deck above the **Fish Pier** is an excellent place to be in the early afternoon to watch returning trawlers unloading their catches. Railway buffs will enjoy the **Railroad Museum**, housed in a Victorian railroad station. Birdwatchers will want to make their way by boat from Chatham to **Monomoy Island**, a National Wildlife Refuge on an 8-mile (13-km) stretch of pristine barrier beach. It's an important resting place for migrating birds.

From Chatham, continue west on State 28 along the Cape's South Shore, passing **Harwich ❾**, where cranberries were first commercially cultivated. Old Harwich, incorporated in 1694, has resisted the overdevelopment that has plagued other towns, and its Winchmere harbor is one of the prettiest on the Cape.

After driving through a honky-tonk area, you reach **Hyannis ❿** after 17 miles (27 km). It and its port are the commercial center and the transport hub of the Mid-Cape, with scheduled airline services to Boston, Martha's Vineyard and Nantucket and ferries to the two islands. A vintage train provides a one-hour sightseeing ride to Sandwich or to Buzzards Bay.

The Kennedy compound

The magnet at **Hyannisport** is the **Kennedy Compound**, yet it is not visible from the road, nor is it open to the public. Visit, instead, the **Kennedy Memorial**, located on Lewis Bay (a pretty walk) or the **John F. Kennedy Museum** on Main Street.

A further 17 miles (27 km) on State 28 leads to elegant **Falmouth ⓫**, whose delightful green is surrounded by 18th- and 19th-century houses shaded by graceful elms. The **Julia Wood House** and the **Conant House Museum** are maintained by the Falmouth Historical Society: the former, dating from 1790, has a genuine widow's walk, while the latter features exhibits of whaling times. Eight miles (13 km) beyond Falmouth, at the southernmost tip of the Cape, is **Woods Hole**, famous for its **Oceanographic Institute**. From here, ferries leave for Martha's Vineyard.

Leave Woods Hole on State 28 and travel north 17 miles (27 km) to **Bourne** at the canal. Either cross the canal by the **Bourne Bridge** and then drive east for 3 miles (5 km) on Interstate 6 to join State 3 or take State 6 on the south side of the canal, which can then be crossed by the Sagamore Bridge. Boston beckons. ❑

Map on page 282

Pilgrim Monument, Provincetown.

BELOW: a good catch.

Map on page 292

THE NORTH SHORE

The delightful, wild coast of Cape Ann is a major attraction.
Characterful seaports such as Gloucester and Marblehead
cast a potent spell. So do Salem's witches

The North Shore – which, at least as far as Bostonians are concerned, ends at Cape Ann – is far more rugged than the South Shore and Cape Cod. This region of seaports, including Salem, Marblehead, Gloucester and Newburyport, features sedate, well-preserved 18th-century houses, as well as a number of 20th-century mansions.

Start your journey by leaving Boston either through the **Callahan** or **Ted Williams Tunnels** or over the **Tobin Bridge**. The traveler who opts for the latter is marginally less likely to encounter airport traffic snarls. Either way, make for Route 1A and the Lynn roundabout. A detour here, to the south on Route 129, is rewarding. Drive along the 2-mile (3-km) causeway which, on the left, is bordered by a not too attractive beach, to **Little Nahant Island**.

Continue across this island and a second, shorter, causeway to **Nahant Island** with its winding roads, fishing coves, **Forty Step Beach** with its rocky cliffs and ledges, and a mixture of summer and suburban homes, some humble, some in the style of Greek temples or Victorian mansions. A sign at **Bass Point** at the tip of the island announces that lawn tennis was played here for the first time in the US in August 1874.

Back at the roundabout, turn right and drive along **Lynn Shore Drive**; this skirts wide, flat **Lynn Beach**, odoriferous at low tide. After about a mile, one reaches **Swampscott** – the transition is quite marked – and the city is left behind. Lynn Shore Drive now becomes Humphrey Street which soon becomes Atlantic Avenue. The sea is no longer visible and the road now passes some grand, white Federal-style homes standing amid beautiful grounds.

Yachties' haven

About 6 miles (10 km) after the roundabout, turn right on Ocean Avenue and drive across the causeway at the base of Marblehead Harbor to arrive at exclusive **Marblehead Neck ❶**. **Harbor Avenue** makes a 3-mile (5-km) loop around the Neck, passing some splendid homes and, on the harbor side, the **Eastern Yacht Club**, the East Coast's most prestigious yacht club – although that statement will certainly be challenged by members of the neighboring **Corinthian Yacht Club**. **Chandler Hovey Park**, in the lee of the lighthouse at the tip of the Neck, is a glorious windswept point from which to watch dozens of white sails scudding in and out of the deep, protected harbor.

Return across the causeway to Ocean Avenue, turn right onto Atlantic Avenue and immediately arrive in **Marblehead ❷** proper, a twisting labyrinth of busy, narrow one-way streets lined by ancient clapboard houses. All is bustle and go.

The **Jeremiah Lee Mansion** on Washington Street,

PRECEDING PAGES:
sunrise, Rockport.
LEFT: lighthouse at
Annisquam Canal.
BELOW: sailing at
Marblehead.

When the Marquis de
Layfayette, who
fought as a major-
general during the
American Revolution,
visited Marblehead
in 1824, a corner of
Lafayette House at
Hooper and Union
streets was removed
to let his carriage
pass through the
narrow streets.

built in 1768, is an excellent example of pre-revolutionary architecture. Its exterior is of wood cut to imitate stone, while its interior has a grand entrance hall, elegant furnishings and original paneling. Also worth visiting is the **King Hooper Mansion**, an early 18th-century building with slave quarters, ballroom and garden.

Two vantage points from which to enjoy the passing scene are **Crocker Park** and **Fort Sewall** at the south and north end respectively of Front Street, which borders the bustling harbor. Another splendid view point, just beyond the Fort, is the **Old Burial Hill**, where 600 Revolutionary war veterans are interred.

Washington Square in the heart of the town is its highest point and provides pleasant views. The square is surrounded by private mansions which once belonged to sea captains and merchants; it is fronted by **Abbot Hall** (tel: 781-631 0528), the town hall, which has earned a niche in history by being home to Archibald Willard's renowned painting *The Spirit of '76*.

Leave the town by **Lafayette Street**; this immediately becomes Route 114, which, in turn, soon joins Route 1A and, after another 3 miles (5 km), enters Salem.

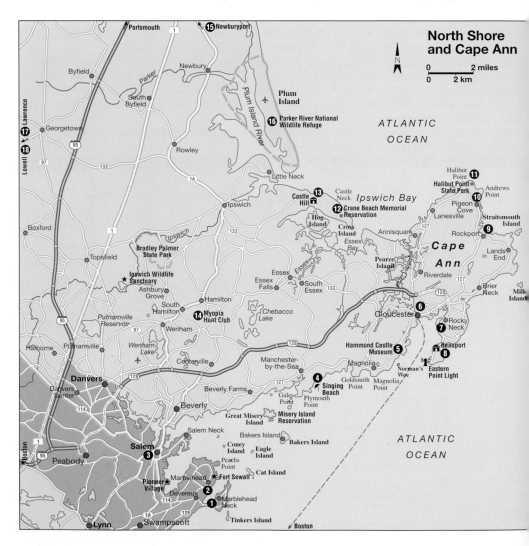

North Shore and Cape Ann

A bewitched seaport

The attractions of **Salem** ❸ – the word is derived from the Hebrew *shalom* ("peace") – make for an rewarding day trip, and its compact area make it possible to tour almost entirely by foot. It is easily reached on the MBTA Rockport commuter rail line from Boston's North Station.

Salem was once one of the nation's great seaports. At its apogee, at the end of the 18th century, many in foreign parts believed that New York was a town in a land that was called Salem. Today, it is a shadow, albeit a delightful one, of its former self, rich in museums and historic sites.

A good introduction to the town and its history is provided at The **Salem Maritime National Historic Site** ❶ which also includes a Visitor Center.

Salem in known for several restored historic houses which cover the evolution of architecture and furnishings in the region from the 17th to the 19th centuries. In a row on Church Street are the **Derby-Beebe summerhouse** (1799), the **John Ward house** and the **Andrew-Safford house** (1819). These are overseen by the **Essex Institute** ❷, whose collection of paintings, decorative objects and household items provides a close look at domestic life in early Essex County. Also nearby are the **Gardner-Pingree** (1805) and the **Crowninshield-Bentley** houses.

Diagonally across from the Essex Institute is the world-class **Peabody Museum** ❸ (Tues–Sat 10am–5pm, Sun noon–5pm; tel: 978-745 9500), whose wealth stems from the fact that, in 1799, 22 Salem men who had sailed beyond Cape Horn and the Cape of Good Hope founded the East India Marine Society, whose mission included forming a "museum of natural and artificial curiosities" to be collected by members on their voyages. How well they succeeded! Ships' models, figure-heads, nautical instruments, charts and maps abound in the Museum's

Maps:
Area 292
Town 295

Low-flying witches.

BELOW: picnicking at Chandler Hovey Park, Marblehead.

Salem's witches

In the mid-1600s, when the fever for witch-killing blew across the North Atlantic from Europe, the colonies of Rhode Island, Connecticut and Massachusetts joined the pack with decrees of death. Connecticut quickly seized and executed nine victims. Bostonians hanged Margaret Jones of Charlestown on a bright June day in 1648, and for an encore on Boston Common they hanged the beautiful and cultured Anne Hibbins, widow of the colony's former representative to England.

Against that lunatic background, the fanatical Rev. Cotton Mather sensed a great opportunity for self-promotion and professional success. He was already the colony's most highly acclaimed clergyman. He was learned, brilliant, ambitious, but he yearned for more. He longed to succeed his father, the Rev. Increase Mather, as the president of Harvard. He decided it would boost his reputation and enhance his career if he could identify assorted witches and promote their executions. So

he went to work and soon focused on a witch-suspect named Goodwife Glover, the mother of a North End laundress. With Mather's help, poor Mrs Glover quickly wound up in the noose of a Boston Common gallows rope.

In that same year, the fever struck Salem. The initial case involved a hot-tempered, trouble-making minister named Samuel Parris. He upset the serenity of his neighbors by arriving in town with two black slaves from the West Indies, a man named John and his wife, Tituba. Within two years, Tituba was teaching voodoo to a pair of young girls, Ann Putnam and Mercy Lewis. When they had learned all they needed to know from Tituba, they turned against the black woman with hysterical charges of witchcraft. And Tituba wound up in jail.

At this point, Salem's witchcraft surge really took off. Tituba pointed the witch-finger against two other Salem women, Sarah Osburn and Sarah Good. They in turn dragged in Rebecca Nurse and Martha Corey. And the madness kept spreading like infection, with every suspect accusing somebody else, until scores of victims awaited death. Between June and September in 1648, the Salemites executed 14 women as witches and six men as warlocks. And, to leave nothing to chance they also convicted and hanged two dogs.

Throughout the year, Cotton Mather was a frequent visitor to the town. He never missed an execution. He was a roaring orator at all hangings. He was quick to gallop his horse to the front of a crowd of onlookers and to leap from his saddle to the gallows platform. There he would rant and rave, preach and pray, devoting most of his performance to berating and denouncing the victim who was waiting to die, and thereafter adding a modest personal bit calculated to move his steps toward the presidency of Harvard.

Such was the situation in 1693 when William Phips, who had been busy fighting the Indians and the French in the northern woods, returned to his duties as the colony's governor. Phips took one disgusted look at the witchery set-up and issued a proclamation freeing all suspects still incarcerated. The madness braked to an abrupt halt. ❑

LEFT: Salem's Witch Museum.

Maritime Department, while the Asian Export Department glitters with porcelain, gold, silver, furniture and textiles created by Chinese, Japanese and Indian artisans in the 19th century. Artifacts from the South Pacific (especially the Solomon Islands) and the Far East (especially New Guinea) abound in the Ethnology Department, which also has an unsurpassed Japanese collection. A department of Natural History rounds off the collection of this, one of the oldest continuously operating museums in the country, which is rich throughout in marine paintings.

West of these museums, elegant homes, many built for sea captains by Samuel McIntire, line **Chestnut**, **Essex** and **Federal streets**. The first of these streets is a National Historic Landmark and justly deserves its accolade as one of the most beautiful and distinguished streets in the nation.

North next to **Salem Common** is the **Witch Museum ⓓ** (Washington Square; daily 10am–5pm; Jul–Aug 10am–7pm; tel: 978-744 1692). It and the **Witch Dungeon and Museum ⓔ** (16 Lynde Street; Apr–Nov 10am–5pm; tel: 978-741 3570), both in former churches, present their versions of the witch hunts which made Salem notorious in 1692–93. Any historic allusion to the witch hunts that plagued the Bay State colonists usually brings up Salem's name, and it's true that the town, where most of the witchcraft trials were held, led the region for exterminations, executing some 20 victims at the peak of the hysteria. However, it was in Boston in 1688 that the wheels of persecution really got rolling, propelled by the most fanatical witch-hunter of them all, the Rev. Cotton Mather. And it was in Boston in 1693 that the order finally was issued by Governor General Sir William Phips, bringing the craziness to an abrupt halt and freeing 150 "witch suspects" from jail – including Phips's own wife.

Witch-killing had been known for hundreds of years before it arrived in Amer-

More "witches" were exterminated in Salem than anywhere else in New England.

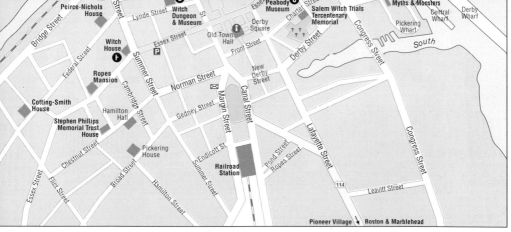

ica. In the early pages of the Bible, Exodus 22:17 demanded: "Thou shalt not suffer a witch to live." Dating from the Roman Inquisition in the year 1200, witch trials were common in Europe. A witch or warlock who confessed under torture would get an "easy" death, like hanging or beheading. But any who refused to confess got burned at the stake. More can be learned about this agitation in the **Witch House ⓕ** (310 Essex Street; Mar–Dec 10am–4.30pm; tel: 978-744 0180), where Judge Corwin questioned more than 200 who were accused of witchcraft.

While visiting the Witch House be sure to visit some other distinguished houses owned by the Essex Institute: the **Peirce-Nichols**, the **Ropes** and the **Cotting-Smith**. The Ropes Mansion is noted for its beautiful gardens and houses a rich collection of Nanking porcelain and Irish glass.

At the other end of town are the **Salem Maritime National Historic Site** (174 Derby Street; daily 9am–5pm; tel: 978-740 1650) and the **House of the Seven Gables ⓖ** (54 Turner Street; tel: 978-744 0991), the setting for Hawthorne's novel of that name. Several other houses at the site include his birthplace.

Across the street are the 1761 **Derby House** (Derby, a ship-owner, was probably the nation's first millionaire) and the 1819 **Custom House ⓗ** with an office once used by Nathaniel Hawthorne. To the southeast are the desolate 2,000-ft (600-meter) long **Derby Wharf**, one of 40 wharves once crowded with merchantmen. Adjacent **Pickering Wharf**, with its many restaurants and stores, including several antiques shops, will delight those who enjoy Boston's Quincy Market. But *caveat emptor:* 200 years ago the English were making and exporting to Salem copies of Chinese export-ware.

All these places can be visited by following the red line painted on the sidewalk. Alternatively, board a trackless trolley for a narrated tour of all the sites,

Arthur Miller based his 1953 play "The Crucible" on the Salem trials, though its real target was the contemporary witch hunts being carried out by Congress against supposed Communists.

BELOW: Ropes Mansion, Salem.

Maps:
Area 292
Town 295

alighting at will and rejoining a later car. Trackless trolleys also make 90-minute trips to the Pioneer Village and Marblehead. Visitors can alight at several stops and rejoin later trolleys. The **Pioneer Village**, 4 miles (6 km) south of Salem and staffed by history interpreters in period costume, introduces visitors to Salem of the 1620s when it was the first capital of Massachusetts. The buildings range from rough dugouts and wigwams to thatched cottages. Crafts demonstrated include making tallow candles and spinning wool.

Seafront mansions

From Salem, travel north on Route 1A to **Beverly**, where, in 1775, the schooner *Hannah* was armed and sent out to harass British shipping, thus giving birth to the Continental Navy. Turn east on Route 127 and drive through Beverly Farms, Pride's Crossing and **Manchester-by-the-Sea**, all of which were, and are, proper places for dyed-in-the-wool Yankees to have summer retreats or year-round homes. **Singing Beach ❹** in Manchester, 31 miles (50 km) from Boston, is especially attractive. It derives its name from the crackling sound made when walking on the sands. (There is parking only at the railway station, half a mile from the beach.)

Six miles (10 km) past Manchester, turn right toward **Magnolia** and immediately sense the former glory which once attracted the rich and the beautiful from New York, Cincinnati and St Louis. Their palatial homes are now guest houses, and Main Street's once elegant stores – the street was known as "Robbers' Alley" – are quite ordinary. Yet a drive along the seafront, where the waves pound the rocks and where many grand buildings still stand, is exhilarating.

Continue in Magnolia along **Hesperus Avenue** and, after a couple of miles, stop at **Hammond Castle Museum ❺** (daily 10am–4pm in summer, Sat–Sun only

Manchester-by-the-Sea (pop. 5,526) was incorporated in 1645 and was the home of many top mariners. It became a fashionable summer community in the middle of the 19th century.

BELOW: clamming.

Gloucester skyline.

Sept–May; tel: 978-283 2080). This massive building was constructed in the mid-1920s with bits and pieces of European châteaux. The eponymous owner was an inventor; the castle was his home, his laboratory and a gallery for his art collection. The castle, which has secret passageways and a 100-ft (30-meter) long hall for the 8,200-pipe organ (advance arrangements can be made for a mini-organ concert), stands on a bluff overlooking the sea and **Norman's Woe**, a surf-pounded rock that is the setting for Longfellow's poem *The Wreck of the Hesperus*.

Hesperus Avenue now rejoins Route 127 and, after 3 miles (5 km), arrives at the drawbridge in Gloucester which spans the **Annisquam Canal**, a boon to sailors who do not wish to round Cape Ann. On the other side of the bridge, those who have perished at sea are honored by a statue of a fisherman, one hand shading his eyes as he peers into the distance, the other firmly gripping a steering wheel.

Gloucester

Gloucester ❻, the nation's oldest seaport, was founded in 1623 by a group of Englishmen who had come "to praise God and to catch fish." How well they succeeded can be observed in the harbor, where hundreds of boats unload their daily catch. Here also, the hauls of fishing boats from Canada, Iceland, Greenland and Scandinavia are processed in preparation for shipping to cities throughout the nation. Many fishermen in this, one of the world's leading fishing ports, are of Portuguese or Italian descent. Whale-watching cruises also leave from the harbor.

In town, visit the **Sargent House Museum**, the handsome Georgian home of Judith Sargent and John Murray at 49 Middle Street (Memorial Day–Columbus Day, Fri–Mon noon–4pm); its rooms are arranged as they might have looked in 1790. The country's first **Universalist Church**, a movement which Murray founded, is across the street. Displayed in a large Federal-style house at 27 Pleasant Street, the headquarters of the **Cape Ann Historical Association**, is an outstanding collection of seascapes by the renowned American marine painter Fitz Hugh Lane. Here, too, is an interesting collection of furniture, silver and porcelain and a maritime room. Farther inland, on Main Street, is the **Portuguese Church of Our Lady of Good Voyage**, readily recognizable by its two blue cupolas.

A recent literary landmark is **The Crow's Nest**, the seedy rooming house featured in Sebastian Junger's 1997 bestseller *The Perfect Storm*.

From the church, drive around the harbor to **East Main Street**, which leads to **Rocky Neck** ❼, an artists' colony looking across the water to Gloucester and containing several lively restaurants. Rudyard Kipling worked on *Captains Courageous* while staying here.

On leaving Rocky Neck, turn right onto **Eastern Point Road**. After about 3 miles (5 km), take the right fork, even though you are entering a private estate. This is the exclusive enclave of **Eastern Point**, which boasts a score of magnificent homes. Notable among these, and open to the public, is **Beauport** ❽ (mid-May–mid-Oct Mon–Fri 10am–4pm; tel: 978-283 0800), built and furnished between 1907 and 1934 by Henry Davis Sleeper, a collector of American art and antiquities. More than half of the 40 rooms, each designed and decorated to cover a different period of American life, can be seen.

Map on page 292

Some of the more popular rooms in what has been called the most fascinating house in America are the Paul Revere room, the China trade room, the pine kitchen, the Strawberry Hill room (a tribute to English Gothic) and the Golden Step room, which offers a breathtaking view of the harbor. Isabella Stewart Gardner and John D. Rockefeller were just two of many American collectors who visited Beauport and were influenced by Sleeper's taste.

At the end of Eastern Point, just beyond **Niles Beach**, are the half-mile **Dog Bar Breakwater** and **Eastern Point Light**, both built with Rockport granite. This is a great place to fish for mackerel, flounder or pollock and to find sea anemones.

Cape Ann

Return to the entrance to Eastern Point, turn right onto **Farrington Avenue** and then left onto **Atlantic Road**. You are now on a counter-clockwise loop of **Cape Ann**, following by land, if not by sea, the exploration made in 1604 by Champlain, the French explorer, and then in 1614 by John Smith, who mapped the area and named it in honor of his queen. Cape Ann is a delight, with its sometimes wild, sometimes caressing coast, dotted with sandy beaches, glorious rocky outcrops and secret coves, plus numerous boutiques, galleries and restaurants.

Good Harbor, **Long** and **Pebble beaches** are immediately passed and, after about 7 miles (11 km), **Rockport ❾** is reached. It's difficult to believe that this bustling, even frenetic, resort was a tranquil fishing village until the 1920s. Then it was discovered by artists and subsequently became a day-trippers' paradise. Most of the town's two dozen galleries, which display works of both local and international artists, are on **Main Street**, but the lure which attracts most tourists is **Bearskin Neck**. This narrow peninsula, jutting out beyond the

BELOW:
Essex attracts antiques collectors.

Rockport's harbor.

harbor, is densely packed with old fishing sheds, many with gardens, which have been converted into galleries, antique stores and restaurants.

A photographers' favorite is a red lobster shack called **Motif No.1** because of the infinite number of times it has been photographed and painted. Magnificent views of the Atlantic can be had from the breakwater at the end of the Neck.

Leave Rockport for **Pigeon Cove** ❿, a couple of miles along Route 127, and turn left to visit the **Paper House**; its walls and furnishings are made of Boston newspapers whose pages were compressed together – 215 sheets for the walls – and then lacquered. One desk is made exclusively of *Christian Science Monitors*, another of accounts of Lindbergh's transatlantic flight.

Return to Route 127 and continue for another couple of miles to **Halibut Point** ⓫. A half-mile walk from the parking lot through blueberry bushes leads to the outermost tip of Cape Ann, where huge tilted sheets of granite and fascinating tidal ponds have their devotees. A former quarry near the parking lot can be explored and attests to the fact that Rockport and its surrounds were once renowned for their granite, seen in many Boston buildings.

Continue on the loop past charming villages and rocky inlets – **Folly Cove**, **Lanesville**, **Plum Cove**, **Lobster Cove** – to **Annisquam**, which borders an inlet at the northern end of the canal of that name. This is a delightful spot freshened by the tang of the ocean. Rather than returning directly to Gloucester, turn west on Route 128 and take Exit 14 to reach Route 133, which leads to the north.

The appearance of **Woodman's**, a rusticated restaurant in **Essex**, belies its contribution to mankind. This is where, on a hot July day in 1916, Lawrence Woodman tossed some clams into a pan of boiling oil and created the heavenly dish of fried clams. Essex's other main draw is its antiques shops, and its huge redstone town hall, which towers above the playing fields, also catches the eye. **Essex Shipbuilding Museum**, at 28 Main Street (Tues–Sun 1–4pm), has drawings, tools, photographs, rigged ship models and 15 builders' half-models, all displayed in an 1834 schoolhouse. The highlight of the Essex Clamfest, held on the second Saturday in September, is a clam chowder tasting competition.

Just before reaching Ipswich, turn right onto Argilla Road, bordered by country estates. After about 3 miles (5 km), it leads to the **Crane Beach Memorial Reservation** ⓬, covering more than 1,400 acres (570 hectares) and with more than 5 miles (8 km) of magnificent white sands and dunes. However, nothing is perfect and the greenfly season from mid-July to mid-August can be hell. The **Pine Hollow Interpretive Trail** is an enjoyable 1-mile stroll over dunes into pine hollows and onto a boardwalk in a red maple swamp. Overlooking the beach is **Castle Hill** ⓭, the Crane estate, whose 59-room mansion may be visited and on whose lovely grounds glorious concerts are held on summer weekends.

Return on Argilla Road to **South Main Street**, which borders the **Ipswich** village green. On the left, at 53 South Main Street, is the dark-brown **John Whipple House** (tel: 978-356 2811), with its lovely 17th-century garden furnished in period style. Across the road at No. 40, the white Federal-period **John Heard House**, built with profits from the China trade, is filled with Chinese and early American artifacts; it

Map
on page
292

has a collection of antique carriages on its grounds. These are just two of 40 restored 17th- and 18th-century houses which permit Ipswich to claim that it has more restored houses from this period than anywhere else on the North Shore.

Backtrack from Ipswich by crossing the **Ipswich River** on the **Choate Bridge**, built in 1764; after a couple of miles, **Appleton Farms**, open to the public, is passed on the right. This glorious estate, which, with its oak trees, is reminiscent of the English countryside, has been farmed since 1640 by the same family.

Horsey types might wish to detour from Ipswich on Route 1A for about 5 miles (8 km) to **Hamilton** and the **Myopia Hunt Club** ⓮ with its renowned polo fields. The club owes its name to the fact that its founders, the Prince brothers, and many of their friends wore glasses.

Anne Bradstreet (1612–72), the first important woman author in America and one of its first poets, lived in Ipswich. Her "The Tenth Muse Lately Sprung Up in America" was published in 1650.

Newburyport

Travel north from Ipswich and, after 12 miles (20 km), Route 1A becomes **Newburyport's** ⓯ elegant High Street, lined by magnificent clapboard Federal-period houses, many with widow's walks. At No. 98, the **Cushing House** (Tues–Fri 10am–4pm, Sat 11am–2pm; tel: 978-462 2681), headquarters of the Historical Society, has 21 splendidly furnished rooms, a varied collection of artifacts and a garden with many plants more than a century old.

Turn right off High Street to reach the **Merrimack River** and the waterfront. The story of the town's nautical heritage – difficult to believe that this charming spot was once home to a large merchant fleet and a thriving ship-building industry – is told in the **Custom House**, now a **Maritime Museum** (25 Water Street; Mon–Sat 10am–4pm, Sun 1–4pm; tel: 978-462-8681).

Between the waterfront and High Street is the reconstructed **Market Square**

BELOW: details
of Motif No. 1.

and **Inn Street Mall**, a pleasing ensemble of early 19th-century three-story brick and granite buildings where it is a delight to stroll, to shop and to dine. Two churches in town are worth visiting. **Old South**, the older (1785), boasts a whispering gallery and a bell cast by Paul Revere; the newer (1801) **Unitarian** is renowned for its delicate wooden spire.

From Newburyport, a 3-mile (5-km) drive across a causeway leads to **Plum Island**, a 4,700-acre (1,900-hectare) reservation, **Parker River National Wildlife Refuge** ⓰, with a 6-mile (10-km) stretch of superb sands which is nirvana for both bird watchers and beach bums. The dunes, freshwater bogs and fresh and tidal marshes are covered with false heather, dune grass or scrub pine, and after Labor Day visitors are permitted to pick beach plums and cranberries. Turtles and toads, woodchucks and rabbits, pheasant and deer can all be seen.

Relics of the Industrial Revolution

From Newburyport, it is an easy 35-mile (56-km) drive back to Boston on Route 1. Alteratively, heading southwest along the I-495 provides an insight into the industrial revolution that transformed Massachusetts in the 19th century. **Lawrence** ⓱ was known as "Queen of the Mill Towns," and, at sunset, views along the Merrimack River, with its red-brick mills and more than a dozen soaring smoke stacks, are stygian. It was here that 30,000 mill workers went on strike for two months in 1912. The "Bread and Roses" strike was marked by murders and mass arrests but finally won wage increases for textile workers throughout New England. The story of Lawrence is recounted in its **Heritage State Park**, located in a mill boarding house (1 Jackson Street; daily 9am–4pm; tel: 978-794 1655).

BELOW: reliving the industrial past.

From Lawrence, travel 4 miles (7 km) east on Interstate 495 and turn south at exit 47 in the direction of peaceful, colonial **Andover**, home of **Phillips Academy**, one of the most prestigious preparatory schools in the nation. Its **Addison Gallery of American Art** (closed Mondays and in August; tel: 978-749 4015) houses a superb collection of 12,000 American paintings and sculptures, including works by Copley, Revere, Eakins, Homer, Whistler, Watkins, Muybridge, Sloan and Hopper.

Lowell ⓲, 8 miles (13 km) southwest of Lawrence, was known as "Spindle City" when it became the world's leading textile producer in the early 19th century. Canals were constructed and the **Merrimack River** was harnessed to power eight major red-brick textile mills. These were staffed with mill girls from the area who, thanks to the owners' Utopian pretensions, boarded in model dormitories and attended the city's handsome **St Anne's Church** each Sunday.

The local girls were replaced by successive waves of immigrants: Irish, French-Canadians, Afro-Americans, Portuguese, Poles, European Jews and, in the 20th century, Armenians, Asians (Lowell has been called the "Cambodian capital of America") and Hispanics. Before long the Utopian philosophy of Francis Cabot Lowell and his co-investors was abandoned and Lowell's sweatshops were no better than those in Europe and Asia.

Exhibits in the **Museum of American Textile History** (491 Dutton Street; tel: 978-441-0400) explain the history of woolen textile manufacturing, stressing

Map on page 292

the transition from hand to machine production during the industrial revolution. Carding, spinning and weaving are demonstrated.

Today, textiles (mainly synthetics) are produced in only two mills and Lowell has fallen on hard times. Recycling of the magnificent mills and boarding houses was introduced just in time and wholesale destruction prevented.

All this and more is recounted by National Park rangers, for much of Lowell is now a **National Historic Park**. The best tour (just over two hours) involves genuine trolley rides, traveling on a barge through canals and locks and some walking. The **Visitor Center** offers varied exhibits and a multi-image slide show; the **Lowell Heritage State Park** shows how canals, water-wheels and turbines worked. The **New England Quilt Museum** *(see right)* has antique and contemporary quilts.

Close to the Visitor Center is the home of American painter James McNeill Whistler's father, where **Whistler's etchings** are displayed. The commemorative **sculpture of Jack Kerouac**, a Lowell man who in his first novel *The Town and the City* captured Lowell in the early 20th century, stands in Eastern Park Plaza.

Those in search of further industrial history should continue toward Boston. The **Saugus Iron Works National Historic Site**, the country's first iron works (1646), is just east of Route 1 about 10 miles (16 km) north of Boston (244 Central Street, Saugus; tel: 781-233 0050). Rangers lead visitors through the impeccably reconstructed plant and explain, step by step, how iron was manufactured in the mid-1600s. The **Iron Works House**, the only surviving structure of the original complex, is a good example of 17th-century American Elizabethan architecture.

On Route 1, the **Hill Top Restaurant**, readily recognized by a herd of life-size plastic cattle bordering the highway, claims the largest turnover of an US restaurant. Seating 1,500 in five dining rooms, it specializes in inexpensive steaks. ❑

The New England Quilt Museum, conceived in 1980, moved in 1993 into a landmark savings bank building at 18 Shattuck Street, Lowell. where it runs exhibitions, lectures and workshops. Open Tues–Sat 10am–4pm (and also Sun noon–4pm in May–Nov).

BELOW:
mill buildings at Lowell National Historic Park.

INSIGHT GUIDES

Travel Tips

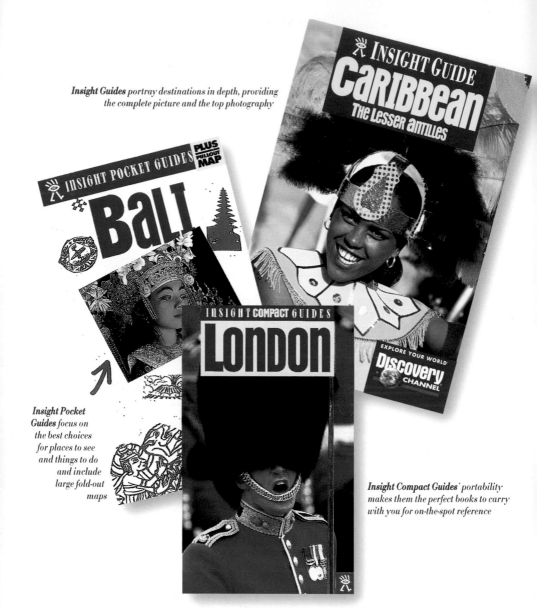

Insight Guides portray destinations in depth, providing the complete picture and the top photography

Insight Pocket Guides focus on the best choices for places to see and things to do and include large fold-out maps

Insight Compact Guides' portability makes them the perfect books to carry with you for on-the-spot reference

Three types of guide for all types of travel

INSIGHT GUIDES Different people need different kinds of information. Some want *background information* to help them prepare for the trip. Others seek *personal recommendations* from someone who knows the destination well. And others look for *compactly presented data* for on-the-spot reference. With three carefully designed series, Insight Guides offer readers the perfect choice. Insight Guides will turn your visit into an experience.

The world's largest collection of visual travel guides

CONTENTS

Getting Acquainted

NOTE: Unless a separate exchange code is shown, all telephone numbers are for Boston (US trunk dialing code 617). 1-800 numbers are toll-free only when dialed from within the US.

The Place

Boston, a port city on the northeastern coast of the US, has a population of fewer than 600,000 and covers an area of 40 sq. miles (105 sq. km). Centered on an historic common, it consists of 14 tight neighborhoods, each of which believes in the territorial imperative. Cambridge, separated from Boston by the Charles River, is a city in its own right, with a shared history and ambiance. Greater Boston, with nearly 100 towns, encompasses 3 million people and covers 1,100 sq. miles (2,850 sq. km).

The city was originally settled on the hilly Shawmut Peninsula, which was almost completely surrounded by water. It was connected with mainland Roxbury on the south by a narrow neck of land where Washington Street runs today. To the west, the extensive mud flats and salt marshes were known as the Back Bay. The North End is the only part of the early town that has been continuously occupied since the settlement in 1630.

The long shoreline encouraged the building of wharves and shipyards, and gradually the marshy coves were filled. Beyond the first settlement lay Boston Common, an area of 45 acres (18 hectares), bought by the town in 1634 and still public space today. In the 17th century, a three-peaked hill rose above the Common, but only

Beacon Hill survives. The other hills were turned into landfill as the city expanded in the 19th century.

Government

The city is governed by a mayor, who is elected for a four-year term, and by a city council of nine members. The government of the Commonwealth of Massachusetts is based in the State House at the top of Beacon Hill and in other buildings adjacent to the Government Center.

Time Zones

Boston runs on Eastern Standard Time. Every spring the clock is turned one hour ahead, and every fall one hour back. Boston is three hours ahead of Los Angeles, one hour ahead of Chicago, five hours behind London and 15 hours behind Tokyo.

Climate

Part of the magic of Boston is that it is a land of seasons. The first snow may fall in November, and intermittent snow accompanied by cold weather – considerably below freezing – will usually continue well into March. The Charles River usually freezes over. Spring, which can be temperamental, spans March into May. This is when magnolias and lilacs bloom and magic fills the air. The summer months – June until September – can be very hot and humid with some real dog-days, although most of the time the weather is just pleasantly hot – in the 70° to 80°F (21°–27°C) range.

The fall encroaches gradually, usually with one last splurge of glorious "Indian summer" days. Starting in September and "peaking" in mid-October, resplendent fall colors can be enjoyed in the outskirts of Boston and even more so in the mountains of northern New England.

In summary, Boston weather can be described in one word: erratic.

Planning the Trip

What to Wear

Boston is simultaneously more formal and less than other parts of the country. The old-guard restaurants and hotels require proper dress (the mayor himself was once refused entrance to the Ritz), whereas in student enclaves, anything goes. Plan – and, if necessary, call – ahead. Remember, too, that it can get very cold in winter and very hot in summer.

Electricity

Boston homes have "standard" electricity which is 110 volts. European appliances require an adaptor because European countries use 220-240 volts. Some hotel bathrooms have electrical outlets suitable for use with European appliances (220–240 volts), but it is useful to pack an adaptor.

Entry Regulations

VISAS & PASSPORTS

To enter the United States you must have a valid passport. Visas are required for all foreigners except Canadians. Vaccinations are not required.

CUSTOMS

Those over 21 may take into the US: 200 cigarettes, 50 cigars, or 3 lbs of tobacco; 1 US quart of alcohol; duty-free gifts worth up to $100. Do not bring in meat products, seeds, plants and fruits. Don't even think about bringing in narcotics. Customs agents in the

US are tough and efficient. The United States allows you to take out anything you wish, but consult the consulate or tourist authority of the country you are visiting next to learn of its custom regulations for entrance.

Health

In the US, health care is very expensive. If you get sick or need medical attention, the average cost for one night in a hospital in a semi-private room is well over $500. If you live in a foreign country and do not have private health insurance, try to obtain insurance for your stay here before leaving home.

Money

The most convenient and safest way to carry large sums of money is travelers checks. The two most widely accepted are American Express and Visa. Almost all stores, restaurants and hotels will accept them. Credit cards such as American Express, Visa, MasterCard, Diners Club and Discover are also widely accepted. If in doubt, be sure to double-check with waiters or clerks before you order dinner or have your purchases tallied up.

Public Holidays

Following is a list of some of the major celebrations which will appeal to visitors. Public holidays are marked with an *.

January
1st – New Year's Day*.
Third Monday – Martin Luther King Day*, ceremony at City Hall.
End of month or early February – Chinese New Year, celebrated in Chinatown with lion and dragon dances and firecrackers.

February
Third Monday – Washington's Birthday*, ceremony held at Washington's statue in the Public Garden.

March
5th – Boston Massacre/Crispus Attucks Day, parade from the massacre site to City Hall Plaza.
Middle of month – New England Spring Flower Show, the oldest annual flower exhibition in the nation lasts for seven days.
Sunday before March 17 – St Patrick's Day Parade, held in South Boston.

April
Easter Sunday* – Parade. Join the throngs who walk to the Common in their finery.
Third Sunday – Eve of Patriot's Day, lantern service at Old North Church
Third Monday – Patriots' Day*, celebrations abound, especially in Concord and Lexington.
Third Monday – Boston Marathon, the most renowned annual marathon in the world.

May
Mid-May – Boston Pops, commencement of a two-month Tuesday to Saturday (8.30pm) season at Symphony Hall.
Mid-May Sunday – Art Newbury Street, festival when art in the galleries is joined by music on the streets: an art lover's nirvana.
Mid-May Sunday – Lilac Sunday, the air at the Arnold Arboretum is redolent with the aroma from 400 varieties of varicolored lilacs in bloom.
Last Monday in May – Memorial Day*, Parade leaves from Copley Square and terminates with a ceremony at the Rose Garden in the Fenway.

June
Second week – Boston Common Dairy Festival. A quartet of cows are tethered on the Common, to commemorate its original purpose. Celebrating their presence (and output), the three-day Scooper Bowl, a charity event, dishes out 14 tons of "all you can eat" ice cream.
First Monday – Parade. Ancient & Honorable Artillery Company (nation's third oldest standing military organization) celebrates.
First Saturday – Back Bay Street

Fair, features food, drink, arts and crafts and great live music.
Sunday before the 17th. – Bunker Hill Day, reenactment of the Battle of Bunker Hill and parades in Charlestown.
Last weekend – Blessing of the Fleet, takes place at both Gloucester and Provincetown: activities peak on the Sunday.

July
Month-long – Boston Pops, free outdoor concerts at the Hatch Memorial Shell on the Esplanade.
4th – Independence Day*, Boston is awash with celebrations including a reading of the Declaration of Independence from the balcony of Old State House.
4th – Harborfest, waterfront activities marked by the turnaround of the U.S.S. *Constitution* and fireworks.
4th – Pops Concert, held at Hatch Memorial Shell on the Esplanade culminates with playing of the *1812 Overture* replete with cannons and fireworks.
Early in month – Chowderfest, an opportunity to sample literally dozens of superb New England chowders.
Most weekends – Religious processions and feasts – the North End lives up to its name of "Little Italy" with the oompah of brass bands and lots of food: best on Sundays.
14th – Bastille Day, celebrated on Marlborough Street in Back Bay with champagne, a buffet supper and lively dancing.

August
Weekends – The North End continues its religious processions and feasts.
Movable – August Moon (Chinese) Festival, prancing lions and dragons and lots of exotic foods in Chinatown.

September
First Monday – Labor Day*.
A Sunday – Art Newbury Street, the city's major concentration of galleries take to the street.
Second Saturday – Back Bay Street

Dance. Marlborough Street is closed as bands and food move in for an evening of gaiety.
Sunday late in month – Charles Street Fair, traditional fall celebration on Beacon Hill's main shopping thoroughfare.

October

Monday closest to the 12th – Columbus Day*, parade in East Boston or North End.
Second last Sunday – Head of the Charles Regatta, the largest one-day crew race in the world attracts oarspeople from everywhere.

November

Monday nearest the 11th – Veterans Day, parade starts on Commonwealth Avenue in Back Bay.
Fourth Thursday – Thanksgiving*.

December

16th – Reenactment of Boston Tea Party takes place at Tea Party Museum.
24th – Carol Singing, Louisburg Square.
25th – Christmas Day*.
3lst – First Night, citywide revels start in the afternoon and continue until the small hours.

Getting There

BY AIR

Logan International Airport leases space to more than several dozen carriers, of which about one-third are international airlines. Currently Logan is the 11th busiest airport in the nation. It is the northern terminal of the world's busiest airline market: the New York–Boston run. The Delta and the US Air shuttles leave hourly throughout the day and guarantee seats.

Although the *Traveler's Guide to Major US Airports* has called Logan "downright hospitable," it is well to remember that in its annual report for the same year the Massachusetts Port Authority confessed that "no-one wants to spend any more time than they have to at the airport."

Logan has five terminals (A – E).

Airline Telephone Numbers

Some useful telephone numbers (call Logan's public information office on: 561-1800 for current terminal locations. Terminals often move about) include:
Aer Lingus, tel: 1-800-474-7424.
Air Atlantic, tel: 1-800-426-7000.
Air Canada, tel: 1-800-776-3000.
Alitalia, tel: 1-800-223-5730.
American, tel: 1-800-433-7300.
British Airways, tel: 1-800-247-9297.
Canadian Airlines International, tel: 1-800-426-7000.
Cape Air, tel: 1-800-352-0714.
Continental, tel: 1-800-525-3273.
Delta, tel: 1-800-221-1212.
Delta Business Express, tel: 1-800-345-3400.

Lufthansa, tel: 1-800-645-3880.
Northwest (International), tel: 1-800-447-4747.
Sabena, tel: 1-800-873-3900.
Swissair, tel: 1-800-221-4750.
TAP Air Portugal, tel: 1-800-221-7370.
TWA (Domestic), tel: 1-800-221-2000; (International), tel: 1-800-892-4141.
United Airlines, tel: 1-800-241-6522.
US Air, tel: 1-800-428-4322.
Virgin Atlantic Airways, tel: 1-800-862-8621
Other useful airport numbers:
Public Information Office tel: 561-1800
Traveler's Aid tel: 542-7286.

Note that domestic and international flights of the same airline do not necessarily use the same terminal. There is a free shuttle bus service between the terminals.

Currency may be exchanged at BankBoston at terminal E. Rental lockers are available at all terminals, except terminal D. (It costs about $1 to rent a cart.) Hotel reservation information is available at the information booths in each terminal. The nearest hotels are the Logan Airport Hilton and Logan Airport Hyatt.

Logan, just 3 miles (5 km) from downtown Boston, is closer to town than any other major airport in the nation: this refers to distance and not to time. Traffic can back up at the tunnels that go under the harbor to connect the airport and city. For up-to-date information on airport traffic conditions, call Massport's Ground Transportation Hotline (tel: 1-800-23-LOGAN), operators are available Monday–Friday 8am–7pm; recorded information is available at the same number on off-hours.

The MBTA Blue Line from Airport Station is the fastest way to downtown (about 10 minutes) and to many other places as well. Free shuttle buses run between all the airport terminals and the subway

station. Cabs can be found outside each terminal. Fares to downtown should average about $20, including tip, providing there are no major traffic jams. Airways Transportation buses leave all terminals every half hour for downtown and Back Bay hotels, and several major bus companies, including Bonanza, Concord Trailways, Peter Pan and Vermont Transit, serve many outlying suburbs and distant destinations.

A delightful way to approach the city and especially useful for those staying in downtown hotels (Boston Harbor, Boston Marriot Long Wharf, Bostonian, Swissôtel and Hotel Meridien) is the Airport Water Shuttle (tel: 1-800-235-6426). The shuttle operates every 15 minutes Monday–Friday 6am–8pm; every 30 minutes on Friday evening from 8pm–11pm; every 30 minutes on Saturday 10am–11pm and Sunday 10am–8pm. The voyage takes 7 minutes and the fare is $10. (Round trip tickets are available for $17.) A free shuttle bus operates between the airport ferry dock and all of the airline terminals.

CAR RENTALS

Car rentals can be arranged at the ground level of all terminals. The following firms are represented: **Alamo** (tel: 561-4100, 1-800-327-9633); **Avis** (tel: 1-800-831-2847); **Budget** (tel: 497-1800, 1-800-527-0700); **Dollar** (tel: 569-8890, 1-800-800-4000); **Enterprise** (tel: 561-4488, 1-800-736-8222); **Hertz** (tel: 1-800-654-3131); **National** (tel: 1-800-227-7368) **Thrifty** (tel: 634-7350).

When serious traffic delays occur at the tunnel, take Route 1A North to Route 16 and thus to the Tobin Bridge and into Boston.

BY RAIL

Boston is the northern terminus of Amtrak's Northeast Corridor ("Shore Line"). Passenger trains arrive at **South Station** (Atlantic Avenue and Summer Street, tel: 482-3660; 1-800-872-7245 or, for the hearing-impaired, 1-800-523-6590) from New York, Washington, DC, and Philadelphia with connections from all points in the nationwide Amtrak system. They also stop at **Back Bay Station** (145 Dartmouth Street, tel: 482-3660).

Nine or 10 trains travel between New York and Boston daily; the average travel time is 5 hours, but some trains make the journey in a tad less than 4 hours. South Station is also the eastern terminus for Amtrak's Lake Shore Limited, which travels daily between Chicago and Boston by way of Cleveland, Buffalo, Rochester and Albany. One train daily makes the journey in 2½ hours.

BY BUS

Several intercity bus companies serve Boston. The two largest, **Greyhound** (526-1800, and 1-800-231-2222) and **Peter Pan** (1-800-343-9999), have frequent daily services from New York City and Albany, NY, as well as services from points within New England. Greyhound serves the entire United States and parts of Canada; it offers unlimited advance purchase fares for 7, 14 or 30-day periods. Nearby destinations are served by smaller bus companies such as

American Eagle, Bloom Bus, Bonanza, C & J Trailways, Concord Trailways, and Plymouth & Brockton. All converge on the handsome new bus station. Both Greyhound and Peter Pan also have terminals at Riverside in Newton, on the "D" Branch of the Green Line.

BY CAR

Getting to Boston

From the west:
Route 90 (Mass. Pike) is the most clear route inbound. Three major exits:
Exits 18–20 – Cambridge/Allston – are best for Cambridge and Charles River locations;
Exit 22 – Prudential Center/Copley Square – is best for Back Bay, Fenway, Kenmore Square and Boston Common (via Boylston, Charles, Beacon, Park and Tremont Streets);
Exit 24 – Expressway/Downtown – is best for Downtown and Central Artery access.

From the south:
Routes 95, 24 and 3 all "feed" into Route 128 East, which leads into Route 93 inbound. Two major exits are:
Kneeland Street/Chinatown – best for Back Bay, Theater District and Boston Common Visitor Center (via Kneeland, Charles, Beacon, Park and Tremont Streets);
Dock Square – best for Airport, North End, Waterfront and Faneuil Hall Marketplace.

From the north:
Routes 95, 1 and 93 enter Boston on elevated highway structures. Four major exits:
Storrow Drive – best for Back Bay, Beacon Hill, Cambridge and Boston Common Visitor Center (via Government Center exit and Cambridge Street, which becomes Tremont Street);
High Street – best for Downtown;
Kneeland Street – best for Chinatown and Theater District.

Getting Out of Boston

To the west:
Route 90 (Mass Pike) best route. From Downtown, enter the "Pike" at **Kneeland Street**; from the Back Bay take **Arlington Street, Copley Square** or **Mass. Avenue** at Newbury Street.

To the south and the north:
Route 93 (Southeast Expressway) serves the South Shore and Cape Cod (via Route 3) and Rhode Island and New York (via Routes 128 and 95). Route 93 (North) serves the North Shore and the New England Coast (via Route 1 and 95), New Hampshire (via Route 93) and Vermont (via Routes 93 and 89).

Useful Addresses

INFORMATION SOURCES

Citywide Reservation Services: 25 Huntington Avenue, tel: 267-7424 or 1-800-HOTEL-93. One-step hotel, B & B and guest house reservation service.

Boston Common Visitor Information Center: Tremont Street side of Boston Common. The booth here marks the start of the Freedom Trail and provides visitor information about Greater Boston, Massachusetts and New England. Daily, 9am–5pm.

Faneuil Hall Marketplace Information Center: on the south side of Quincy Market.

Massachusetts Office of Travel & Tourism: 10 Park Plaza, Suite 4510, tel: 727-3201. "MOTT"can supply details on the state and day trip information. Monday–Friday 9am–5pm.

Prudential Visitor Center: on the west side of the Prudential Plaza, tel: 536-4100. The center is operated by the Greater Boston Convention & Visitors Bureau and provides information on Greater Boston, Massachusetts and New England. Monday–Saturday 9am–5pm, Sunday 1–5pm.

Massport International Information Booth: Logan International Airport (terminal E). Provides visitors assistance to International visitors.

Summer, noon–8pm; winter, noon–6pm.

National Park Service Visitors Center: 15 State Street, opposite Old State House, tel: 242-5642. Starting point for free Freedom Trail walks. The Center offers services, including information, displays and sales on historic Boston and Massachusetts; rest rooms; telephones, and handicapped accessiblity. Daily 9am–6pm.

Cambridge Discovery Inc: Located at booth in the center of Harvard Square, tel: 497-1630. Source of comprehensive Cambridge-specific information. Tours for groups by appointment. Monday–Saturday 9am–6pm.

Harvard University Information Office: Holyoke Centre in Harvard Square, tel: 495-1573. Source of Harvard-specific information. Monday–Saturday 9am–7pm. Summer Sunday 12–5pm.

Travelers Aid Society: Offices at 17 E Street, tel: 542-7286. Booths at Greyhound Bus depot at South Station and at Logan Airport, Terminals A and E.

Bostix Ticket Booth: Faneuil Hall and Copley Square, tel: 723-5181. This is Boston's official entertainment and cultural information center, providing tickets and information for more than 100 attractions. On the day of a performance, half-price theatre tickets are sold here. Tuesday–Saturday 10am–6pm, Sunday 11am–4pm.

Practical Tips

Weights & Measures

The US uses the Imperial system of weights and measures. Metric is rarely used. Below is a conversion chart.
1 inch = 2.54 centimeters
1 foot = 30.48 centimeters
1 mile = 1.609 kilometers
1 quart = 1.136 liters
1 ounce = 28.4 grams
1 pound = 0.453 kilograms
1 yard = 0.9144 meters

Business Hours

Most offices are open Monday–Friday 9am–5pm, although some offices open at 8am.

Banks are open Monday–Friday 9am–3pm and often later. On Thursday they remain open until 5pm and often later. Saturday hours are generally 9am–2pm.

The main Post Office is at 25 Dorchester Avenue (tel: 654-5001), behind South Station. Post Office hours are Monday–Friday 8am–5pm and Saturday 8am–noon.

The Post Office at Logan Airport is open until midnight. Stamps are also available in vending machines located in airports, hotels, stores, bus and train stations. If you do not know where you will be staying, mail can be addressed to

General Delivery, Main Post Office, Boston.

Tipping

Tipping is voluntary. Gratuities are not automatically tallied into the bill. Here are a few tipping guidelines:
Waiters are usually given 15 percent of the bill. For above-average service, tip 20 percent.
Taxi cab drivers usually get 15 percent of the fare.
Doormen, skycabs and porters receive one dollar a bag.
Hairdressers, manicurists and masseurs usually receive 10 to 15 percent of the total charge.

Media

NEWSPAPERS & MAGAZINES
Boston Globe: daily newspaper. Thursday supplement gives complete events listings for the next seven days.
Boston Herald: daily newspaper. Friday supplement contains listings for following week.
Boston Magazine: a slick and informative monthly of local interest.
Boston Phoenix: a thick Thursday alternative weekly with intelligent articles plus listings and comments on the local entertainment scene.
Christian Science Monitor: a prestigious daily newspaper published in Boston on weekdays. Strong on international news, light on local news.
The kiosk in the middle of Harvard Square (tel: 354-7777) is *the* place at which to purchase national and international publications.

RADIO STATIONS
Radio stations in the area include:
WEEI on 590 AM for sports;
WRKO on 680 AM for talk;
WCRB on 102.5 FM for classical music;
WBCN on 104.1 FM for rock music;
WJIB on 96.9 FM for popular music;
WGBH (Public Radio – classical music) on 89.7 FM;
WBUR (Public Radio – news and information) 90.9 FM .

Essential Telephone Numbers

Police in Boston/Cambridge: tel: 911.
Medical Hot Line: Beth Israel Hospital, tel: 667-3300.
Boston Evening Medical Center: tel: 267-7171.
Eye & Ear Infirmary: tel: 523-7900.
Massachusetts General Hospital: tel: 726-2000.

Credit Cards Lost or Stolen:
American Express tel: 1-800-528-2121;
Diners Club/Carte Blanche tel: 1-800-525-9150;
MasterCard tel: 1-800-826-2181;
Visa 1-800-227-6811.
Weather: tel: 936-1234.

TELEVISION STATIONS

These include: channel 2 (**WGBH**) and channel 44 (**WGBX**) for public television, (**PBS**);
CBS can be viewed on channel 4 (WBZ);
ABC on channel 5 (WCVB);
NBC on channel 7 (WNEV);
Fox on channel 25 (WXNE).

Fax Facilities

Fax machines can be found at most hotels. Public fax companies are located throughout the city, so check the phone directory under "Facsimile" for the fax service nearest to you.

Embassies and Consulates

Canada: 3 Copley Place, tel: 262-3760.
Chile: 79 Milk St, tel: 426-1678.
Denmark: 20 Park Plaza, 542-1415.
Dominican Republic: 20 Park Plaza, tel: 482-8121.
Finland: tel: 654-1800
France: 31 St. James, tel: 542-7374.
Great Britain: 600 Atlantic Ave, tel: 248-9555.
Greece: 86 Beacon St., tel: 523-0100.
Haiti: 545 Boylston St, tel: 266-3660.
Ireland: 535 Boylston St, tel: 267-9330.
Israel: 1020 Statler Office Building, tel: 542-0041.
Japan: 600 Atlantic Ave, tel: 973-9772
Pakistan: 393 Commonwealth Ave, tel: 267-5555.
Portugal: 899 Boylston St, tel: 536-8740.
Spain: 545 Boylston St, tel: 536-2506.
Sweden: 286 Congress St, tel: 350-0111.
Switzerland: 3 Center Plaza, tel: 720-6310.
Venezuela: 545 Boylston St, tel: 266-9368.

Getting Around

General

Boston, it is justly claimed, is a walker's city – a good thing, for it is certainly not a driver's city. The city planners, as Emerson noted, were the cows, and it has been suggested that the Puritan belief in predestination extended even to urban design. Streets appeared where Providence chose to lay them – along cow paths, Native American trails and colonial wagon tracks – and are linked by crooked little alleys.

City planners, however, did come into their own in the middle of the 19th century, and the Back Bay, South Boston, to a lesser extent, the South End have impeccable grid systems.

If you attempt to drive in the city, and feel frustrated and inadequate, be consoled that many Bostonians feel the same way. Being faced by cars coming the wrong way on a one-way street, being stuck in a traffic jam, getting lost and then being unable to find a parking space is about par for the course. It's said that indicating a turn is considered "giving information to the enemy."

PARKING

Conveniently located public parking facilities are found at **Government Center**; **Post Office Square**; the **Public Garden**; the **Prudential Center**; on **Clarendon Street** near the **John Hancock Tower**; and elsewhere. Private lots are scattered here and there.

A number of parking garages are situated close to **Harvard Square** in Cambridge. Try **Charles Square Garage**, 1 Bennett Street; **Church Street Parking Lot**, Church Street; **Harvard Square Garage**, JFK and

Eliot Streets; and **Holyoke Center Garage**, access via Dunster and Holyoke Street.

Better by far to use the subway (a.k.a. rapid transit or "T") and bus services provided by the **MBTA** (**Massachusetts Bay Transportation Authority**). For general MBTA travel information, telephone 222-3200 or 1-800-392-6100, for the hearing-impaired 722-5146, weekdays 6.30am–11pm, weekends 9am–6pm. For customer service telephone 222-5215; and for MBTA police emergency telephone 222-1212.

Transport

RAPID TRANSIT

For easy reference, see the subway map facing inside back cover.
Ever since it was inaugurated in 1897, the subway (nowadays the rapid transit or, as it is usually called, the "T") has been a source of amusement for Bostonians. One ditty, "The Man Who Never Returned," revived by folksingers in the 1960s, tells of poor Charlie who was "doomed to ride forever 'neath the streets of Boston" because he lacked the nickel fare necessary to alight.

However, despite severe overcrowding during rush hours the "T" is a fairly efficient, clean and user-friendly system.

The four rapid transit lines – Red, Green, Orange, Blue – that radiate out from downtown Boston cling to the name "subway" even though all lines run above ground for part of their route.

There are more than 75 rapid transit stations, usually named for a nearby square, street, or landmark. In addition, Green Line trains stop at many street corners along the surface portion of their routes. All four lines intersect in downtown Boston. Transfers between lines, at no extra charge, are possible at: **Park Street** – Red and Green Lines (with underground walkway to the Orange Line at Downtown Crossing). **Downtown Crossing** – Red and Orange Lines (with underground

walkway to the Green Line at Park Street).
Government Center – Blue and Green Lines.
State – Blue and Orange Lines.
Haymarket and North Station – Green and Orange Lines. (This connection is considerably more convenient at Haymarket than at North Station).

"Inbound" is always towards downtown Boston – Park Street, Downtown Crossing and Government Center. "Outbound" means away from downtown. Outside of central Boston, both the Red and Green Lines have branches. Check the sign on the front of the train. Green Line trains (also called streetcars or simply cars) carry letters to indicate different branches: B – Boston College; C – Cleveland Circle; D – Riverside; E – Heath Street or Arborway. A red line through the letter on a sign means that the train goes only part way on that branch.

Turnstiles in the underground stations of the "T" accept only tokens. These can be purchased at the collectors' booths. One token (currently under $1) permits travelers to ride as far as they wish without extra payment. When boarding the "T" at surface stations one token or the exact change is necessary. Getting there on the "T" can be less expensive than getting back. Although most outbound fares (except to Quincy Adams and to Braintree), irrespective of distance, are 85 cents, an inbound journey from outlying stations can cost $2 or more.

The Rapid Transit operates 20 hours each day – from shortly after 5am until past 1am On Sundays, service begins about 40 minutes later than on other days. Last trains leave downtown Boston at 12.45am.

BY BUS

The majority of the MBTA's 160-plus bus routes operate feeder services linking subway stations to neighborhoods not directly served

by the rapid transit system. Some crosstown routes connect stations on different subway lines without going into downtown. Only a few MBTA buses actually enter downtown Boston, and most of these are express buses from outlying areas. One service that visitors might wish to use is Route 1, which travels along Massachusetts Avenue (at the western end of the Back Bay) across the Charles River to MIT and onto Harvard Square. MBTA buses also serve Lexington (board the T-62 or T-76 at Alewife) and Marblehead (board the T-441 or T-442 at Haymarket).

The basic MBTA bus fare is 60 cents. On a few relatively long routes, zone fares – charges per additional zone, up to $2 – are imposed. Express bus fares range from $1.25 to $2.25, depending on the length of the route. Exact change is required on buses, and dollars bills are not accepted. MBTA tokens are accepted, but change is not returned.

COMMUTER RAIL

The MBTA Commuter Rail extends from downtown Boston to as far as 60 miles away and serves such tourist destinations as Concord, Lowell, Salem, Ipswich, Gloucester and Rockport. Trains to the north and northwest of Boston depart from North Station, while trains to points south and west of the city leave from South Station.

All south side commuter trains, except the Fairmount Line, also stop at the Back Bay Station. For information contact South Station (tel: 345-7456) or North Station (tel: 722-3600).

Commuter rail fares are zoned from a minimum of 85 cents to a maximum of $6. A trip from Boston to Salem, for example, costs $2.50. Tickets are sold at the railway stations or can be purchased on the train, subject to a surcharge.

Passport Visitor Pass
A one–day Passport costs $5; three-day, $9; seven-day, $18.

Children's Passports (age 5–11) are half the adult price. Passports permit unlimited use on the "T," on MBTA buses up to $1.50 fare (additional fare, if any, payable in cash), and commuter rail zones IA and IB. Passports also earn discounts at some tourist attractions and restaurants. Passports are sold at the Airport, three railway stations; Visitor Information Center on Boston Common; Faneuil Hall Marketplace Information Center; Harvard subway station and at some hotels. Tel: 222-3200 for further details.

CAR RENTALS

There are a wide variety of car rental companies:
Alamo, tel: 1-800-327-9633
Avis, tel: 1-800-831-2847
Budget, tel: 1-800-527-0700, 497-1800
Dollar Rent A Car, tel: 1-800-800-4000
Enterprise, tcl: 1 800 325 8007
Hertz, tel: 1-800-654-3131
National, tel: 1-800-227-7368
Rent-A-Wreck, tel: 1-800-535-1391, 542-8700
Thrifty, tel: 1-800-367-2277

LIMOUSINE SERVICES

A & A, tel: 623-8700
Cap's, tel: 523-0727
Commonwealth, tel: 1-800-558-5466, 787-5575
Escort, tel: 926-6900
Fifth Avenue, tel: 1-800-343-2071, 884-2600

COMMUTER BOAT

The Navy Yard Water Shuttle (this is a delightful way to reach the U.S.S. *Constitution* and the Bunker Hill Monument) sails from Long Wharf to the Charlestown Navy Yard daily; the voyage takes 10 minutes and the fare is about $1.

The Hingham commuter boat sails from Rowes Wharf, Monday–Friday: the one-way fare is about $4.

OTHER FERRIES, BUSES AND PLANES

Boston Harbor Cruises (tel: 227 4320) offers transport to **Georges Island** (time 45 minutes). The service operates from **Long Wharf** daily from mid-June to Labor Day and on weekends only from early-May until mid-June and from mid-September until late-October. During the summer months and on weekends in May and September the Boston Harbor Islands State Park runs a free water taxi service from Georges Island to half a dozen of the other Harbor Islands. Each island is visited two or three times daily, with increased service on the weekends.

A delightful way to reach **Provincetown** during the summer months is to board the **Bay State Cruise Company's** (tel: 748-1428) ferry at **Commonwealth Pier** near the World Trade Center at 8am and arrive at Provincetown 2½ hours later. The ferry leaves Provincetown

Taxicabs

Taxi stands are common at popular tourist sites.
Companies to call include:
Bay State Taxi Service, tel: 566-5000
Boston Cab Association Inc, tel: 262-2227
Checker Taxi Co., tel: 536-7500
Independent Taxi Operators Association, tel: 426-8700
Metro Cab, tel: 242-8000
Red Cab, tel: 734-5000
Town Taxi, tel: 536-5000

Tolls for bridges and tunnels are paid by the passenger. There is no extra fare for additional passengers. The driver may charge extra for trunks or unusual cargo (e.g., crocodiles). For trips over 12 miles from downtown flat rates are charged – currently, a bit over $2 per mile plus tolls. Tipping is not mandatory but it is a brave (or callous) soul who does not add 15 percent to the fare.

for Boston at 3pm. It runs daily from mid-June to Labor Day and on weekends from Memorial Day to mid-June and Labor Day to mid-October. Reservations are strongly recommended.

The **A.C. Cruise Line** (261-6633) ferry departs daily (except Sunday) at 10am from late-June to Labor Day and at weekends from Memorial Day to mid-June from 290 Northern Avenue for **Gloucester (Rocky Neck)**. The voyage takes 3 hours; the boat arrives back in Boston at 5.30pm.

For **Plymouth** board the **Plymouth–Brockton** bus at South Station. The trip takes under one hour. Unfortunately, the majority of buses do not stop in Plymouth itself but at the North Plymouth Bus station, which is 2½ miles from the tourist attractions. The same company offers a fairly frequent service to **Hyannis**: the trip takes about 1½ hours. Connecting buses leave from Hyannis for **Provincetown**, a journey of about 90 minutes. **Bonanza** buses and travel via Falmouth, Wareham, Buzzard's Bay to **Woods Hole**.

Cape Air (tel: 1-800-352-0714) offers direct flights from Logan Airport to Hyannis and Provincetown, Nantucket and Martha's Vineyard, as well as between these points. Flights are brief – less than 30 minutes.

TOURS

Bus companies run daily tours during the summer months. These cover not only Boston and its environs but venture farther afield and visit many destinations mentioned in this book's Day Trips chapters.

Brush Hill Transportation (tel: 781-986-6100) offer tours of Lexington, Concord, Greater Boston, Cambridge, Plimoth Plantation, Salem and Cape Cod, departing from several downtown hotels.

Throughout the year **Beantown Trolley** (tel: 781-986-6100) and **Old Town Trolley** (tel: 269-7010) run trolley tours covering Beacon Hill,

Newbury Street, Downtown, the Waterfront, and the Bunker Hill Pavilion in Charlestown, passing close to many of the Freedom Trail sites. The uninterrupted tour lasts 90 minutes, but passengers can alight as often as they wish and board a later trolley from the same company.

Old Town Trolley also runs a **Cambridge** tour, which leaves Harvard Square every hour on the hour.

A relatively new addition are the popular **Boston Duck Tours** which offer narrated historic tours of the city and the Charles River on World War II vintage amphibious vehicles. Tours leave from the Prudential Center (tel: 723-3825).

A wide variety of **harbor cruises**, ranging from one hour sight-seeing to lunchtime cruises, evening outings and "booze" cruises with dinner and/or musical entertainment, are organized by the **Bay State Cruise Company** (tel: 748-1428), **Boston Harbor Cruises** (tel: 227-4320) and the **Massachusetts Bay Lines** (tel: 542-8000). Vessels of Boston Harbor Cruises leave from Long Wharf; those of the Massachusetts Bay line from Rowes Wharf; and those of the Bay State Cruise Company leave from Commonwealth Pier near the World Trade Center.

Cruising and dining can also be enjoyed on the Odyssey (tel: 654-9700) out of Rowes Wharf. Five-hour **whale-watching** cruises, run by the New England Aquarium (tel: 973-5200) and accompanied by Aquarium naturalists, cast off from Central Wharf daily at 9am on Monday–Friday and at 8am and 2pm on Saturday and Sunday from May until October. They also sail on weekends (departure 11am) in April and October.

Both Boston and Cambridge are ideal for **walking**. Many walking tours, both general and for the specialist, are available.

Boston by Foot (tel: 367-2345). Offers a wide variety of regular scheduled tours May–October. History and the city's architecture are highlighted. Most tours start at

10am or 2pm and last for 90 minutes. Meet your guide in front of Faneuil Hall at the statue of Samuel Adams.

Cambridge Discovery Tours (tel: 497-1630). Morning and afternoon tours leave from the Cambridge Discovery Information Booth in the heart of Harvard Square.

Cambridge Historical Society (tel: 547-4252). Offers year-round tours with a variety of themes and routes.

Historic Neighborhoods Foundation (tel: 426-1885). Has a variety of regular scheduled tours May–November. The Kennedy Roots Tour focuses on North End sites associated with the family of John F. Kennedy. Other tours include a Chinatown, the Financial District and a sunset stroll through Beacon Hill. Small children will adore the "Make Way for Ducklings" stroll, based on the classic book, in the Public Garden on Saturdays at 11am.

Victorian Society in America (tel: 267-6338). Organizes walking tours on spring and fall Sunday afternoons. Emphasis is on architecture, landscape and women's achievements.

The **National Park Service** (tel: 242-5642). Offers frequent free tours of the **Freedom Trail** from mid-June to mid-October. A half dozen Freedom Trail sites are visited in a tour which lasts about 90 minutes.

Boston Center for Adult Education (tel: 267-4430). Some of the courses consist of unusual ways to get acquainted with the city: e.g., harbor kayak tours, or glimpses into Newbury Street galleries. Call for a catalog.

Where to Stay

General

The city of Boston is fairly well endowed with hotels, although one might be tempted to question this during spring and fall when conventions are in full swing. Hard facts are that the metropolitan area boasts more than 21,000 hotel rooms, of which two-thirds are in Boston and Cambridge. Bed and breakfast accommodations are becoming increasingly popular and can be of a high standard. And then, of course, there's the inevitable "Y" and youth hostels.

Some visitors might prefer the rarified atmosphere of Cambridge a quick trip (5–10 minutes) from Boston and easily reached by public transport. Another alternative is to stay in one of the many hotels in Greater or Metropolitan Boston and join the MBTA (Massachusetts Bay Transportation Authority) commuters for a 30–40 minute journey every morning and evening. These suburban hotels, most of which belong to major chains, tend to be less expensive than city center hotels.

Boston Hotels

Back Bay Hilton
40 Dalton Street
Tel: 236-1100. Fax: 867-6158
www.bostonbackbay.hilton.com
335 rooms. Across the road from the Hynes Convention Center and the Christian Science Complex. Close to Massachusetts Avenue and bus to Cambridge. **$$$**

Best Western
342 Longwood Avenue, Boston
Tel: 731-4700. Fax: 781-6273
www.bestwestern.com
152 rooms. Situated in the heart of

the city's major medical complex and adjoining the Longwood Galleria, which has a food court and some retail stores. Also close to the Fenway with its colleges and museums. A bus stop at the hotel door means that downtown Boston is only minutes away. Some units are kitchenette studios. **$$**

Boston Harbor Hotel
70 Rowes Wharf
Tel: 439-7000. www.bhh.com
230 rooms. Board the airport water shuttle at Logan and, seven minutes later, step into the luxury of the city's foremost waterside hotel. Bedrooms all have either harbor or skyline views. Eighteen rooms are specially designed for the physically handicapped. A museum-quality art collection decorates the public areas. Across the road is the Financial District, while minutes away (on foot) is the Aquarium and Quincy Market. **$$$$**

Boston Marriott Copley Plaza
110 Huntington Avenue
Tel: 236-5800. Fax: 236-5885
www.marriott.com
1,149 rooms. Handsome bedrooms in this hotel, which has 36 rooms suitable for the handicapped. Not only is the hotel linked to the Copley Place shopping mall with its upmarket stores, but it is also connected by a glassed-in walkway with the Prudential Center, where there is still more shopping and restaurants. **$$$$**

Boston Marriott Long Wharf
296 State Street, Long Wharf
Tel: 227-0800. Fax: 227-2867
www.marriott.com
400 rooms. Situated at the waterfront immediately next to the Aquarium and within a minute's walk of Quincy Market. Ideally situated for all water activities. Most rooms in this architecturally unusual hotel have panoramic views of the harbor. Step out of the hotel and into the subway. **$$$$**

Boston Park Plaza Hotel & Towers
64 Arlington Street
Tel: 426-2000. Fax: 426-5545
977 rooms. This excellently located, middle-of-the-road, bustling hotel began life in 1927 as the flagship of the Statler chain. It is

convenient for the Theatre District and the Green Line "T." **$$$**

Colonnade
120 Huntington Avenue
Tel: 424-7000. Fax: 424-1717
www.colonnadehotel.com
280 rooms. A charming, European-style hotel which prides itself on its multilingual staff. All the bedrooms are L-shaped, with distinct sitting, sleeping and dressing areas. Situated very close to the Prudential Center and the Christian Science Complex and with a subway stop at its doorstep. **$$$**

Copley Square
47 Huntington Avenue
Tel: 536-9000. Fax: 267-3547
www.copleysquarehotel.com
150 rooms. This modest and moderately priced hotel was opened in the 1890s. Bedrooms vary enormously in size. Copley Plaza, the Prudential Center and the Public Library are all close by. **$$**

Fairmont Copley Plaza
138 St James Avenue
Tel: 267-5300. Fax: 267-7668
www.fairmont.com
393 rooms. It is still, with its European style, "*la grande dame*" of Boston hotels. Some rooms, many decorated with period furniture, are on the small side. Since it opened in 1912, it has reputedly been visited by every President. Situated in Copley Square, it is close to most tourist attractions and public transport. **$$$$**

Four Seasons
200 Boylston Street
Tel: 338-4400. Fax: 423-0154
www.fourseasons.com
288 rooms. This 15-story red-brick hotel, which overlooks the Public Garden, is devoted to elegance and sybaritic living. The service and cuisine set standards city-wide. **$$$$**

Holiday Inn–Government Center
5 Blossom Street
Tel: 742-7630. Fax: 742-4192
www.HIselectBoston.com
300 rooms. Situated at the foot of the "wrong" side of Beacon Hill, (but next to the Massachusetts General Hospital) and with the river just a few yards away. **$$**

Lenox Hotel
710 Boylston Street
Tel: 536-5300. Fax: 267-1237
www.lenoxhotel.com
220 rooms. Modest and moderate traditional family hotel built in 1900. Bedrooms, some with functional fireplaces, have been redecorated in French Provincial, Oriental or Colonial decor. Just a few steps from the Prudential Center and the Public Library, and a block from the subway. **$$**

Price Categories

A very approximate guide to current room rates for a standard double per night is:
$$$$ = over $200
$$$ = $150–200
$$ = $100–150
$ = under $100

Le Meridien
250 Franklin Street
Tel: 451-1900. Fax: 423-2844
www.lemeridienboston.com
326 rooms. A superb recycling in the early 1980s of the Federal Reserve Bank, which was patterned after a 16th-century Roman palazzo, brought France to Boston. The hotel is in the heart of the Financial District yet close to Quincy Market. **$$$$**

Midtown Hotel
220 Huntington Avenue
Tel: 262-1000. Fax: 262-8739
www.midtownhotel.com
160 rooms. Near Symphony Hall, Christian Science Complex and Prudential Center. Bus to Cambridge and subway to downtown nearby. **$$**

Omni Parker House
60 School Street
Tel: 227-8600. Fax: 227-2120
www.omnihotels.com
541 rooms. Reportedly the oldest continuously operating hotel in America (since 1854); however, the present building, which has frequently been renovated, dates only from 1927. Some rooms have showers only. Malcolm X and (allegedly) Ho Chi Minh both worked here. A favorite with politicians, and

possibly the most centrally located hotel in the city. **$$$**

Radisson Hotel Boston
200 Stuart Street
Tel: 482-1800. Fax: 451-2750
www.radisson.com
350 rooms. An indoor heated pool adds to the allure of this hotel located in the heart of the Theater District and within walking distance of most tourist attractions. Free-indoor parking, with direct access to your room. **$$**

Regal Bostonian Hotel
Faneuil Hall Marketplace
Tel: 523-3600. Fax: 523-2454
www.regal-hotels.com
152 rooms. Continental elegance and intimacy are the keynotes here. The Harkness Wing, an original 1824 building, has rooms with working fireplaces, exposed beamed ceilings and brick walls. The newer wing is more contemporary in style. The location, though central, can spell trouble for light sleepers. The hotel offers complimentary limousine service to the airport and other parts of Boston. **$$$$**

Ritz-Carlton
15 Arlington Street
Tel: 536-5700. Fax: 536-1335
www.ritzcarlton.com
278 rooms. Not quite as glitzy as the Four Seasons, but in its own way every bit as luxurious. Some bedrooms overlook the Public Garden. Forty-one of the units are suites, including a presidential suite and one for kids with specially scaled-down fixtures and the latest toys. The Back Bay, with its stores, galleries and restaurants, is just outside the door. Complimentary limousine service within the city on weekday mornings. **$$$$**

Sheraton Boston Hotel & Towers
39 Dalton Street
Tel: 236-2000. Fax: 236-1702
www.ittsheratonboston.com
1,250 rooms. New England's largest hotel, adjacent to the Hynes Convention Center and the Christian Science Complex. Don't be put off by the exterior of the twin 29-story towers. The top four floors are superior and more expensive than those below. **$$$$**

Swissôtel Boston
One Avenue de Lafayette
Tel: 451-2600. Fax: 451-0054
www.swissotel.com
500 rooms. In the heart of
Downtown and close to everything.
This grand and elegant hotel rises
above Lafayette Place, a shopping
complex currently in transition;
Downtown Crossing, with its large
stores, is two blocks away. Upper
floors offer superb views of the
waterfront and Beacon Hill. Twenty-
five rooms specially designed for
the physically handicapped. **$$$$**

Tremont House
275 Tremont Street
Tel: 426-1400. Fax: 423-0374
www.wyndham.com
281 rooms. Situated in the very
center Theater District and within
walking distance of most tourist
attractions. **$$**

Westin Hotel, Copley Place
10 Huntington Avenue
Tel: 262-9600. Fax: 424-7502
www.westin.com
804 rooms. Rooms in Boston's
tallest hotel – it has 36 stories –
are among the city's largest and
have superb views of the river. Forty
rooms are specially designed for
the physically handicapped. Hotel is
linked by skybridge to the Copley
Place shopping mall, with its
cinemas and restaurants. **$$$$**

B & B Agencies

The Massachusetts Office of Travel
and Tourism, 10 Park Plaza,
Boston, MA 02116, tel: 727-3201,
(www.massvacation.com) publishes
a free *Bed and Breakfast Guide,*
which lists guest houses throughout
the state.
  In Boston and Cambridge, B & B
accommodations run from about
$60 to $100 or more for a double.
Central organizations to contact
are:

Bed & Breakfast Agency of Boston
47 Commercial Wharf, Boston,
MA 02110
Tel: 720-3540, 1-800-248-9262.
Fax: 973-8525
www.boston-bnbagency.com
Offers late 19th-century town-

Price Categories

A very approximate guide to
current room rates for a
standard double per night is:
$$$$ = over $200
$$$ = $150–200
$$ = $100–150
$ = under $100

houses, furnished condos and
much more.

Bed & Breakfast Associates Bay Colony
Tel: 720-0522, 1-800-347-5088.
Fax: (781) 449-5958
www.bnbboston.com
Lists homes in metropolitan Boston
and throughout the eastern part of
Massachusetts.

Bed & Breakfast Cambridge and Greater Boston
262 Beacon Street, Boston 02116
Tel: 720-1492. Fax: 227-0021
www.bedandbreakfast.baweb.com
Accommodations in private homes
in Boston, Cambridge and
surrounding towns.

Boston Reservations
1643 Beacon St, Waban, MA 02168
Tel: 723-8839. Fax: 332-5751
www.bostonreservations.com
Accommodations in private homes
in Boston and Cambridge.

Boston B & Bs

A Cambridge House
2218 Massachusetts Avenue,
Cambridge, MA 02140
Tel: 491-6300, 1-800-232-9989.
Fax: 868-2848
A delightful historic home with 9
A/C rooms, some with shared bath.
An exercise room is also available.
Breakfast is included and parking is
also available.

Anthony's Town House
1085 Beacon Street, Brookline
02246
Tel: 566-3972. Fax: 232-1085
A four-story turn-of-the-century
brownstone townhouse with 14
rooms decorated with Queen Anne
and Victorian style furnishings.
Situated on the Green Line of the
"T": 15 minutes to downtown
Boston.

Baileys Boston House
P.O. Box 130, Boston 02199
Tel: 262-4543. Fax: 278-9736
A European-style B & B home in the
heart of the Back Bay.

Beacon Inn
1087 Beacon Street, Brookline
02246
Tel: 566-0088. Fax: 264 7948
15 rooms. Close to Fenway Park
and Boston University and on the
Green Line of the "T"; 15 minutes
to downtown.

Newbury Guest House
261 Newbury Street, Boston 02215
Tel: 437-7666. Fax: 262-4243
14 rooms. On a fashionable street
in the heart of Back Bay.

Hostels & "Ys"

Berkeley Residence Club
40 Berkeley Street, Boston 02116
Tel: 482-8850. Fax: 482-9692
Located close to Copley Square and
South Station, this 200-room club
run by the YWCA offers single and
doubles for women only. Pleasant
garden and public rooms. $51 for
singles; $78 for doubles, $90 for
triples.

Boston International Youth Hostel
12 Hemenway Street, Fenway
Tel: 536-1027. Fax: 424-6558
www.bostonhostel.org
Well located at the western fringe of
the Back Bay and very close to
public transport. 220 beds in 4–6
bed dormitories: bring or rent
sheets. Currently around $20 a
night for members and $23 for
non-members.

Greater Boston YMCA
316 Huntington Avenue, Fenway
Tel: 536-7800. Fax: 267-4653
www.ymcaboston.org
Clean rooms with color TV run $41
for singles; $61 for singles with
baths; $61 for doubles (with double
bed); with three- and four-person
accommodations for $80 to $95.
This includes hot breakfast and
maid service. Maximum stay is 10
days. Guests have full use of all
athletic facilities. The "Y" is well
situated within walking distance of
the Christian Science Complex, the
Prudential Center, Museum of Fine
Arts and Symphony Hall. The Green

Line of the "T" stops at the door and downtown is only 10 minutes away.

Cambridge Hotels

The majority of Cambridge hotels are situated near Harvard University or at the extreme eastern end of the MIT campus.
In the former group are:
Charles
1 Bennett Street
Tel. 864-1200. Fax: 864-5715
www.preferedhotels.com
299 rooms. A touch of class is provided on the edge of Harvard Square at Cambridge's answer to the Four Seasons. Its Regattabar is consistently rated as the best jazz scene in the region, and Rialto is a highly regarded restaurant. A shopping mall is attached to the hotel, and shops and restaurants are all around. **$$$$**
The Harvard Square Hotel
110 Mount Auburn Street
Tel: 864-5200. Fax: 864-2409
72 rooms. A six-floor motel in the heart of Harvard Square. All rooms with picture windows; a complimentary continental breakfast. **$**
The Inn at Harvard
1201 Massachusetts Avenue, Cambridge 02138
Tel: 491-2222, 1-800-528-0444.
Fax: 491-6520
www.innatharvard.com
113 rooms. Graham Gund's playful design, with a four-story atrium/library, creates the sense of an ever-shifting salon. **$$**
Sheraton Commander, 16 Garden Street, tel: 547-4800, 1-800-325-3535. Fax: 868-8322
www.sheratoncommander.com
176 rooms. An old-fashioned but well-kept hotel near Cambridge Common and Harvard Square. Some rooms have Boston rockers and four-poster beds, and some have kitchenettes. **$$$**
Among the hotels at the extreme eastern end of the MIT campus are:
Marriott Cambridge
2 Cambridge Center
Tel: 494-6600. Fax: 494-0036
www.marriott.com

431 rooms. A 25-story hotel with a modest adjacent shopping complex. A subway stop at the hotel entrance means that both Downtown Boston and Harvard Square are just minutes away. **$$$**
Royal Sonesta
5 Cambridge Parkway
Tel: 806-4200. Fax: 806-4232
www.sonesta.com
400 rooms. On the banks of the Charles and offering great views of the Boston skyline. Closest of all hotels to the Science Museum. Practically next door is the CambridgeSide Galleria, a popular shopping mall. Free shuttle service into Boston. **$$$**

Other Cambridge hotels include:
DoubleTree Guest Suites
400 Soldiers Field Road, Boston
Tel: 783-0090. Fax: 783-0897
www.doubletreehotels.com
310 suites. All accommodations are in two-room suites with two telephones and two TV sets. Great for families because the living rooms contain sofa-beds and children under 18 are free. Breakfast is included in room rate. Next to the Harvard Business School and on the banks of the Charles. A 10-minute stroll leads to Harvard Square. **$$**
Howard Johnson Hotel Cambridge
777 Memorial Drive
Tel: 492-7777. Fax: 492-6038
www.hojo.com
204 rooms. This modern motel, popular with tour groups, is situated on the Cambridge side of the Charles River about equidistant from Harvard College and MIT and across the river from Boston University. Many rooms offer splendid views of the Boston skyline. **$$**
Hyatt Regency
575 Memorial Drive
Tel: 492-1234. Fax: 491-6905
www.hyatt.com
500 rooms. The "pyramid on the Charles" is situated on the Cambridge side of the river somewhat closer to MIT than to Harvard College, and across the bridge from Boston University; some great views of the Boston

skyline. Fifteen rooms specially designed for the physically handicapped. **$$$$**

Greater Boston Hotels

Best Western–Terrace Inn
1650 Commonwealth Avenue, Brighton
Tel: 566-6260. Fax: 731-3543
www.bestwestern.com/terraceinn
75 rooms. A complex of motel units suitable for families because of two-room suites and because children under 16 are free. Free use of kitchenettes, although dishes and utensils are not provided. Boston University is nearby and Downtown Boston is reached in 15 minutes on the Green Line of the "T." **$**
Holiday Inn-Boston at Brookline
1200 Beacon Street, Brookline
Tel: 277-1200. Fax: 734-6991
www.holiday-inn.com
208 rooms. Small, comfortable rooms and free underground parking in a residential neighborhood 15 minutes from downtown Boston on the Green Line of the "T," which runs alongside the hotel. Coolidge Corner, with excellent shopping and a variety of restaurants, is only a short stroll. **$$**
Howard Johnson Hote
575 Commonwealth Avenue, Boston
Tel: 267-3100. Fax: 424-1045
www.hojo.com
179 rooms. Practically situated in the outfield of Fenway Park, home of the Red Sox, and close to Boston University, this typical Howard Johnson's is near Kenmore Square with its stores and restaurants catering to sports fans and students. Downtown is about 5 minutes by "T." **$**

Where to Eat

Where & What To Eat

Many claim that Boston has the best seafood in the nation, and it is certainly a great town in which to indulge in all sorts of fish. Boston specialties include clam chowder (made with cream, not tomatoes), scrod (not a separate species of fish but the name given to small tender haddock or cod) and steamers (clams served with broth and melted butter). Baked beans, once synonymous with Boston, and Boston brownbread are not especially popular and may be difficult to find.

In the late 1980s a renaissance of Boston cuisine occurred which was spearheaded by a cluster of imaginative chefs – Jasper White, Lydia Shire of Biba, Gordon Hamersley of Hamersley's, Michela Larson, Chris Schlesinger of the East Coast Grill and Todd English of Olives. Contemporary New England cuisine reflects the bounty of the region.

The Back Bay, especially Newbury and Boylston Streets, has many sidewalk cafés and restaurants, pleasant for people-watching. A recent hotbed of haute cuisine, mainly contemporary American, is the South End, home to many yuppies and gays. Other high concentrations of restaurants include Faneuil Hall Marketplace, Chinatown and the North End. Also, excellent international dining can be enjoyed in nearly all major hotels.

In Cambridge, restaurants are concentrated around both Harvard, Central, Inman and Kendall squares. Many of these are small, inexpensive, ethnic eateries. However, not all the enormous floating student population is impecunious, and, especially as many are from abroad, they significantly contribute to the restaurant scene.

As time passes, the dress code at restaurants becomes less and less formal, although a few bastions remain. Traditionally, Bostonians are not late diners and restaurants are fairly busy by 7pm. Reservations, when accepted, are always a good idea, and the more advance notice, the better. Hot spots often book weeks ahead.

In a survey of the average price of a meal in 17 major American cities, Boston was two-thirds as expensive as New York and on a par with Los Angeles, Philadelphia, Washington DC, San Francisco and Chicago. However, Boston's culinary fame is certainly earned, both at the high end of the price range and, thanks in large part to a wide range of ethnic eateries, at the low end as well.

Restaurants

Rough guide to prices for a three-course dinner excluding beverages, tax and tip: **$** = under **$**20; **$$** = **$**20–**$**35; **$$$** = **$**35-**$**50; **$$$** = over **$**50. On top of this there is a 5 percent state meal tax. As a general rule, a tip of 15 percent is pretty much *de rigueur*; tips of 20 percent or more reward exceptional service.

LANDMARK

Anthony's Pier 4
140 Northern Avenue (on Pier 4)
Tel: 423-6363.
This 1,000-seat restaurant, situated on the waterfront, probably attracts more tourists than any other Boston restaurant. Portions are large; good wine list. Jacket and tie. No reservations, and lines can be long. Limited outdoor dining if weather suitable. Free parking. **$$$**

Durgin Park
340 North Market Street (Faneuil Hall Marketplace)
Tel: 227-2038.
Yankee cooking attracts flocks of tourists to this legendary old dining

hall, where they are seated with others at long, picnic-cloth-covered tables and insulted by the waiters. Try Brontosaurus-sized prime ribs. No reservations; long waits. **$$**

Jacob Wirth
31 Stuart Street
Tel: 338-8586.
A time-warp in the Theater District. Since 1868 wurst, sauerkraut and beer have attracted visitors to this institution with sawdust on the floor. **$–$$**

Locke-Ober
3 Winter Place
Tel: 542-1340.
This "bastion of Brahmins" with a gentlemen's club atmosphere opened in 1870. Some of the waiters may have been there since then. Highlights include the Lobster Savannah and the Baked Alaska (order ahead). Outstanding wine card. Naturally, jacket and tie. If this is your scene, the place is a "must." **$$$$**

The Ritz Dining Room
Ritz-Carlton Hotel, 15 Arlington Street
Tel: 536-5700.
The cuisine aspires to – and attains – cutting-edge sophistication. Another draw is the sumptuous scenery – including midnight-blue chandeliers, the Public Garden twinkling outside, and Boston socialites scintillating within. **$$$$**

Union Oyster House
41 Union Street (near Faneuil Hall)
Tel: 227-2750.
Daniel Webster dined here, where traditional steaks and seafoods are served in the old-fashioned way in atmospheric rooms with creaky floors, low ceilings and wooden booths. A popular raw bar. No reservations and an irritating PA system. **$$$**

RESTAURANTS WITH A VIEW

Bay Tower Room
60 State Street
Tel: 723-1666.
Beautiful glass-walled room on the 33rd floor. Tables arranged so that all enjoy view of Faneuil Hall Marketplace, the harbor and airport. Accomplished contemporary American cuisine. Jacket and tie. Reservations advised. **$$$$**

Rowes Wharf Restaurant
Boston Harbor Hotel
70 Rowes Wharf
Tel: 439-3995.
Excellent contemporary American cuisine served in a luxurious dark-paneled dining room with superb views of the hotel's marina and Boston harbor. Jacket and tie. Reservations advised. **$$$$**

The Sail Loft
1 Memorial Drive, Cambridge
Tel: 225-2222.
Seafood served overlooking the river and the Boston skyline. **$$**

Spinnaker Italia
Hyatt Regency Hotel
575 Memorial Drive, Cambridge
Tel: 876-7746.
This revolving rooftop restaurant serves up adequate, if not dazzling, North Italian cuisine and stunning views of the river and the Boston skyline. Reservations advised. **$$$$**

Top of the Hub
Prudential Center, Back Bay
Tel: 536-1775.
Glass walls on three sides of the 52nd-floor restaurant offer grand views of Boston with, in the distance, the harbor and airport. The New American cuisine achieves comparable heights. Reservations advised. Great place for Sunday brunch. **$$$**

SEAFOOD

Daily Catch
323 Hanover Street, North End
Tel: 523-8567; also at
261 Northern Avenue
(adjacent to Boston Fish Pier)
Tel: 338-3093.
Small cramped "Little Italy" outpost redolent with garlic. **$$–$$$**

Jimmy's Harborside
242 Northern Avenue (adjacent to Boston Fish Pier)
Tel: 423-1000.
Great harbor views from downstairs main dining room and sunny Merchant's Club on upper level. Simplify life by ordering one of the shore dinners. No reservations. Valet parking. **$$$**

Legal Seafoods
26 Park Square
Tel: 426-4444; also at
5 Cambridge Center, Kendall Square, Cambridge
Tel: 864-3400;
Prudential Center
Tel: 266-6800; and
Copley Place, 100 Huntington Avenue
Tel: 266-7775.
What started as a small Cambridge fish store now has a justly deserved international reputation. Enormous variety. No reservations and waits can seem interminable. **$$–$$$.**

No-Name
15½ Fish Pier (off Northern Avenue)
Tel: 338-7539.
In spite of the name, an extremely popular, modestly priced restaurant. No frills: just large portions. Majority of dishes are fried. No reservations. **$$**

Skipjack's
500 Boylston Street
Tel: 536-3500.
Also at 2 Brookline Place (off Boylston Street, Route 9), Brookline, tel: 232-8887. Snappy takes – including Cajun – on the freshest of fish. No reservations. **$$–$$$**

Turner Fisheries
Westin Hotel, 10 Huntington Avenue, Copley Place
Tel: 424-7425.
On a par with Legal Seafoods (see above), although slightly more expensive. Reservations accepted. **$$$**

AMERICAN

Ambrosia on Huntington
116 Huntington Avenue
Tel: 247-2400.
Anthony Ambrose is one of Boston's hottest young chefs, combining solid training with unflapping creativity. Reservations advised. **$$$$**

Aujourd'hui
Four Seasons, 200 Boylston Street
Tel: 451-1392.
Some truly superb contemporary dishes accompanied by excellent wines in an opulent dining room overlooking the Public Garden. Jacket and tie. Valet parking. **$$$$**

Back Bay Brewing Co.
755 Boylston Street
Tel: 424-8300.
Surprisingly polished food in a cool, centrally located brewpub.

Biba
272 Boylston Street
Tel: 426-7878.
Bold flavors of this contemporary New England cuisine matched with bold décor. Some tables overlook the Public Garden. A fun place. Reservations essential. **$$$**

Black Rose
160 State Street, near Faneuil Hall
Tel: 742-2286.
Irish pub-restaurant with lively atmosphere. Entertainment in evenings may be Irish, but the food, including prize-winning chowder, is American. **$.**

Blue Room
1 Kendall Square, Cambridge
Tel: 494-9034.
Eclectic cuisine in a jazzily updated mill building. **$$$**

Cafe Louis
234 Berkeley Street
Tel: 266-4680.
Exquisite New American concoctions in a historic Back Bay building. Reservations advised. **$$$$**

Capital Grille
359 Newbury Street
Tel: 262-8900.
Seafood and dry-aged steaks in an opulent, business-oriented setting. **$$$$**

Club Café
209 Columbus Avenue
Tel: 536-0966.
Innovative dishes, served until 1.30am, in a bright restaurant which is part of a gay complex. **$$**

Commonwealth Brewing Company
138 Portland Street (near North

Station)
Tel: 523-8383.
Light meals among glistening copper kettles and pipes. Seasonal brews. **$**

Division 16
955 Boylston Street, Back Bay
Tel: 353-0870.
Long lines often gather outside this former police station – not so much for the food, which is mostly burgers and the like, as for the lively ambiance. No reservations. **$$**

Grill & Bar 23
161 Berkley Street
Tel: 542-2255.
Club-like upmarket dining room with an excellent wine list. Valet parking. **$$$$**

Hamersley's Bistro
553 Tremont Street, South End
Tel: 423-2700.
A South End charmer where friendly service accompanies exciting and delightful contemporary New England cuisine. Reservations essential. **$$$–$$$$**

Hard Rock Café
131 Clarendon Street
Tel: 424-7625.
Good hamburgers and the like served amid rock 'n' roll memorabilia. Lots of decibels. Long lines. **$**

Harvest
44 Brattle Street, Harvard Square, Cambridge
Tel: 492-1115.
Contemporary New England cuisine served in a vibrant, lively setting. Excellent wine list. Outdoor courtyard. Reservations advised. **$$$**

Henrietta's Table
Charles Hotel, 1 Bennett Street, Cambridge
Tel: 661-5005.
Generous, well-priced renditions of American classics – and classics in the making. Reservations advised. **$$**

Hilltop Steakhouse
855 Broadway, Saugus
Tel: 233-7700.
Drive north on Route 1 for 20 minutes and look for the herd of plastic life-sized cattle on the left. This mammoth steakhouse is always packed and the line often long. No reservations. Cash only. **$**

Hungry i
71½ Charles Street
Tel: 227-3524.
Tiny, romantic, some say claustrophobic, downstairs restaurant which serves contemporary American cuisine. Imaginative menu. Delightful courtyard. Reservations required. **$$$–$$$$**

Mercury Bar
116 Boylston Street
Tel: 482-7799.
Where the glamorous set goes to nosh. **$$$**

Marketplace Grill and Cafe
North Market, Faneuil Hall Marketplace
Tel: 227-1272.
Bracing New American fare in a calm outpost overlooking the milling throngs. **$$**

Morton's of Chicago
1 Exeter Place, Back Bay
Tel: 266-5858.
A tasteful retreat for red meat-lovers. Top cut: the 24-ounce Porterhouse. **$$–$$$**

Parker's
Omni Parker House
60 School Street
Tel: 227-8600.
A New England tradition since 1854: home of Parker rolls and Boston Cream Pie, with formal and attentive service. **$$$–$$$$**

Providence
1223 Beacon Street, Brookline
Tel: 232-0300.
Worth a detour for elegant ambiance and a truly ambitious menu. Reservations advised. **$$$$**

Salamander
1 Atheneum Place, Cambridge
Tel: 225-2121.
Vigorously spiced New American cuisine influenced by a wide range of cultures. Reservations advised. **$$$**

Seasons
Bostonian Hotel, Faneuil Hall Marketplace
Tel: 523-3600.
A dining experience. Jacket and tie. Reservations advised. **$$$$**

Sonsie
327 Newbury Street
Tel: 351-2500.
More a place to be seen than to do serious eating, but nonetheless fun. Reservations advised. **$$$**

Upstairs at the Pudding
10 Holyoke Street, Cambridge
Tel: 864-1933.
Romantic cuisine served in the beautiful dining room of Harvard's Hasty Pudding Club. Reservations suggested. **$$$$**

SOUTHERN

Cottonwood Café
222 Berkeley Street
Tel: 247-2225; also at
1815 Massachusetts Avenue, Cambridge
Tel: 661-7440.
Southwest American *nouvelle* in an exciting atmosphere. Reservations recommended. **$$**

Dakota's
34 Summer Street
Tel: 737-1777.
Marble floors and rarefied Texas-style *nouvelleries* pack in the business-lunchers. **$$$**

East Coast Grill
1271 Cambridge Street
Tel: 491-6568.
Long lines testify to the high regard

Restaurant Guidelines

● **Prices** are approximate, but for a three-course meal for one (excluding beverages, tax and tip), the following guidelines may prove helpful:

    $$$$ = over $40
    $$$ = $28-40
    $$ = $15-28
    $ = under $15

● **Meal tax** varies from state to state, but it is customary to tip 15 to 20 percent on the pre-tax total.

● **Credit cards** The more expensive establishments generally accept credit cards, but call ahead to check just in case.

● **Reservations** Most restaurants, except for the clearly casual, appreciate reservations (some require them).

in which this restaurant's open-grill barbecues are held. A fun place. No reservations. **$$$**

House of Blues
96 Winthrop Street, Cambridge
Tel: 491-2583.
The flagship nightclub serves authentic down-home food, including a dynamite gospel brunch. Reservations advised. **$$**

Magnolias
1193 Cambridge Street, Cambridge
Tel: 576-1971.
Small menu written on blackboard in snug dining room. Closed Sunday. **$$$**

Redbones
55 Chester Street, Somerville
Tel: 628-2200.
The decor doesn't come any plainer, or ribs juicier. **$**

MEXICAN/SPANISH

Casa Romero
30 Gloucester Street
Tel: 536-4341.
Delightful romantic ambiance. Mission-style decor. No tacos or burritos here but unusual, well-prepared, dishes. **$$$**

Dali
415 Washington Street, Somerville,
tel: 661-3254.
Authentic *tapas* and a festive atmosphere. **$$**

Sol Azteca
914A Beacon Street, Brookline
Tel: 262-0909.
Explosively hot food in a casual basement restaurant. Ignore the Tex-Mex and traditional Mexican food here and go for the specialties. **$$$**

FRENCH

Carambola
663 Main Street, Waltham
Tel: 781-899-2244.
An adventurous menu of French and Cambodian appetizers; no entrees. **$$$**

Chez Henri
1 Shephard Street, Cambridge
Tel: 354-8980.
French classics with a fresh Cuban twist, a short stroll from Harvard Square. Reservations advised. **$$$**

Elephant Walk
900 Beacon Street (on the Brookline-Boston town line)
Tel: 247-1500; also at 2067 Massachusetts Avenue, Cambridge
Tel: 492-6900.
Justly celebrated dual French and Cambodian menus. **$$$$$**

Julien
Le Meridien, 250 Franklin Street
Tel: 451-1900.
The city's most exquisite – and authentic – French cuisine, in the former boardroom of a bank. Look for the N.C. Wyeth murals in the adjoining bar. **$$$$**

L'Espalier
30 Gloucester Street
Tel: 262-3023.
Imaginative cuisine served in three elegant, intimate dining rooms – each different – in a 19th-century Back Bay town-house. Excellent wine list. Valet parking. Dinner only. Closed: Sunday. **$$$$**

Les Zygomates
129 South Street
Tel: 542-5108.
The perfect little bistro/wine bar in the artsy Leather District. Reservations advised. **$$$**

Maison Robert
45 School Street
Tel: 227-3370.
Romantic elegance and adventurous French cuisine in the upstairs dining room in the French Second Empire Old City Hall building. Jacket and tie are required. **$$$$ Ben's Café**, on ground floor and with patio dining, is more traditional (and more affordable).

ITALIAN

Alloro
351 Hanover Street
Tel: 523-9268.
Intimate North End fixture with excellent food. No reservations. **$$**

Ciao Bella
240-A Newbury Street
Tel: 536-2626.
Upscale spot for the trendy crowd serving some excellent Southern Italian cuisine. Outdoor dining. Valet parking. **$$**

David's
123 Stuart Street
Tel: 367-8405.
A stylized trattoria in the Theater District serving Mediterranean cuisine primarily. **$$**

La Piccola Venezia
263 Hanover, North End
Tel: 523-3888.
Large helpings with lots of red sauce attract gourmands rather than gourmets to this restaurant. **$$**

Mamma Maria
3 North Square
Tel: 523-0077.
Unconventional *nuova cucina* menu served in several charming small rooms in a three-story townhouse. Upstairs rooms have best ambiance and view. Reservations advisable. Valet parking is available. **$$$ – $$$$**.

Olives
10 City Square, Charlestown
Tel: 242-1999.
Great chefs have converted a small shop in this trendy part of town into a country Italian restaurant. No-reservations policy can mean long lines. **$$$**

Pignoli
91 Park Plaza
Tel: 338-7500.
Lydia Shires's lesser-known restaurant. Exquisite regional dishes. Reservations are advised. **$$$$**

Rialto
Charles Hotel, 1 Bennett Street, Cambridge
Tel: 661-5050.
An elegant setting and outstanding cuisine make this Boston's *numero uno* restaurant. Outstanding wine list. Jacket and tie. Reservations advised. **$$$$**.

Ristorante Toscano
41 Charles Street
Tel: 723-4090.
Wonderful food at the foot of Beacon Hill. **$$$–$$$$**

Tuscan Grill
361 Moody Street, Waltham
Tel: 781-891-5486.
Outstanding Northern Italian food, including scrumptious pastas make the trip to this small suburban bistro rewarding. Reservations advised. **$$$**

Stellina
47 Main Street, Watertown
Tel: 924-9475.
This charming spot, with luscious food, is definitely worth the trek. Reservations advised. **$$$**
UVA
1418 Commonwealth Avenue, Brighton
Tel: 566-5670.
A gem of a modern trattoria, with an enticing wine list. Reservations advised. **$$$**

CHINESE

Carl's Pagoda
23 Tyler Street
Tel: 357-9837.
Unpretentious upstairs restaurant serves great Cantonese food. Ask Carl to choose the menu. **$$**
Changsho
1712 Massachusetts Avenue, Cambridge
Tel: 547-6565.
Cantonese standbys in a dramatically decorated space. **$$**
East Ocean City
27 Beach Street
Tel: 542-2504.
Marble floors, tablecloths and exotic seafood raise this Chinatown restuarant a notch above the competition. **$$**
Imperial Seafood
70–72 Beach Street
Tel: 426-8439.
Large busy Cantonese restaurant where the main attraction is *dim sum* served daily from 9am to 3pm. **$–$$**
Mary Chung
460 Massachusetts Avenue, Cambridge
Tel: 864-1991.
Cozy spot for Mandarin and Szechuan specialities. **$$**

JAPANESE

Kaya
581 Boylston Street
Tel: 236-5858; also at
1366 Beacon Street, Brookline,
Tel: 738-2244; and
1924 Massachusetts Avenue, Cambridge
Tel: 497-5656.

Good traditional Japanese fare. **$$–$$$**
Roka
1001 Masssachusetts Avenue, Cambridge
Tel: 661-0344.
Superior specialties and sushi. **$$**
Takeshima
308 Harvard Street, Brookline
Tel: 566-0200.
Small location with very high quality. **$$–$$$**
Tatsukichi-Boston
189 State Street
Tel: 720-2468.
Consistently one of the top Japanese restaurants in town. Interesting specials. **$$$**

THAI

Bangkok Cuisine
177A Massachusetts Avenue, Boston
Tel: 262-5377.
Boston's oldest Thai restaurant is nothing fancy but turns out the favorites. No reservations. **$$**
Singha House
1105 Massachusetts Avenue, Cambridge
Tel: 864-5154.
Impressive food amid contemporary decor. **$$**
Thai Dish
259 Newbury Street
Tel: 437-9611.
Subtly spiced food amid subdued decor. **$$**

INDIAN

Indian Club
1755 Massachusetts Avenue, Cambridge
Tel: 491-7750.

Restaurant Guidelines

● **Prices** are approximate, but for a three-course meal for one (excluding beverages, tax and tip), the following guidelines may prove helpful:
$$$$ = over $40
$$$ = $28-40
$$ = $15-28
$ = under $15

A trendier Cambridge restaurant more likely to appeal to Harvard faculty than their students. **$$**
India Pavilion
17 Central Square, Cambridge
Tel: 547-7463.
A hole-in-the-wall restaurant frequented by both Indians and students who enjoy the tandooris. **$$**
Kebab-N-Kurry
30 Massachusetts Avenue
Tel: 536-9835.
Pleasant intimate ambience with helpful waiters. **$$**
Shalimar of India
546 Masssachusetts Avenue, Cambridge
Tel: 547-9280.
Friendly service and wailing music behind the curtained windows of a shopfront. **$**

PERSIAN

Lala Rokh
97 Mount Vernon Street
Tel: 720-5511.
Rarefied cuisine in a romantic Beacon Hill hideaway. Reservations advised. **$$$$**

KOSHER

Milk Street Café
50 Milk Street
Tel: 542-3663.
Popular with business people; breakfast and lunch only. **$**
Rubin's
500 Harvard Street, Brookline
Tel: 731-8787.
Best chopped liver in town. No reservations; long line on Sundays. **$**
Zaftigs Eatery
335 Harvard Street, Brookline
Tel: 975-0075. A friendly bustling community deli and restaurant. Prepare for long lines on weekend mornings. **$-$$**

PIZZA

Bertucci's
799 Main Street, Cambridge
Tel: 661-8356; also at
21 Brattle Street, Harvard Square
Tel: 864-4748;
Faneuil Hall Marketplace
Tel: 227-7889; and elsewhere.

A pizza chain which cooks great thin-crust pizza in traditional brick ovens and puts almost anything on it. **$**

Pizzeria Regina
11 Thatcher Street, North End
Tel: 227-0765.
A fixture in the Italian hub of Boston. **$**

Pizzeria Uno
731 Boylston Street, Back Bay
Tel: 267-8554; also at
Faneuil Hall Marketplace
Tel: 523-5722; and
22 John F. Kennedy Street, Cambridge
Tel: 497-1530; and elsewhere.
Deep-dish crust with fresh and gooey toppings. Good appetizers. **$**

Attractions

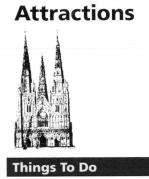

Things To Do

HIGH SPOTS

A view from the top is a good way to "case the joint." The two in the heart of the city are especially worth visiting.

John Hancock Observatory, Copley Square, tel: 247-1977. The observatory on the 60th floor of New England's tallest building (740 ft) has "funscopes" focused on famous landmarks and a collection of exhibits. The sonorous voice of the late Walter Muir Whitehill narrates a historical commentary. Monday–Sunday 9am–10pm. **$5** adult admission.

Prudential Skywalk, 800 Boylston Street, tel: 536-1775. Situated on the 50th floor of the city's second-tallest building; provides a 360-degree panorama of the city and beyond. Monday–Sunday 10am–10pm. The lounge and restaurant on the 52nd floor are well worth visiting at sunset, and the Sunday brunch is also popular.

The Freedom Trail

Free Freedom Trail maps are available at the National Park Visitor Center at 15 State Street next to the Old State House.) The entire trail can be walked in one day, but it's probably wiser to do it more leisurely over two days.

Ben Franklin's Statue and Site of First Public School, School Street.
Boston Massacre Site, Congress and State streets, tel: 242-5642. Where five patriots were killed by the British.

Bunker Hill Monument, Monument Square, Charlestown, tel: 242-5641. Daily 9am–4.30pm. Obelisk, whose 294 stairs can be climbed, marks site of first major battle of the Revolution. Small museum.
Copp's Hill Burial Ground, Snowhill Street, North End. Daily 9am–5pm. Distinguished Americans, including blacks, buried here. Some of the gravestones still show evidence of having been hit by British bullets.
Faneuil Hall, Quincy Market, Congress Street. Daily 9am–5pm. Meeting hall on second floor dubbed "Cradle of Victory" because protests of British policy voiced here.
The Boston Globe Store (The Old Corner Bookstore), corner of School and Washington streets, tel: 367-4000. Monday–Saturday 9am–9pm, Sunday noon–6pm. Center of 19th-century literary Boston: Emerson, Longfellow, Hawthorne and Oliver Wendell Holmes met here.
Granary Burying Ground, Tremont Street, tel: 536-4100. Daily 8am–4pm. Many notables are buried here, including Paul Revere, signatories of the Declaration of Independence and "Mother Goose."
King's Chapel and Burying Ground, 58 Tremont Street. Mondays, Tuesdays, Fridays and Saturdays 9am-4pm; Sundays 1pm-4pm. The present church building dates from 1754. Many notables are interred here.
Old North Church, 193 Salem Street, tel: 523-6676. Daily 9am–5pm. From the steeple two lanterns were hung to warn that British were on their way to Concord.
Old South Meeting House, 310 Washington Street, tel: 482-6439. April–October daily 9.30am–5pm; November–March 10am–4pm. Often used as town meeting site. From here enraged citizens set off to the "Boston Tea Party."
Old State House, 206 Washington Street, tel: 720-3292. Daily 9am–5pm. Oldest public building in Boston. Place where the Declaration of Independence was first read to citizens of Boston.

Park Street Church, One Park Street, tel: 523-3383. July–August Tuesday–Saturday 9am–3pm; September–June by appointment. William Lloyd Garrison gave his first antislavery speech here, and in 1831 "America" was sung publicly for the first time.

Paul Revere House, 19 North Square, North End, tel: 523-1676. November to mid-April daily 9.15am–4.15pm; mid-April to October daily 9.30am–5.15pm. The hero and his family lived in this, the oldest house in downtown Boston.

State House, Beacon and Park streets, tel: 727-3676. Monday–Friday 8:45am–5pm. Bulfinch masterpiece. Frequent tours.

U.S.S *Constitution*, Charlestown Navy Yard, tel: 242-5670. Daily 9.30am–3.50pm. Thousands want to explore "Old Ironsides," which means long lines.

Culture

Places Of Interest

IN BOSTON

Alexander Graham Bell Room, New England Telephone Company Building, 185 Franklin Street, tel: 743-4747. Open daily. Where the telephone began.

Boston Athenaeum, 10½ Beacon Street, tel: 227-0270. A bibliophile's delight in an Italian palazzo. Currently undergoing major renovation.

Boston Marine Society, National Historic Park, Building No. 32, Charlestown Navy Yard, tel: 242-0522. Monday–Friday, 10am–3pm. Maritime history of the region, with lots of model ships.

Boston Public Library, Copley Square, tel: 536-5400. Monday–Thursday 9am–9pm, Friday and Saturday 9am–5pm, Sunday 1–5 (October–June). Call for tour information. Relax in tranquil courtyard after viewing ornamentation of the interior.

Boston Tea Party Ship and Museum, Congresss Street Bridge, tel: 338-1773. Daily 9am–dusk; 9am–5pm (Spring and Fall). Toss a tea chest into the harbor from a replica, the *Beaver II*.

Bunker Hill Pavilion, 55 Constitution Hill, Charlestown, tel: 241-7575. April–November daily 9.30am–4.30pm. A 25-minute multimedia show re-creates the Battle of Bunker Hill.

Children's Museum, 300 Congress Street, Museum Wharf, tel: 426-8855. Daily 10am–5pm, with extended hours until 9pm on Friday. Laid-back, hands-on, fun museum.

Dorchester Heights National Historic Site, Thomas Park near G Street, tel: 242-5642. Open daily 9am–5pm. Impressive tower, which

may or may not be open, in small park.

First Church of Christ, Scientist, Huntington and Massachusetts avenues, tel: 450-2000. The **Mapparium** allows visitors to walk through the world on a glass bridge. It will reopen in 2001.

Frederick Law Olmsted National Historic Site, 99 Warren Street, Brookline, tel: 566-1689. Friday–Sunday 10am–4.30pm. Buildings in which Olmsted lived and worked, together with his drawings and plans.

Gibson House Museum, 137 Beacon Street, tel: 267-6338. Hourly tours: Wedneday–Sunday 1–4pm. Guided tours of only historic Back Bay house open to visitors, Victorian furnishings.

Harrison Gray Otis House, 141 Cambridge Street, tel: 227-3956. Wednesday–Sunday 11am–5pm. Enter this Bulfinch house, the headquarters of the Society for the Preservation of New England antiquities and be transported to 18th-century Boston.

Institute of Contemporary Art, 955 Boylston Street, tel: 266-5152. Wednesday–Sunday 11am–5pm, Thursday extended hours until 9pm. Temporary art exhibits, no permanent collection.

Isabella Stewart Gardner Museum, 280 The Fenway, tel: 566-1401. (For concert information, tel: 734-1359). Tuesday–Sunday 11am–5pm. A glorious Venetian palazzo filled with an idiosyncratic art collection.

John F. Kennedy National Historic Site, 83 Beals Street, Brookline, tel: 566-7937. April–November 10am–4.30pm. Birthplace of John F. Kennedy.

John F. Kennedy Library and Museum, Columbia Point, tel: 929-4500. Daily 9am–5pm. The President's papers and memorabilia.

Massachusetts Archives, Columbia Point, tel: 727-2816. Monday–Friday 9am–5pm, Saturday 9am–3pm. All you ever wanted to know about Massachusetts.

Mugar Memorial Library of Boston University, 771 Commonwealth

Avenue (5th floor), tel: 353-3696.
Monday–Friday 9am–5pm. Personal
papers and memorabilia of
hundreds of prominent 20th-century
figures, including Theodore
Roosevelt, Bette Davis and Martin
Luther King Jr.
**Museum of Afro American
History/African Meeting House**, 46
Joy Street, tel: 739-1200.
Monday–Friday 10am–4pm. In
June–August additional hours on
Saturday and Sunday 10am–4pm.
Information on the Black Heritage
Trail and Boston's black history.
Museum of Fine Arts, 465
Huntington Avenue, tel: 267-9300.
Monday, Tuesday, Thursday and
Friday 10am–4:45pm. Wednesday
10am–9:45pm. Saturday and
Sunday 10am–5:45pm. West wing
open until 9:45pm on Fridays.
(Telephone for tour information.).
Rates second only to New York's
Metropolitan Museum, superb
paintings; magnificent Oriental and
Old Kingdom Egyptian collections.
Excellent restaurant and gift shop.
**Museum of the National Center for
Afro-American Artists**, 300 Walnut
Avenue, Roxbury/Jamaica Plain, tel:
442-8014. Call for hours. Changing
exhibits.
**Museum of Science, Hayden
Planetarium and Mugar Omni
Theatre**, Science Park, tel: 723-
2500. Saturday–Thursday
9am–5pm, Friday 9am–9pm;
extended evening hours
Saturday–Thursday in July and
August. Exciting and exhausting
look-and-touch museum. Splendid
shop.
Museum of Transportation, Larz
Anderson Park, Brookline, tel: 522-
6547. Tuesday–Sunday 10am–5pm.
Superb collection of vintage
automobiles.
New England Aquarium, Central
Wharf, tel: 973-5200.
September–June Monday–Friday
9am–5pm, Saturday, Sunday and
holidays 9am–6pm; July–August
Monday, Tuesday and Friday
9am–6pm, Wednesday and
Thursday 9am–8pm, Saturday and
Sunday 9am–7pm. Watch scuba-
divers feeding sharks and their
friends in giant tank. Dolphin and

sea lion shows.
**New England Historic Genealogical
Society**, 101 Newbury Street, tel:
536-5740. Monday–Saturday
9am–5pm, extended hours
Wednesday and Thursday until 9pm.
Trace your family tree.
New England Sports Museum,
Causeway Street (at the Fleet
Center), tel: 624-1234.
Tuesday–Saturday 10am–5pm,
Sunday noon–5.00pm. Features
sports memorabilia of the local
scene. There are also magnificent
life-size and life-like wooden
carvings of local deities.
Nichols House Museum, 55 Mt
Vernon Street, tel: 227-6993.
Tours: noon–5pm on various days
depending on time of year. House
designed by Bulfinch; mid-Victorian
furnishings.
Trinity Church, 206 Clarendon
Street, Copley Square, tel: 536-
0944. Daily 8am–6pm. H. H.
Richardson's masterwork enriched
by the work of his contemporaries.
U.S.S. Constitution Museum,
Charlestown Navy Yard, tel: 426-
1812. Daily, spring and fall
10am–5pm; summer 9am–6pm.
Meet members of the crew; take
the wheel; and much more.

IN CAMBRIDGE

Hart Nautical Galleries,
Massachusetts Institute of
Technology, 77 Massachusetts
Avenue, tel: 253-5942.
Monday–Friday 9am–8pm. Model
craft.
**Harvard's Collection of Historical
Scientific Instruments**, Science
Center, Harvard University, tel: 495-
2779. September–June
Tuesday–Friday 10am–4pm.
Exhibits illustrating the history of
instrumentation in a broad range of
subjects.
Harvard University, Holyoke Center,
1350 Massachusetts Avenue, tel:
495-1573. Campus tours:
October–May Monday–Friday 10am,
2pm, Saturday 2pm; June–August
Monday–Saturday 10am–3pm,
Sunday 1.30pm and 3pm. Student-
led tours.
Harvard University Art Museums,

32 Quincy Street, tel: 495-9400.
Monday–Saturday, 10am–5pm,
Sunday 1pm–5pm. The **Fogg**, the
Sackler and **Werner Otto Hall**
feature, among them, outstanding
and varied art from most periods.
**Harvard University Museums of
Natural History**, 26 Oxford Street,
tel: 495-3045. Monday–Saturday
9am–5pm, Sunday 1–5pm. Four
museums, including the oldest
Archaeology and Ethnology Museum
in the nation. See the glass flowers
in the Botanical Museum.
Harvard Semitic Museum, 6
Divinity Ave, tel: 495-4631.
Monday–Friday 10am–4pm, Sunday
1pm–4pm. Main attraction – old
Middle East photographs.
**Henry Wadsworth Longfellow
House**, 105 Brattle Street, tel: 876-
4491. Daily 10am–4.30pm.
Virtually as it was in Longfellow's
time.
Hooper-Lee-Nichols House, 159
Brattle Street, tel: 547-4252.
Tuesday and Thursday 2–5pm.
Home of the Cambridge Historical
Society.
List Visual Arts Center, Wiesner
Building, Massachusetts Institute of
Technology, tel: 253-4680.
Weekdays noon–6pm, weekends
1–5pm. Closed in summer.
Temporary exhibits of contemporary
art.
MIT Museum, Massachusetts
Institute of Technology, 265
Massachusetts Avenue, tel: 253-
4444. Tuesday–Friday 10am–5pm,
Saturday and Sunday noon–5pm.
Highlighting MIT's extraordinary
creative output, past and present.
Mount Auburn Cemetery, 580 Mt
Auburn Street, tel: 547-7105. Daily
8am–4.30pm; summer till 7pm.
Progenitor of all garden cemeteries.
Many greats interred here.
**Schlesinger Library on the History
of Women in America**, Radcliffe
Quadrangle, 3 James Street, tel:
495-8647. Monday–Friday
9am–5pm. Country's top research
center devoted to women's studies.
Culinary library.

IN THE WEST

American Jewish Historical Society, Brandeis University, Waltham, tel: 891-8110. Call for times. Extensive documentation.

Battle Road Visitors Center, Route 2A, Concord, tel: 781-862-7753. Daily 9am–5pm. Audiovisual introduction to the opening salvos of the Revolution.

Buckman Tavern, 1 Bedford Street, Lexington Green, Lexington, tel: 781-862-5598. Mid-April to November Monday–Saturday 10am–5pm, Sunday 1–5pm. Where the Minutemen waited the arrival of the Redcoats.

Cardinal Spellman Philatelic Museum, 235 Wellesley Street, Weston, tel: 781-768-8367. Thursday–Sunday noon–5pm. Custom-built museum for display of stamps. Also Lincoln memorabilia and tributes to President John F. Kennedy.

Charles River Museum of Industry, 154 Moody Street, Waltham, tel: 781-893-5410. Monday–Saturday 10am–5pm. History of American Industry from 1800 to the present, with emphasis on steam.

Codman House, Codman Road, Lincoln, tel: 781-259-8843. June to mid-October Wednesday–Sunday 1am–5pm. Eighteenth-century house and furnishings; tours on the hour.

Concord Museum, 200 Lexington Road, Concord, tel: 978-369-9763. Monday–Saturday 9am–5pm, Sunday 11am–5pm. Ralph Waldo Emerson's study with original furnishings; Paul Revere's lantern; decorative arts and domestic artifacts from Concord area.

Davis Arts Museum, Wellesley College, Route 135, Wellesley, tel: 235-0320, ext, 205l. Tuesday–Saturday 11am–5pm, Sunday 1–5pm. Closed summer and school vacations. Distinguished art collection.

DeCordova and Dana Museum and Sculpture Park, Sandy Pond Road, Lincoln, tel: 781-259-8355. Tuesday–Sunday 11am–5pm. Rotating bimonthly exhibits.

Sculpture exhibited on grounds. Summer weekend concerts.

Fruitlands Museums, 102 Prospect Hill Road, Harvard, tel: 978-456-3924. Mid-May to mid-October l0am–5pm. Closed Monday except holidays. American Indian Museum, 19th-century American paintings, 1794 Harvard Shaker House, memorabilia of Bronson Alcott's short-lived commune.

Gore Place, 52 Gore Street, Waltham, tel: 781-894-2798. April 15–November 15 Tuesday–Saturday 11am–5pm, Sunday 1–5pm. Guided tours only. One of New England's great Federal estates.

Gropius House, 68 Baker Bridge Road, Lincoln, tel: 781-259-8098. June–October 15 Wednesday–Sunday 11am–5pm; rest of year Saturday and Sunday 11am–5pm. Guided tours only. The first building designed by Gropius when he arrived in the US.

Hancock-Clarke House, 35 Hancock Street, Lexington, tel: 781-861-0928. Mid-April–October Monday–Saturday 10am–5pm, Sunday 1–5pm. Where Paul Revere met up with John Hancock and Samuel Adams.

Lexington Visitor's Center, 1875 Massachusetts Avenue, Lexington, tel: 781-862-1450. May–October daily 9am–5pm; November–April call for hours. Diorama; artifacts.

Lyman Estate, The Vale, Lyman and Beaver Streets, Waltham, tel: 781-891-4882. Monday–Saturday 9am–4pm. A McIntire house and conservation center.

Minute Man National Historical Park, North Bridge Visitors Center, 174 Liberty Street, Concord, tel: 978-369-6993. Daily 9am–sundown. Where "the shot heard round the world" was fired.

Munroe Tavern, 1332 Massachusetts Avenue, Lexington, tel: 781-862-1703. Mid-April–October Monday–Saturday 10am–5pm, Sunday 1–5pm. This was the headquarters of the Redcoats during the local skirmish.

Museum of Our National Heritage, 33 Marrett Road, Lexington, tel: 781-861-6559. Monday–Saturday 10am–5pm, Sunday noon–5pm.

Frequently changing exhibits of Americana.

Nashoba Valley Winery, 100 Wattaquadoc Hill Road, Bolton, tel: 508-779-5521. Open daily; tours Saturday and Sunday 11:30am–4:00pm. Taste wines made from peaches and pears, cranberries and blueberries.

Old Manse, Monument Street, Concord, tel: 978-369-3909. Mid-April–October Monday–Saturday 10am–5pm, Sunday and holidays noon–5pm. Home of Rev. William Emerson. Nathaniel Hawthorne and Ralph W. Emerson also lived in this house, which contains furnishings from the Revolutionary War period.

Old Sturbridge Village, Route 20, Sturbridge, tel: 508-347-3362. April–October daily 9am–5pm; November–mid-February Saturday and Sunday 10am–4pm; mid-February–March daily 10am–4pm. Sights, sounds and smells of a New England village in the 1830s.

Orchard House, 399 Lexington Road, Concord, tel: 978-369-4118. April–October Monday–Saturday 10am–4.30pm, Sunday 1–4.30pm; November–March Monday–Friday 11am–3pm, Saturday 10am–4.30pm, Sunday 1.30–4.30pm. Louisa May Alcott wrote Little Women here. Also home of Bronson Alcott's School of Philosophy.

Rose Art Museum, Brandeis University, Waltham, tel: 781-736-3434. Tuesday–Sunday noon–5pm, Thursday noon–9pm. Permanent collection and exhibits of outstanding contemporary American art.

Thoreau Lyceum, 156 Belknap Street, Concord, tel: 978-369-5912. March–December Monday–Saturday 10am–5pm, Sunday 2–5pm. Memorabilia of the great man and a replica of his Walden Pond cabin.

The Wayside, 455 Lexington Road, Concord, tel: 978-369-6975. May–October Thursday–Tuesday 10am–4.30pm. The Alcotts, Hawthorne and Margaret Sidney lived here in succession.

Wayside Inn, Boston Post Road (Route 20, 5 miles west of Route

126), Sudbury, tel: 978-443-1776. Said to be America's oldest operating inn.

IN THE NORTH

Abbot Hall, Washington Square, Marblehead, tel: 781-631-0528. Tuesday and Wednesday 8am–9pm, Friday 8am–6pm, Saturday 9am–6pm, Sunday 11am–6pm. A big attraction is A.M. Willard's painting *The Spirit of '76*.
Addison Gallery of American Art, Phillips Academy, Main Steet, Andover, tel: 978-749-4015. September–July Tuesday–Saturday 10am–5pm, Sunday 1–5pm. American paintings and sculpture.
Beauport Sleeper-McCann House, 75 Eastern Point Boulevard, Gloucester, tel: 978-283-0800. Mid-May–mid-October Monday–Friday 10am–4pm. Twenty-six rooms furnished with American and European decorative arts.
Cape Ann Historical Museum, 27 Pleasant Street, Gloucester, tel: 978-283-0455. Tuesday–Saturday 10am–5pm. Renowned Fitz Hugh Lane collection, antique furniture and silver in historic house.
Cushing House Museum, 98 High Street, Newburyport, tel: 978-462-2681. Tuesday–Friday 10am–4pm, Saturday 11am-2pm. Furnished rooms with collection of artifacts, a carriage house and a French garden.
Custom House Maritime Museum, 25 Water Street, Newburyport, tel: 978-462-8681. Monday–Saturday 10am–4pm, Sunday 1–4pm. Exhibits on maritime history, tools and paintings.
Essex Institute Museum and Neighborhood, 132 Essex Street, Salem, tel: 978-744-3390. Tuesday–Friday 10am–5pm, Saturday and Sunday 9am–6pm. Monday 9am–5pm, June–October only. Paintings and domestic life in early Essex County. Restored houses in grounds showing architecture and furniture of 17th to 19th centuries.
Hammond Castle, 80 Hesperus Avenue, Gloucester, tel: 978-283-2080. Summer: daily 10am–4pm.

Closed Monday–Friday September–May. Castle with collection of Roman, Medieval and Renaissance art and giant pipe organ.
House of the Seven Gables, 54 Turner Street, Salem, tel: 978-744-0991. September–June daily 10am–5pm; July–Labor Day daily 9am–6pm. Made famous by Hawthorne's classic tale.
Jeremiah Lee Mansion and Museum, 161 Washington Street, Marblehead, tel: 781-631-1069. Monday–Saturday 10am–4pm, Sunday 1–4pm. Colonial furnishings and decorations in a Georgian house.
John Heard House, 40 South Main Street, Ipswich, tel: 978-356-2811. Seasonal Tuesday–Sunday. Eighteenth-century China trade mansion with Chinese and early-American furnishings. Also has a collection of restored carriages.
John Whipple House, 53 South Main Street, Ipswich, tel: 978-356-2811. Seasonal Tuesday–Sunday. Seventeenth-century house filled with antiques. Delightful herb garden.
King Hooper Mansion, 8 Hooper Street, Marblehead, tel: 781-631-2608. Monday Saturday 10am–4pm, Sunday 1–5pm. Closed: Janurary and Feburary. Eighteenth-century house.
Lawrence Heritage State Park, 1 Jackson Street, Lawrence, tel: 978-794-1655. Daily 9am–4pm. Story of industrial revolution in Lawrence.
Lowell National Historical Park and Visitor Center, 246 Market Street, Lowell, tel: 978-970-5000. Daily 9am–5pm. Remains of the nation's most significant planned industrial city have become the nation's first industrial state park.
Museum of American Textile History, 491 Dutton Street, Lowell, tel: 978-441-0400. Tuesday–Friday 9am–4pm, Saturday and Sunday 10am–4pm. Exhibits demonstrate the evolution of woolen textile manufacture.
New England Quilt Museum, 18 Shattuck Street, Lowell, tel: 978-452-4207. Tuesday–Saturday 10am–4pm, with additional hours

May–November on Sunday noon–4pm. Features both historic and contemporary examples of the art of quilting.
Peabody Museum of Salem, East India Square, Salem, tel: 978-745-9500. Tuesday–Saturday 10am–5pm, Sunday noon–5pm. Superb museum with comprehensive maritime, ethnological, Asia export and natural history collections.
Rockport Paper House, 50A Pigeon Street, Pigeon Cove, Rockport, tel: 978-546-2629. Any reasonable hour. House and furnishings completely built from paper.
Ropes Mansion and Garden, 318 Essex Street, Salem, tel: 978-744-0718. May–October Thursday and Saturday 11am–3pm. Important collections of Nanking porcelain and Irish glass.
Salem Maritime National Historic Site, 174 Derby Street, Salem, tel: 978-740-1650. Daily 9am–5pm. Waterfront wharves and buildings from Salem's years as foremost American seaport.
Salem Witch Museum, 19½ Washington Square North, Salem. tel: 978-744-1692. Daily 10am–5pm; July and August 10am–7pm. Multimedia presentation recreating 1692 witch hysteria.
Saugus Iron Works National Historic Site, 244 Central Street, Saugus tel: 781-233-0050. April–October daily 9am–5pm; November–March daily 9am–4pm. America's first successful iron works.
Witch Dungeon Museum, 16 Lynde Street, Salem, tel: 978-741-3570. April–November 10am–5pm. Live presentations of witch trials and recreated dungeon.
Witch House, 310½ Essex Street, Salem tel: 978-744-0180. March–December 10am–4.30pm. Restored home of Jonathan Corwin, one of judges of Salem witch trials.
Whistler House Museum of Art, 243 Worthen Street, Lowell, tel: 978-452-7641. March–December Wednesday–Saturday 11am–4pm, Sunday 1–4pm. Whistler's father's home and the artist's etchings.

IN THE SOUTH

Adams National Historic Site and the Adams Presidential Birthplace, 135 Adams Street, Quincy, tel: 773-1177; 1250 Hancock Street, Quincy, tel: 770-1175; 131 and 141 Franklin Street, Quincy. Mid-April–mid-November 9am–5pm. Guided tours. Home of the Adams family for 140 years, now decorated with their furnishings and memorabilia.

Cranberry World Visitor Center, 225 Water Street, Plymouth, tel: 508-747-2350. May–November 9.30am–5pm. All there is to learn about cranberries. Free juice tastings.

Daniel Webster's Law Office, Winslow House, Careswell and Webster streets, Marshfield, tel: 781-837-5753. Seasonal. Workplace of the great orator.

Heritage Plantation of Sandwich, 130 Grove Street, Sandwich, tel: 508-888-3300. Mid-May–mid-October daily 10am–5pm. Eclectic collection of Americana in several buildings among 76 acres of gardens rich in rhododendrons and daylilies.

Jabez Howland House, 33 Sandwich Street, Plymouth, tel: 508-746-9590. Late-May–mid-October; call for times. The only surviving house in Plymouth in which a Mayflower Pilgrim lived.

New England Fire and History Museum, Brewster, tel: 508-896-5711. Mid-May–mid-September Monday–Friday10am–4pm, Saturday and Sunday noon–4pm; mid-September–mid-October Saturday and Sunday noon–4pm. Outstanding collection of antique fire equipment and memorabilia.

Old Ship Church, 107 Main Street, Hingham, tel: 781-749-1679. Seasonal. Oldest building in the nation in continuous ecclesiastical use.

Pilgrim Hall Museum, 75 Court Street, Route 3A, Plymouth, tel: 508-746-1620. Daily 9.30am–4.30pm. Closed in January. Oldest public museum in the nation. Pilgrim memorabilia.

Pilgrim Monument and Provincetown Museum, Winslow Street, off Bradford Street, Provincetown, tel: 508-487-1310. (1-800-247-1620) Call for hours. Observation tower can be ascended. Exhaustive museum with dioramas showing arrival of Pilgrims, whaling section and much more.

Plimoth Plantation, Plymouth, tel: 508-746-1622. April–November daily 9am–5pm. A re-creation of the Pilgrims' village populated by interpreters dressed and speaking in character. Also a Wampanoag campsite as it would have appeared in the 1620s.

Plymouth National Wax Museum, 16 Carver Street, Plymouth, tel: 508-746-6468. March–November 9am–5pm. Twenty six life-size dioramas illustrating Pilgrims' story.

Provincetown Art Association and Museum, 460 Commercial Street, Provincetown, tel: 508-487-1750. November–April Saturday and Sunday noon 4pm; May Friday–Sunday noon–5pm; June–August noon–5pm and 8pm–10pm; September–October Friday and Saturday noon–5pm and 8pm–10pm. Exhibitions by emerging and established artists.

Provincetown Heritage Museum, 356 Commercial Street, Provincetown, tel: 508-847-7098. Daily 10am–6pm. Eclectic exhibits of the region's culture.

Sandwich Glass Museum, 129 Main Street, Sandwich, tel: 508-888-0251. May–October daily 9.30am–4.30pm; November–December Wednesday–Sunday 9.30am–4.30pm; Closed January; February–April Monday and Tuesday 9.30am–4.30pm. Locally produced 19th-century glass.

United First Parish Church, 1306 Hancock Street, Quincy, tel: 617-773-1290. Mid-May–Labor Day 10am–4pm daily except Sunday. Contains remains of John Adams and John Quincy Adams and their wives.

Expedition **Whydah** Sea Lab, 16 Macmillan Wharf, Provincetown, tel: 508-487-7955. The continuing reclamation of a pirate ship wrecked in 1717.

Yesteryear's Doll Museum, Main and River streets, Sandwich, tel: 508-888-1711. Seasonal. Call for times. Two floors of beautifully costumed dolls, tiny shops and miniature rooms.

Parks

Arnold Arboretum, 125 Arborway, Jamaica Plain, tel: 524-1718. Daily sunrise to sunset. The jewel of Olmstead's "Emerald Necklace" dates from 1872. Over 7,000 kinds of trees and shrubs cover the Arboretum's 265 acres. Bonsai pavilion has dwarfed trees, some of which predate the Revolution.

Franklin Park Zoo, Franklin Park Rd, tel: 442-2002. Monday–Friday 10am–5pm, Saturday–Sunday 10am–6pm. Situated in Boston's largest public park, the zoo includes a children's zoo, Birds' World and a rainforest exhibit.

George's Island, Boston Harbor, tel: 727-5293. June–October daily 9am–sunset. Ferries leave from Long and Rowes wharves on the waterfront. Picnicking, fishing, tours of Fort Warren (a Civil War landmark) and a free water taxi (late-June to Labor Day) to other harbor islands. No alcohol.

Lovells Island, Boston Harbor, tel: 727-5295. June–Labor Day daily 9am–sunset. Take ferry from Long or Rowes Wharf to Georges Island and then free water taxi. Swimming, picnicking and free water taxi to other islands. No alcohol.

World's End Reservation, Martin's Lane, Hingham, tel: 781-749-8956. 8am–sunset. This 250-acre peninsula, 14 miles south of Boston, was landscaped by Frederick Law Olmsted. Stroll over 200 acres of magnificent landscaping, examine shells on the shore, look for horseshoe crabs in the water. Grand spot for birdwatchers and for great views of the Boston skyline.

Entertainment

Classical Affairs

As befits the "Athens of the North," Boston is, considering its size, the most musical city in the nation. This it owes to tradition and also to its many educational institutes.

Chamber music groups and choral groups abound. Among the former are the Cambridge Society for Early Music and the Boston Camerata; among the latter is the Handel and Haydn Society, America's oldest musical organization, which first performed in 1815, and the upstart Boston Cecilia, whose chorus first sang in 1875. (Not to be forgotten are the choirs of churches such as Emmanuel Church, King's Chapel and First Church in Cambridge Congregational.) Then there is the Boston Symphony Orchestra or simply Symphony, the most illustrious of the city's musical organizations, and the Boston Philharmonic Orchestra.

The city's premier dance company is Boston Ballet, whose repertory includes classical and modern works. Other dance groups include Ballet Theatre of Boston, a newer group which presents the works of both masters and innovators, and Dance Umbrella, the most active New England presenter of contemporary and culturally diverse dance. Boston is home to several innovative choreographers who perform regularly in venues large and small.

The renowned Sarah Caldwell and her financially beleaguered Opera Company of Boston have been bringing innovative and popular opera to Boston for nearly half a century, lapsing only in the past few years. The Boston Lyric Opera Company is trying to pick up the slack, with standards and premieres featuring up-and-coming talent.

And, all the while, playing, singing and dancing, as much for your pleasure as for their own, are students from most of the 50 colleges and universities in Greater Boston.

Some venues where classical performances can be enjoyed are:

Ballet Theatre of Boston, 186 Massacusetts Avenue, tel: 262-0961. Mounts a pared-down *Nutcracker*, as well as new and classic works.

Berklee Performance Center, 136 Massachusetts Avenue, tel: 266-7455. Owned by the Berklee School of Music, this 1,200-seat auditorium is best known for its jazz concerts. A multitude of excellent musical events, at very reasonable prices, are mounted by college students and faculty.

Boston Center for the Arts, 539 Tremont Street, tel: 426-5000. This cluster of small theatres in the South End is used for a wide variety of productions.

Boston Lyric Opera Company, 45 Franklin Street, tel: 542-4912. Three major productions per season (October–March).

Gardner Museum, 280 The Fenway, tel: 566-1401. Chamber music concerts in the Tapestry Room at 1.30pm on Saturday and Sunday.

Hatch Memorial Shell, The Esplanade. Renowned for its free May–September concerts and dance performances. Most famous are the Boston (Symphony) Pops concerts in July.

Jordan Hall at the New England Conservatory of Music, 30 Gainsborough Street, tel: 536-2412. Considered an acoustic marvel, this hall is home to the Boston Philharmonic Orchestra, who put on a number of concerts throughout the winter. Many other performances – classical and otherwise – are presented.

Longfellow House, 105 Brattle Street, tel: 876-4491. Chamber music in the garden in summer on Sunday afternoons.

Museum of Fine Arts, 465 Huntington Avenue, tel: 267-9300. A concert series takes place in the Remis Auditorium, and summer brings sounds into the courtyard.

Sanders Theatre, Memorial Hall, Cambridge & Quincy Streets, Cambridge, tel: 496-2222. This 1,200-seat theater is renowned for its Gothic architecture and for holding, for over a century, a wide variety of musical and literary events.

Symphony Hall, 301 Massachusetts Avenue, tel: 266-1492. Home of the Boston Symphony Orchestra, who present concerts in the winter and move to Tanglewood (in Lenox) for the summer, letting the Boston Pops take over. The hall is also used for a variety of other classical performances, including a celebrity series.

Wang Center for the Performing Arts, 270 Tremont Street, tel: 482-9393. A big stage and huge auditorium make this a favorite venue for ballet, opera, concerts and Broadway plays. It is the home of the Boston Ballet, the foremost dance company in the area.

Theater

Boston theater runs the gamut from Broadway shows to amateur and professional college productions by way of repertory and experimental theater. It has long played the role of a tryout town for pre-Broadway productions.

Note that theater tickets for major theaters can be purchased, subject to availability, for half-price on the day of performance at the Bostix booths at the Faneuil Hall Marketplace and in Copley Place. Credit cards are not accepted. Bostix is open Tuesday–Saturday 10am–6pm and on Sunday 10am–4pm. Call 723-5181 for recorded information on the day's offerings.

American Repertory Theatre, Loeb Drama Center, 60 Brattle Street,

Cambridge, tel: 547-8300. The ever-controversial ART, Harvard's repertory troupe, presents neglected works of the past, as well as new American plays and modern interpretations of the classics.

Back Alley Theater, 1253 Cambridge Street, tel: 576-1253. Home of an innovative group producing new and experimental plays, including premieres.

Charles Playhouse, 74 Warrenton Street, tel: 426-6912. Cabaret-scale musicals known for their record-setting runs.

Colonial Theatre, 106 Boylston Street, Theater District, tel: 426-9366. Boston's oldest theatre, with a richly restored turn-of-the-century proscenium. Features pre- and post-Broadway productions.

Emerson Majestic Theater, 219 Tremont Street, Theater District, tel: 824-8000. This jewel box of a theatre which belongs to Emerson College has been lovingly restored. Presents very professional productions of musicals by Emerson students and other non-commercial, non-profit groups including Dance Umbrella, Boston Lyric Opera and Ballet Theatre of Boston.

Huntington Theatre Company, 264 Huntington Avenue, tel: 266-0800. Boston University's resident company mounts five professional productions, which include such varied delights as Gilbert, Sullivan and Lillian Hellman.

Lyric Stage, 140 Clarendon Street, tel: 437-7172. Boston's oldest residential professional theatre company presents serious 20th-century plays including New England and American premieres.

Publick Theatre, Brighton, tel: 782-5425. From Shakespeare to Gilbert & Sullivan, all under the stars (summer only).

Shubert Theatre, 265 Tremont Street, tel: 482-9393. This 1910 theatre is frequently the setting for pre-Broadway tryouts and for touring Broadway companies.

Wilbur Theatre, 246 Tremont Street, tel: 423-4008. Opened in 1914, this intimate and elegantly restored theatre can boast several world premieres, including *A Streetcar Named Desire* and *Our Town*.

Movie Theaters

The city and suburbs have a fair number of cinemas, many with multiple screens. The Boston Public Library, tel: 536-5400, and the Museum of Fine Arts, tel: 267-9300, regularly show classics. Some commercial cinemas in the city are:

Cheri, 50 Dalton Street (near Hynes Convention Center), tel: 536-2870. Four screens.

Copley Place, 100 Huntington Avenue, tel: 266-1300. Thirteen screens.

Nickelodeon, 606 Commonwealth Avenue (near BU), tel: 424-1500. Five screens; specializes in independent and foreign films. Future is uncertain.

IN CAMBRIDGE

Brattle Theatre, 40 Brattle Street, Harvard Square, tel: 876-6837. *Casablanca* with Bogie and Bacall plays at least yearly. This former theatre plays reruns of the classics and frequently mounts film festivals and author readings. One screen.

Harvard Square, 10 Church Street, tel: 864-4580. Five screens catering to Harvard sophisticates.

Kendall Square, 1 Kendall Place, tel: 494-9800. Well-selected independents. Eight screens.

Nightlife

Although Boston does not have an especially distinctive night life, its 250,000 students ensure that it has a busy one. Bars and nightclubs, discos and comedy clubs abound in both Boston, especially in the Back Bay, and in Cambridge. Most remain open until 2am on weekdays and 1am on Saturdays, although Cambridge nightspots tend to close earlier than their Boston counterparts. Those under 21 cannot be served liquor, but this does not mean they will be denied admission. (The distinction between the different categories in which the following nightspots are listed is often blurred.)

Comedy Clubs

Few cities in the nation harbor as many comedy clubs as Boston. Those over 35 may feel uncomfortable, for nearly all who visit these clubs are students. Some clubs serve light snacks as well as drinks (bar and tables); all have a cover charge, and at some the show is continuous while at others there are discrete showtime hours, especially when big names perform. Most clubs have an "open mike" night when the audience may take to the stage. Call for details and hours. Clubs include:

Dick Doherty's Comedy Vault, 124 Boylston Street, tel: 482-0110. Set in an old bank vault below Remington's Eating and Drinking Exchange.

Nick's Entertainment Complex, 100 Warrenton Street, tel: 482-0930. Largest comedy shop around. Now a nightclub as well as a restaurant and comedy club.

Dance Clubs

Avalon, 15 Landsdowne Street (near Fenway Park), tel: 262-2424. Huge bars and dance floor. The ultimate spot for dancing to loud music, videos and lasers. Live music on occasions. Young crowd often in bizarre dress.
Jillian's, 145 Ipswich Street, tel: 437-0300. From classy pool rooms to computer games.
Man Ray, 21 Brookline Street, Cambridge, tel: 864-0400. Ultra-alternative.
M-80, 969 Commonwealth Avenue, tel: 562-8800. A favorite with the "Euros," Boston's well-heeled exchange students.
Middle East, 472 Massachusetts Avenue, Cambridge, tel: 864-3278. The best place to catch up-and-coming bands.
The Roxy, 279 Tremont Street, tel: 338-7699. A huge ballroom with theme nights and some major special events.

Listening Rooms

House of Blues, 96 Winthrop Street, Cambridge, tel: 491-2583. "Blues Brother" Dan Aykroyd backed this venue, site of nightly concerts and a soul-stirring Sunday Gospel Brunch.
Johnny D's, 17 Holland Street, Somerville, tel: 776-2004. The best local jazz, blues, and occasional folk.
Paradise, 969 Commonwealth Avenue, tel: 562-8800. National pop, rock, jazz and more bands regularly perform here in a clean tropical atmosphere. Young college crowd. Dress wild.
Passim, 47 Palmer Street, Cambridge, tel: 492-7679. A survivor from the far-off 1960s which has given many folk greats their first chance and on which much of Boston's reputation as a folkie mecca rests. No alcohol is served.
Regattabar, Charles Hotel, 1 Bennett Street, Cambridge, tel: 661-5000. Consistently obtains the nod as the best jazz club in the region. Frequented by thirty-

something crowd. Top names and great hors d'oeuvres.
Ryles, 212 Hampshire Street, Inman Square, Cambridge, tel: 867-9330. For many years a favorite featuring the best of New England's jazz musicians in both its upstairs and downstairs lounges. Dinner served.
Scullers Lounge, Guest Quarters Suite Hotel, 400 Soldiers Field Road, Brighton, tel: 783-0090. Hotel jazz club which attracts big names.

Pubs

Black Rose, 160 State Street, tel: 742-2286. This classic Irish pub, close to Faneuil Hall Marletplace, teems with Boston business people released from the office. Live Irish music nightly and weekend afternoons.
Boston Beer Works, 61 Brookline Avenue, tel: 536-2337. A big, brash brewpub, conveniently located across from Fenway Park.
Bull & Finch, Hampshire House, 84 Beacon Street, tel: 227-9605. Tourists come to gawk at what is, in reality, nothing like what they see on TV in *Cheers*.
Casablanca, 40 Brattle Street, Harvard Square, tel: 876-0999. "Here's looking at you, kid" seated in rickshaw-shaped wicker booths around copper tables among other beautiful people. A Harvard institution.
Cornwall's, 510 Commonwealth Avenue, tel: 262-3749. Bracing food and a truly international gamut of brews.
Daisy Buchanan's, 240A Newbury Street, Back Bay, tel: 247-8516. Although there's no cover, proper dress is required at this well-established bar and restaurant with a great rock juke-box. Thirty-something crowd.
Division 16, 955 Boylston Street, Back Bay, tel: 353-0870. Lines form up to enter this dimly lit, upbeat restaurant and bar.
John Harvard's Brew House, 33 Dunster Street, Cambridge, tel: 868-3585. A micro brewery with well priced and prepared fare.

Miracle of Science, 321 Massachusetts Avenue, Cambridge, tel: 828-2866. The tables are black lab tables, the ashtrays are petri dishes, and the burgers are miraculous.
The Plough and Stars, 912 Massachusetts Avenue, Cambridge, tel: 441-3455. A tiny but beloved Irish bar with a wide range of music, from bodhran to blue grass. Massachusetts Governor William Weld boasts of having been a regular in his not entirely misspent youth.

Gay Scene

Boston Ramrod Room, 1254 Boylston Street, tel: 266-2986. Popular with the leather crowd.
Chaps, 100 Warrenton, tel: 695-9500. Levi-clad clones frequent this disco.
Club Cafe, 209 Columbus Avenue, tel: 536-0966. Live performances in a gay complex with restaurant, cocktail bar and gym.

Shopping

Chic and funky, trendy and traditional, state-of-the-art and secondhand, antique and ethnic, bargain-basement and rarified gentility: it's all to be found when shopping in Boston. Three major shopping areas attract strollers as well as serious shoppers. They are the Back Bay (anchored by Newbury Street), Downtown Crossing and Faneuil Hall Marketplace. Most stores open between 9 and 10am and close at 6 or 7pm, although some, especially at Faneuil Hall Marketplace, stay open later. Some stores, especially those in malls and tourist areas, are open on Sundays from noon until 5 or 6pm. The state sales tax does not apply to clothing under $175.

Faneuil Hall Marketplace, more than 150 shops and restaurants attract more than a million visitors each month. Food stalls fill the Quincy Market Building flanked by colorful pushcarts from which handmade crafts and souvenirs are sold. The North and South Markets are bursting with shops and still more restaurants, as is the newer Marketplace Center with its soaring steel, glass and neon canopy.

Celtic Weavers has a wide array of imported caps and capes, kilts and shawls and hand-knit fisherman sweaters, while **Dupre** features funky junior sportswear. And no fashionable wardrobe is complete without nightwear or lingerie from **Dalliance** or **Victoria's Secret,** whose selections range from demure to provocative. **Cuoio** features costume jewelry and accessories as well as imported Italian shoes and boots.

Turning to the home rather than self, there's **Whippoorwill** for crafts and the **Faneuil Hall Heritage Shop**, with magnificent pewter sculpture.

Downtown Crossing is a brick pedestrian zone, the heart of which is the intersection of **Washington** and **Winter Streets,** where souvenirs and jewelry are sold from pushcarts. A number of well-established jewelry shops – **DePrisco**, **De Scenza Diamonds**, **The E.B. Horn Company** – can also be found here. And here, dominating a score of small stores, is **Filene's** – don't miss **Filene's Basement** for unbeatable bargains – and **Macy's**, one of the largest department stores in New England. Here, too, is what is said to be the world's largest **Woolworth**, as well as **Borders** and **Barnes and Noble** bookstores and an **HMV** music outlet.

Back Bay, with its eight-block-long stretch of Newbury and Boylston streets, is considered Boston's premier shopping area. The young and the not-so-young make for the ultra-trendy, yet historic **Newbury Street** not only to shop but to sit at the many chic sidewalk cafés and to watch the world pass by. The part of Newbury Street closest to Massachusetts Avenue tends to attract the young and outrageous; the section closest to the Public Garden and Arlington Street is geared primarily to Boston's moneyed old guard and international visitors. Boston's best galleries – e.g. Alpha, and Barbara Krakow – are clustered at this high-priced end of the street.

Start your safari at **Firestone and Parson**, a gem of a jewelry store in the lobby of the **Ritz-Carlton** hotel. On exiting from the hotel, further gems can be found in **Dorfman Jewelers**, and then one passes, in short order, **Burberry's**, **Charles Sumner**, and **Brooks Brothers.** Cross **Berkeley Street** to reach **Louis**, the most elegant men's store in Boston, which occupies a handsome free-standing building that was originally the Museum of Natural History. Priceless furnishings surround shoppers in

this elegant altar to chic. The clothes are trendy but not gimmicky, the service impeccable, the prices astronomical.

Haute couture on this part of the street is amply represented by **Tatiana** and **Divino** for women, and **Alan Bilzerian** for men. **Laura Ashley** specializes in fashion with that homespun look.

Simon Pearce offers an impressive array of tastefully designed glassware and pottery from his Vermont workshop.

Across **Clarendon**, the fashion show continues at **Serenella**. Several boutiques, including **Country Road**, offer reasonably priced essentials, and both **Rodier** and **Pierre Deux** take a last stab at the chi-chi crowd with ultra-elegant, ultra-expensive watches, jewelry, china and housewares.

In the next block, the shops tend to get smaller and more specialized. **Alianza Contemporary Crafts** features innovative ceramics, glassware and jewelry, and **Anokhi** stocks hand-printed Indian clothing. The **Society of Arts and Crafts** is a wonderful showcase for American artists working with glass, wood, ceramics and about 100 other less conventional media.

Beyond **Exeter** is **Armani**'s upscale outpost, several fine galleries specializing in contemporary and modern works, including **Pucker Safrai** and the **International Poster Gallery**. Relax and enjoy fine Italian fare at **Ciao Bella** or **Davio's**, which are priced well, considering the neighborhood, and attract an interesting local clientele.

Across **Hereford Street**, **Emack & Bolio's Ice Cream** draws a crowd even on the coldest winter nights. The **Avenue Victor Hugo Book Shop**, with its comfortable clutter of used books and magazines, makes for a great afternoon of browsing. The more modern **Trident Bookstore**, across the street, hosts readings and offers delectable café fare. Beyond this street ends with **Tower Records** (open till midnight) which is one of the largest record stores in the nation.

One street over (to the south) from Newbury, and lacking that street's charm, is **Boylston Street**, dominated by the soaring **Prudential Tower.** Here can be found ever dependable **Lord & Taylor** and **Saks Fifth Avenue** and a score of other shops. The new Prudential Center shopping mall, under the tower, has a dozen shops, restaurants and a varied Food Pavilion. Three notable restaurants are **Legal Seafoods**, the **California Pizza Kitchen** and **Dick's Last Resort** (a get-down-and-dirty barbecue joint whose theme is the staff's ability to be incredibly rude to customers).

Closer to town, the action heats up and becomes quite rarified. **FAO Schwartz** appeals to children of all ages and **Shreve, Crump & Low**, long New England's favorite jewelry store, also carries antique furniture, silver, porcelain and more. Readily ignored in this elevated company are the boutiques of the non-profit

Women's Education and Industrial Union, which sell delightful gifts, cards, needlework and even antiques and other collectibles.

Cross **Arlington Street** and arrive at the **Heritage on the Garden** complex, where **Hermès** elegantly displays absurdly expensive items.

A shoppers' delight is **Copley Place**, an indoor shopping mall at the southeast corner of **Copley Square**. Built at the start of the 1980s, this elegant and glitzy cornucopia houses about 100 stores and restaurants and a nine-screen cinema, and links the Westin and Marriott hotels. The stores radiate from a skylight atrium with a 60-ft-high waterfall sculpture circled by pink marble floors. **Nieman-Marcus** is the anchor tenant; other outstanding shops are **Bally of Switzerland**, **Gucci**, and **Louis Vuitton**. Jewelers are headed by **Tiffany**, while the less traditionally inclined will marvel over the pieces at **The Goldsmith.**

Then there are **Crabtree & Evelyn**, **Brookstone** and **Sharper Image**. All this may be enjoyed while nibbling **Godiva** chocolates, purchased by the unit rather than by weight.

Gays and lesbians flock to the well-stocked **Glad Day Gay Liberation Bookshop** at 673 Boylston Street and whodunit lovers will search out **Spencer's Mystery Bookshop** on Newbury.

BEACON HILL

Charles Street, at the foot of the hill, is Beacon Hill's main commercial street. Its brick sidewalks and gas-lit street lamps correctly suggest that it is the place to look for antiques. You might also wish to check out the handcrafted furniture, toys and utensils at some of the local craft stores. Popular is **Helen's Leather**, with New England's largest selection of genuine leather goods, and **Linens on the Hill**, with beautiful items from around the world. **Rouvalis Flowers**, with its witty and tasteful arrangements of gorgeous fresh blooms, is one of Boston's best florists.

CAMBRIDGE

The area in and around **Harvard Square** is chock-a-block with stores, most of which, not unexpectedly, have a youthful appeal. Some stores are gathered in mini-malls. Four such covered complexes are **The Garage** and the **Galleria**, both on **John F. Kennedy Street**, **Atrium Arcade** on **Church Street** and **The Shops at Charles Place** on **Bennett Street**.

Gentlemen will make for the long-established **Andover Shop** and **J. Press**, while those who absolutely demand the Harvard look will stock up on casual wear at **J. August Co**. Women will find elegant clothes at **Ann Taylor**, **Clothware**, and the almost ubiquitous **Laura Ashley** and **Talbot's**. Armchair travelers and others will enjoy exploring the **Banana Republic.**

On Brattle Street, **Motto/MDF** carries cutting edge accessories

Comparing US and European Clothing Sizes

The table below gives a comparison of American, Continental and British clothing sizes. It is always best to try on any article before buying it, however, as sizes can vary.

Women's Dresses/Suits

American	Continental	British
6	38/34N	8/30
8	40/36N	10/32
10	42/38N	12/34
12	44/40N	14/36
14	46/42N	16/38
16	48/44N	18/40

Women's Shoes

American	Continental	British
4½	36	3
5½	37	4
6½	38	5
7½	39	6
8½	40	7
9½	41	8
10½	42	9

Men's Suits

American	Continental	British
34	44	34
–	46	36
38	48	38
–	50	40
42	52	42
–	54	44
46	56	46

Men's Shirts

American	Continental	British
14	36	14
14½	37	14½
15	38	15
15½	39	15½
16	40	16
16½	41	16½
17	42	17

Men's Shoes

American	Continental	British
6½	–	6
7½	40	7
8½	41	8
9½	42	9
10½	43	10
11½	44	11

(fashion and home), while **Jasmine/Sola** has the latest looks for men and women – and shock-effect window displays. Across the street and up one block, the magnificent **Crate and Barrel** showcases with all one could wish for the home: yuppiedom in a nutshell.

Those who want to show that they have been to Harvard – even if only as a tourist – will delight in the **Harvard Shop**, which is crammed with Harvard insignia merchandise. More of the same and practically everything else can be found in the **Harvard Coop Society** (which began in 1882 as a non-profit service for students and faculty) in the heart of the Square.

Then there are the bookstores. It is claimed – and who will contest it? – that here is the greatest concentration of bookshops in the nation. Most are in and around the Square, and some are open until midnight. Some of the more unusual bookshops are **Grolier**, which carries the largest selection of poetry books in the country, **Robin Bledsoe** for out-of-print books on art, architecture and design, and a large selection on women artists, and the **Globe Corner Bookstore,** specializing in travel. For foreign books, used as well as new, visit **Schoenhof's Foreign Books**, more an institution than a bookstore.

Stroll a little further and reach **Ahab Rare Books**, with antique volumes on eclectic subjects; and **The Million-Year Picnic**, whose comic book selection plus books on rock 'n' roll, T-shirts, and unusual cards are astonishing. New books can be found at **WordsWorth**, which offers books at a discount. For used books, trek west to Huron Avenue where the **Bryn Mawr Bookshop** sells stock donated from alumni.

Stores are not restricted to the region close to the Square but extend eastward along Massachusetts Avenue to Central Square, with the quality falling along with the rents. Worth noting is **Oona's**, crammed with an intriguing selection of "experienced" clothing.

Bowl and Board has an extensive selection of affordable housewares.

Also in the vicinity are several furniture stores catering to ex-students who can't bear to move away. **Keezer's** in **Central Square** has been supplying pre-worn tuxes to Harvard undergrads for generations.

A cluster of stores around 1750 Massachussets Avenue (the northern arm of this thoroughfare) near **Porter Square** will delight those – men and women – searching for vintage clothing and collectibles. Try **Vintage Etc**.

In the same neck of the woods, the tailored bohemian will make for **Susanna**, while even more elegant and expensive women's garments can be found at **Pepperweed**.

Over in **East Cambridge** (alight at **Kendall Square** on the Green Line of the "T") is the **CambridgeSide Galleria**, a popular shopping mall. Anchor tenants here are **Sears** and **Filene's**.

More appealing to the dilettante is the well-heeled upmarket **Abercrombie and Fitch**, tops for after-shave lotions. Those who enjoy the feel of cotton will make for **The Gap**. **The Limited** carries a wide colorful variety of trendy Euro-look clothing.

One of the most under-used and most handsome shopping mall in Greater Boston is the **Atrium** on **Route 9** at **Chestnut Hill** which mostly pulls in a suburban crowd but is a joy to visit. Here are a number of major national retailers from **Benetton, J. Crew, Nine West,** for clothing as well as a **Borders** bookstore, **Pottery Barn** and **Cheesecake Factory**.

Sport

Spectator

Sports-mad Boston has major league teams in baseball, football, basketball and hockey. Tickets for the last two sports are difficult to obtain, although 2,500 general admission tickets are available for every game. Baseball and football usually don't present too much of a problem, especially early in the season.

Tickets can be purchased at Bostix, Faneuil Hall Marketplace and Copley Square, tel: 723-5181, Tuesday–Saturday 10am–6pm, Sunday 10am–4pm.

For an overview, see "A Passion for Sports" on pages 71–77.

Baseball: Boston Red Sox, Fenway Park, Yawkey Way, tel: 267-8661. (Tickets may be purchased on a 24 hour line at 482-4769.) This cozy park which was built in 1912 still has grass rather than artificial turf. The Kenmore Square (Green line of the "T", branches B, C, D) and Fenway (Green line, branch D) are only a short distance from the Park. Box office open Monday–Friday 9am–5pm.

Basketball: Boston Celtics, FleetCenter, 150 Causeway Street, tel: 624-1000 (recording). Accessible by the Green or Orange lines of the "T".

Hockey, Boston Bruins, FleetCenter, 150 Causeway Street, tel: 624-1000 (recording).

Football: New England Patriots, Sullivan Stadium, Foxboro, tel: 1-800-543-1176. Special "T" commuter trains to all Patriots home games from South Station, Back Bay Station, Hyde Park, Route 128 Station. By car take Route 3S (the Southeast Expressway) to Route 128N on to Route 95S. Take exit 9 and follow route 1S for about 3 miles (5 km) to the stadium – a total distance of about 25 miles (40 km).

Each year Boston is host to three major sporting events:

Boston Marathon, tel: Boston Athletic Association at 236-1652. Held on third Monday (Patriots Day) in mid-April. The finish line is at Copley Square, but the Copley Station of the "T" is closed on Marathon day. To reach the final stretch, take the Orange Line to Back Bay Station or the Green Line to Auditorium or Kenmore; or the Green Line (C branch) to any stop on Beacon Street.

Head of the Charles Regatta. Held on the second-to-last Sunday of October, when thousands of oarspeople from throughout the world race their shells on the Charles. Take the Red Line of the "T" to Harvard Square and walk south on J.F. Kennedy Street to the river. Alternatively, board the Green line (B branch) to Boston University campus and walk across the Boston University Bridge.

United States Pro Tennis Championships, tel: 731-4500. Held at the Longwood Cricket Club during the second week in July. Professionals from throughout the world. The Green line (D branch) of the "T" stops next to the Club.

Participant

Golf: the Massachusetts Golf Association, tel: 781-891-4300, represents more than 200 clubs in the state and will provide up-to-date information on which courses are open to the general public. Two public 18-hole golf courses supervised by the Parks and Recreation Department are:
Franklin Park, 1 Circuit Drive, tel: 265-4084.
George Wright Golf Course, 420 West Street, Hyde Park, tel: 361-8313.
Other public courses close to the city:
Newton Commonwealth Golf Course, 212, Kenrick Road,

Newton, tel: 630-1971. Call for weekend reservations.
Pine Meadows Country Club, 255 Cedar Street, Lexington, tel: 781-862-5516. Nine holes.
Bicycling: lots of opportunities to cycle along the banks of the Charles or through Olmsted's Emerald Necklace. You can rent a bike from Community Bike Shop, 496 Tremont Street, tel: 542-8623. Monday–Saturday 10am–8pm, Sunday 10am–5pm.
Sailing: Boston has produced some great sailors, and yachting on the Charles is sheer bliss. Less blissful, but possibly more exciting, is sailing in the harbor.
Boston Sailing Center, 54 Lewis Wharf, tel: 227-4198. A varied 45-boat fleet. "Learn to Sail Vacation Week" is exactly that.
Community Boating Inc. 21 Embankment Road, tel: 523-1038. Become a temporary member; prove you can sail and 100 boats await you. No reservations required. April to October Monday–Friday 1pm–sunset, Saturday and Sunday 9am–sunset.
Jamaica Pond Boathouse, 507 Jamaica Way, tel: 522-6258. Sailboats available during summer months for sailing on a pretty suburban lake.
Canoeing: Charles River Canoe and Kayak Center, 2401 Commonwealth Avenue, Newton, tel: 965-5110. Canoes, kayaks and rowing shells for hire. Instruction available. April–October Monday–Friday 10am–sunset, Saturday and Sunday 9am–sunset.
South Bridge Boat House, 496 Main Street, Concord, tel: 369-9438. Canoes and rowboats for exploring the Sudbury, Assabet and Concord rivers. April–October 9.30am–sunset.
Billiards: Jillian's Billiard Club, 145 Ipswich Street, tel: 437-0300. Features 39 Brunswick Gold Crown tables. Café serving snacks. Monday–Saturday 11–1am, Sunday noon–1am.
For public **tennis** courts, **swimming** pools and **skating** rinks, contact the Metropolitan District Commission, 20 Somerset Street, tel: 727-1300.

Further Reading

Non-Fiction

Bainbridge Bunting. *Houses of Boston's Back Bay* (Harvard University Press, 1967)
Robert Campbell and Peter Vanderwarker. *Cityscapes of Boston* (Houghton Mifflin, 1992).
Joseph Garland. *Boston's North Shore* (Little, Brown, 1978).
Joseph Garland. *Boston's Gold Coast* (Little, Brown, 1981).
Max Hall. *The Charles – The People's River* (Godine, 1986).
Jane Holtz Kay and Pauline Chase-Herrell. *Lost Boston* (Houghton Mifflin, 1980).
Christopher Leary, et al. *The Nature of Massachusetts* (Audubon Society/Addison-Wesley 1996).
Anthony J. Lukas,. *On Common Ground: A Turbulent Decade in the Lives of Three American Families* (Alfred A. Knopf, 1985).
David McCord. *About Boston* (Little, Brown, 1973).
Shaun O'Connell. *Imagining Boston: A Literary Landscape* (Beacon Press, 1990).
Thomas H. O'Connor. *Bibles, Brahmins, and, Bosses* (Public Library, Boston, 1991).
Simon Schama. *Dead Certainties* (Knopf, 1990).
William Schofield. *Freedom By the Bay* (Branden Publishing Company, 1988).
Susan & Michael Southworth. *A.I.A. Guide to Boston* (Globe Pequot Press, 1989).
Louis Leonard Tucker. *The Massachusetts Historical Society: A Bicentennial History, 1791–1991* (Massachusetts Historical Society, 1996).
Walter Muir Whitehall. *Boston: A Topographical History* (Belknap Press of Harvard University Press, 1968).
Henry Wiencek. *The Smithsonian Guide to Historic America – Southern New England* (Stewart,

Tabori & Chang, 1989).
Scott Turow. *One L* (Warner Books, 1988).
Susan Wilson. *Boston Sites and Insights* (Beacon Press 1994).

Fiction

Louisa May Alcott. *Little Women* (Simon & Schuster, 1988).
Robin Cook. *Coma* (New America Library, 1977).
Esther Forbes. *Johnny Tremain* (Dell, 1987).
Gerald Green. *The Last Angry Man* (Amereon Ltd, 1976).
Nathaniel Hawthorne. *The Blithedale Romance* (Oxford University Press, 1991).
Nathaniel Hawthorne. *The Scarlet Letter* (Knopf, 1992).
George Higgins. *The Friends of Eddie Coyle* (Viking Penguin, 1987). Also several other mysteries such as *Cogan's Trade*, *Impostors*, *Outlaws*, *Penance for Jerry Kennedy* in an ongoing series based in Boston.
William Dean Howells. *A Modern Instance* (Penguin, 1984).
William Dean Howells. *The Rise of Silas Lapham* (Random House, 1991).
Henry James. *The Bostonians* (Knopf, 1993).
Henry James. *The Europeans* (Viking Penguin, 1985).
Jane Langton. *Memorial Hall*

Murder (Gollancz, 1990).
John P. Marquand. *The Late George Apley* (Little, Brown, 1965).
Sue Miller. *The Good Mother* (Dell, 1987).
Edwin O'Connor. *The Last Hurrah* (Little, Brown, 1985).
Robert B. Parker. *Godwulf Manuscript*, *Promised Land* and other Spenser mystery novels.
Sylvia Plath. *The Bell Jar* (Bantam, 1975).
George Santayana. *The Last Puritan* (Macmillan, 1981).
May Sarton. *Faithful Are the Wounds* (Norton, 1986).
Jean Stafford. *Boston Adventure* (Harcourt, Brace, 1986).

For children

Robert McCloskey. *Make Way for Ducklings* (Penguin, 1976).
E.B. White. *Trumpet of the Swan* (Harper Collins, 1973).

Other Insight Guides

More than 190 *Insight Guides* cover every continent. In addition, a companion series of more than 100 *Insight Pocket Guides* provides selected, carefully-timed itineraries for the traveler with little time to spare and include a full-size fold-out map. And more than 100 *Insight Compact Guides* provide ideal on-the-spot companions, with text,

maps and pictures all carefully cross-referenced.
Titles which highlight destinations in this region include:

Insight Guide: New England (above) is a lavishly illustrated companion to the present book, and *Pocket Guide: Boston* provides recommendations and a full-size city map.

Boston, *Cape Cod*, and *Martha's Vineyard & Nantucket* are covered in detail by three Compact Guides.

ART & PHOTO CREDITS

AllSport 70, 71, 74L, 74R, 76
Ping Amranand 241
Tony Arruza 66, 81, 135, 137, 169, 231
Bank of Boston 21, 22L, 32
Boston College/Gary Gilbert 86
Bostonian Society Library 6/7, 27, 38, 39
Boston Public Library 34L, 99
Brandeis University 88, 89
Marcus Brooke front flap bottom, back left, 2BL, 8/9, 10/11, 26, 30, 36, 52, 57, 60L, 62, 75, 83, 84, 92/93, 102/103, 104/105, 114, 118L, 118R, 120R, 121, 129, 130, 130T, 132/133, 134, 140, 141T, 142L, 142R, 143, 143T, 145, 145T, 150, 151, 153T, 154R, 155, 156L, 157R, 162, 163, 164, 165, 167, 168, 168T, 171, 176/177, 178, 180, 181, 184/185, 186, 187, 190T, 191, 194, 194T, 195T, 198, 198T, 199, 201L, 201R, 202, 204T, 210, 213L, 213R, 216, 218/219, 221, 223, 224T, 225, 228, 232L, 232R, 233, 234, 235, 239, 242, 243, 246, 247, 247T, 252, 253, 255, 256, 257L, 257R, 258L, 258R, 258T, 259, 259T, 260/261, 262/263, 267, 270, 271, 272R, 273, 273T, 276, 277, 278, 279, 280, 283, 290, 293, 294, 296, 298, 300, 302, 304
John Brunton front flap top, 1, 19, 46/47, 51, 72, 127, 128, 208/209
Cullen Bryant 22R
Computer Museum/Jack McWilliams 168
Church of Christian Science 200
Jeffrey Dunn 42, 153, 179, 214, 215
Steve Dunwell 12/13, 78/79, 80, 160/161, 211, 217, 220, 236/237, 248
Essex Institute, Salem 25
Kimberly Grant spine center, back center, back bottom, 2/3, 4BL, 4BR, 5BL, 14, 43, 44, 45, 53, 63, 65, 68/69, 90, 94, 119, 122, 125L, 126, 139, 144, 146L, 147L,

147R, 148/149, 156R, 157L, 192, 193R, 195, 196, 197, 203, 212, 24, 226/227, 229, 249, 251, 254, 272L, 303
Blaine Harrington spine top
Brownie Harris 20, 23, 24
Carlotta Junger 280T, 284T, 285
Catherine Karnow 297, 299, 301
Teresa Lopas 138R
Ken Mallory 172, 173
Massachusetts General Hospital 91
Massachusetts Historical Society 16/17
Museum of Fine Arts 35, 54/55, 56, 59
Richard T. Nowitz 48/49, 64, 85, 96, 106, 138L, 159
Gene Peach 87, 100/101, 117, 131, 222, 238, 250, 266, 288/289, 291
Peter Newark's American Pictures 28
Arthur Pollack 41L, 41R
Frank Radway 37, 40
Mark Read back top right, back flap bottom, 5BR, 67, 73, 82, 95, 97, 99, 115, 117T, 118T, 120L, 120T, 121T, 123, 124, 124T, 125R, 125T, 126T, 127T, 128T, 131T, 137T, 146R, 154L, 155T, 158, 164T, 166, 166T, 180T, 181T, 182L, 182R, 183, 183T, 189T, 190, 191T, 193L, 202T, 204, 205, 222T, 241T, 242T, 244, 245, 248T, 249T, 251T, 253T, 257T, 268, 268T, 269T, 271T, 274/275, 279T, 280T, 282T, 283T, 284, 286L, 286R, 286T, 287, 287T, 293T, 95T, 298T, 300T

Cartographic Editor **Zoë Goodwin**
Production **Stuart A Everitt**
Design Consultants
Carlotta Junger, Graham Mitchener
Picture Research **Hilary Genin**
Proofreading **Penny Phenix**

Stanley Rowin 281
Kathy Tarantola 50, 77, 189
Stephen Trimble 4/5, 98, 141

Picture Spreads

Pages 110-111
Top row, left to right: Stephen Trimble, John Brunton, Richard T. Nowitz, Mark Read. *Centre row:* Marcus Brooke. *Bottom row: all by* Mark Read
Pages 112-113
Top row, left to right: Mark Read, Marcus Brooke, Kimberly Grant, Kimberly Grant. *Centre row:* Mark Read, Peter Newark's American Pictures. *Bottom row:* Richard T. Nowitz, Blaine Harrington, Mark Read, Mark Read, Mark Read
Pages 174-175
Top row, left to right: Kindra Clineff/The Picture Club, Mark Carwardine/Innerspace Visions, Bob Glasheen/Photophile, Kendal Whaling Museum. *Centre row:* James D. Watt. *Bottom row:* Marcus Brooke, Tony Arruza, Mark Read, Francois Gohier
Pages 206-207
Top row left to right: Mark Read, Bequest of John T Spaulding – Courtesy of Museum of Fine Arts Boston, Mary Stevenspm Cassatt – Courtesy of Museum of Fine Arts Boston, Marcus Brooke. *Centre row, clockwise from left:* Marcus Brooke, Picture Fund – Courtesy of Museum of Fine Arts Boston. *Bottom row:* Pauline Revere Thayer Collection – Courtesy of Museum of Fine Arts Boston, Hervey Edward Wetzel Fund- courtesy of Museum of Fine Arts Boston

Map Production
Colourmap Scanning Ltd

©2000 Apa Publications GmbH & Co
Verlag KG (Singapore Branch)

Index

Numbers in italics refer to photographs

The World of Insight Guides

400 books in three complementary series cover every major destination in every continent.

Insight Guides

Alaska
Alsace
Amazon Wildlife
American Southwest
Amsterdam
Argentina
Atlanta
Athens
Australia
Austria
Bahamas
Bali
Baltic States
Bangkok
Barbados
Barcelona
Bay of Naples
Beijing
Belgium
Belize
Berlin
Bermuda
Boston
Brazil
Brittany
Brussels
Budapest
Buenos Aires
Burgundy
Burma (Myanmar)
Cairo
Calcutta
California
Canada
Caribbean
Catalonia
Channel Islands
Chicago
Chile
China
Cologne
Continental Europe
Corsica
Costa Rica
Crete
Crossing America
Cuba
Cyprus
Czech & Slovak Republics
Delhi, Jaipur, Agra
Denmark
Dresden
Dublin
Düsseldorf
East African Wildlife
East Asia
Eastern Europe
Ecuador
Edinburgh
Egypt
Finland
Florence
Florida
France
Frankfurt
French Riviera
Gambia & Senegal
Germany
Glasgow

Gran Canaria
Great Barrier Reef
Great Britain
Greece
Greek Islands
Hamburg
Hawaii
Hong Kong
Hungary
Iceland
India
India's Western Himalaya
Indian Wildlife
Indonesia
Ireland
Israel
Istanbul
Italy
Jamaica
Japan
Java
Jerusalem
Jordan
Kathmandu
Kenya
Korea
Lisbon
Loire Valley
London
Los Angeles
Madeira
Madrid
Malaysia
Mallorca & Ibiza
Malta
Marine Life in the South
China Sea
Melbourne
Mexico
Mexico City
Miami
Montreal
Morocco
Moscow
Munich
Namibia
Native America
Nepal
Netherlands
New England
New Orleans
New York City
New York State
New Zealand
Nile
Normandy
Northern California
Northern Spain
Norway
Oman & the UAE
Oxford
Old South
Pacific Northwest
Pakistan
Paris
Peru
Philadelphia
Philippines
Poland
Portugal
Prague

Provence
Puerto Rico
Rajasthan
Rhine
Rio de Janeiro
Rockies
Rome
Russia
St Petersburg
San Francisco
Sardinia
Scotland
Seattle
Sicily
Singapore
South Africa
South America
South Asia
South India
South Tyrol
Southeast Asia
Southeast Asia Wildlife
Southern California
Southern Spain
Spain
Sri Lanka
Sweden
Switzerland
Sydney
Taiwan
Tenerife
Texas
Thailand
Tokyo
Trinidad & Tobago
Tunisia
Turkey
Turkish Coast
Tuscany
Umbria
US National Parks East
US National Parks West
Vancouver
Venezuela
Venice
Vienna
Vietnam
Wales
Washington DC
Waterways of Europe
Wild West
Yemen

Insight Pocket Guides

Aegean Islands★
Algarve★
Alsace
Amsterdam★
Athens★
Atlanta★
Bahamas★
Baja Peninsula★
Bali★
Bali Bird Walks
Bangkok★
Barbados★
Barcelona★
Bavaria★
Beijing★
Berlin★

Bermuda★
Bhutan★
Boston★
British Columbia★
Brittany★
Brussels★
Budapest &
   Surroundings★
Canton★
Chiang Mai★
Chicago★
Corsica★
Costa Blanca★
Costa Brava★
Costa del Sol/Marbella★
Costa Rica★
Crete★
Denmark★
Fiji★
Florence★
Florida★
Florida Keys★
French Riviera★
Gran Canaria★
Hawaii★
Hong Kong★
Hungary
Ibiza★
Ireland★
Ireland's Southwest★
Israel★
Istanbul★
Jakarta★
Jamaica★
Kathmandu Bikes &
   Hikes★
Kenya★
Kuala Lumpur★
Lisbon★
Loire Valley★
London★
Macau
Madrid★
Malacca
Maldives
Mallorca★
Malta★
Mexico City★
Miami★
Milan★
Montreal★
Morocco★
Moscow
Munich★
Nepal★
New Delhi
New Orleans★
New York City★
New Zealand★
Northern California★
Oslo/Bergen★
Paris★
Penang★
Phuket★
Prague★
Provence★
Puerto Rico★
Quebec★
Rhodes★
Rome★
Sabah★

St Petersburg★
San Francisco★
Sardinia
Scotland★
Seville★
Seychelles★
Sicily★
Sikkim
Singapore★
Southeast England
Southern California★
Southern Spain★
Sri Lanka★
Sydney★
Tenerife★
Thailand★
Tibet★
Toronto★
Tunisia★
Turkish Coast★
Tuscany★
Venice★
Vienna★
Vietnam★
Yogyakarta
Yucatan Peninsula★

★ = Insight Pocket Guides
with Pull out Maps

Insight Compact Guides

Algarve
Amsterdam
Bahamas
Bali
Bangkok
Barbados
Barcelona
Beijing
Belgium
Berlin
Brittany
Brussels
Budapest
Burgundy
Copenhagen
Costa Brava
Costa Rica
Crete
Cyprus
Czech Republic
Denmark
Dominican Republic
Dublin
Egypt
Finland
Florence
Gran Canaria
Greece
Holland
Hong Kong
Ireland
Israel
Italian Lakes
Italian Riviera
Jamaica
Jerusalem
Lisbon
Madeira
Mallorca
Malta

Milan
Moscow
Munich
Normandy
Norway
Paris
Poland
Portugal
Prague
Provence
Rhodes
Rome
St Petersburg
Salzburg
Singapore
Switzerland
Sydney
Tenerife
Thailand
Turkey
Turkish Coast
Tuscany
UK regional titles:
   Bath & Surroundings
   Cambridge & East
      Anglia
   Cornwall
   Cotswolds
   Devon & Exmoor
   Edinburgh
   Lake District
   London
   New Forest
   North York Moors
   Northumbria
   Oxford
   Peak District
   Scotland
   Scottish Highlands
   Shakespeare Country
   Snowdonia
   South Downs
   York
   Yorkshire Dales
USA regional titles:
   Boston
   Cape Cod
   Chicago
   Florida
   Florida Keys
   Hawaii: Maui
   Hawaii: Oahu
   Las Vegas
   Los Angeles
   Martha's Vineyard &
      Nantucket
   New York
   San Francisco
   Washington D.C.
Venice
Vienna
West of Ireland

"I was first drawn to the Insight Guides by the excellent "Nepal" volume. I can think of no book which so effectively captures the essence of a country. Out of these pages leaped the Nepal I know – the captivating charm of a people and their culture. I've since discovered and enjoyed the entire Insight Guide series. Each volume deals with a country in the same sensitive depth, which is nowhere more evident than in the superb photography."

Sir Edmund Hillary

Boston Subway

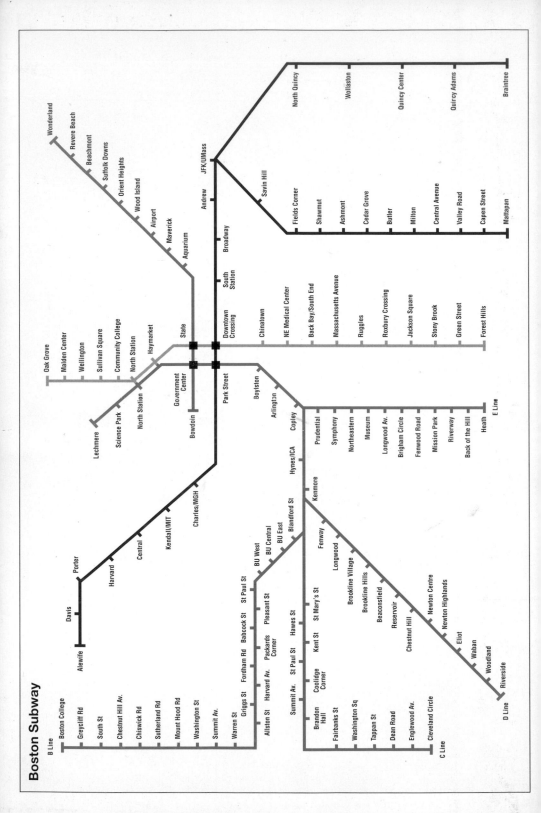